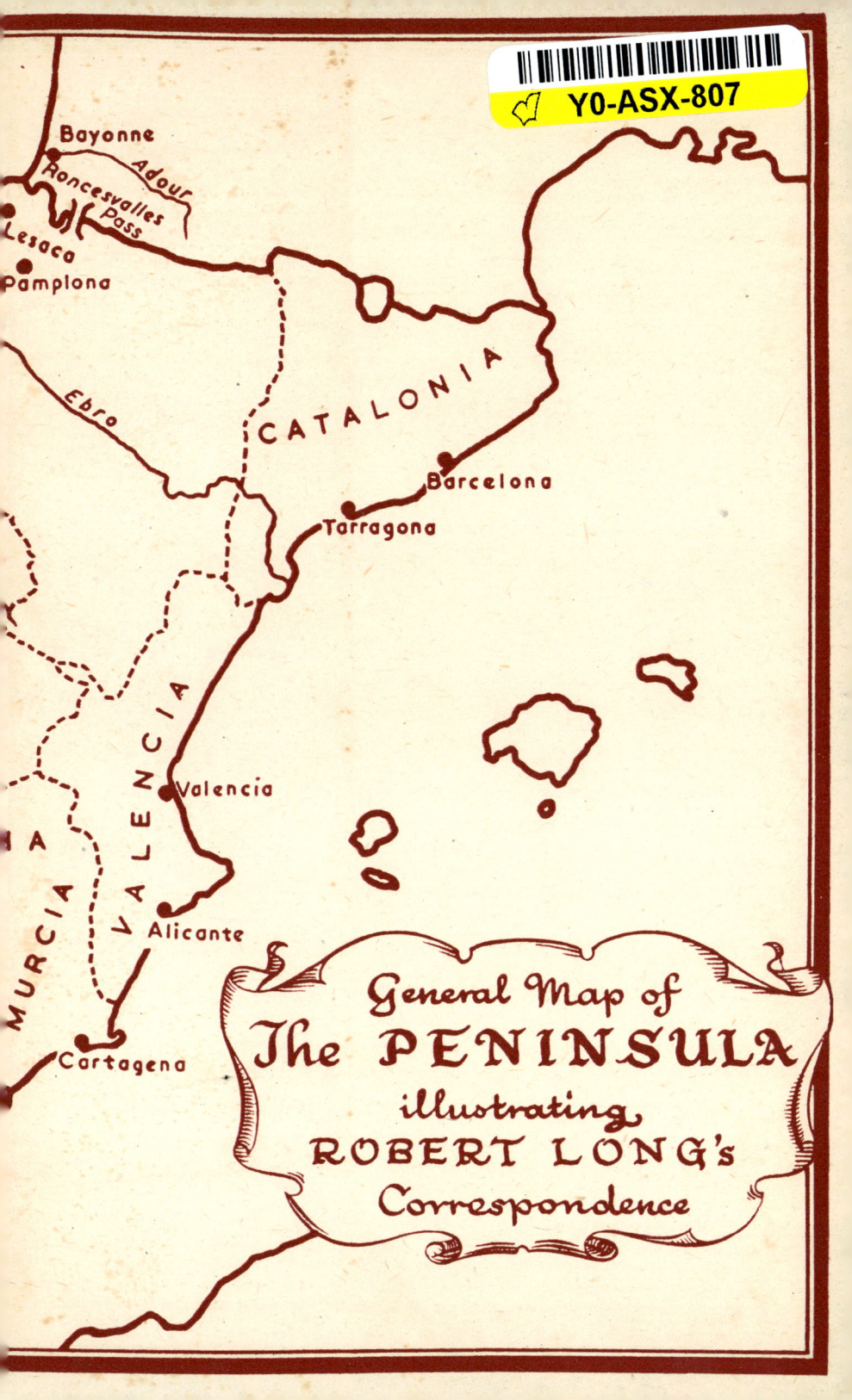

General Map of The PENINSULA illustrating ROBERT LONG's Correspondence

PENINSULAR CAVALRY GENERAL

ROBERT BALLARD LONG
(1771–1825)

PENINSULAR CAVALRY GENERAL (1811-13)

*The Correspondence of
Lieutenant-General Robert Ballard Long*

Edited with a Memoir by
T. H. McGUFFIE

GEORGE G. HARRAP & CO. LTD
LONDON   TORONTO   WELLINGTON   SYDNEY

For

my Wife and Son

First published 1951
by GEORGE G. HARRAP & CO. LTD
182 High Holborn, London, W.C.1

Dewey Decimal classification: 923.542

Composed in Fournier type and printed by Western Printing Services, Ltd,
Bristol. Made in Great Britain

A SOLDIER'S EPITAPH

The Thanks of the Country

to

ROBERT LONG
Major-General and Cabbage Planter

Who had luck enough to do his public duty
Sense enough to know when he had done it
and
Wisdom enough to prefer Cabbage Planting
to
Dependence upon Princes or Power
for
More substantial Happiness

Bello finito
Requiescat in Pace!

NOTE. This mock epitaph was prepared by Robert Long himself when discussing his attitude to the Army and its possible reward. (Letter of July 9, 1811, at p. 124.)

Chronological Outline of the Peninsular War 1808–14

1808. *February and March.* French seize Pamplona, Barcelona, and Madrid.
May. Outbreak in Madrid against Murat. Napoleon makes brother Joseph King of Spain.
June. Portugal rebels against French domination.
July. Dupont and 18,000 Frenchmen surrender at Baylen to a Spanish army.
August. Sir Arthur Wellesley lands in Portugal and wins battle of Vimiero. French (Junot) evacuate Portugal.
October—December. Moore advances to Salamanca, draws off Napoleon from Southern Spain, and withdraws towards Vigo and Coruña.

1809. *January.* Battle of Coruña (Soult), and subsequent British concentration in Portugal.
May. Wellesley retakes Oporto (Soult).
July. Wellesley advances with the Spanish and fights battle of Talavera (Victor).
December. British troops back in Portugal.

1810. *April.* French (Victor) open siege of Cadiz.
July. French (Masséna) take Ciudad Rodrigo and invade Portugal.
September. French advance (Ney) held up by battle of Bussaco.
October. French (Masséna) halted before Lines of Torres Vedras.

1811. *March.* Soult captures Badajoz. Battle of Barrosa (Graham beats Victor). French (Masséna) withdraw from Portugal. Wellington pursues and detaches Beresford to hold back Soult. Combat of Campo Mayor.
April. Siege of Badajoz begins.
May. Battle of Fuentes de Oñoro (Masséna). Battle of Albuera (Beresford beats Soult).
August. Ciudad Rodrigo blockaded.
September. Combat of El Bodon. Wellington retreats again to Portugal.
October. Hill surprises Arroyo dos Molinos.

1812. *January.* Wellington storms Ciudad Rodrigo.
April. Wellington storms Badajoz.
May. Hill destroys Bridge of Almaraz.
August. Wellington enters Madrid.
September. Siege of Burgos begun.
November. Wellington driven back to Ciudad Rodrigo.

1813. *May.* Wellington begins the final advance.
June. Battle of Vittoria (Joseph).
July. Pamplona blockaded. St Sebastian besieged.
July and August. Battles of the Pyrenees (Soult). French field army abandons Spain.

1814. *April.* Battle of Toulouse (Soult). End of the war.

Preface

THE letters and documents which form the bulk of this book are to be found in nine volumes of the Manuscript Library of the Royal United Service Institution, Whitehall, London, S.W.1. They first came to my attention during the 1939–45 War while I was engaged on some research on Combined Operations. On investigation they proved to be a hitherto unnoticed collection of private correspondence and copies of military documents covering almost the whole career of Robert Ballard Long, who commanded a cavalry brigade in the Peninsula under Beresford and Wellington from early in 1811 until the summer of 1813, and who died a lieutenant-general in 1825. The papers, mostly personal letters written home at weekly intervals to a twin-brother, deal in the most objective and accurate way with the war in Spain as Long saw it, along with much acute comment on the general situation in Europe and at sea, on the political issues in England, and with private family and domestic affairs. It has been possible to get much additional information from many regimental histories and autobiographies, from the great works of Fortescue and Oman, and from a two-volume book on the Long family, published by R. M. Howard, entitled *The Longs of Longville, Jamaica, and Hampton Lodge, Surrey*. Mr Howard printed many interesting letters and pedigrees concerning the family, with other information. It is sad to record that the great mass of Long papers which Mr Howard possessed seem to have been destroyed, the only surviving documents being R. B. Long's military papers, which were the only documents Mr Howard did not use; while the family homes in Surrey, Berkshire, Sussex, and Hampshire no longer know their former owners, whose sole memorials now consist of some neglected monuments in country churches.

There are over five thousand folios in the original papers, and much cutting and editing has been necessary to produce the present single volume. Long frequently spelt Peninsular place-names in several differing manners, apparently varying them as he heard them spoken by different people, or discovered them on different maps; place-names have therefore been standardized, as far as it has proved possible to identify them, on the text and maps of Oman's *History of the Peninsular War*. Generally speaking, the letters in Part II are as Long wrote them, though shortened by the omission of certain repetitive and speculative passages. The only parts of the documents previously published are to be found in two little pamphlets published in the 1830's by Long's nephew, C. E. Long, defending the general's memory from the vicious and inaccurate attacks of Beresford during his pen-and-ink war with Napier, and in certain short articles and notes published by the present editor in the Journal of the Society for Army Historical Research.

It is a pleasure to acknowledge the help given me by many friends. Particular mention should be made of the Trustees of the Leverhulme Research Fund. Special credit must be given to Lieutenant-Colonel P. S. M. Wilkinson, Secretary and former Librarian of the Royal United Service Institution, for his generous and complete co-operation in permitting investigation and research, and to Mr Antony Brett-James, for valuable service and advice.

Robert Long came out from his papers to me as a vigorous, intelligent, generously prejudiced man, soldiering well, but abhorring bloodshed, an honourable gentleman who kept his own code and who would sooner be sacked than servile. I hope the readers of this book will enjoy his company as much as I have.

T. H. McGUFFIE

July 1951

Contents

Part I: A General Officer in the Making

CHAPTER		PAGE
I.	Robert Ballard Long Himself	11
II.	Schooldays	15
III.	First Commission and Active Service	18
IV.	Foreign Regiments and Ireland	25
V.	First Cavalry Command	28
VI.	The 15th Light Dragoons and the Duke of Cumberland	32
VII.	Coruña	37
VIII.	The Walcheren Expedition	40
IX.	Posting to the Peninsula	44

Part II: A General Officer in Action

I.	Arrival in the Peninsula	49
II.	Cavalry in Action at Campo Mayor	70
III.	Advances, Skirmishes, and Retreat before Albuera	82
IV.	Albuera	95
V.	Retreat from Badajoz	111
VI.	A Spanish Summer, 1811	121
VII.	Arroyo dos Molinos	137
VIII.	A Quarrel with Beresford	146
IX.	Observations on War by an Unwilling Soldier	158
X.	The Bridge of Almaraz and Operations of May–July 1812	182
XI.	Salamanca and Victory: Madrid and Retreat	210
XII.	The Prospect for 1813	241
XIII.	The Campaign of Vittoria, May–June 1813	268
XIV.	The Pyrenees and the End of Long's Active Career	277
	Epilogue	297
	Index	301

Illustrations

In Half-tone

Robert Ballard Long .... *frontispiece* (PAGE)

Maps and Diagrams

The Action at Campo Mayor, March 25, 1811, adapted from Plans in Robert Long's MS. Journal 77

The Star as it appeared just under Ursa Major, and as sketched by Robert Long 129

General Map of the Peninsula illustrating Robert Long's Correspondence .... *front endpaper*

Sketch from Memory of the Ground about Albuera, with Original Position of Allied Army, May 16, 1811 .... *rear endpaper*

PART I

A GENERAL OFFICER IN THE MAKING

I

Robert Ballard Long Himself

ROBERT BALLARD LONG was a professional soldier, one of those who helped Wellington to win the Peninsular War. In this successful venture, when the armies of Napoleon were driven from Portugal to the Pyrenees and beyond, and when one after another of Napoleon's marshals was worsted in battle, Long played a prominent part. He served as a cavalry brigadier during the years 1811 to 1813, at the very moment when the crisis of the war was reached.

With few exceptions, the British cavalry leaders in the Peninsula have received a bad Press; most of them had black marks scored against them. Probably the best was Le Marchant, a brilliant and original soldier, but the fact that he did not smirch a good reputation may be due to his early death in the great cavalry charge at Salamanca. Sir Stapleton Cotton was little better than a dashing dandy. Jack Slade went from one piece of reckless idiocy to another, until at last 'promoted' home out of harm's way. Sir William Erskine went mad, and threw himself to his death from an upstairs window in Lisbon. Others became sickly or applied for transfer, finding it better to be elsewhere than under Wellington's chilly glance. Robert Long himself was recalled from the Peninsula in what he felt to be a humiliating and disgraceful manner.

His career reveals many contradictions, for in certain ways the two sides of the man—the military and the personal—reacted one upon the other and were not compatible. He had well-placed and powerful friends in the Army; but his enemies proved even better qualified in the end. He was hard-working, enthusiastic, and efficient, yet his final command in the field, though he held the rank of major-general at the time, was reduced to a single regiment of fewer than four hundred sabres. He was never involved in any action which was a total failure, and he was present in command at several brilliant cavalry skirmishes where the finest troops of France were broken and defeated. Nevertheless, when Spain had been cleared of the enemy and when at last the British regiments gazed down from the heights of the Pyrenees over the long plains and winding streams of France, it was then, fresh from the final battles, that the blow fell, and Long was recalled to England.

Long was a misfit in the Army of his day, and did not fit squarely into the conventional pattern of a soldier. His military forecasts of strategy and political warfare were often remarkably accurate, and on occasions his tactical actions displayed brilliance. But with this marked ability for the theory and practice of war he combined an abhorrence of all that war entailed. He fundamentally disliked bloodshed; the endless suffering of the troops and, still more, of the helpless civil population of Portugal and Spain wrung his heart.

Both as a regimental and general officer Long was conscientious and hard-working, caring intensely for the welfare of the regiments under his command. He appears to have lived on good terms with those immediately about him, with his subordinate officers and his servants. The 13th Light Dragoons, who served with him almost without interruption through three long campaigns, parted from him with marked affection and regret.

It was with those above him that Long's relations were dangerously uncertain, for he never hesitated to tackle with vigour anyone, even a commander-in-chief or a royal prince, whom he considered guilty of injustice. So high and well defined was his conception of honour that he was unsparing in his condemnation of infringements of what was, in many respects, a very personal and difficult code. Whoever offended, however unwittingly, received outspoken comment. He was as disgusted with Beresford as he was with Napoleon, and equally careless in using the cutting and critical remarks which brought down unremitting hostility from those he attacked. On such occasions his language tended to be immoderate, and he threw himself on the spears of circumstance with unnecessary zeal.

He never shrank from adopting an unconventional line. Nor was he ever content to have his mind made up for him on any point.

The basic tenets of his attitude have been set out in two letters written home to his twin-brother, Charles, from the Peninsula. The first is dated June 26, 1811.

> I was not cast in the mould that secures fortune by acts of servility and sycophancy, and I am not blessed with the ability to command her graces by personal endowments. I must be satisfied to relinquish the theatre of glory to more aspiring candidates for favor, satisfied if my conscience and my friends accuse me of no dereliction of duty, in discharging the debt I owe to my Country.

Robert Long wrote the second of these letters on March 14, 1812.

> Those who follow a military life from natural predilection and preference, are, in the very execution of their duty, prosecuting their sweetest pleasures. To some its attractions are paramount to those of any other

calling. They know no greater happiness than when thus following the bent of their inclinations. To minds not formed in the same mould, the feelings are widely different. To me the day of Cateau was one of mourning, that of Albuera of deep affliction. I felt pain where others found pleasure. Their joys were to me tears, their sunshine darkness, their happiness misery. I dislike butchery in all its forms and shapes, and of all kinds of butchery that of the human species is to me the most odious. No ambition, no love of reputation can conquer this feeling. A Profession that is at constant war with one's feelings cannot be an agreeable one; Lord W. talks of *expending* such and such Battalions in such and such affairs, as you would talk of expending so much shot and powder on the 1st Sept. To him, War must have every charm that can fascinate a man's heart. He is a *thorough-bred* soldier. I make a distinction between the duty that summons every man to the field to defend his own country and rights; but Armies which are formed for other purposes (and all of them are) should be made up of Volunteers, those who adopt the profession from preference and predilection, who love War as a trade, in all its forms and features, and follow what they like. I say honestly that *I* have no business among *this* class of men, for I dislike the thing, and always have. You cannot, therefore, be surprised at my anxiety to see an end to what I abhor, and more particularly so when I feel as assured of the future recompense that avails my toils and sacrifices, as I do of your being my well beloved brother. I have really nothing to hope for or look to but what you call the bubble reputation, which with us is, nine times out of ten, the *gift of fortune*, and, generally speaking, as easy to be lost as acquired. Ambition should be made of sterner stuff than any I possess, therefore I discard it from my heart, and in all humility seek the only consolation I ever can enjoy, that of living and dying, unmolested, among those who are most dear to me. In the meantime, and waiting this most desirable consummation, we will endeavour to discharge a painful duty to the best of our abilities, in the hope of deriving from this reflexion, hereafter, a comfort that even Princes cannot deprive us of.

The results on his military career might have been and probably were expected. The troops under Long's command shone in successful actions, and he personally was capable of great energy and of long-continued exertions. It is true that like all soldiers, through the very conditions of their calling, he was guilty of mistakes; but his work with Sir Rowland Hill, his constant duty in advance-guard or rear-guard actions, and his behaviour in the heat of battle were at least as creditable as those of any other of Wellington's cavalry generals, and a good deal better than most.

Yet for all this, his mind and character, with the defects of a generous nature, left him vulnerable both in his heart and in his professional life. Long does not seem to have been very happy in his relations with women, for his letters reveal signs of uneasiness in their direction.

His quarrels with the Duke of Cumberland and Beresford were justified, for the first was a detestable person and the second undoubtedly mishandled his field campaigns. But in both cases—and especially when Long came to realize that Beresford blamed Long personally for the bulk of his own military errors—Long's anger and the immoderation of his language were excessive.

This was not, of course, the first or last occasion on which enmity between brother officers exceeded the dislike which each felt for the official enemy; yet the upshot was, though it may be hard to realize for those who held less exalted rank, that a soldier who became a lieutenant-general was still, almost without doubt, a fundamentally disappointed man.

II

Schooldays

ROBERT BALLARD LONG was the elder of twin-sons born at Chichester on April 4, 1771, to Edward Long, a member of a family which, though it originally hailed from Wiltshire, owned extensive plantations in Jamaica. These West Indian connexions dated back to a seventeenth-century ancestor who, having sailed there with the Commonwealth forces, had risen to be Chief Justice. From the Longville estates on the Mino river flowed a torrent of wealth which, helped by wise marriages among other leading Jamaican landowners, maintained the Long family in easy affluence for centuries. The South Sea Bubble, in the early part of the eighteenth century, had, it is true, trapped an earlier Long into a wild-cat "Jamaican Gold and Silver" scheme, but the results had been small, and the Long fortunes remained steady and serene.

Edward Long, on leaving Gray's Inn, had gone to Jamaica, where in due course he became Chief Judge of the Admiralty Court and married into another well-known and wealthy Jamaican family, the Beckfords. On his return to England he lived in various districts round London, until the death of his wife, in 1797, caused him to retire finally to Park House, Arundel. Here in Sussex Edward Long settled down to write his *History of Jamaica*, which for many years remained the standard work, and to be the centre of interest for his devoted and well-beloved children.

All things taken together, fate dealt kindly with Edward Long, and he dealt kindly with those about him. Besides three sons—the eldest, Edward Beckford, had been born in Jamaica—he had three daughters, Jane Catherine, Charlotte Mary, and Elizabeth. They all married happily and well: Elizabeth to a Lord, a younger son of the Norfolk Howards; Charlotte Mary to an admiral who became a baronet; and Jane, a headstrong girl, to a young man whose father protested vigorously but in vain against the match on the grounds of lack of money on each side.

As youngsters both Robert and Charles attended a Dr Thomson's school in Kensington, and from there followed their elder brother, in 1780, to the school on the hill—Harrow. That the two boys were only nine years old when they entered did not necessarily mean that they were the youngest, since newcomers were sometimes mere children of eight. At this time the Headmaster of Harrow was the great Benjamin Heath, whose appointment nine years before had caused one of the great Harrow rebellions, because "a school of this reputation ought not to be considered an appendix to Eton" (where Heath had been a master). Heath, "a well-behaved man, and reckoned very severe in his school," set Harrow on the extraordinarily successful path followed and maintained by his successor and brother-in-law, Joseph Drury. The school grew from the 139 boys it numbered when the Long twins entered to the 345 present in 1803. Five future Prime Ministers, five dukes, two marquises, and thirteen earls (not to mention Lord Byron) attended in that Golden Age. Harrow became a school of peaceful prosperity, great prestige, and a healthy atmosphere, prompting the Sheridans to settle at the Grove near by, and there to maintain their witty, hospitable, and cultured circle.

The fact that Harrow had a considerable connexion with West Indian families probably influenced Edward Long to send his sons there. Nor were the fees high. Sums mentioned for a boy in 1779 total £64 18s. 0d. a year, plus books, servants, clothing, and fencing, all of which accounted for a further twelve guineas or so. This total included not only tutor, entrance-fee, washing, French, writing, and dancing, but also "a bed for himself": Heath was putting on a firm and recognized basis the boarding-house system we know to-day.

The school was in many ways surprisingly enlightened in its treatment of the boys. If Heath began by being "very severe" he grew more charitable; while Drury developed a truly liberal outlook, and went so far as to forswear the birch for the older boys. Even a little Euclid was allowed to be taught in the Sixth Form, though the main education was exclusively classical. A translation of the first four lines of Ovid, preserved by his father, shows that Robert Long made a shaky start as a Latinist.

The Long twins' schoolday began at seven o'clock in the morning, and lasted till after six in the evening, when prayers were held. Robert and Charles, whether sharing a corner of the great Fourth Form room,[1] where on dark mornings each master gathered his group round his own small candle, or in the Shell in the attic under the roof-tiles, grew up in an atmosphere which developed no 'types' and produced no stock pattern. Variety of character flourished in a rich growth. "None so narrow the range of Harrow," indeed. That Robert Long in particular took advantage of this opportunity to go his own way is testified by his later career.

[1] The names of several Longs are to be found carved in the panels of the old Fourth Form room; "R. B. Long" is among those to be seen.

Long seems to have enjoyed his schooldays. After he left Harrow, in 1789, at the age of eighteen, he always took an interest in the Speech Days, whether his own nephews were taking part in them or not, and he was a steward at the Harrow Dinner in 1797. In later years it was natural that some of his closest military friends, such as Robert Brownrigg and Harry Calvert, should have been Old Harrovians.

One of our general's nephews, Edward Noel, while at school became attached to Byron. In the years 1804 and 1805 these two were among the Harrow 'speakers,' and at Littlehampton, where his friend was holiday-making, Byron turned up complete with horses, retinue, and his dog Boatswain. Together they bathed and played cricket, and terrified the neighbourhood with pistol-practice on the sands. Byron, when both were at Trinity College, Cambridge, used to look in at Harrow and demoralize Noel's younger brother with five-guinea tips. Subsequently Noel, an ensign in the Coldstream Guards, was swept overboard and drowned in a collision off Lisbon between the transport he sailed in and an American brig. This was in March 1809, when the young soldier, full of advice from his war-wise uncle Robert, and diligently writing up his daily journal, was not a week past his twenty-first birthday. Byron gave himself up to the most violent grief. The lines which he wrote of Noel, under the character of Cleon in the poem "Childish Recollections" in his first published work, *Hours of Idleness*, form the most permanent memorial to his school friend:

> No vice degrades that purest soul serene.
> On the same day, our studious race begun,
> On the same day, our studious race was run;
> Thus, side by side, we pass'd our first career,
> Thus, side by side, we strove for many a year,
> At last, concluded our scholastic life,
> We neither conquered in the classic strife . . .
> To soothe a youthful Rival's early pride,
> Though Cleon's candour would the palm divide;
> Yet Candour's self compels me now to own
> Justice awards it to my Friend alone.

Other Longs went on after schooldays to Oxford or Cambridge, to write little historical monographs, to become soldiers or Justices of the Peace, and to live the quiet, honourable, rather complacent lives of good nineteenth-century country landlords and gentle sportsmen.

Robert's brother Edward, after Harrow and Trinity Hall, toured the Continent, keeping careful note of his experiences. He then settled to a life of broad acres and estate management at Hampton Lodge, near

Seale, in Surrey. Charles followed Harrow with Christ Church, Oxford. A boyhood illness, when a nasty tumour developed, left him permanently scarred, and caused him throughout his adult life to wear a black patch on the right cheek and side of the nose. After marriage he took up a retired but sporting life at Langley Hall, near Newbury.

III

First Commission and Active Service

ROBERT LONG appears early in life to have settled on a soldier's life. There was a degree of tradition in this choice. The family fortunes had been founded by an ancestor serving as a lieutenant in Colonel Edward d'Oyley's Regiment during the conquest of Jamaica. And Robert Long's great-grandfather Samuel had been in his youth Captain of a troop of Horse Guards, in special favour with Queen Caroline, by whom he was affectionately called "her handsome Captain."

In December 1790 Robert went to study French at Orbe, in Switzerland, under a Monsieur Louis Constançon, who has been recommended to the Long family by the Samuel Whitbreads,[1] with whom brother Edward, in particular, was on friendly terms. Robert disliked his first taste of foreign travel. The weather was wet, and one window of his coach was broken, so that he travelled inside in partial darkness at an average rate of three miles an hour. The inns in France, he wrote home, were "very wretched."

After a short time at Orbe Robert Long moved to the University of Göttingen, where he took a course of military instruction. This university, one of the more recent foundations, was celebrated for the comparative freedom of its curriculum from the traditionalism common to most universities in Germany. Its numerous English colony numbered among its members, some years after Long had left, an even more famous Light Dragoon, called on his papers, during a short military life, Silas Tompkyns Comberbatch, but better known by his proper name of Samuel Taylor Coleridge. Among this colony were also, at various times, several of the sons of George III, including Ernest, Duke of Cumberland, with whom Long was later to come into close and unhappy contact.

On May 4, 1791, Robert Long was gazetted to a cornetcy in the King's Dragoon Guards, commanded by Sir George Howard, who, as it happened, was married to one of Long's cousins.

In those days the officers of the British Army were almost all men of means or the sons of such people. Commissions were purchased,

[1] Samuel Whitbread (1758–1815), politician, brewer, Negro-emancipator, and Parliamentary reformer.

and the social standing of the buyers was fairly reflected in the status of the regiments they entered. The Guards, both Horse and Foot, were the *crême de la crême*, since they dwelt usually in London or at Windsor, where the best society was to be found. They went abroad only on actual campaigns in full-scale wars, and usually served not far removed from our own coasts.

Next in standing came the cavalry, ranged in order of raising; and last the foot regiments of the line, which might be, and often were, dispatched to the fever-ridden and distant ends of the earth. Usually, the lower the regimental number the older and more distinguished was the regiment. Some attempt was made to give regiments a district affiliation, but the exact value of this varied greatly. Recruiting parties foraged for men where they could, ranging Ireland and Scotland, and competing with one another in height of cap-feathers, brilliance of sashes, and length of tales among the ploughmen and the alehouses of our own country. Within the general framework of the Army there were the manifold minute distinctions in which the English heart delights. And over all existed the many exceptions to the general rule, so that through territorial ties or family tradition or ancient custom it was possible to find almost any social rank holding any position in any regiment without society being outraged. The First, or King's, Dragoon Guards gave a young man a very satisfactory standing.

Robert Long had a good chance to settle down in his regiment before the long war against the French started. In 1791, with years of peace how mistakenly prophesied by the Prime Minister, the standing army was treated rather as a cadre than as a full-sized affair. The officers were always more numerous in peacetime in proportion to other ranks than during a war. Nor were their duties heavy. Leave was freely given, and a very full and delightful life could be led by a young man fond of hunting, shooting, fishing, dancing, gaming, and entertainment.

The prospect of war at the end of 1792, and its actual outbreak in the following January, was marked by the habitual frantic search for recruits. One generalization that it is more than usually safe to make about the British Army in the eighteenth century is that the other ranks were drawn from the lower classes of society, and from the lowest ends of those classes. Unemployment was the great recruiting sergeant. Yet the men were certainly not Wellington's "scum of the earth," "fellows who have enlisted for drink." And those obtained in the ranks were infinitely better than anyone in authority had a right to expect, for the grant of money for the Army was normally both reluctant and inadequate.

Some of the earliest of the papers kept by Long dealt with these hurried recruiting activities. He was told, in 1792, that each recruit would bring him £5, of which £2 18s. was to go at once to the man. In February 1793 the order went out that the ranks of the 1st Dragoon Guards were to be filled. Long kept his copy of the regimental recruiting order, his recruiting permit, and his instructions. These last told him that only Protestants and natives of Great Britain were to be enlisted. No apprentices, seamen, marines, militia men, "colliers, stragglers or vagrants," or possible deserters, were to be considered, nor any man "not perfectly straight, well-featured, in every way well-made, and not heavy limbed." The men were to be not older than thirty and not younger than seventeen, though "any fine boy" of over sixteen might be accepted. Examination had to prove each recruit free from "fits, rupture, broken bones, sore legs, scaled head, blear eyes or running sores." Men over twenty years old should be at least five feet seven inches tall. The bounty was then fourteen guineas.

Long's first return as a recruiting officer gives the names and particulars of eight men enlisted by his party in two months. It seems that this little group, with subsistence, allowances, and expenses, cost the country over £144, apart from the pay of the sergeant, six troopers, and Long himself.

During 1793 Long advanced in rank, becoming a lieutenant. He also had a swift and invigorating taste of active service against the infant French Republic during the campaigns in the Low Countries and North Germany which began the long and deadly struggle that was to close at Waterloo.

These initial campaigns were full of dashing incident and military adventure. It is true that their final unhappy ending, when the whole force, or what was left of it, was evacuated in complete failure, has obscured our national memory. The only name usually associated with these days is of the "Noble Duke of York," and the persistent and unhappy "up the hill" jingle. The fact that British regimental flags still hang among French trophies has made men forget many brave fights, especially of our cavalry, when the raw Republican armies were harried and dispersed, their guns and camps captured, and deep thrusts made towards Paris itself. Divided counsels among our allies, political reasons which caused the British forces to be used against Dunkirk, too complicated plans, and, above all, the invincible determination of the French not to be beaten lost us all the fruits of the early victories.

But these early battles were among the most successful and dashing cavalry actions in our history. At Villers-en-Cauchies, in April 1794, three hundred men of the 15th Light Dragoons attacked and dispersed five thousand Frenchmen. At Beaumont[1] the 1st Dragoon Guards

[1] This action is also known as Le Cateau, and this was the name Robert Long generally used.

also came into action, when they, with the 3rd and 5th Dragoon Guards, the Blues, Royals, and 16th Light Dragoons, together with six squadrons of Austrian Cuirassiers, burst upon the flank of over 20,000 Frenchmen and in a few minutes whirled them away in a torrent of destruction.

On this glorious day Long, with most of the first squadron, began by falling in a deep ditch, where he was overrun by our supporting troops, but escaped unhurt. His horse, Conqueror, was not so fortunate. In Long's own words, used when writing home, Conqueror "received a wound in his off foot near the hoof, by a musket shot which a scoundrel, whom I had pardoned the instant before on condition of his laying down his arms, fired at me. My sword soon gave him the reward which such Criminal Ingratitude justly merited."

A few days before this fight, in what was little more than a rather ill-managed scuffle designed to drive the French out of their camp at Prémont, the Brigade Major, Captain Carlton, was killed by Long's side. Long took over his duties, and remained a staff officer for the rest of the campaign. He finished as Deputy-Adjutant-General, and when he sailed from Cuxhaven in the first weeks of 1796 was one of the last to leave Germany.

That Long had begun his life of active service in the comfortable conditions suited to his position in life can be seen from his bill for camp equipage. The total cost of £47 17s. 4d. included a marquee and tent, cot and case, hair-mattress, bolster, pillow, sheets, blankets, counterpane, bedside carpet and floor-cloth, stool, table, and a round tent for his servant ("which in case of necessity may answer for the officer himself").

Not even complete triumph, however, consoled Robert Long for the horror and barbarism he found in war. "Victory," he confessed in a letter to his father, was "a most enchanting enthusiasm and Glory a very fine thing," but "the manner in which every principle of humanity, religion and honor" was violated made him "not anxious of becoming too often a spectator of such scenes of murder and distress."

In spite of early triumphs in May 1794 the Allied arms suffered a serious blow at the battle of Tourcoing, where the Duke of York himself escaped the French Dragoons only through the speed of his horse, and where nineteen of our twenty-eight guns were captured.

One disaster followed another, and mistakes multiplied. By February 1795 all our early gains, all the towns taken in Northern France, were gone, and what was left of the British forces lay in North Germany about the river Ems. A shockingly hurried and mismanaged retreat had rushed our troops from positions round Arnhem (of more recent fame). Thousands of sick had been abandoned. It was at this stage that Walmoden,[1] then joint-commander, for the Duke of York had been recalled, wrote what is probably the most bitter comment ever penned on a British force. "Your army is destroyed," he said, "the officers, their carriages, and a large train are safe, but the men are destroyed." Thirty-three battalions could muster only 6000 fighting men.

Among these regiments was the 33rd Foot—now the Duke of Wellington's Regiment—commanded by a very young lieutenant-colonel, Arthur Wesley (or Wellesley), who commented: "I learned more by seeing the faults and defects of our system in the campaign in Holland than anywhere else." Also present, and duly noted in a staff-order which Long preserved, were the Commissariat Train, commonly known as the "Newgate Blues" from the colour of their uniform, their presumed recruiting-ground, and their unfortunate habits.

Thus Robert Long saw the war's early promise fade into defeat and misery, until what was left of our forces came home again, leaving the Continent on the point of falling completely away from us and into the hands of our enemies.

[1] Walmoden was a Hanoverian commanding the foreign troops in British pay; Lieutenant-General Harcourt commanded the British regiments, and the supreme command at this difficult moment was shared.

IV

Foreign Regiments and Ireland

THE staff post had opened new possibilities to Long, and he was appointed Major of Brigade on the Home Staff, a position he retained until he became A.D.C. to the Right Hon. Sir William Pitt, with whom he served in the Southern Command, and where he made a firm and lifelong friendship with a fellow-officer called John Peter Addenbrooke.

It was during this period that Long's mother died, in July 1797, but apart from this loss the time must have been very happy and pleasant for the young captain. He got on famously with Pitt, and began a friendship which was to prove most helpful in those days of patronage. As headquarters for the South-western Command were often to be found in Portsmouth, a famous gathering-ground for news and rumour, Robert's letters home were usually well informed and lively. In making himself a sort of travelling correspondent, he laid the foundations for the fascinating record of his Peninsular experiences.

Interesting and varied as an A.D.C.'s life was, however, Long did not make the mistake of becoming a Bond Street warrior, unable to tear himself away from the delights of society. He was intelligent, able, and ambitious. He spoke German and French, and so turned his attentions to the prospects offered by the foreign corps in British pay.

There were many of these regiments, and their ranks were filled by what was often an extremely odd collection of men. The King's German Legion, in a class by itself, was in fact the King's Hanoverian Army, comprising horse, foot, and artillery, and Long was to command some of the excellent Hussars of the Legion in Spain, where they won great renown. There were sundry others: French emigrants, Italians, Minorquins, Dutch, Swiss, Corsicans, Greeks, and Albanians. There were also the Royal Americans, which, by Long's time, apart from one noble battalion which served under Wellington, had become practically a penal corps, condemned to die of fever in the West Indies. Other regiments, each with a highly individual and usually short-lived history, and generally uniformed in an exciting fashion, had been raised in various places in and round the borders of the old Holy Roman Empire.

England became the refuge to which fled many who were hostile to the revolutionary ideas preached by the French republicans. As the nations and kingdoms of the Continent fell and were overrun, the British Government recruited and supported an increasing number of foreign regiments. In these corps, employed either under their own officers or sometimes under British command, promotion tended to be cheaper and more rapid than in our own army.

It is true that Long was far from penniless, and had useful friends. But something about these regiments attracted him, and in July 1797 he was gazetted major in the York Rangers. Long must have seen them in their dark uniforms with yellow facings on outpost work in the Low Countries and North Germany. Whether he actually served with them is doubtful, for in 1796 they were in the West Indies, where ultimately the difficulties of finding continual fresh drafts of recruits brought about the final reduction of the regiment in the following year. It is probable, then, that although Long may have worn their uniform and donned their handsome light-infantry cap (complete with a fox's brush crest worn transversely and a green plume on the left side) it was only to decorate Sir William Pitt's immediate surroundings and to delight Lady Pitt's elderly but susceptible heart.

After the reduction of the York Rangers Robert Long concluded what he regarded as a shrewd stroke of business; he bought the lieutenant-colonelcy of the Hompesch Mounted Riflemen from their proprietor, Baron Hompesch. Long paid £2000 down for this—or rather his father Edward did, for Robert depended on him for all extraordinary expenditure, as well as for a regular quarterly allowance.

There were several Hompesch Regiments, of fusiliers, light infantry, hussars, or chasseurs. Their reputation stood high, and they gave good service under various titles in Flanders, Germany, the West Indies, Egypt, and the Peninsula.

John Gaspard Le Marchant, one of Long's closest military friends, also served in Hompesch's. They corresponded regularly, and, like all Long's correspondence, it was at length. They exchanged not only views on current affairs of military and personal importance, but memoranda and regular essays on regimental and national matters. Like Long, Le Marchant was an unconventional officer who bent a keen intellect upon Army affairs, and so offended and upset some of his superiors. But he had the good fortune to be thought well of by George III himself.

The particular Hompesch unit which fell to Long's command was not formed until January 1798. Robert became its first Lieutenant-Colonel, gazetted on March 3, 1798. On being sent to Ireland a month or so later the Regiment became heavily involved in the terrible events of '98. The Mounted Rifles served in Sir John Moore's "advanced corps," and did sterling work. But Long was not there at the most exciting times, for Hompesch himself, the full Colonel, was present and in command. If this circumstance did not gratify Robert it mightily pleased his sister Elizabeth, who wrote that Colonel Hompesch was "certainly the proper Officer to go with his regiments where danger calls, for with his horrible moustache and evil looking countenance, he must keep them under better command than poor Robert's milk and water face could do. I hope our Bobus will escape all these dangers he is so eager to encounter."

Long did not sail from England until August 11, 1798, and on arrival in Ireland he sent back the news that a force of French had landed. These were too late to help the Irish rebels, whose resistance was already broken; but under their gallant leader, Humbert, they routed the opposing forces at Castlebar, and were a dreadful nuisance until finally rounded up at Ballinamuck. Hompesch and his men took part in this, but Long was still at Clonmel, commenting on the cruelty of the war and the immense amount of baggage which hampered the Army's progress.

The Mounted Rifles stayed in Ireland for two years, only returning home in the spring of 1800. This was a shocking period in the history of Ireland. Looting, flogging, the burning of villages, the butchery of stragglers, and the massacre of prisoners on one side were matched with dreadful skill on the other. Long was indignant at the conduct of the "miscreant savages" of Irish, yet bitterly hostile to the official view, with its barren policy of suppression. The whole business was "enough to break the heart of a civilized being and of an Englishman," being little more than "a war between Protestants and Catholics."

It was a bad time, too, for discipline. The fear of creeping murder and the encouragement of reprisals, with the overhanging threat of further French intervention and the ferment of revolutionary ideas, brought about some disgraceful episodes. So ferociously were the Irish peasants treated that the memory is still green. The behaviour of one regiment of fencibles was such that it had to be disbanded. Another more noble regiment was swept from the Army List, when the 5th Royal Irish Dragoons were broken and most of the officers placed on half-pay. Finally, the Carbineers were also drafted out. In this turmoil Robert Long did what he could to mitigate the dreadful severity shown towards the Irish, and was remarked upon for his leniency. That he came out of the episode a firm advocate of Catholic emancipation illustrates the nature of the man.

An event in 1799 affords a further example of his rather unusual character. Sir William Pitt still maintained his warm friendship with his former A.D.C., and corresponded also with Edward Long. During this year there are frequent references in the family correspondence to a military appointment which Robert Long declined, and which it was said the Duke of York himself, besides the King and the Princesses, wished him to accept. This was almost certainly the lieutenant-colonelcy of his old regiment, the 1st Dragoon Guards. But Long was reluctant to take command over men who had formerly been his fellow-officers, and in some cases his superiors. Sir William Pitt, at this time Colonel of the Regiment, apparently favoured acceptance. But Long would not be moved. His reasons satisfied those in authority; even, it was said, they might serve to promote rather than obstruct his future advancement. Yet the note of difference had been firmly struck. When Robert Long found a good personal reason of honour for any course of behaviour, however odd or unusual, he could not be budged from his chosen line.

A change of regiment was not long delayed, for in May 1800 Long transferred to a new command, leaving Hompesch's Mounted Rifles to be shipped off on an expedition to Ferrol and Cadiz, and, when this adventure failed, to take part in the campaign which destroyed what was left of Napoleon's Egyptian Army.

In 1802, with many other units of similar antecedents, the Hompesch Regiments were for the greater part disbanded, the men returning to Germany, save those infantry who joined the 5th Battalion of the 60th Foot (now the King's Royal Rifles).

A few of the Mounted Rifles are said to have re-enlisted in the 20th Light Dragoons, but as a whole Long's first command disintegrated without trace. The Regiment's green jacket, with broad red strips running from throat to waist, vanished along with the black shako enlivened with a red 'turban' round it. Even the tradition of mounted riflemen disappeared; almost a century was to elapse before these extraordinarily useful troops were restored to active service.

V

First Cavalry Command

THE York Hussars was the regiment to which Robert Long was gazetted as lieutenant-colonel on May 30, 1800. Raised originally in 1794, when Baron de Wydenbruck had recruited a mounted unit of "Uhlans" dressed in Polish fashion, these Hussars had served with distinction both in North Germany and the West Indies. When plague and yellow fever had cut down these foreign regiments beyond their power to replenish themselves through their limited recruiting resources the York Hussars had been kept alive, cannibalistically, by absorbing what was left of other corps, including the Guernsey and Dutch Emigrant brigades. In some respects it was a favoured regiment, receiving as it did permission to recruit in England and being placed on the British Establishment. While Long commanded them the Hussars were usually at Weymouth or on the Isle of Wight—both fashionable places, and expensive for the officers.

Baron de Wydenbruck proved troublesome to Long by claiming persistently that money was still due to him for the initial recruitment the Hussars. He declared that, "as Chamberlain of the Elector of Cologne, Uncle of the Emperor of Germany," he had been a major-general. His German income was lost, and in 1800 he was in prison, confined under arrest for debts of £50,000, with "an alarming perspective to starve in prison." Long sent the correspondence to his schoolfriend Brownrigg at the Horse Guards, and received it back with the comforting assurance that the Duke of York thought the Baron "an Adventurer and a great Rogue."

It was at this point in his career that Robert Long began a systematic collection of military papers. He had, as Lieutenant-Colonel, executive control over his regiment, and between certain very wide general limits could do what he pleased with it. In 1800, being obliged practically to refound the York Hussars,[1] Long put it in good order according to his own ideas. Details of dress, drill, and discipline were largely at the Lieutenant-Colonel's discretion. It is true that General Dundas had recently introduced the 'eighteen manœuvres,' which were to be the solid core of uniformity among the troops, and which gave him

[1] Among the troopers at the time was Sergeant Landsheit, who later wrote an account of his military adventures which is at least racy if not entirely accurate. He finished his active life as hall porter to the Royal United Service Institution when it was first founded.

the nickname of "Old Pivot." But most Commanding Officers were still enjoying a pretty free hand.

The York Hussars were always spoken well of under Long's command, and his papers provide many indications of his serious devotion to his duty. When the bounty for recruits was raised from six to twelve guineas Long rewrote the recruiting instructions, using as his model those regulations of the King's Dragoon Guards already described. No men were to be taken "in-kneed, bow-legged, subject to fits, with ruptures, running sores, scaled heads, defects in sight, speech or hearing or with any visible complaint or bodily infirmity whatsoever"; nor any man who had received corporal punishment. Labourers or men bred to the plough were to be preferred.

The officers of the York Hussars were a mixed lot, as might have been expected. At one time several of them were Irish and had formerly served in the Irish regiments of the French Army; they had taken service with the hereditary enemy when the first émigré formations had been recruited. When Long took over he listed six names of "officers unfit for their situations." The chief crime of four was their ignorance of the German language; another as a regimental officer was "scarcely worth his pay," while the sixth, a cornet, was brusquely described as "an ignorant and wretched officer, and much unfit for his present situation. Indeed he appears the worst of the whole." These two last on the list were removed from the Regiment, and allowed to sell out for whatever sums they had actually paid for their commissions.

Long also kept his orders for that most unhappy of regimental duties—the execution of deserters by their comrades. It appears there were six culprits, of whom two corporals were shot, each receiving ten bullets at three or four paces, kneeling beside their graves. They were taken to the place of execution in a cart, with their officers, each unhappy man "in his white stable waistcoat and overalls." After death the Regiment filed past the graves, and then listened to an address by their Lieutenant-Colonel. As a copy of his speech was preserved it is possible to hear again of the "melancholy and afflicting spectacle," and the account closes with an exhortation to the ranks to "chuse between a life of Honor or a death of Disgrace."

Among other innovations Long inaugurated a regimental mess in the York Hussars. The length of the war was consolidating what had been merely a convenience into tradition, and officers' messes were becoming common. Long began by gathering in copies of the rules of already existing messes. Having studied the twenty-four messing articles governing the 17th Light Dragoons, the fifteen of the 1st Battalion 30th Foot, and the eight of the 12th Light Dragoons, Long launched his own scheme. He did the thing very completely: he began with a circular to the officers, put four main points before them, and took a vote. A committee was then formed, and twenty-one regulations laid down for guidance. This proclaimed the subscriptions, the first wine allowance (one half-bottle, or pint, of wine daily for each member), and the duties, accounts, and forms necessary. He also sent out specimen sheets giving concrete examples. One form shows that in a single week forty-six bottles of red wine (at 3s. 3d. each) and seven of white (at 3s. 9d.) were drunk. In another form twenty-five officers are shown as spending between them £21 12s. 1¾d. on drink in a week in November 1801. Porter is charged at 8½d. a bottle, "cyder" at 6d., tea or coffee at 1s. 0s. a cup.

A sergeants' mess was also started, providing "a good and sufficient meal consisting of soup, at least ¾lb of meat, vegetables and good table beer," the bread being supplied by each member for himself.

That Long's proposals were well received not only by his own men, but by his superiors is shown by the many notes in the Brownrigg Letter Books, now in the War Office Library, approving Long's suggestions for promotion, recruitment, and the augmentation of the regiment. One letter gave him a personal assurance that though the York Hussars would not be sent to Egypt in 1801, yet, as whichever regiment was sent would sail dismounted, this need not be regretted.

Long also preserved a note explaining his personal expenditure at Weymouth in 1801. He gives amounts under various headings: Forage, Music, Bills, Messing (£713 18s. 8d. in all). The single item "Cash Advanced" comes to £344 1s., explained as being for washing, powder, pomatum, stabling, or turnpikes; all spent by himself, his servant William, or James Lynch, the groom. The wine bill, which was not given exactly, is described simply as "very high," because of "the visit from the Royal Family, and in expectation of a second in Camp." Another item is for "full dress uniform, £41 18s. 10d." The York Hussar uniform consisted of a scarlet jacket with green facings and a green pelisse, the breeches red by some accounts and by others green. Cloaks and boots *à la Polonaise* were worn, and each man carried a sword, a carbine, and a pair of pistols. In Long's day the original white chapska had been replaced by a black mirliton, or watering-cap, with a red 'flame' and white plume. It is little wonder that Princess Charlotte, daughter of the future George IV, remembered Robert Long so well, for in 1802 she was six years old, and the friendly young colonel must have been an impressive and brilliant figure.

By the end of 1801, however, these fineries had been laid aside, for the war faded away into a short-lived peace. Long stalked the streets of Weymouth, scowling at the illuminations which the inhabitants put on in celebration, and grumbling to his brothers about the idiocy and shortsightedness of those who really believed that the war to date had settled anything whatever.

The Peace of Amiens sounded the death-knell for many of the foreign corps, and in June 1802 the York Hussars left Weymouth for West Cowes to be disbanded. Of the 331 rank and file 272 went to Cuxhaven to take their discharge. The officers were placed on half-pay, and the Regiment finished its existence. The final official comment was that the horses handed over to the Government were in "capital condition." As a mark of appreciation the York Hussars gave their Lieutenant-Colonel a handsome presentation sword which Long cherished exceedingly.[1] The last paper connected with the Regiment he kept was a pathetic letter written on the subject of half-pay by one of the officers from Long's 'black list.' He declared himself to be working steadily away at translations, inquired about the sword "anonymously voted him by the Regiment," and obviously craved for some help to get back on the active list.

Robert Long did not waste the short interlude of peace, for he enrolled as a student in the Royal Military College. This new foundation, one of the many valuable moves of the Duke of York in his capacity as Commander-in-Chief, became the forerunner of Sandhurst. It trained officers for staff duties, and the senior department, which Long joined, was then at High Wycombe, occupying the Antelope Inn in the main street. The first directors were the émigré General Jarry and Long's friend Le Marchant.

Amiens was really a truce rather than a peace, and soon the swords were drawn again. In December 1803 Robert Long was gazetted Lieutenant-Colonel of the 2nd Dragoon Guards, or Queen's Bays. He bade them farewell in Ireland two years later. These years he appears, from the last order published to them, which he kept among his papers, to have enjoyed. He was, however, just embarking on that part of his military career which is not only the most important from the historical point of view, but also that which became personally most disastrous to him.

One unhappy result—and a sort of shadow sent before of his subsequent career—of his association with the Queen's Bays was that he became involved in a long and complicated argument. This one was about the regimental accounts. These accounts, and indeed all the financial arrangements of our Army were peculiarly susceptible to trouble. Long's records show that the quarrel between himself, the Regiment, his successor, and the Irish tradesmen concerned was still going strong as late as June 1816. The bills remained unpaid, and no one was satisfied.

[1] This sword is still in the possession of a member of the family.

VI

The 15th Light Dragoons and the Duke of Cumberland

ON leaving Ireland Long was nominally posted to the 16th Light Dragoons. But almost immediately he was transferred to the 15th Light Dragoons. The move was said to have been at the particular desire of George III and on the recommendation of the Colonel of the Regiment, the Royal Prince, Ernest Augustus, Duke of Cumberland, later King of Hanover.

The 15th Light Dragoons was a famous regiment. They were the first British Light Dragoons, and a year after their formation, in 1759, were granted the title Royal. Their gallantry on July 16, 1760, at Emsdorff (near Marburg, in Germany) resulted in the capture of five battalions of French infantry complete with their sixteen colours and nine guns. The resulting battle-honour, "Emsdorff," was the first ever given to a British regiment. In the 1794 campaign they had fought side by side with the Dragoon Guards at Villers-en-Cauchies, and at Willems.

The Duke of Cumberland, their Colonel, was an unusual prince. Alone among his brothers he was thin, elegant, and intelligent to a degree. His early training, like Long's—they were the same age— had been received at Göttingen and in the Army. At the battle of Tournai he had lost an eye and gained a horrid scar, which in later life he covered with an enormous growth of whiskers and moustache. In the same campaign of 1794 he also indulged in a ferocious display of personal bravery, culminating in his returning to his own lines with a French dragoon under one arm as a trophy.

He had also shown a less desirable side of his character when, on being shown over a convent, he had attempted to kiss the Abbess and had leered at the nuns in a marked manner.

Cumberland was a thoroughly unpopular man. The mere possibility, at a later stage in his career, that he might succeed to the British throne was enough to throw political parties into a panic. Where his brothers' vices were public property and on the whole publicly approved Cumberland's weaknesses were reputed to be of the unmentionable type. Public opinion, against all the evidence, in 1810 declared that Cumberland had murdered his valet, Sellis, who was supposed either to have been blackmailing his master or to have been betrayed by him. Greville described the Duke as "a mixture of narrow-mindedness, selfishness, truckling, blustering and duplicity with no object but self, his own ease and the gratification of his own fancies and prejudices." Cumberland had deeply offended his own family by a sudden, ill-considered marriage to a widow of thirty-seven who had already married twice and who had jilted his younger brother the Duke of Cambridge into the bargain. Cumberland was also suspected of incest with his sister the Princess Sophia; and it was generally accepted, not without a good deal of supporting evidence, that no woman of any age or position dare trust herself alone in a room with him. When at the age of sixty-six he succeeded to the throne of Hanover he was advised by the Duke of Wellington, "Go, before you are pelted out."

In contrast to his Whig brothers Cumberland was a most uncompromising Tory, one of the sort that made the most right-wing Englishman appear a milk-and-water Radical. It was inevitable that Robert Long and his new Colonel should come cross-ways-on. One trouble was that Cumberland, unlike most full colonels, had a deep personal interest in his regiment. He generally dressed in uniform, and frequently took direct command of the men. A strict discipline in the 15th Light Dragoons was inevitable, and Cumberland succeeded in retaining, against all law and custom, the inhuman punishment of picqueting, whereby a trooper who had offended against the military code was suspended by his wrists, his only possible support a pointed stake fixed beneath his bare feet.

Up to the year 1805 Long had made good progress. He had seen active service, served in a variety of interesting and important cavalry regiments, acted as a staff officer at home and abroad, and shown his zeal by enrolling among the first students of our first Staff College. He had influential friends, and was on good personal terms with the King and members of the Royal family, including the Commander-in-Chief.

That Long's actual career finished in frustration was very largely due to the conflict which rapidly developed between himself and Cumberland. Long was fundamentally a liberal man in his outlook and of a friendly nature. Cumberland was not. They became bitter though hidden enemies.

Cumberland interfered with everything. Even through the tone of official documents Long, who wielded a too-ready pen and tended to cherish grievances, made his subordinate position plain, and demonstrated his resentment. He issued an acidly phrased regimental order saying that as he had "been required to enforce greater attention to uniformity in the dress and appearance of the officers" he had obtained a pattern boot, spur, hat, and feather from the Duke for inspection.

Under Long's command the 15th was turned into Hussars. Long's experience with this then hardly known form of light cavalry placed him on the board of five experts which reported on Hussar equipment and methods. But this did not prevent Cumberland from constantly giving special instructions. He even laid down the law as to when and whether officers should or should not wear moustaches; these were generally compulsory in Hussar regiments at that time (reinforced with bootblacking when nature would not serve). He also charged that the long locks usual in foreign hussars should be retained; and it took a special order from Headquarters to reverse this and to bring the 15th into line with other British regiments.

As German officers were generally more servile than British, they were naturally preferred by this devilish and overbearing character. Whatever else Long was he was not servile. The climax was reached when Cumberland is said to have threatened one of the 15th's officers with a cane, if not to have actually beaten him. The whole position was intolerable.

* * *

Long's professional interest in his regiment is movingly attested by the great mass of papers he preserved. It is easy from these to build up the actual daily life and conditions of his command.

Very little was directly commanded from the Horse Guards—headquarters of the Commander-in-Chief in London—and Long carefully laid down the rules and regulations governing the 15th Light Dragoons. In two introductory addresses, one to the officers and the other to the N.C.O.'s and men, he struck the keynote by which he meant to govern everything he did. Valour and discipline were his watchwords to the troopers, whom he called "The Heroes of Emsdorff." To the officers he went into more detail. "Prompt and punctual obedience" was to be both observed and enforced. He stressed the value of thorough and careful training. The setting of a model of behaviour by the officers to their men received attention, along with a willingness to receive suggestions. And, very typically, he urged all his officers to recollect that theory was as essential as practice.

In order to ensure uniformity Robert Long issued many regimental orders. Barrack-room regulations forbade the throwing of filth, dirt, or herring-gut against the walls of the rooms, or the stopping of ventilators with straw against draughts, or the burning of candles or lights after ten o'clock at night. The position of women was also regulated, for those were days when the only privacy a married man had was a blanket to screen his bed in the long dormitory.

Kit inspection was carefully detailed, each article being given its set place and condition. The ordering and execution of repairs and the correct management of stable routine received attention. Another paper described the function and the detailed instructions for the proper ordering of marches. Long kept lists of the artificers in the regiment, and a schedule showing the alternation of daily and weekly duties and responsibilities among the troops and squadrons.

During the year 1804 a regimental inquiry was held into the expenses of a subaltern in a regiment of Light Dragoons. The initial expenditure was carefully calculated under several headings. £151 19s. 6d. went for horses and horse appointments, £50 5s. 6d. for camp equipage, £169 10s. 0d. for dress, £61 4s. 0d. for arms and accoutrements, £25 2s. 6d. for sundries. A cornet's first outlay was reckoned at £458 1s. 6d. in all. Further calculations for annual expenditure and upkeep worked out at £5 19s. 5d. a week for board and lodging; wear and repair for horses and appointments cost £36 11s. 6d; £124 10s. 0d. went for upkeep of dress, and £13 annually for wear and repair of arms and accoutrements. An annual income of £510 1s. 2d. was regarded as a minimum amount, towards which a subaltern's net pay was £129 a year. This yearly expenditure allowed only one pint of wine a day, and did not provide at all for a private servant (regarded as essential) or any expenditure outside the regiment on civilian clothes, pocket-money, or amusements. It seems a heavy price to pay to bring into the field of battle one pair of pistols and a sword. Perhaps the 170 buttons and 110 yards of silk and silver lace on an officer's jacket and pelisse of those days compensated for their cost by their magnificence.

When the 15th was changed from Light Dragoons to Hussars[1] during 1807 and 1808 Long noted down the order in which the different items of dress and equipment should be gradually changed, and made an analysis—article by article and piece by piece, complete with details of the materials used and tailors' and makers' charges— of the various jackets, pelisses, cloaks, pantaloons, waistcoats, overalls, stable clothing, trousers, gaiters, caps, accoutrements, and saddlery required. Further documents went to show that, on a comparison of actual outlay and the Government allowances, the lieutenant-colonel would make a steady income. He might be 17s. 0d. a head out of pocket on each man for saddlery, but was 13s. 11d. up for accoutrements, while on clothing he gained throughout as much as £3 and

[1] Although the 15th changed their name from "Light Dragoons" to "Hussars" at this period, they are referred to by either of these titles in contemporary memoirs.

over for every trooper, and a little less on a sergeant. This profit would be repeated every two years. Besides throwing a light on contemporary prices and materials, the figures kept by Long illustrate the typical attitude of the times towards public money, which was regarded as fair game by anyone smart enough to collect it.

The 15th was (and is) a first-rate regiment, and added to its past glories when it went out to the Peninsula. True it is that Long never had the good fortune to be directly in command during action, but it cannot be doubted that the Regiment's nobly won honours were largely due to his careful and intelligent control.

Long was to remain the Lieutenant-Colonel of the 15th for the rest of his life. Lieutenant-Colonel was in fact the highest paid permanent rank to which most successful soldiers attained. It is true that each regiment had one full colonel, and that this post was most eagerly sought after. But by the nature of things these appointments were few in number. It is also true, of course, that the higher ranks, from brevet colonel to general, were paid when actually employed on the staff. But in peace-time there were few staff vacancies, so that many a general drew for the greater part of his life only the pay of what we would probably call to-day his substantive rank of lieutenant-colonel.

However hard Long worked with his regiment, a break with Cumberland was inevitable. Both were proud and determined men, but the final result could not fail to be what it was: the retreat of the Lieutenant-Colonel from an untenable position before the assaults of the Royal Prince.

VII

Coruña

IN 1808 Robert Long was gazetted colonel by brevet on the staff. This meant that he was not the colonel or proprietor of a regiment, with all the control over and profit from the regimental cash which that implied. It simply meant that Long was promoted outside Cumberland's direct sphere of influence. The arrangement was come to after Sir Harry Calvert, the Adjutant-General to the Forces from 1799 till 1818, had submitted for Long's approval and alteration the official letter of appointment. In return, Long's letter of acceptance was sub-edited by Calvert.

The truth is that, while Long was recognized as an able cavalry officer, matters had come to such a personal pass between him and Cumberland that the good of the Regiment demanded a change. Long in his acceptance of his new appointment stressed "the peculiar circumstances" governing the situation. He certainly had Calvert's approval and support, and most probably that of the Duke of York also, who bore no special affection for his violent brother.

Long's place in active command of the 15th Light Dragoons was taken by Colquhoun Grant,[1] a more fortunate soldier than Long proved to be, and favoured throughout his life by the friendship not only of Cumberland, whose Groom of the Bedchamber he was, but of Wellington, under whom he had served at Seringapatam in 1799. Once again in the years ahead Long and Grant were to meet directly, when for the second time Grant was to take over Long's command under even more unfavourable and distasteful circumstances.

In October 1808 Long was appointed to the staff of the Army in Spain, where our commander was his friend and former chief, Sir John Moore.

British troops had landed in Portugal during the previous August under Sir Arthur Wellesley, and had cleared Junot and the French out of Portugal in a brisk little campaign which included the actions of Roliça and Vimiero. Vimiero, on August 21, was marked not only by complete victory, but by the fact that on that notable day the British forces had no fewer than three commanders—Sir Arthur Wellesley,

[1] Sir Colquhoun Grant (1764?-1835) had been A.D.C. to the Prince Regent. He should not be confused with Wellington's brilliant intelligence officer and 'escapist' of the same name and the same period.

Sir Harry Burrard, and Sir Hew Dalrymple. Junot had been able to gain evacuation from Lisbon on the favourable terms agreed to at the Convention of Cintra, which shocked the public at home and was denounced as humiliating. But the Spanish resistance against the French occupation of their country had strengthened and flamed up once more. Then Napoleon himself had swept over the Pyrenees, and thundered down to restore the French position and suppress what he regarded as rebellion.

The French thrusts to the south of the Peninsula were, however, disrupted by an astonishing advance of the British forces from their bases in Portugal on to the French rear and lines of communications. As all three commanders at Vimiero had been recalled to explain to Parliament just how they had managed to win and waste a victory, Sir John Moore was the man responsible for this daring move.

Argument is unending as to whether Moore knew what he was about or whether whatever he did was well or ill done. To Napoleon the presence of the British red-coat on his own soil (and Spain had been given to brother Joseph) was electrifying. From Germany and Italy he hurried veterans of the Grand Army, and by the beginning of November he had one hundred and twenty thousand troops in Spain, which he hurled at Moore's army.

This was the position when Long set off to take up his new appointment. By the time he arrived in Spain the great retreat to Vigo and Coruña had begun. Long traversed scores of leagues searching Northern Spain for Headquarters. The British forces had tarried at Salamanca until there was no chance of returning once more to Portugal. A dreadful rapid rush was made to the north-western corner of the Peninsula. Gallant rear-guard actions were fought, including a cavalry fight at Sahagun, on December 21, where the 15th Hussars did great work. A French regiment of Chasseurs were annihilated, and the enemy commander seems to have been petrified by the beautiful accuracy and quick manœuvres of the men whom Long had trained. Colquhoun Grant was present, and was wounded in this affair.

Long's travels brought him to Vigo, where he had news of the arrival there of Major-General Robert Crauford and his Light Brigade, who had separated from Moore and marched under shocking conditions of haste, snow, and hunger, but comparatively unmolested by the French. Here Long also had sound information that Moore himself was marching for Coruña, hotly pursued by the French. Napoleon was no longer leading the chase, for, when he discovered that it was improbable that the British could be caught, he had handed over the pursuit to Soult, and hurried back to Paris to cope with a conspiracy hatched by those wily intriguers Talleyrand and Fouché.

Also at Vigo were the British transports, stormbound there on their passage to Coruña. Long sailed with them, and landed on January 14, 1809, two nights before the famous battle. He found Moore, and dined with him. Next morning they rode the outposts together before the fighting began. Long had no command during the engagement, and was throughout the day at Moore's side. In the faded and damp-stained notebook which he used as a diary during these times he wrote in rapid pencil this account:

Monday, 16th January 1809. At about $\frac{1}{2}$ past 3 P.M. the French began an attack which lasted until dark at night. Sir John Moore desperately wounded and Sir D. Baird[1] the same. When the action was over returned to Coruña and attended Sir J. Moore in his last moments. He died precisely as the evening gun fired on board the Admiral's ship— 8 o'clock.[2]

Next day, after the hurried funeral on the ramparts, the British sailed for England before Soult's beaten troops could rally and prevent them. Long's diary goes on to record the gathering of the fleet, days of high winds and storm, dangers of shipwreck, the topmast of a ship floating by with a body lashed to it, and final arrival off the English shore on January 27, 1809.

[1] Sir David Baird (1757–1829) had commanded the 18,000 troops sent direct to Coruña from England, and became second-in-command to Moore.

[2] Also present among the small group round Moore's death-bed were three others whom Long was to meet again: Colquhoun Grant, Henry Hardinge, and Sir Thomas Graham.

VIII

The Walcheren Expedition

THERE was a brief pause after the return from Coruña before Long found fresh active service by appointment as Adjutant-General to the Walcheren Expedition in the summer of 1809. It was during this pause that his nephew, young Edward Noel, the son of brother Edward and Byron's friend, was lost. His uncle had watched with great interest the young Coldstreamer's baptism of fire in the Danish Expedition of August–September 1807, sent to seize the Danish fleet lest it be used by Napoleon against Britain.

It is typical of Robert Long that he envied all who went to Denmark because of the experience they gained, that he rejoiced in the wide and varied aspects of military life which his nephew was meeting, and that he abominated the expedition itself, which he called "this violent measure and outrageous attack on the confidence, honor and independence of a nation at amity with us."

By the end of March 1809 the news had reached England of the night collision off Lisbon which caused the death of young Long. The Coldstream's transport *Prince George* had first run down and sunk an American brig and almost immediately afterwards run foul of the 50-gun ship H.M.S. *Isis*. When the mizzen-mast went overboard, there was some natural confusion and many tried to get aboard the *Isis*; with some others, Edward Noel fell between the two ships and was lost.

It was at the same time that the Cabinet began to make definite inquiries about the possibility of an expedition to descend upon Flushing and Antwerp, to seize the French squadron there, and lay to waste the defences, harbour, and shipbuilding improvements upon which Napoleon was just then concentrating much of his energies. There was also the strong possibility that such a descent would act as a powerful diversion to aid our Austrian allies, whose white uniforms were once again in the toils: after worsting Napoleon at Aspern-Essling, they had been defeated at Wagram, and were on the point of surrender.

Castlereagh and Canning, already jealous and at cross-purposes, were War Minister and Foreign Minister in the ailing Duke of Portland's Cabinet which planned this expedition. The proposal to attack the island of Walcheren, in the river Scheldt, aroused great doubt in both military and naval minds as to the chances of success. Between these and other handicaps the Walcheren Expedition had little real opportunity of succeeding.

The military commander was Pitt's brother, the Earl of Chatham, able, indolent, indifferent, and at least as much interested in the welfare of the live turtles he carried round with him in a water-cart for soup-making purposes as in defeating the French. Sir Richard Strachan, the naval commander, was as bustling as Chatham was statuesque. But neither was up to the job before him. An enormous armament was collected, and over 40,000 soldiers took part. It was in fact one of the biggest armies ever despatched abroad by this country until the last fifty years.

Long's position as Adjutant of this force was thus extremely onerous and responsible. Recrimination and almost unbridled abuse were ultimately showered on the heads of all who took part, both by those who were their colleagues and by those in England who sat in judgment in Parliament and the Press. It is therefore noteworthy that Long's share escaped challenge. The staff work in fact was well done.

The initial instructions and the higher command could not and did not escape censure. The islands of Walcheren and South Beveland, in the mouth of the Scheldt, were captured, it is true, and Flushing reduced after a successful fortnight's siege, by mid-August 1809. Some 8000 prisoners were taken, and our own loss was under 800, including missing. But time had been lost, the defences and garrison of Antwerp strengthened, and the French squadron had reached the city without difficulty; though their masts and rigging were clearly visible among the spires and roofs they might have been at Brest for all the power we had of taking them. As for acting as a diversion to take the French pressure from the Austrians, that had ceased with the collapse of our Allies, who had signed an armistice on July 25. Austria eventually signed the peace treaty of Vienna with France on October 14, 1809.

The Walcheren Expedition furnished a striking and in many ways unusual example of the failure of our combined-operations technique. Chatham and Strachan were soon at daggers drawn, each hinting that the other should do more, each resenting even the slightest shadow of interference with his own affairs. Then, when the damp heat and mists of the islands brought on the local 'low fever,' Chatham and the Army had to worry about more pressing matters than their quarrel with the Navy or, for that matter, than their quarrel with the French, who on the whole disturbed us very little. Chatham ceased to exchange angry and difficult letters with Strachan and turned his attention to the rapid and irresistible advances in the figures showing men sick.

On August 6, 1809, under 700 men were shown under this heading. By September 3, 1809, there were over 8000 in hospital, and the dead and ill were both growing in numbers. A council was held, and early in September Chatham, his staff, and all except 15,100 troops sailed away to England. The garrison left on Walcheren was so decimated by sickness that on December 23 the island was abandoned after Flushing harbour had been destroyed.

Altogether there died over 4000 men of Chatham's force; and six months later 11,000 men were still officially returned as sick. There was a tremendous public row and a Parliamentary inquiry. Chatham was accused, quite correctly, of having submitted a private and personal report on the whole affair direct to the King. Strachan was proved guilty of having made some extremely critical comments in his official correspondence about the military commander. Castlereagh and Canning came to blows and fought a duel on September 21, Canning receiving a slight wound. The Government collapsed, and journalists, officers, and politicians had a glorious time. The Duke of Portland died, and was succeeded by Spencer Perceval.[1]

It was too much to expect that Long could stand aside. He embraced the Army cause with great fervour, abused the Navy right and left, and drafted notes for Chatham's use in his defence at the inquiry. His mind when dealing with a situation which was dangerous never took count of the possibilities of reaction on his own career, but solely on what he considered the merits of the case. Over Walcheren Long had no doubts. In the first place the thing was probably impossible (and most military and very many naval men agreed with him), and in the second place the Admiral's behaviour stultified the whole programme. Mistakes were no doubt made, both before and during the expedition.

Long's loyalty did him little good. The inquiry dragged on for over two months early in 1810. Long himself, from all the evidence which he and others gave, had no reason to be ashamed of his own share. From his first sailing in H.M.S. *Venerable* to his return in September his work appears to have been impeccable. But Chatham's secret and certainly unconstitutional narrative, put before the King in practically a private capacity, compelled his resignation from the office of Master-General of the Ordnance.

Three great volumes of Long's correspondence concern this Walcheren Expedition. From these papers much detailed information can be gained, for he preserved an almost complete set of embarkation forms and weekly states, with many other returns. He also kept copies of the circular letters governing the conduct and arrangements of the troops "embarked on Foreign Service": baggage, horses, absent officers, inspections, embarkation, ammunition, women and

---

[1] Spencer Perceval, K.C. (1762–1812), after serving as Solicitor-General, Attorney-General, and Chancellor of the Exchequer, succeeded the Duke of Portland as Prime Minister in 1809. He was assassinated in the lobby of the House of Commons on May 11, 1812, by a bankrupt merchant named John Bellingham, who thought the Tory Government to blame for his difficulties.

children (and their allowances), staff appointments, chaplains, medical staff, Royal Artillery and drivers, Royal Engineers, Royal Military Draftsmen, Royal Military Artificers, commissariat, sick certificates, and records of paroles and counter-signs. For possible prize money Long also collected nominal rolls of many regiments, which are to be found bound up with letters dealing with the purchase of twenty-five sheep for hospital stores on the voyage out, memoranda on hospital-ship accommodation (significantly revised on August 27, 1809), the names of all the French prisoners and deserters taken in the various actions and captures, notes on alleged plundering by troops, reports on suspected spies, and a copy of Long's official journal of his proceedings from July 19 to September 10, 1809.

One series of letters concerns a rebellious junior chaplain accused of blurting out, apropos of an order of Chatham's which regulated divine worship, that if Lord Chatham "could not conduct the affairs of the Church better than he had those of the Army he would prove himself very deficient in sense." Though there were doubtless a great many of the expeditionary force who might agree with this comment, such language could not be tolerated. One forced apology was rejected as being insufficiently complete, and finally a most abject and humiliating withdrawal was extracted from the erring clergyman.

Sir Harry Calvert also exchanged a few personal and private letters on the campaign, as from the Horse Guards Adjutant-General to the Adjutant of the Force Abroad, and as from one Old Harrovian to another. These letters give a fair view of contemporary opinion in highly placed quarters on both the Peninsular and Walcheren Expeditions. Calvert trembled for Wellesley in Spain, where Talavera had just been fought. After this victory we had been forced to abandon our wounded to the French and march rapidly away from the scene of our triumph, and this made Calvert fear to think what might happen next. The Scheldt excursion was written off completely. Calvert agreed with Long that, "with a pair of compasses, a map, a little knowledge of the nature of the country and a little insight into the history of the Dutch wars," people in Downing Street might well have been convinced of the true prospects facing our men. As much had been done as had ever been expected, and Lord Chatham had "conscientiously discharged his duty like an honest man." He wound up with a friendly hint that though spirits were both detrimental and dangerous as a preservative against the effects of the Walcheren climate bitters were highly recommended.

Whatever the truth about the expedition to Walcheren (and controversy is still engaged in assessing its feasibility and execution) it was unfortunate that Long should have been forced into another personal bicker with authority.

IX

Posting to the Peninsula

AFTER keeping himself at the disposal of Parliament in the spring of 1810 Robert Long saw no more service for months. From a negative aspect he was fortunate in that he appears to have escaped the dreaded fever which thinned the ranks of all the Walcheren regiments and caused many an officer to carry with him on all future campaigns a bottle of "bark" (or quinine) instead of a pistol in one of his saddle holsters. Long wore flannel under-waistcoats till June 1810 it is true, but more as a precaution than a cure, and he was afterwards able to dispense with them.

Most of this period of enforced idleness Long spent with his twin-brother, Charles, at the latter's home at Langley Hall. This house being a fine centre for sport, Charles appears to have spent his days in the open air, hunting, shooting, and coursing. The Bramshill Foxhounds was his favourite pack; he kept his own greyhounds; and he brought his five children up to ride far and fast like himself. There is a record than in his fiftieth year he was "in despair" on the Thames bank near Streatley, because the fox and hounds swam the stream and he missed the kill.

Langley Hall vanished in flames nearly a century ago and was replaced by a farm built on the old foundations, so that although there is, in the neighbouring village of Beedon, an inn still called Langley Hall no trace remains of the house which Robert Long used as his headquarters except a derelict and overgrown set of gates at the entrance to an abandoned drive.

In early January 1811 Robert was writing gossip to his father. He discussed the draughts that whistled through his brother's home, talked of pattern shoes and a patent paste for mending china and glass, and of the visit of an old officer of the York Hussars to Langley. But fireside chats in the 'Siberian' winter and a wistful cry for some lovely petticoat to visit him and desultory talk about the Regency Bill and thawing snow began to fade from the picture when, on January 16, a summons to London arrived from Colonel Henry Torrens, the Military Secretary to the Commander-in-Chief.

Long's first reaction was typical. He would not consider any offer unless "proper to be accepted." Nor would he have "anything to do with Marshal Beresford and his Portuguese Heroes." It would have been far better for Long to have stuck to this resolution, but the zeal of the man carried him away. Within five days of receiving this call to an interview Robert had carried brother Charles off to Thomas's Hotel, in Berkeley Square, seen Torrens, accepted the explanation that the staff appointment in question was offered in a manner fitting both to the service in general and to Long in particular, been gazetted brigadier-general, and was busy interviewing possible A.D.C.'s. It was true, he wrote to his father, that the brigade he was to take out to Portugal was an infantry command. It was also true that he had no time for proper preparation, because the troops were already embarking. But it was all in the cause of duty, and Long was eager to go, whatever his earlier doubts had been, and however dubious he felt about the possibilities of ultimate success in the Peninsula.

A brief note to his sister Elizabeth, besides finding room for a few patriotic sentiments, shows the departing soldier puting his affairs in order. "Tell Mary's[1] nurse," he wrote, "I can have no objection to *father* any production of hers. You must find a Proxy, and if there is any tax let me know the amount, and I will furnish you with the means of discharging it."

* * *

The results of Wellington's opening campaign of 1808 and of Moore's winter marches before Coruña had almost brought about the complete evacuation of the Peninsula by our forces: many, particularly the Whigs, considered the enterprise to be hopeless. But in 1809 Wellington had returned in command, and once again led out our Army from its strong-point in Lisbon. He, and our Tory Government at home, received encouragement in this line of action because the Spanish would not accept defeat in their struggle against the French. Town after town broke out in angry resistance, and one Spanish army after another was brought into the field. It is also true that these same armies often ran like hares or lay dormant for lack of food and transport until they either disintegrated of their own accord or were dispersed by the enemy. Many Spaniards of the upper and middle classes were prepared at some time or other to accept French domination, and often the Spanish masses merely endured life in silent misery.

But somewhere in Spain at any time during the long fight which raged from the famous 2nd of May 1808[2] to the final defeat of the

---
[1] The Mary mentioned was Elizabeth Howard's second daughter and third child, in 1811 aged four.
[2] This spontaneous outburst by the people of Madrid against the French occupying forces ended in Spanish disaster that day, but it marked the opening of implacable armed resistance.

French, in 1814, however black the outlook and however triumphant the French eagles, there were to be found Spaniards in arms against their foe. They might be few and scattered, and without hope, or they might only consist of guerrilla bands, without uniforms or artillery—bloody-minded ruffians who were ready to enjoy committing the most foul outrages on any who came within reach of their knives, cords, or roasting fires. Their British allies nearly all despised them openly, and thought bitterly of Spanish promises not kept, Spanish boasts unfulfilled, of treachery and cowardice often displayed, of General Cuesta's immobility at Talavera, and wounded comrades stripped and murdered.

The British Army by itself, however, could never have hoped to win the Peninsular War. Wellington's recognition of this fact indicates as clearly as do his military victories the strength of his mind and his patient determination. During 1810 he had learned quite firmly that while he must act alone the French armies could never act together. Forced to withdraw before a great French concentration under Marshal Masséna, Wellington had constructed the Lines of Torres Vedras, knowing that with the Royal Navy behind him his own supplies were safe, and that Spanish turbulence and unquenchable hostility would be sure to cause hunger, shortage, and retreat to the French.

He had learned other things too. The many volumes of his published dispatches abound in examples of his care on all points of detail, of letters dealing with boots, cartridges, mules, money, beehives, and camp-kettles, besides affairs of State and official accounts of pitched battles. He had learned French tactics and perfected his own technique, opposing his double lines of red-coats behind a thick screen of riflemen to the French columns and skirmishing light infantry. He had come to accept the shocking facts that he would always be short of artillery, always lack an adequate battering-train, always be in danger of losing his supplies or men because another diversion somewhere outside the Peninsula might be mounted by the Government. He had grown to know with what immense reliance he could depend on the British infantry regiments in battle and how little discipline might be expected in retreat.

By March 1811 he had come to certain definite conclusions about the British cavalry. The one thing they could be relied upon to do was to gallop far and fast against the enemy—too far and too fast, for they would neither arrange supports nor be trusted to rally and reform. No cavalry general he had met by the time of Robert Long's arrival had inspired any confidence.

At the end of the war, when the fighting was over, Wellington went to the trouble of writing a long and excellent memorandum for the use of his cavalry generals on the proper handling of cavalry. In various ways, by exhortation, by criticism, or slighting comment, but rarely by praise, he tried to indicate the lines of conduct that English horse-regiments should pursue. There were never enough regiments of either light or heavy cavalry. Horsemastership left much to be desired, particularly among the English, so that it was with difficulty that every cavalryman was provided with a horse, and maintained in that desirable situation. Moreover, Wellington was constantly threatened with the almost complete loss of such cavalry units as he possessed. Either they might be lured into an ambush or hurled against unbroken French infantry squares. Both these disasters, luckily on a small scale, were practically annual occurrences. Yet quite frequently when Wellington needed his horsemen in a hurry the general commanding the cavalry, probably still smarting under some well-deserved rebuke for rash galloping and reckless assaults, would be loathe to move without definite instructions.

It is possible that at their first meeting Wellington took Robert Long for a possible solution to his difficulties. The Commander-in-Chief's secretary, Colonel Torrens, had written a confidential letter describing the new brigadier as "an active and most intelligent officer, and possessed of no ordinary share of talents. I am confident he will give you satisfaction." It is true that their first meeting in the flesh may have given rise to some doubts, because Long in his early letters displays quite freely the somewhat critical attitude to the "Hero of Talavera" typical of most Whiggistically-inclined officers of the day. There never seems to have been any chance of the two men taking warmly to one another. And though it is a fact that Wellington did not often establish really close relations with other men there were some who managed it, like his brother-in-law Edward Pakenham; and there were many whom he dealt with on equal and very friendly terms, as for instance Beresford and Rowland Hill. Later in his Peninsular career Long was to become an enthusiastic admirer of Wellington's genius, but by that time it was too late. Too much damage had been done behind the scenes.

Apparently Long's first communication was a complaint, since he believed he was to be given an infantry brigade. In truth, however, he was destined for a noble command, and took over three British and two Portuguese regiments of cavalry in a great detached force under Beresford.

When Long landed at Lisbon on March 3, 1811, the general position was most complicated. In the south of Spain Allied forces were defending Cadiz against Marshal Victor. Soult was invading Estremadura; he had dispersed a Spanish army, and was on the point of receiving the surrender of Badajoz under unhappy circumstances of near-treachery by the Spanish commander. Various other French forces were operating in the north of Spain and along the eastern seaboard, performing what were practically police duties in a manner frequently marked by great cruelty and oppression. Masséna was on the point of withdrawal from before the Lines of Torres Vedras, where his men had lain, hungry, exasperated, and helpless, for the winter months.

Wellington had divided his forces. He followed Masséna himself, and sent Beresford across the Tagus to relieve Badajoz and to do what he could to delay, defeat, or fend off Soult.

Within the next three months the French were to be driven out of Portugal after Wellington's hard-won victory at Fuentes de Oñoro, and the battle of Albuera was to be fought between Beresford and Soult. The French troubles were, in fact, about to increase and multiply, and the balance of victory begin to tilt towards Allied triumph. The thing was not certain or settled, but by the end of the summer of 1811 final success in Spain for Napoleon was all but impossible.

PART II
A GENERAL OFFICER IN ACTION

I

Arrival in the Peninsula

Last Letter from London before embarking
TO HIS FATHER, EDWARD LONG

Berkeley Square
Friday, 25 Jan., 1811

I have received all your communications to date and have to thank you for all the good wishes they contain. I *hope* you are mistaken in supposing my selection for the service I am about to be employed upon as originating in any wish to injure or annoy me. I have now every reason to be of a contrary opinion, and if the assurances of Public Men, professing themselves to be my friends, are to be trusted, I am bound to maintain this opinion till I see further reason to alter it. I consider myself as going to Portugal to command a Brigade of Cavalry, and that it is only from the scarcity of General Officers for duty, that I am required to take charge of a Brigade of Infantry, till it arrives at its post. Had another officer been found (M. General Ackland was the last applied to) I should have gone out independently. It is clear that opening for the Cavalry is occasioned by General Fane's[1] return to this Country with no apparent intention of going back again; and this opening I expect to fill. I think 3 months will decide the business in Portugal one way or another. . . .

It would of course, be a melancholy pleasure to me to receive your personal blessing before I embark, and if I could away from Town tomorrow I would not fail to make the detour by Arundel for this purpose. But I feel persuaded that my departure from hence cannot take place before Sunday morning next, and on *that* day, I *must* be at Portsmouth in order to embark on Monday, and have a few minutes to give directions about my Horses, etc., from which I shall, unfortunately, be separated, they going in Transports, whilst I am directed to go in the "Victory." The Troops, generally speaking, proceeding in Line of Battle Ships, not an unnecessary moment will be lost in putting to sea, and I saw a letter yesterday from Mr. Yorke,[2]

---

[1] Major-General Henry Fane (1778–1840), M.P. for Lyme Regis from 1796 until 1818, later returned to the Peninsula, and fought at Vittoria.
[2] Charles Philip Yorke (1764–1834) was First Lord of the Admiralty.

urging expedition in the strongest terms. Consequently, should the wind be fair, I think it likely that the first Division will sail on Monday. You see, therefore, My Dear Sir, the necessity of my being prepared against such a contingency, and that I am not in a situation to dare to run any risk. After all, Leave-takings are only bitter trials, consolatory certainly in the end but disorganising the whole system at a time when composure is most to be desired. I should, and shall, nevertheless, embrace with pleasure the adoption of your proposal if the power of doing so is afforded me. But I candidly confess my hopes on this point are very slender indeed.

I must beg you to say everything kind for me to your gallant Colonel[1] when he returns. Being on the wing I have not replied to his communications but I feel most sincerely gratified by his affectionate wishes and attentions.

The Passage to the Peninsula is arranged

TO HIS FATHER, EDWARD LONG

George Inn, Portsmouth

Sunday, 27 Jan., 1811

I arrived here this evening from Town which I quitted this morning at ½ past 8, leaving poor Carolus behind and with a sad London cough upon me. I wish it had been in my power to have taken Arundel in my way, but the doing so merely to go through the painful process of leave-taking, and without the power of remaining with you for an hour, appeared to me an object rather to be avoided than coveted. Still I feelingly regret quitting the Country without receiving your blessing, and if I had found that a possibility of excursing from hence to Arundel without risk of losing my passage I should not hesitate doing so. I hear, however, that it is determined to proceed to sea as soon as the 36 Regt.[2] is embarked, and this will take place tomorrow. If the wind is fair they will probably sail in the night or early on Monday morning next. All officers are ordered to sleep on board tomorrow, the preparatory signal for sailing, and it is in consequence my intention to be on board to dinner. I told you that the "Victory"

---

[1] Colonel Howard, Robert Long's brother-in-law by his marriage to Elizabeth Long. He was an M.P. and later became Lord Howard.

Note on the Names of Military Officers mentioned in the Manuscript. Readers who are interested in the details concerning the many officers mentioned by Robert Long, from subalterns to generals, and in the British or Portuguese Forces, can satisfy their curiosity, for those not in the *Dictionary of National Biography*, by consulting the remarkable card-index entitled *The Peninsular Roll Call*, compiled by Captain Lionel S. Challis, and now deposited in the library of the Royal United Service Institution.

[2] The Worcestershire Regiment.

is to furnish me with a berth, and I am not concerned to hear that the Admiral, Sir Joseph Yorke,[1] has hoisted his flag in the "Vengeur," instead of the "Victory" as reported.

I was so hard pressed for time as to be obliged to give up the whole of last night to wind up my concerns. Mr. Greenwood's[2] extreme liberality and kindness have enabled me to make my equipments upon a credit with his House, but I have promised that he shall receive the allowance I have been in the habit of drawing from Messrs. Rutherford and Wagstaffe. I therefore beg you will have the goodness to give them directions accordingly.

The officer who accompanies me as my Aide de Camp is Capt. Dean, a natural son of Lord Rivers.[3] The Hove family take such an interest in his welfare that I could not resist so favourable an opportunity of making them a small return for all their kindnesses and attentions to me. He is not, perhaps, *exactly* the sort for a Cavalry A.D.C., but he will not be long in learning the secret and he seems willing and intelligent.

I have received no orders whatever to take under my command any of the Corps embarking, and I heartily rejoice at the circumstance. It will leave me at liberty to repair immediately, on my arrival at Lisbon, to Lord W.'s Head Quarters and arrange I hope at once the situation I am to continue to fulfil. . . .

Gossip down Channel in the "Victory"

TO HIS FATHER, EDWARD LONG

"*Victory,*" *Off Culver Cliff*
Isle of Wight
30 *Jan.*, 1811. ½ *past* 11 A.M.

The Admiral has made the signal of an opportunity offering to send letters ashore. I therefore avail myself of it to give you the latest information in my power of our movements. We weighed from Spithead at 8 this morning and have been beating up ever since against a strong breeze at S.E. As soon as we weather the Isle of Wight we shall have a glorious race of it and if the wind continues as it now is

---

[1] Admiral Sir Joseph Yorke (1768–1831) was Lord of Admiralty, and for many years M.P. for Reigate.
[2] Mr Greenwood, the banker. His firm, Greenwood and Cox, became the well-known military bankers—Cox's Bank.
[3] George Pitt, Baron Rivers of Stratfieldsaye (1751–1828), was a nephew of Long's late friend and former commanding officer, Sir William Augustus Pitt, who had died on December 29, 1809. It was an odd coincidence that Stratfieldsaye, where Long retired for a time when the war was over, should later have become Wellington's estate.

shall be in the mouth of the Channel by this time tomorrow, and off the Tagus perhaps by Sunday next. If you can bear therefore a pinch for three or four days we shall be most happy to be favored with a continuance of this keen cutting weather. The "Victory" is not in high trim. Two hundred of her men are performing quarantine in the Harbour in consequence of their having been sent to assist the "Elizabeth," on board of which a violent fever caught from French prisoners had shewn itself. The Captain, Dumaresq, is a young man, and having always lived with the Admiral and of course kept no table of his own, he has been put to great inconvenience in making the necessary arrangements for our accommodation within the time limited. He is to receive however £150 for each of the two Brigadiers on board, and I hope that will secure him from loss. The 36th Regiment are on board and you would hardly believe that there are upwards of 90 officers, of various descriptions, accommodated with berths. Such is the elasticity of a Line of Battle Ship.

The spot where poor Nelson stood when he received his fatal wound is marked by a bit of lignum vitae let into the deck, and what with his arms and various other tokens, the ship is sufficiently designated to have been the Theatre of the Hero's immortality.

Capt. D. told me a circumstance yesterday that I knew not before: viz. that as the gallant Admiral was bringing home the cask wherein he was deposited, being overfilled with brandy, suddenly burst, and up bounced the Admiral to the great surprise and terror of the Sentry standing over him. Of all the crew that served on that glorious occasion the Gunner alone remains now on board.

I had a sad mishap yesterday at Portsmouth. One of the horses I bought in Town was claimed by the owner as stolen property. I have endeavoured to arrange it as well as I could, but I fear I must lose the sum originally given for the animal.

We are all in high spirits, and tho' I see little prospect of Lord W. being able to get out of the cul de sac in which he is placed,[1] and still less that Masséna[2] will think it worth his while to force him, I hope, nevertheless, that I may soon have something to announce.

[1] Wellington, by defeating the French at Busaco on September 27, 1810, had been able to withdraw his outnumbered army into the hilly district north of Lisbon, between the Tagus and the coast, and had held the Lines of Torres Vedras. The starving French had hesitated to attack: Wellington would not be drawn into sallying forth. "I could," he remarked, "lick those fellows any day, but it would cost me ten thousand men, and, as this is the last army England has, we must take care of it." After a month Masséna had given up any attempt at blockade, and had slipped away one night in mid-November to Santarem, on the Tagus, some fifty miles from Lisbon.

[2] André Masséna (1756–1817), nicknamed "l'Enfant chéri de la Victoire," had gained distinction in the battles of Rivoli (1797), Essling and Wagram (1809), and had been made Duc de Rivoli and Prince d'Essling by Napoleon. Masséna was, at the beginning of 1811, commanding the French troops in Portugal.

Windbound in English Coastal Waters
TO HIS BROTHER CHARLES BECKFORD LONG

H.M.S. Victory (Steering for Torbay)
1st Feb., 1811

Our commencement has not been so propitious as we had reason to hope, as will appear by the following Journal of our proceedings....

Wednesday, Jan. 30

The Admiral, Sir J. Yorke, in the "Vengeur" and the "Victory" both weighed from Spithead at 8 A.M. and beat down to St. Helens to join the remainder of the fleet, which was not accomplished before ½ past 11. About that hour the whole fleet assembled round the Admiral and sent a boat on board for instructions. At ½ past 12 received the order to take the order of sailing, and at 20 minutes past 1 o'clock P.M. the Admiral bore up on a S.W. course followed in succession by the Squadron in two lines. The wind at S.E. blew fresh, but the Squadron carried but little sail. The wind southerned during the night, and for what purpose I know not the Squadron lay to for 4 hours.

Thursday, 31 Jan.

The wind shifted more to the westward. Fell in with the convoy that sailed under the Franchise from Spithead on Tuesday, ships very much dispersed. The wind freshened towards noon, breezed suddenly round about ½ past 4 P.M. to the North Westerly taking all the fleet aback at the same moment. The "Pompée" had her fore topsail split, the "Orion" sprung her main topgallant mast. Continued to blow very hard all night. Every ship close reefed and carrying only fore and mizzen topsails, and main storm-staysail. In the morning the wind having shifted again to the South West, and the appearance of the weather being bad the signal made to bear up for Torbay at ½ past 8 A.M.

Friday, 1 Feb.

8½ A.M. bore up for Torbay, the Franchise convoy doing the same. At this time the Squadron was to the *westward* of the *Lizard* point, so that had we sailed from St Helens on Tuesday, or even made the most of our time on Wednesday, we should probably have cleared the Channel and been at this moment with a fair wind in the Bay. At this moment ½ past 12 P.M. we are between the Dodman and Plymouth Sound, the land about 10 or 12 leagues on our larboard beam. We expect to reach Torbay about 4 P.M.

Nothing particular has occurred since our departure but the loss of one man who fell down the main hatchway into the hold and died of his bruises a few hours afterwards on Wednesday. Yesterday he was committed to the deep, and it was the first instance I had ever seen of a salt-water burial.

The body was sewn up in a hammock, with two shot at the feet, then placed upon a narrow grating (like what they cover the hatchway with) and there covered with the union flag, which flag was tied fast to the grating by a rope secured to the side of the ship, which also held fast the grating. When the burial was to take place, the bell was tolled, and the body brought up on the deck and placed at the entrance of the gangway, the feet towards the sea. The service was then read by the Purser, and, at the proper prayer, the grating with the corpse was heaved overboard into the sea, the body slipping through the colours as it reached the water, and disappearing. The grating and colours were then hauled on deck, and thus the ceremony ended.

The weather had been unpleasant since we came on board with a good deal of wet, and motion. I have been, as usual, a little squeamish but not sick. I feel the want of sleep most from the confounded squeaking of the bulkhead. Our daily assembly at dinner consists of Captain Dumaresq and the Purser who head the table. Brigadier General Byrne, Lt.Col. Cameron of the 79th[1] (a very gentlemanly man), Lt.Col. Turner of the West India Rangers, Lt. Col. Cochrane (Lord C.'s[2] brother) of the 36th, Major Nickson, two Aides de Camp and the Lieutenant of the watch. Our fare is not magnificent, nor under such circumstances could we expect it. We have as much as we want, and that is all we can require. The "Victory" is in very bad trim for a voyage in consequence of the absence of 200 of her best seamen who are now doing Quarantine in Portsmouth Harbour in consequence of a fever on board the "Elizabeth" to which ship they were detached to give their assistance. This misfortune has thrown the Captain all aback in the navigating the ship and the Crew are as awkward as those of a Transport. We therefore are obliged to be very cautious and make all snug before the night sets in. This circumstance however prevents our carrying sail, and of course delays the fleet.

We never saw the land after quitting the Isle of Wight on Wednesday till this morning, when we found ourselves to the South-westward

---

[1] Cameron was killed leading the 79th (the Cameron Highlanders) at Fuentes de Oñoro, May 5, 1811.
[2] Thomas Cochrane, styled Lord Cochrane (1775-1860), was at this time on half-pay as a result of his attacks on abuses in the Navy from which he was expelled, in 1814, on false charges of fraud. He was successively Admiral of the Chilean, Brazilian, and Greek Navies, until in 1832, having succeeded to the Earldom of Dundonald, he was reinstated in the British Navy.

of the Lizard, much further down Channel than was supposed. We shall have all this ground to go over again, but as the weather looks dirty and it blows hard, I do not know that a berth in Torbay will not be as pleasant as beating about in the chops of the Channel. The last time I was ever in that bay was with Edward in the year 1789, the year I left Harrow. What a distance of time to look back to, and yet how accurately I recollect the transactions of that period.

We are at this moment (1 p.m.) scudding past the Eddystone Light House going about 12 knots an hour in a heavy squall. It *lightens* strong in the south-east, but is clearing up in the west. I distinguish the plantations at Mount Edgecumbe, but the anchorage in Cawsand Bay is not sufficient for above 8 or 9 Line of Battle Ships, and the Sound is a bad anchorage. I feel very glad that my horses have been detained a day longer at Portsmouth instead of being exposed to the unnecessary beating they would have sustained had they been with us on this last cruise. Lord knows how long we shall now be detained, but I hope on every account as short a time as possible. I shall not close this account till we reach our Anchorage. Your kind and affectionate Scrib written on Sunday and sent with the Maps I never opened till this morning. The parcel arrived when we were all in a bustle, and I desired Ifland[1] to pack it up in statu quo in my Portmanteau, where it has ever since lain. Wishing to refer to the plans this morning, I then found your letter packed up in them, and it was a most agreeable surprise.

There is a grammar of the Portuguese language, published the day before I left Town by a person called *C. Laisne*, and sold by Dulau in Soho Square and Decorby in Bond St. It is very small and I wish therefore you would commission R. Dawkins[2] to purchase it for me, and get General Brownrigg to frank and send it by the Post to me. A Packet sails every Tuesday.

Torbay, Sat., 2nd Feb.

The squadron reached this anchorage yesterday evening at 6, and after the rough treatment we had received in the Channel we passed a delicious night. Everyone is now scribbling and working away to prepare for a second start the moment the wind favors. It has got round to the S.E. and as no boat is allowed to quit the Ship we may be off in an hour or detained here for a week. I have just seen a paper of the 30th containing rather unpleasant news from Portugal, as the Editor terms it. I see nothing in Drouet[3] scouring the country of the Guerrillas but the common precaution which every General should

---

[1] A manservant. [2] A brother-in-law.
[3] Jean-Baptiste Drouet, Comte d'Erlon, commanded the French 9th Corps.

take. Nor can I doubt but that the English Army will act like a besieged and the French one like a besieging force. It will rest with Masséna to determine whether having established satisfactorily his investment he will, in the first instance direct his attention to the taking of Abrantes, Badajos and Elvas, as a preliminary step to the complete subjugation of Portugal, *or* if he will disregard these fortresses and make every effort to assemble the greatest possible force he can muster to bring things to a termination by one determined effort upon Lord Wellington's position. Whatever he may determine upon I consider Lord W. as reduced positively to the defensive until a decisive blow has been struck somewhere. I cannot bring myself to believe that Lord W.'s *lines*[1] are of the description they are represented to be, or that he can defend them against an Enemy determined at any risk or loss to carry them. ... In every view of the subject, therefore, I can scarcely bring myself to think that our Army will long continue in Portugal. But time will shew much and will depend upon the extent of supplies which both sides are able to procure. It will be now my business however to leave the General to his own responsibility and confine myself to mine; and I shall have enough to do. Like an old rusty sword long put by, I feel that I have to begin everything again, and must go back to A.B.C. I shall not be sorry therefore if after my arrival we should remain unmolested sufficiently long to enable me to overhaul a little the *old* history, before I am called upon to put it in practice before a well exercised and experienced antagonist. A man, destined for service, should never be left two months unemployed! It throws him back sadly!

Write to Pater and acquaint him where I am and tell him I sent a Portmanteau to Park House,[2] which I request may have a quarter there till it can be conveniently returned to Langley to remain with my other things. I shall enclose the key of it in this letter.

And now, by best beloved Bro., I again take my leave, wishing you and yours from the bottom of my heart all health and every happiness this world can afford.

Life on Shipboard

TO C. B. LONG

Torbay, Tuesday Night

5 *Feb.*, 1811

I wrote you a letter this morning but the man to whom I intended entrusting it left the Ship before I was aware of it, and therefore I enclose it with this.

---

[1] The Lines of Torres Vedras, the secret of which was so well-kept that English as well as French were completely surprised.   [2] Edward Long's home at Arundel.

We weighed at ½ past 8 A.M. with the wind at S.E. blowing strong with a heavy sea, and after an eight hours attempt to beat out of the Bay, returned to our anchorage again at ½ past 3 P.M. The result of these unsuccessful efforts, if repeated much oftener, will oblige us to return to Portsmouth to refit. The "Ganges" this day was compelled to cut her cable to get under weigh. This is the fourth that has been lost since our arrival. The "Orion" sprung her fore-top-mast and spritsail-yard, and we split our fore-top-sail to pieces. The swell was so heavy that scarcely a ship could tack without wearing. I had a fine opportunity of seeing the coast where I used to ramble about so much in the year 1789. Teignmouth appears to be grown to an immense comparative size. Dawlish and Exmouth shew equal marks of increasing prosperity.

The wind has got round again to the westward of South, and I really think it likely that we may be detained here for weeks to come, for a prevalence of westerly and south-westerly winds is to be looked for. It is probable that my horses started from Portsmouth this day thro the Needles. Had we been at St. Helens, we should have run more than half down Channel, but Torbay is so much to leeward there is no getting out of the bite if it blows strong. We enjoy, under our misfortunes, the pleasure of a quiet berth for eating our dinner, and resting in our cots, and I have introduced a game of whist every evening which serves admirably to pass away the lingering hours of the evening, for as we dine at 4 P.M. some such resource is indispensable. I shall leave this open to give you the latest intelligence tomorrow, so for the present goodnight, and a good run to you with the C.C.[1] before I resume.

My Journal

Weds. 6 Feb.
Still at anchor with the wind at S.W. and a thick fog. No chance therefore of moving.

When at Langley I directed the Carpenter to make me a *Roughrider*, the article employed in breaking young horses and bitting old ones. It was intended for Le Marchant, to whom I request you will have the goodness to forward by directing it in the first instance to Major Wright at Marlow Place, Great Marlow, Bucks; to be left at the Swan Inn, Maidenhead, and forwarded thence to Marlow. Write a note at the same time to Wright to apprise him of the circumstance.

It is a sad thing to be so near the land and to hear so little of what is going on ashore! Very like a Prison, except in the treatment or

[1] Possibly the Craven Hunt.

rather behaviour of the Gaolers. Capt. Dumaresq is all civility and attention. A different character would give us the blue devils and bilious attacks from which we are happily free! I have a pleasure in thinking that you are better off, and at this moment perhaps enjoying your liberty in its pleasantest attire! Long may you continue so to do!

I forgot to apprise you of a promise I made Farmer Matthew that he should have the South American breed of pigs when Old Suck lay in. You must discharge this obligation for me.

A Brigadier applies for his Allowance
TO HIS FATHER, EDWARD LONG

H.M.S. *Victory*
Torbay, 6 *Feb.*, 1811

I am concerned still to have to announce our continued detention at this anchorage. We have made two efforts to put to sea, but ineffectually. These attempts have caused the squadron some injury in the loss of anchors and cables, masts sprung and sails torn to pieces. Indeed I had no conception that Ships of War could sustain under such circumstances casualties like those we have experienced, and they tend to confirm the truth of the reports I hear of the new system of economy adopted in the Dockyards, by which, to save the rigging, the loss of the Ships is risked.

We were beating yesterday for eight hours, trying to weather the start, and the threedeckers could scarcely get clear of the Berry Head. We split our foretopsail to pieces, and then returned quietly to our anchorage for the night. The wind is now S.W. with a thick fog.

Greenwood has behaved so liberally to me on a recent occasion, that I cannot forbear requesting you will be as punctual as your circumstances admit, in placing in his hands such pecuniary assistance as you can afford me. I have been obliged to anticipate the first Quarter, with a view not to be perfectly unprovided on my arrival at Lisbon. The remainder I wish him to receive in order to meet his advances to me.

Soldiering (in England at least) is a beggarly profession, and if I did not think my continuance in it involved your peace of mind, more than my own, I should long ago have pulled off my hat to it. As it is, we must fight on to the best of our ability till a Gaol or cannon shot puts an end to the speculation.

First Letter Home from the Peninsula
TO C. B. LONG

Lisbon, 4th March, 1811

Altho' dead tired and more than half asleep and purposing to set off tomorrow to Cartaxo to pay my obeisance to Lord W. I cannot go to bed without announcing to you my arrival in the Tagus yesterday after a most long and tempestuous voyage during which we experienced two severe gales of wind, one in the Channel the night we quitted Torbay for the last time, viz. the night of Friday the 15th Feby., and one more off Cape Finisterre during the night of the 23 and morning of the 24 Feby. After the latter breeze, we were obliged to stand back across the Bay of Biscay having the day before made the land near to Coruña (being distant from Cape Villana only about 2 leagues) to the latitude nearly of Ushant, as we had before been driven up Channel close to Portland.

But the Journal of these proceedings will be forwarded to you by the first opportunity after my return from Cartaxo. I landed this day about 10, and have employed the whole morning in running about after the first preliminaries.

I have got a good Quarter (where General Fane resided) but for a short continuance I propose going tomorrow at 5 A.M. by water to Villano and thence by the best means I can find to Cartaxo.

Reports this evening state the Enemy in movement. If so I shall have some difficulty in finding the Peer of Talavera.[1] But in war we should believe nothing of what we hear and only half of what we see.

Lord W. I am told is much disappointed by the delay attending our arrival, having proposed to employ this Force under Marshal Beresford[2] in raising the blockade or rather siege of Badajos, which event is now looked for as inevitable.

Reports today insinuate the supposition of the Enemy being about to retire from Santarem. If so I conjecture it will only be pour mieux sauter.

Lisbon is the Sink of Sinks, and I was much disappointed on entering the River[3] from the description I had heard of it. I shall be glad to take my departure.

The American ships are pouring in with provisions and the Army

---

[1] Talavera, fought on July 28, 1809, was a victory for British and Spanish arms. Sir Arthur Wellesley was raised to the peerage and became Viscount Wellington of Talavera.

[2] Since the spring of 1809 Sir William Beresford had been Generalissimo of the Portuguese armies.

[3] Tagus.

have now a supply of 8 months flour in store. I see no other marks of scarcity than the price of provisions, having had this day for dinner a bowl of soup, a joint of beef, a fowl and a dish of fish with very good wine. But this can only last at Lisbon, and the news from the frontier in this respect is most *faminous*. We shall nevertheless find enough to keep body and soul together, and that must suffice.

I found a letter from Slade[1] in the post office, stating that Lord W. had acquainted him with my appointment, and that his lordship intended giving me six squadrons of German Hussars for my command. It is not a very *large* one, but in quality most *excellent*, and I mean to make no difficulties—particularly till I get a little into the practice of the thing.

As I think the Enemy will still manoeuvre by the left bank, it only remains for me to say that the Town of Lisbon and the right bank of the Tagus as far as Belem can be bombarded from the opposite bank. Below Belem and Fort St. Julian, a considerable number of ships may be anchored out of gunshot, but in an unpleasant situation with a S.W. wind.

Works are going up round Fort St. Julian and Ozeras and also along the heights on the left bank; the former are not very formidable and the latter too extensive to be of much use.

I hope the "Victory" will sail before the packet and I entrust this note to Capt. Dumaresq accordingly.

State to my beloved Pater what I have written, and tell him he shall have a long dispatch on my return from Cartaxo.[2]

God bless you my best beloved and all belonging to you.

Affecly,
R.L.

PS. Blink asleep.

First Impressions of Portugal
TO C. B. LONG

Lisbon, Sat. 9th March, 1811

I wrote you two lines I think on the 5th inst. which announced my intention of going the next day to Cartaxo to see the Commander in chief.

I did so, but, chemin faisant, I learned that the Army was in movement in consequence of the retreat of the Enemy from their position at Santarem. Notwithstanding the uncertainty arising out of this state

---

[1] Major-General Jack Slade.

[2] It was at this moment that Edward Long made the suggestion that "our General's" letters should be kept and circulated by copies among the family and their friends, and it was thus that the present collection came to be preserved.

of things I persevered, and reached Santarem at 8 o'clock the same evening, where I was introduced to, and had an audience of, the Hero of Talavera. I found that he had directed me in orders to assume the command of an Infantry Brigade. I represented my disappointment at such an arrangement, and was told that it had taken place *in consequence of a supposed and previously arranged plan at the Horse Guards*.[1] His Lordship however assured me that it was his intention to provide for me otherwise, and seemed to insinuate a wish for my immediately joining the Army. I told him that I had come to Headquarters with only the shirt on my back to pay him my respects and receive his orders, but that nevertheless if I could be provided with a horse and the means of existence I would not return to Lisbon, otherwise it was impossible for me to undertake the duties of a General Officer, without first making the preparations necessary so to do, arising out of the absence of my horses, servants, etc.

It was then suggested that I should be furnished with an order to be accommodated with two horses temporarily from the Prince Regent's stables, that I should return to Lisbon to obtain them and join him with all convenient dispatch, or as he expressed his wish within three days.

I returned accordingly on Thursday night (day before yesterday) employed all yesterday in accomplishing with difficulty this arrangement, which was only completed this day at 12 o'clock when I dispatched my horses to Villafranca, with orders to proceed tomorrow and hope to be with his Lordship as soon after as the distance he may have advanced from Santarem will permit. Where this junction will be effected I know not because no information whatever of his Lordship's movements or of those of the Enemy has been received at Lisbon since I quitted Santarem and at that time it was perfectly unknown what line of retreat or operation Masséna had in contemplation. But it was conjectured that he meant to fall back on the Mondego, and take a position on the Alva between which river indeed and Espinhal the ground is very favourable for defensive warfare. That line of retreat would draw our Army from the Tagus and of course increase the difficulty of procuring supplies and in some measure serve as a diversion in favor of the siege of Badajoz. A very short time will elucidate all these points and therefore I shall not say more upon the subject because I have not had a moment to look at the map and form my own conjectures upon it.

I understand it was intended, had the reinforcement we brought out arrived as it was expected it would have done some weeks ago, to have

---

[1] The offices of the Commander-in-Chief and his staff were at this address in London. It is now the headquarters of London District.

sent them to Marshal Beresford and proceeded to the relief of Badajoz,[1] the fate of which Town will I fear be decided against us, particularly since the death of the Governor and the loss of the Spaniards in that direction are events likely to accelerate such a calamity. . . .

The Army is in high health, spirits and courage, and full of confidence in its Leader. Every hope may naturally be indulged from these circumstances.

What the thoughts of the Enemy may be I cannot speak for a certainty, but from a very intelligent Deserter (a Corporal), whom I saw at Santarem I learned that their sickness had been excessive and their loss in men proportionate, that they had experienced great distress from the want of provisions, having often nothing for bread but Indian corn beat to a pulp with stones, and an allowance in meat of one goat to 15 or 20 men for a week, that they lived a good deal upon vegetables, and that but for the difficulty attending the attempt to desert from the nature of their position, a very considerable number indeed would have come over to us.

The position of Santarem is so strong by nature, that I think Lord W. may congratulate himself in having been prevented making the attack he meditated in that direction. The greater part of the Town which I saw is in a complete state of Ruin, from the houses having been completely gutted by the Enemy in order to procure firewood, in addition to which, the day previous to their departure they burned down the large Nunnery there with some adjacent buildings. . . .

All the Spaniards are gone to the neighbourhood of Badajoz. General Beresford with one Division of English Troops and a considerable number of Portuguese is in the Alemtejo. His force is now in movement but in what direction I have not learned, tho' I think they could not be better employed than in marching towards Badajoz to raise the siege of that place.

Provisions here are not so scarce as you may think. The River is filled with Americans, and flour is in *abundance*. The *Army* has never been better supplied, and I saw several droves of cattle following it, sufficient to insure a continuance of its good condition. Everything however is very *dear*.

I had hoped to have sent you a regular Journal of what has occurred since I left Torbay, but I have neither had time to eat, drink or sleep, and I must sacrifice a night's rest to give you this scrawl, and write to other friends by this opportunity. I fear my correspondence will not be quite so regular and continued as it used to be, but no effort of mine shall be wanting to be as sociable as possible.

The Ships with the remainder of the Troops and my horses, etc.,

---

[1] Marshall Soult had laid siege to Badajoz on January 26th.

have not yet made their appearance. I therefore have Capt. Dean at Lisbon to wait their arrival and conduct them to the Army. Never was a poor devil so hard pressed in every way, but I hope I shall have strength and health enough to get thro' it without going to the Hospital.

Lord W. is exceedingly annoyed at the number of General Officers who have thought proper to go home *on pleasure*, and I do think we have reached a point beyond the mark of delicacy and high honor, when men of that rank persevere in such defection under a positive understanding that their requests for leave of absence had his *permission*, but *not his inclination*. . . .

Send this scrawl to Pater and Edward, and believe me always, my dearest Bro.,

Yrs most Affectly,
R.L.

Note to a Brother
TO C. B. LONG

Chamusca, on left bank of Tagus
17th March, 1811

I have not had a moment my dearest C. to write you since my last communication from Lisbon which place I quitted this day to rejoin Lord Wellington. On arriving at Villafranca I found troops had been ordered to Leiria. Conceiving therefore the Enemy to be in march for the Mondego, I directed my course accordingly and overtook his Lordship in the moment when he was making preparations and movements to dislodge the Enemy from Condeixa. The Army had had a beautiful field day the day before, at Redinha, at which I regret not having been present, but I was gratified with a repetition of the same exhibition on the following day between Condeixa and Miranda de Corvo. The fighting was principally confined to the light troops, the movements that dislodged the Enemy from their successive positions being performed by columns of the line. We have lost about 200 men, the Enemy about 1000, but they effected their retreat in a *masterly*, tho' barbarous, manner.

Every town they passed thro' was burned to the ground, and men, women and little children were equally the objects of their insatiable cruelty. Their orgies in this particular out-rivalled those of the most savage Indian tribes, and will reflect eternal disgrace on the Troops and the officers who connived at such a iniquitious proceedings. Mothers were hung up with the children by their sides, and fires lighted below them. Men and children, half-murdered, thrown upon the burning embers of the houses they had set on fire. In short murder and desolation mark their track in letters that ought never to be forgotten by the Portuguese for generations to come.

Lord W. will I suppose see them fairly across the Alva, and then perhaps join us in the Alemtejo. The force is now about to assemble at Portalegre, and will proceed to dislodge the Enemy from the southern frontier, and perhaps attempt the recapture of Badajoz. I am to command all the cavalry stationed on this side, consisting of 3 British and 2 Portuguese Regiments. I shall do my best to deserve the honor. I have had nothing with me but one blanket and one shirt for the last 8 days and have really not had an opportunity of writing to anyone.

I am off tomorrow for Portalegre. I have as yet heard no news of my servants and horses, but still they may be at this moment at Lisbon, where I have left Capt. Dean to take care of and escort them to me when ready to March.

As our campaign will I think be a short one, when it is over I will devote my first leisure moments to committing to paper a regular journal of my proceedings. In the meantime be assured I am well and happy and most anxious to give the Barbarians a good drubbing, coûte que coûte.

The First Full Budget of News

TO C. B. LONG

Portalegre
Thursday, 21st March, 1811

This is the first day's halt I have had, and I take advantage of it to send you a brief account of my movements since I last left Lisbon; viz. on Sunday, 10th March, of which I gave you intimation in a former letter. I likewise wrote you a scrawl from Thomar.

Having obtained on Saturday, the 9th inst., the assistance of two horses from the Prince Regent's stable and two mules from the Waggon Train I sent them on one day's journey to Villafranca, intending to follow the next day by water and push them on to Villada, a small Town on the riverside a short distance from Santarem conceiving that Lord Wellington could not perhaps be at a great distance from Thomar. The Enemy's movements and intentions were unknown to me.

Sunday, 10th inst.

I left Lisbon in a boat lent me by Sir John Gore with the intention of proceeding in it to Villada, but the wind and weather were so much against me I was obliged to stop at Villafranca. On arrival there I found the 85th Regt. of Foot[1] had received route to march to Leiria Concluding from this circumstance that the Enemy were returning upon the Mondego, I abandoned my original intention of going to Santarem, and as soon as I could get every thing arranged I set off with my baggage to Alemquer, which place I reached about 8 o'clock and remained there for the night in the house occupied by Masséna when his Head Quarters were there. The French had marked upon the wall "Les Quartiers de M. le Prince D'Eslingen;"[2] under which some wag added, "Qui a fait plus de bruit en battant ses tambours qu'en battant les Anglais."

Monday, 11 March

I proceeded from Alemquer over a barren country but upon a very good road by N.S. de Mexoeira and Alcoentre to Rio Major, a miserable village completely gutted by the Enemy. Here I learned by a letter from Santarem that Lord W's Hd. Qrs. were at Peracha on the road from Thomar to Pombal.

Tuesday, 12th March

I left Rio Major and proceeded to Leiria, 8 leagues, where I again met General Houston[3] who had been detached there to assemble the 7th Division, a great part of which I had passed on the road. Here I learned that Lord W. had driven the Enemy out of Pombal and that it was supposed they were retiring upon Coimbra with the intention of passing the Mondego, and taking up a position in the north side of the river.

Feeling convinced that if such an attempt was made a general action would take place before it could be carried into effect, I felt anxious to close with our Army and accordingly on

Wednesday, 13th March

I mounted a Dragoon's horse and proceeded as rapidly as I could by Pombal and Redinha, and never stopped till I overtook his Lordship and the Army at his heels. The head of his column was then within 1½ miles of Condeixa, which was occupied by the Enemy; but on the appearance of a column destined to turn their left flank, they retreated precipitately on the road towards Miranda de Corvo, but took up a position about 2 miles from Condeixa, and our advanced guard was between them and the Town.

[1] The King's Shropshire Light Infantry.
[2] Masséna had been made Prince d'Essling in honour of his victory over the Austrians there in 1809.
[3] William Houston (1766–1842) had served at Minorca, in Egypt, and on the Walcheren Expedition, and commanded the 7th Division in the Peninsula, 1811–12.

General Slade was kind enough to do the duties of hospitality on this occasion, and I took up my quarters with him near Condeixa. I had nothing with me but a blanket and a clean shirt, and of course could not be otherwise than dependent upon some friend or other. My baggage, which I deserted, I have not seen since [sic] yesterday, when it joined me here about 8 o'clock P.M.

I have to regret not arriving a day sooner with the Army in order to witness the movements of the two Armies, which took place on Tuesday on the heights and plains between Pombal and Redinha, and altho' the operations in question scarcely ended in smoke, nevertheless as a field day of manoeuvre I understand the spectacle was most gratifying. The fighting was confined to skirmishes with the light troops of each Army, the line never coming into contact, for as soon as the offensive movements on our part indicated danger they generally decamped. The operations of this description cost however some men on both sides at Pombal, Redinha and Alca de vique. I observed a tolerable display of sacrifices in each of these places, and on the road leading thro' them.

Thursday, 14th March

I moved on with the advanced guard and at about 2½ or 3 miles from Condeixa we found our adversaries, strongly posted behind a village, I believe Alca de vique. Sir Wm. Erskine[1] directed the light troops to dislodge them, and a most severe skirmish took place accordingly, which cost a good many lives. I think this operation was premature, for the Enemy's whole Rearguard, consisting of a corps of their Army, was concentrated on most favourable ground, and to force them with a light division of our Troops only could not fail to be an unnecessary sacrifice. After some time this was discovered, and Lord W. having come up directed operations in columns on both flanks which effected the desired object of compelling them to retire, but the whole day was spent in consuming ammunition to little purpose. Had the ground favored the operations of Cavalry, or had our movements been less circuitous, I think the Enemy's loss on this

---

[1] Sir William Erskine (1769–1813), a cavalry general, in March 1811 commanded the cavalry of the Light Division. He later was placed in command of all the cavalry south of the Tagus, and led a division until his mind gave way and he committed suicide after being relieved of his duties.

It was on receiving the news of the appointment of Sir William Erskine and General Lumley to the Army in Portugal that Wellington wrote: "The first I have generally understood to be a madman.... Really, when I reflect upon the characters and attainments of some of the General officers of this army, and consider that these are the persons on whom I am to rely to lead columns against the French Generals, and who are to carry my instructions into execution, I tremble; and, as Lord Chesterfield said of the Generals of his day, 'I only hope that when the enemy reads the list of their names he trembles as I do.'"

day would have been very severe indeed; but the ground everywhere favored them, and they availed themselves most ably of such advantages. After being driven to an almost unassailable position in front of Miranda de Corvo, both Armies gave up the idea of further molestation. The loss up to this date was reported to be about 800 on the part of the Enemy and 200 on our side; Major Stuart of the Rifle Corps, a most excellent officer unfortunately killed, and some others whose names I do not know shared the same fate, or were badly wounded. The fatigue of the Troops was at this time very great, and their supplies not very regular, nor could they be under the circumstances of so rapid an advance. Nevertheless it was determined to follow them up with activity, and the Army was accordingly directed to move at day-break.

Friday, 15th March
A thick fog which lasted till nearly 10 o'clock prevented the Army from marching. The Enemy in the meantime had sent off his baggage at 12 o'clock the night before, and followed soon afterwards, so that on advancing we found the coast clear. On this occasion, however, they felt themselves so hard pressed as to be obliged to destroy several ammunition and other waggons, and I strongly suspect some artillery (which was probably thrown into the River) for the guns were not found; the limbers were. The road was also strewed with dead men, horses, mules, etc. I continued with the Army for about 8 miles, but having been desired by Lord W. to repair to this quarter, I left them on this side of the Ceira River, where I understand they had another skirmish more fatal in point of loss to the Enemy than the preceding ones. Having turned my horse about, I proceeded solus to Espinhal, slept in a stable about 8 miles beyond it on the road to Thomar, and on

Saturday, 16th March
I reached Thomar where Marshal Beresford arrived the same evening. At his invitation I joined his escort, and continued with them till our arrival here yesterday morning, having marched

> On Sunday (17th) to Chamusca, crossing the Tagus at Tancos;
> Monday (18th) Ponte de Loro;
> Tuesday (19th) Crato;
> Wednesday (20th) Portalegre.

Such it the outline of my movements. A considerable force is now assembling here for the evident purpose of offensive operations on the side of Badajoz, of which the Enemy possessed himself prematurely by the treachery or cowardice of the Spanish Commander who succeeded to the command on the death of the old Governor.[1] They are now besieging Campo Mayor, but it depends entirely on the will of our chief how long their molestations are to be continued in that direction. The fact is that the Corps d'Armée now collecting here will not be assembled before tomorrow and I have reason to believe that if not prevented by some unexpected circumstance Lord W. purposes being here himself to direct the operations in person. The amount of the force here will be I conjecture between 15 and 20,000 men. The Cavalry will consist of the

 3rd Dragoon Guards,
 4th Dragoons,
 13 Light Dragoons,
 2 Regiments of Portuguese,

scarcely amounting to 2000. One or both of these Brigades are to be under my command, for altho' the arrangement still waits Lord Wellington's sanction; I was nevertheless told by Col. Pakenham, the D. Adjutant-General,[2] that I was to have the command of the Cavalry in the Alemtejo. At present Marshal Beresford has only put me in orders to superintend the Division lately commanded by General Fane. I expect to March tomorrow towards Elvas or Campo Mayor, but this is not yet quite certain. To this hour I have heard nothing of my horses, etc., and therefore am opening the Campaign in an unpleasant kind of manner. I make however no difficulties. I get on, I shall continue to do so, as well as I can.

From the devastation and murder which mark the progress and line of march of the Barbarians (for they cease to make war like Frenchmen) I am inclined to think they have little hope or expectation of making the conquest of this Country, and indeed supplied as the Capital now is, and with such a formidable barrier round it of bayonets and entrenchments, the attempt would be almost hopeless, unless the rest of the Peninsula was subdued. I must however do them the justice to say that their retreat as far as I can judge has been made in a masterly and soldierlike manner, with reference to it as a military movement of extreme difficulty.

The appearance of the Portuguese Troops has really astonished me. It is in every respect equal to our own, and in some instances finer, and their conduct hitherto before the Enemy has commanded the

---

[1] Badajoz was surrendered to Soult on March 10, after six weeks of siege. Imaz, who had succeeded Menacho as governor, capitulated without having withstood a single assault—with food and ammunition to last a month, and with the knowledge that Beresford and two divisions were on the way to relieve Badajoz.

[2] Colonel Edward Pakenham, the Deputy Adjutant-General and Wellington's brother-in-law.

most decided approbation. From the three days intercourse I have had with Marshal Beresford I am inclined to like him most exceedingly.[1] I find him unreserved, affable, open, sociable and obliging, and the revolution he has affected here bespeaks his ability. The Army is in high health, confidence and courage and altho' it is difficult to foresee the results of warfare, I think they will accomplish as much as can be expected of them.

Whilst I am writing an officer has just come in from Elvas. He tells me Ballesteros has given the Enemy a drubbing in the neighbourhood of Lanz de los Cavalresos (towards Seville[2]) that Campo Mayor is besieged by about 3 or 4,000 men only, and that there are not above 600 left in Badajoz. If so, and the Governor holds out till the day after tomorrow, we shall soon save them the trouble of further operations in that Quarter. An unpleasant dilemma has, however, between ourselves, occurred. Beresford expected and is waiting for further instructions from Lord W. An envelope has arrived properly sealed but on opening it no contents were found. I hear that he is nevertheless determined to attempt to cut off the force before Campo Mayor as soon as General Cole's[3] Division of British Troops arrives, and they are expected here tomorrow.

God bless you, my Dearest Bro. It is with difficulty, from incessant interruptions, that I have been able to write, and have no time now to read over this scrawl. Dean is still at Lisbon, but I have not heard a word from him since we parted, nor indeed was it possible. Had I but my horses, I should be perfectly satisfied. I feel the want of them most miserably.

[1] Long's high opinion of Beresford was soon to alter sharply.
[2] On March 2 and 9, 1811, Francisco Ballesteros, commanding a Spanish division, defeated the French General Remond in two small actions. Though he failed to take Seville, his campaigns in 1811 were on the whole successful.
[3] Major-General Galbraith Lowry Cole (1772–1842) commanded the 4th Division between 1809 and 1814. He was later to be appointed Governor of Mauritius and of Cape Colony. He had been a former rival for the hand of Kitty Pakenham, whom Wellington married in 1806.

II

Cavalry in Action at Campo Mayor, March 25, 1811

ON Wednesday, March 20, 1811, about noon, Robert Long took over his brigade of some 2000 men. He was in charge of the 3rd Dragoon Guards, 4th Dragoons, 13th Light Dragoons, and two Portuguese regiments. His Commanding Officer was William Carr Beresford.

At this time Beresford was forty-three years old, and had been in the Army since the age of sixteen. A natural son of the Marquess of Waterford, he enjoyed special privileges, and his promotion had been rapid. He was a rugged character, strongly opinionated, of great physical strength and courage. His active service experiences were many and varied. He had been at Toulon in the early and unsuccessful operation designed to seize the French fleet and provide a rallying ground for Royalist sympathizers. He had led a division in a wild march from the Red Sea across the desert against Napoleon's armies in Egypt. Engaged in the capture of the Cape of Good Hope, he, with others, had been carried off to take part in a disastrous adventure in South America and had been forced to sign a capitulation, subsequently dishonoured, at Buenos Aires. He had been in the Coruña retreat, and in 1809 had served in the Oporto campaign.

His work in charge of the Portuguese Army had been remarkable, and by hard work and determination he had succeeded in equipping and training infantry fit to stand in the battle-line with British battalions. It is true that at no time were the Portuguese cavalry to be trusted; if sometimes they stood firm, at others they would refuse to charge and take to their heels.

Beresford enjoyed the full confidence and friendship of Wellington, who held him in the highest regard, and at a later date named him as second-in-command. In 1811 Beresford was holding his greatest and, as it proved, his last independent command. As a leader of troops he was excellent in training and disciplining men, but in the field he did better as a subordinate than in complete charge. During the months of March, April, and May 1811 Beresford made many bad errors of judgment that were patent to his own officers and men, while his mistakes at Albuera were flagrant.

Like the Duke of Cumberland, Beresford had lost an eye. The tremendous efforts he made while founding the Portuguese Army had, moreover, sapped his health. During 1811 he was not physically well, and it was not until 1812 that he became really sound in body again.

By the time Long and Beresford had arrived at Portalegre Portuguese and British horse, foot, and artilllery were gathering, until a total of 18,000 were concentrated less than forty miles to the north-west of Badajoz. The French had seized this old, strongly fortified town, well placed on the left, or south, bank of the river Guadiana, on March 11, and a few days later

Marshal Soult had hurriedly departed towards the south, to Seville and Cadiz, for news had reached him of a battle won by the Allies against Marshal Victor at Barrosa, near Cadiz. Eleven thousand men were left behind under Marshal Mortier,[1] and these were not idle.

They moved out of Badajoz to cross the Portuguese frontier and assault the little frontier fortress of Campo Mayor, which surrendered on March 21 after a full week's resistance. Considering how old-fashioned the defences were, and how antique many of its fifty guns, this was a very creditable performance by the Portuguese, and gave time for Beresford to move forward.

This approach by a British force apparently surprised Mortier, who had left some 2400 men in Campo Mayor under General Latour-Maubourg.[2]

Long and the light cavalry crossed the river Caya and advanced towards Campo Mayor on the morning of March 25. Reconnaissance early in the morning showed two or three French pickets, who, though they had been aware for the past few days of the presence of hostile cavalry, contented themselves with a short gallop or two, and did not alarm Campo Mayor. Hard rain fell. Beresford pressed on. Latour-Maubourg at last took fright, hastily evacuated the town, and marched off towards Badajoz. Sixteen guns and their wagons went first, followed by the infantry, under the protection of some 900 dragoons and hussars. Although the day continued showery at intervals, this does not appear to have affected the manœuvre. Long took the Portuguese and the 13th Light Dragoons (two and a half squadrons), left the Heavy Brigade under the command of Colonel de Grey, and under Beresford's orders threw a cast round the walls of Campo Mayor and went ahead to close the French. Both at the time and afterwards, when Napier (who hated and despised Beresford) exposed the whole truth, there was an outbreak of controversy, with pamphlets and correspondence giving each side's experiences and arguments, so that the details of this action (and that of Albuera) are largely recoverable.

Long, in circling the little Portuguese town, had to avoid an obstacle variously described as a ravine, swampy ground with a ditch, or an ugly gully, and swerved away from the walls. Beresford, mindful of Wellington's warnings and anxious to keep his cavalry in hand, twice sent aides-de-camp to order a closer approach.

When some two miles from Campo Mayor and ten from Badajoz the French cavalry drew out to guard their retreating infantry. Long saw behind him his two heavy cavalry regiments and the columns of infantry and guns coming up at a fast pace, and judged the moment ripe for a decisive charge. Colonel Head gathered in his skirmishers and, with support from two Portuguese squadrons under Colonel Otway, drove at the French in two decisive charges. He cut through the French horse, beat off more cavalry approaching on his left, and dispersed all the enemy mounted troops in sight, except for a squadron or so of hussars immediately attached to the French infantry column, which, having nothing better to do and apparently very little to hope for, slogged away down the Badajoz road for all they were worth.

---

[1] Edouard-Adolphe Mortier (1768–1835), Marshal of France.
[2] Marie-Charles, Comte de Latour-Maubourg (1757–1831).

Head and Otway, seeing these fellows marching rapidly along and beside the road, and the artillery and baggage pressing on ahead, set off in hot pursuit. In vain the French infantry fired a shot or two. The Light Dragoons were soon among the guns. They pressed on, sabred the gunners, immobilized the wagons, guns, and caissons, and cut down the flying enemy cavalry. Not until they actually reached Badajoz did they halt, and then only because grapeshot and canister were fired at them from the ramparts. One of our men was wounded when actually on the wooden bridge leading into the town, almost ten miles from the scene of the original charge.

Head thereupon re-formed his men, and, seeing no supports at hand, set off back along the Campo Mayor road to rejoin the army.

Long, meanwhile, seeing the 13th Light Dragoons vanish into the distance, gathered the remaining Portuguese cavalry about him, and sent a staff officer back to bring up the Heavy Brigade. To him, and to all those about him, including the French, it seemed as though the fighting was over.

But Beresford had come forward to see what was happening. On inquiry he found to his horror that the 13th and some of the Portuguese had disappeared, none knowing their fate. One officer reported to him that they had been surrounded. This information Beresford later declared came from Long himself, but here he is surely wrong: an aide named Baron Tripp was responsible. Beresford had fresh in his mind a letter that had just arrived from Wellington giving a special warning about the need of keeping his cavalry in reserve and *en masse*, to be thrown in only for a decisive blow, and until then nursed and protected, being impossible to replace. Beresford really knew nothing of Long's capabilities, and he determined to keep at least the heavy regiments in hand. He therefore drew them across the road and halted them.

The result was that when Long took his remaining Portuguese squadrons forward to charge and halt the French in preparation for the final blow he was entirely unsupported. The French fired, the Portuguese refused to charge and broke back, and Long (who was mounted on a dragoon's horse, his own being still on board ship) snapped a stirrup-leather and was almost unseated. Two British guns (King's German Legion six-pounders) were brought up and fired a few rounds into the enemy, but Beresford missed his chance and ordered everything to halt until he knew just what was happening. The French gave a shout of joy and in some cases picked up the muskets they had grounded in anticipation of surrender. They then set off again rapidly towards Badajoz. As they went they gathered about them the cavalry scattered by Colonel Head's charge, and ultimately approached Head himself. That officer at first refused to believe that any of the enemy could have escaped, but in the end had to abandon the guns and other trophies he had collected, and leave the road. There he watched the French march past, under the guard of their cavalry, which twice made as though to attack him, only to turn about without pressing the charge. On regaining the army, which had remained halted about Campo Mayor, at about half-past six in the evening Head was very coldly received.

The 13th Light Dragoons lost about sixty killed, wounded, and missing;

the Portuguese over a hundred. On the French side, where squadrons of three regiments had been ridden down and badly beaten, their losses were certainly far heavier than those of the Allies; among the dead was Colonel Count Chamorin of the 26th Dragoons, slashed through the skull by Corporal Logan of the 13th. Yet most of their prisoners were retaken, and of all those trophies captured the British finally retained only one six-inch howitzer and a few waggons.

Beresford and Long quarrelled publicly over this business. Long was furious at being let down, and Beresford confused by all that had occurred. The Marshal told the Brigadier that the latter had made a bad business of it, and that the errors of the day were to be attributed to "want of practical experience in the field." This outburst also apparently included the phrases "Damn it, sir, why did you not do *something*? Why did you not support them, or send to bring them back?" and "The loss of one regiment is enough."

The whole action of Campo Mayor was a bitter disappointment to the British forces, whose confidence in Beresford as a commander in battle was heavily shaken. Energetic action might even have led to a *coup-de-main* at Badajoz, which was to be a long weary time in falling. It was time the over-confident French received a check, but this golden chance of a heavy blow was not taken.

The Commander of the Forces issued a stong censure, embracing the 13th Light Dragoons and Colonel Otway, which was couched in stinging terms. The squadrons concerned were compared to an armed rabble. Long discharged his duty by reading this reprimand to the Regiment, and then declared, very typically, to the 13th Light Dragoons that he would not permit it to be entered in their Orderly Book.

The publication of Sir William Napier's account of Beresford's 1811 campaign caused a furious outburst of letters and pamphlets, in which Beresford cast all the blame for Campo Mayor and the preliminaries of Albuera on Long, who was dead. Robert Long's nephew, Charles Edward, his twin's eldest son, published two booklets to justify his uncle, and quoted some of his letters and journal. Although Beresford received some support, Long's side received as much, and the contemporary witness of British officers was overwhelmingly on Long's side. Unfortunately, Long's undisguised anger, the tone of his letters home to his family and friends, and the semi-public nature of the dispute brought Long at once to the unfavourable attention of Wellington, who no doubt put him down as merely another brainless galloper like Jack Slade.

Campo Mayor
TO C. B. LONG

St. Vicente, near Elvas

March 28, 1811

My last to you was written, I think, on the 21st or 22nd instant, from Portalegre, and it announced the probability of approaching operations against the force besieging Campo Mayor and afterwards perhaps against Badajoz. The desire of doing too much prevented our accomplishing anything. It was not thought sufficient to raise the siege of Campo Mayor (an object of great importance with a view to the Town, its inhabitants and the supplies of corn deposited there). Nothing would satisfy us but taking or destroying *all* the Enemy's force collected there, but for this purpose 20,000 men were to be assembled, and to do this required time, and time produces delay, delay produces failure. So it happened. A breach being made, the Governor was obliged to surrender at a moment when 12 to 15,000 men were within a day's march of him, and might have been there much sooner. Well! this business being so settled, all that remained for us to do was to retake the said Town of Campo Mayor. And for this purpose our united force assembled at Arronches on the 24th instant, and marched, with the exception of one division, to a bivouac on the left bank of the Caya river, our right close to the ford which is passed in going from St. Olaia to Campo Mayor. The enemy was reconnoitred early the next morning and the report made them very strong in cavalry, so much so as to induce Marshal Beresford, after having planned the march of my division in two separate columns, to unite them again in one. Having left our bivouac about 10 o'clock A.M. on the morning of the 25th, a march of about three miles brought us out of the wooded into the open country, and we came in contact with the enemy's picquets.

The arrangements for our further progress were here made, and I was directed to move circling round a considerable height over which the infantry marched, but from whom I was separated by a deep ravine. The heavy dragoons were again separated from me, and marched in column on my right flank. I trotted away with the light gentry, and having driven the enemy's picquets from the positions they occupied, I at length passed over a considerable plain which brought me to a small ridge, from whence I looked down on the town of Campo Mayor, distant about 1,200 yards. Here I first saw their cavalry (a part of them at least), drawn up in line of battle under the protection of the works. I immediately formed my line and waited further orders, not knowing what were the Marshal's intentions. During this time they began to move and manoeuvre, and I did the same, to counteract any project they might have in contemplation. I had expressly asked the Marshal in the morning, if it was his wish that I should attack, if practicable, wherever I might meet them. His answer was, that they were very strong, I must not commit myself; but, that if a favorable opportunity of striking a blow should occur, to avail myself of it. I soon after had orders to lead the column of light cavalry (five troops of the 13th Light Dragoons, and five weak squadrons of Portuguese) so as to turn and gain the rear of the town. This I did, and the enemy, alarmed at the movement, soon began to retire, and formed in the valley behind the town, on the road to Badajoz, their order of march en retraite. As soon as I observed this, I determined to gain their flank and rear, and then to act as circumstances might prompt me. The heavy cavalry now joined me, and as the route upon which I was marching intersected, at about one mile and a half, the road upon which the enemy was retiring, the further I advanced the more of course we closed. At length I found myself, for the first time, in sight of their whole force, consisting of eight squadrons of cavalry, 10th Hussars, some chasseurs, and, I believe, the 26th Dragoons, and two battalions of infantry, in close column. The column of infantry had a squadron of hussars at its head, and another in its rear, and in this way they were retiring in perfect order. Six squadrons in two divisions en potence covered their retreat. Considering myself quite strong enough to show my adversaries the way to Campo Mayor, I determined at least to attempt it. The heavy brigade had joined me, and the force now under my immediate command consisted of

  8 squadrons 3d dragoon guards, and 4th dragoons,
  2½ ditto, 13th light dragoons,
  5 very small squadrons of Portuguese,

in all, perhaps, about 1,200 swords. At this time the enemy's position was thus (see plan).[1]

To oppose which, I made the disposition as above (see plan), and my orders and instructions were, in the first instance, to get rid of the covering force of the cavalry A and C [on plan], and then to dispose of the rest, who, deprived of their support, would no doubt fall an easy conquest. I marched the light division by the left in columns of ranks by threes, and when I had approached sufficiently near, I directed the 13th dragoons to disengage from their right from the rear of the column, and having gained the flank of the enemy's corps C, to charge them, whilst my movements with the remaining five squadrons of Portuguese was directed against the corps A, to cover at the same time the left flank of the 13th dragoons and to endeavour to cut them off completely from their point of retreat; the heavy dragoons to support this movement in the situation you see described. Two squadrons covered my left flank, and interposed between the enemy and the point of his retreat.

[1] At this point Long included a rough sketch of the position. This has been omitted, and in its place are given the two plans of the action (p. 77), which are also from Long's journal.

It is necessary to observe, that I led the light division over a ridge of heights and broken ground, which overlooked the valley in which the enemy were formed, and through which ran a nasty boggy and almost impassable kind of ditch. My intention was, that the heavy cavalry should continue to move straight on, their left towards the heights I occupied, their right as low down as the ground permitted.

Everything being thus situated and arranged, I directed the attack to be made. The moment the enemy C saw the two columns moving on parallel lines to outflank and attack them, they changed their positions to the left on their left squadron. The 13th formed immediately to their front, and both proceeded with determined gallantry to the charge, the 13th receiving a partial fire from the infantry as they passed. As the movement of the 13th dragoons was made with the rapidity characteristic of the army, and as the pace of the Portuguese ponies could not be very extended, consistent with the preservation of that order which, with ill-formed troops, is with difficulty maintained at any pace, I found, at the moment of the attack of the 13th, that the head of the three squadrons I led was only just in a line with the attacking corps, which, having completely broken the enemy's ranks, the whole of the corps A and C dispersed and fled in confusion towards Badajoz. I followed as rapidly as I could to support this attack, still supposing the heavy brigade in my rear, occupying the attention of the remaining part of the enemy's force, but, to my utter astonishment, when, at the point where I first met the Badajoz road, I halted, and looked round to see what was next done to be, I found they had quitted altogether the line of direction I had pointed out, and at the suggestion of one of Marshal Beresford's aides-de-camp, had marched by their right to the other side of the valley and road, and were halted a mile and a half off, on the opposite and elevated ground, quite abandoning me to myself, and completely oversetting all my plans. In consequence of this unfortunate occurrence, the enemy's infantry column had kept on retreating uninterruptedly, and the whole of the 13th Dragoons having dispersed in pursuit of the flying and beaten cavalry, and every effort of mine to stop them proving useless, I felt myself obliged to detach two squadrons of the Portuguese to support and rally them, under the orders of Colonel Otway, formerly of the 18th Dragoons. They, however, instead of obeying my orders, broke also away in pursuit and continued unsupported till they reached the bridge of Badajoz. The rapidity with which this ill-judged pursuit was made absolutely left as many of the enemy behind as they were driving before, so that soon after I had halted, I found two squadrons of them rallying on the road upon a small rise, within 200 yards of my left flank, and just at the same moment came up the

The Action at Campo Mayor
March 25 1811
adapted from plans in Robert Long's M.S. Journal

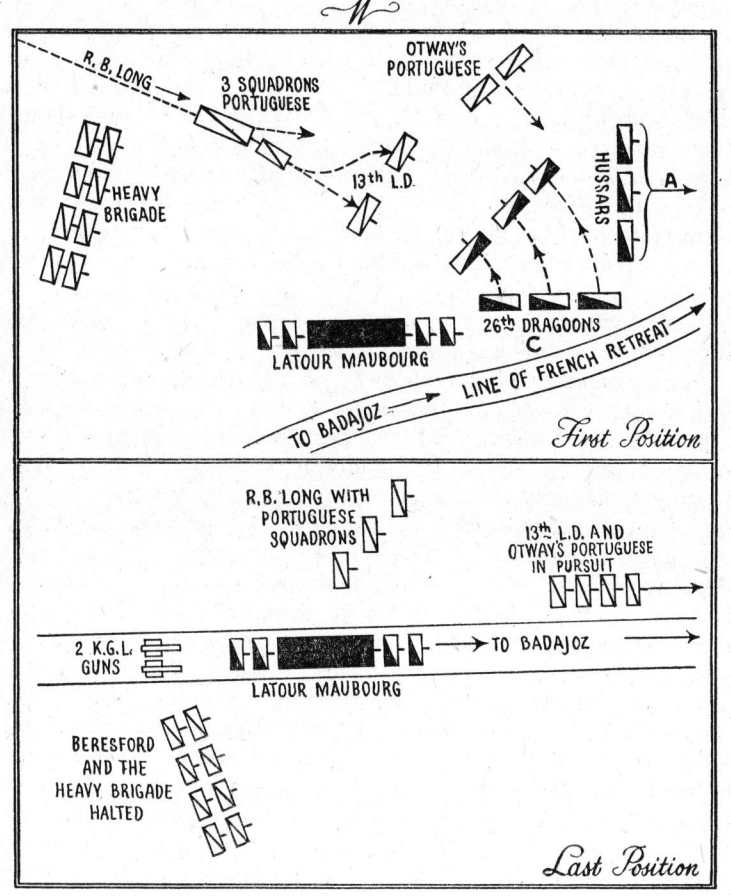

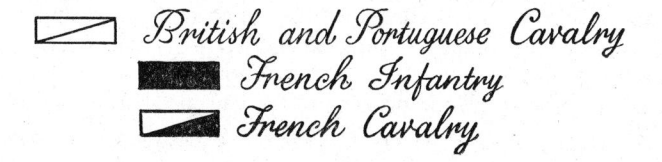

First Position

- R.B. LONG
- 3 SQUADRONS PORTUGUESE
- OTWAY'S PORTUGUESE
- HEAVY BRIGADE
- 13th L.D.
- HUSSARS — A
- LATOUR MAUBOURG
- 26th DRAGOONS — C
- TO BADAJOZ → LINE OF FRENCH RETREAT

Last Position

- R.B. LONG WITH PORTUGUESE SQUADRONS
- 13th L.D. AND OTWAY'S PORTUGUESE IN PURSUIT
- 2 K.G.L. GUNS
- LATOUR MAUBOURG → TO BADAJOZ
- BERESFORD AND THE HEAVY BRIGADE HALTED

Key:
- British and Portuguese Cavalry
- French Infantry
- French Cavalry

infantry columns, headed and closed by two squadrons of hussars on my right flank. I felt the critical situation I was in, and saw but one way of getting out of it, that of making a rapid change of position, throwing back my left flank. As soon as I could get the Portuguese to understand me, I put their ranks by threes to the right, and was in the act of conducting them to the point I intended, when some of the enemy's infantry and flankers firing, and a troop of their cavalry advancing and shouting, my Portuguese friends got alarmed, broke away and fled in disorder. The French hussars, encouraged by the spectacle, pursued and got among them. After great difficulty I rallied them, with the assistance of Captain Doyle, of the Quarter-Master-General's department, and led them back, posting myself on the enemy's left flank, within 200 yards, and continuing to march parallel with them, with the view of preventing them from acting against the corps of the 13th and Portuguese, that were at this time still between them and their point of retreat—Badajoz. I at that time sent Captain Doyle to order the immediate advance of the heavy cavalry, determined, on its arrival, to lose not a moment in accomplishing the defeat and surrender of this column of infantry.

For the first time I learned from Captain Doyle that Marshal Beresford himself was with the brigade of heavy cavalry, and had himself halted them in the situation I have described. I had nothing further to say! Soon after I saw them in motion at a very slow pace in two lines, keeping to the right of the road on which the enemy were retreating. At length they approached the right flank of the enemy's column, indicating an apparent intention to attack, bringing up at the same time two pieces of artillery, which no earthly obstacle prevented firing into the French column at such a distance as they chose. I hung upon their left flank with my valiant runaways. The country was beautifully open and favorable for the movements of both artillery and cavalry. The enemy had still several miles to go to their point of retreat, and between them were interposed the four squadrons of British and Portuguese, who had pursued their adversaries to the bridge of Badajoz, taking all the artillery they had with them and had employed at the siege of Campo Mayor, about twelve or fifteen pieces of cannon.[1] In such a state of things I did not conceive it possible for the enemy to exist ten minutes longer, and I really am convinced that, had they been summoned, an immediate surrender would have taken place. After parading and escorting them in this manner for some distance, judge my *astonishment* at seeing all the troops, artillery, etc., *halted*, and the enemy permitted to retire without molestation before us, taking with them all the prisoners they had made from us, retaking

---

[1] Actually the total French artillery consisted of sixteen guns, at one time all captured.

all their guns, and absolutely threatening the safety of the dragoons in advance, who were then returning from their pursuit, tho' their exact situation was unknown, and to speak the truth, I augered but ill of their fate from the unsupported manner in which they had pushed forward, and which, though displaying great gallantry, was a sad proof of want of order and discipline both in officers and men. The heavy brigade, by some improper though perhaps well-meant interference, had left me to myself, and the subsequent retreat of my three squadrons, with the loss sustained, obliged me to leave the others almost to their fate; but the defeat of the enemy's column would have ensured safety to the whole, and would have wound up as brilliant a little field-day as fortune could have delighted my hearers with. Had Marshal Beresford not interfered, you may rely upon it I should have accomplished it (not merely *attempted*) but positively accomplished, for it was impossible they could resist the force of 11 squadrons which I should have had at my disposal to bring against them. It was only necessary to charge, and beat, and throw into confusion the cavalry at their head and rear, (and which if British dragoons could not do, they have no business here,) and the object was accomplished. But I am convinced, that had a determination to annihilate them been shown, and steps taken accordingly, they would have surrendered at the first summons.

Such is my decided opinion, and I believe (with the exception of Marshal Beresford) that of every officer present on the occasion. The motives of his conduct were I dare say excellent, but sure I am that Lord W. himself would never have conferred such an honor on the enemy and entailed such a disgrace on his own troops, as to suffer two battalions of infantry and four squadrons of cavalry to bid defiance to and retreat in safety before eight squadrons of British and three of Portuguese cavalry, two pieces of artillery and a large column of infantry that were following the same route, and were within a couple of miles of the scene of action, and this in a country so favorable to the operations of cavalry, and after the whole of the enemy's covering force of cavalry had been charged, broken and pursued for nearly nine miles. The thing speaks for itself, therefore I shall say no more.

After keeping away from me above half my force (and that of the best quality, too) upon which I had relied, and founded all my intended operations upon, because I could not exactly inform him what might under the existing circumstances be the fate of the Dragoons who had so improperly pursued, without adequate support, and against my order, His Excellency, I say, was pleased to remark that I had made a bad business of it. First of all, under the actual circumstances I think it was a brilliant day for the small corps with which the attack was made, and the killing of the Colonel of the 26th Regiment of Cavalry, Count Chamorez [sic], with many of their men and horses, taking 15 pieces of artillery and several ammunition waggons, the bringing away of all which depended upon the mere ipse dixit or will of the Marshal himself, the beating and cowing of two of their best Cavalry Corps, are in my opinion no symptoms of a bad business, even though our loss in prisoners by the flight of the Portuguese has been considerable, the retaking of whom however likewise depended upon the Marshal. But suffering 2 battalions and squadrons to escape from before a Field Marshal with 11 squadrons at his disposal, 2 pieces of artillery and a column of Infantry in the rear, is in my opinion as bad a performance as ever disgraced a theatre of war. With this remark I shall conclude, namely, that if Marshal Beresford had known the powers of Cavalry as he certainly does those of the Infantry, I think he would not have lost so favorable an opportunity of striking a severe blow with a very paltry sacrifice of men; and had he heard the remarks of the private dragoons as I did on their inglorious return, he would have regretted the extreme care he took of their bodies in preference to their credit.

We returned to Campo Mayor after the skirmish and thence on the 26th to this place, and St. Olaia, where we are awaiting further orders. I expected we should have moved to the attack of Badajoz, but nothing indicates the immediate accomplishment of this intention, tho' I do not believe they have more than 6 or 7000 men altogether in the neighbourhood.

I hear not a word of what is going on in the side of the Mondego, and at this moment am as ignorant of what is passing in this country as a child of two months.

I enclose a bill on the Treasury for £147 1s. 0d., which I request you will forward to Greenwood to be placed to my credit, taking his receipt for the same. The second [bill] of exchange shall be forwarded as soon as you have acknowledged the receipt of the first.

I wish you would be good enough to buy me a ten guinea watch made by Barweis in St. Martin's Lane. I hear he manufactures excellent ones for service at that price, and I am not anxious to risk a more valuable one in a country of thieves. Draw upon Greenwood for the amount, and send it by any convenient opportunity in which Brownrigg may assist you.

I have had an unpleasant bowel complaint for the past 4 days and am doctoring for it. I hope in a day or two to be myself again. My horses are arrived safe, and now on their road from Lisbon to join me.

Make Mrs. Nesbitt[1] acquainted with the contents of this scrawl, and tell her it was not *my* fault that my first effort against the Enemy was not a triumph worthy of her congratulations. The *opportunity* was one of Fortune's best smiles, but my evil genius interfered to moderate my pretensions and disappoint my too sanguine expectations. I rode a Troop Horse and nearly had an unpleasant accident. Just as I gave the order to attack and was going off, my right stirrup leather broke, and I was as near as possible falling to the ground with it. *I did not stop to pick it up again, however,* but the want of it distressed me much throughout the day, and what is worse occasioned the annihilation almost of a good pair of overalls, an article not easily replaced.

Not a letter have I received since I left Torbay, tho' I *hear* some have arrived at Lisbon and have been forwarded to Hd.Qrs., but everything being now on the move, regularity of communication is not to be expected.

The Beans are all in full bloom, the wallflowers in their gayest attire, and altho' we have been annoyed by wet latterly, the weather is nevertheless very fine. I have written a letter to Sir John Gore, telling him what I have been about, and begged him to forward it to Howard, for Pater's information, not having time to write more.

---

[1] Mrs Nesbitt was the widow of a major-general of Long's acquaintance, and a close personal friend.

III

Advances, Skirmishes, and Retreat before Albuera

AFTER this action at Campo Mayor the main object of Beresford's force was to recover Badajoz. The troops advanced to the river Guadiana at Jerumenha, some twenty miles downstream from the city, and there threw a ferry-bridge and crossed over it. Each load took about a hundred men or twenty-five horses, so that it was a slow process. The country near the river was beautifully wooded, and while charming to see was not easy to reconnoitre or guard. During the night of April 6, 1811, the 13th Light Dragoons had a mishap. One squadron was passed across in the evening, and took up their quarters in, as they thought, a safe situation. After three o'clock in the morning, however, the French hussars, who had observed the operations closely, launched a surprise attack, and cut off this outlying squadron, some of whom were in their night-shirts. Confusion spread deep into the British camp, and the French got clean away.

The fault seems to have been with the staff officer who placed the squadron. At any rate it was a most complete disaster, if on a small scale, for, apart from a cornet who escaped in his night-cap and another who jumped into a stream and hid, there was taken a whole squadron, to the total of fifty-two officers and men, one wife, and sixty-five horses, with three wounded left on the ground.

Years afterwards, when the publishing fever was on him, Beresford tried to attribute this loss to "some mistake or other which occurred in giving or carrying out Major-General Long's orders." But this was long after the event, and at the time there was no such suggestion.

To Long this disaster provided an interesting item of news for his regular budgets home. These letters were copied by his father or brothers, and circulated to their families or friends, so that Long's opinions of Beresford's capacity received pretty wide publicity. There can be no doubt that both Beresford and Wellington in due time came to know of this. Long in fact was one of the "writing officers" whom Wellington disliked and mistrusted. It is a fact that he had good cause to complain, for in 1812 his own Quarter-Master-General[1] was sending confidential information home to newspapers, and these were eagerly searched for accurate knowledge of British movements by the French. Our enemies could not rely on getting their own messages across the Pyrenees, and so found the British Press invaluable. "Every man who can write, who has a friend who can read," said Wellington, "used his pen to good effect." Long's friends were numerous and well placed, Long's

[1] Colonel Willoughby Gordon, who was responsible for some serious supply disasters, and was as incompetent as he was arrogant.

family assiduous in spreading round his regular communications, and his comments were pungent, bitter, and well worth reading.

Between lack of stores, pontoons, and food Beresford's movements were very slow. He was held up for a few days at a little tumble-down fortress called Olivenza, and then cleared the ground south of Badajoz of the enemy by pushing his cavalry towards the Sierra Morena. On April 16 Long was engaged again, when the light cavalry again overthrew the French.

This skirmish was at Los Santos, on the vast plains south of Badajoz and Albuera. These were to be the scene of much of Long's active service. At Los Santos the Marshal himself was up, and when some 600 French cavalry showed front and moved to the attack Beresford, Long, and the 13th Light Dragoons, with two heavy cavalry regiments in support, delivered two strong charges, to the cheers of the Spanish inhabitants, and dispersed the enemy. The French finally broke up.

Order in our own ranks, however, was strictly maintained. It seems from the tone of Long's description that nothing more was done than was ordered, and that no particular impetus was given to the attack. Guns, which Long considered of great value in the open plains, were missing. Generally speaking, Long did little more than lead a squadron. He obviously annoyed Beresford, and found a malicious pleasure in formal adherence to the letter of his orders. Beresford later said it was at Los Santos he first began "to suspect the military qualifications of General Long." In actual fact the skirmish was a decided British success, since we did not lose a man, whereas the enemy's losses were considerable.

Advance on Badajoz:
Disaster overtakes a Squadron of the 13th Light Dragoons

TO C. B. LONG

Bivouac near Algueta

12 April, 1811

The position I now write from is in front of Algueta, which place is on the direct road from Badajoz to Seville. The date of my last letter I cannot recollect, but if I did not send you a communication from Villa Vicoza I fear the last you received from me was written from Vicente on the 28th March, but if my memory does not altogether fail me, I think I must have dedicated a few minutes to you at Villa Vicoza.

1 *April*

It was on this day that we received an order to march immediately to Villa Vicoza, which was done accordingly. The Town itself is one of the neatest and cleanest I have yet seen in Portugal, and the surrounding country very pretty.

2 and 3 April
    Remained at Villa Vicoza.

4 April
    Marched from Villa Vicoza thro a wild but romantic and pretty country down to the right bank of the Guadiana, where the Army was collected and bivouacked near Jerumenha, N.W. of that Fort. Nothing could be more beautiful than the ground occupied by the Troops. As I can neither paint with pencil nor pen I must leave what I would otherwise describe, to your imagination. I did not forget the day [their common birthday], and drank you many many returns of it with a daily diminution of the ills and an increase of the blessings of life.

5 April
    Remained in bivouac. Received at night a pacquet of letters from England from all my friends. A Ferry bridge having been established across the Guadiana a Division of Infantry and some squadrons of cavalry passed over during the evening and succeeding night to the left bank.

6 April
    The Infantry continued to pass the River during the preceding night and the whole of this day in a ferry carrying about 100 men or 25 horses. In the Evening I received orders to pass the whole of the Cavalry without delay, and the 13th Light Dragoons commenced their march accordingly about 6 o'clock P.M. but were not all got over till nearly 2 o'clock A.M. of the 7th April.
    I went over with the 2 squadrons about 9 or 10 o'clock, and rode forward to reconnoitre the ground on which the Troops were to be stationed as they successively crossed. The Infantry were posted on an extensive range of hills, partly wooded, and the rest covered with the gum cistus, their right resting upon a small village called Villa Real, their left brought down to the Guadiana; the whole about 2 or 3 miles from the Ferry opposite Jerumenha.
    Waiting the arrival of the Troops General Stewart recommended me to take up my quarters in a small house near him that was about 200 yards in front of Villa Real, but on the other side of a small brook. I went to examine the situation and I confess from the manner in which the advanced picquets appeared to me to be placed and which I could observe by their lights I thought it too exposed, and therefore went to Villa Real, where I waited the arrival of the 13th Dragoons. As they did not make their appearance by 1 o'clock A.M. I mounted my horse and rode back to the Ferry to hasten them, and when assembled

I proceeded with them to their ground, directing them to continue bridled up and went back to Villa Real to get my own horse fed and watered ready for anything that might occur after daybreak, a report having been circulated by the Enemy that they intended to attack us. General Cole's Division (one Regiment of it at least) had in the meantime reached Villa Real, and were lying down near their arms. Scarcely had my horse returned from water and was unbridled when I heard an alarm. I immediately ran out, and saw the Enemy attacking with loud shouts our picquets stationed at the house where General Stewart recommended me to go, and as I passed on to get the Infantry under arms (for they were all asleep by their fires) up came some of the 13th Dragoons in a state of complete dispersion, the Enemy at their heels, firing as hard as they could, and having the boldness to come into the very village where our Troops were posted. One of their horses was killed about 10 yards from the house I had been sitting in. Not knowing what their force was, and thinking it certain that if in any strength they would immediately try to get amongst the Infantry and avail themselves of the confusion arising out of such a surprise, I hastened afoot to the spot where I had stationed the 13th Dragoons, got upon a troop horse and brought them rapidly to the point threatened, and placed them in a situation to cover the Infantry. In the meantime the Troops, generally alarmed, had taken up their positions of defence, and we waited quietly for break of day to show us what all this meant, or rather what it was to lead to, but I was soon, unfortunately, made acquainted with the unpleasant fact that a whole squadron of the 13th Dragoons stationed in advance with General Lumley, had been surprised and cut off.

Upon these occasions it is difficult to get at the truth. It appears there was some great misapprehension upon the subject between General Lumley and Major Morris, the officer commanding the squadron. The latter had occupied a different situation during the preceding day, and at 9'oclock at night received orders to remove from that situation, and to consider himself as a reserve to be stationed near the house "where the General had met Major Morris in the morning." Unfortunately they had met in more places than one, and Major Morris, putting his own construction upon this order, crossed the little brook near Villa Real, and posted himself near a small house about 1½ miles from the house which had been recommended to me for my quarter. Arriving on his ground very late, and conceiving that the Portuguese Light Cavalry were in his front, Major Morris seems to have been thrown off his guard so far, as not to have paid that attention to the nature of the ground he occupied which it deserved, and besides to have suffered his men to dismount and even unbridle at the very time they should have been prepared for such a rencontre as shortly afterwards took place. The French, on the look out, discovered, probably, these errors, and moved out of Olivenza a detachment of Infantry, supported by artillery, and I suppose about 400 hussars to attempt the capture of this squadron. Their plan was well laid and ably executed. At about 3 o'clock A.M. they succeeded in enveloping the Major and his squadron and after pursuing some of the fugitives into Villa Real as above described, they carried off one Major, 1 subaltern, 3 sergeants, 2 Trumpeters, 49 men and 65 horses, all belonging to the 13th Dragoons. They likewise wounded a few more, and took about 3 prisoners from the *Infantry Picquet* stationed at the house where I might, also, but for a kind of presentiment, have been quartered and shared their fate. This was a sad blow upon us, a glorious triumph to the Enemy. They got a beautiful lot of horses (officers and privates) worth in this country £2,500. But what I regret most is the temporary advantage they obtained over a Corps which had a short time before given them a specimen of superiority they will not soon forget. It is serious enough that on the day following the French Cavalry left Olivenza and went to Valverde taking with them their booty, and on the night of the same day *they* had a false alarm, which threw them into confusion, and away they ran from Valverde, leaving behind them the horses of the 13th which they had taken. They rallied after some time and returned, but remained the whole night under arms.

7 April

The 3 Dragoon Guards and 4th Dragoons crossed the water during the day and the Artillery and Portuguese Cavalry during the following night.

Captain Dean with my horses from Lisbon joined me; all well, the big bât horse excepted, which having been strained by some accident in the loins, and otherwise showing symptoms of bad humours flying about him was sent to Elvas to keep Palafox company, and there they now remain. A little mule I bought at Portsmouth for £10 turns out remarkably well, so that I am now getting on admirably.

8 April

The whole Army remained in disposition, the Cavalry suffering a good deal from the heavy rains which fell throughout the day, exposed as they had been for several days in a plain with not a bush or tree to shelter them. The Infantry were better off.

9 *April*
　The Army marched in two columns (or rather three) upon Olivenza without seeing a soul. As soon as they arrived before the Town it was summoned, but the Commandant refused to surrender arguing that altho his force was small he was in expectation of sufficient assistance being sent him to resist the meditated attack. Having no artillery for a siege with us, some was, in consequence, sent for to Elvas, and on the following day at 2 P.M. the Cavalry and Light Division of Infantry marched to Valverde and bivouacked for the night. The inhabitants appeared rejoiced at their deliverance, but the troops behaved very ill owing to the precariousness of their supplies having made them outrageous for bread, which they seized on indiscriminately whenever they could meet with it.

11 *April*
　The Cavalry and Light Division moved to Albuera, and one Division being left before Olivenza to carry on the siege, the rest of the Army assembled in front of the Village and took up the bivouac from which I am now writing.

12 *April*
　The Army continued in its position. The Rear Guard of the Enemy passed thro Albuera about an hour before we reached it. They were only 80 horse.
　This day (13 April) the Heavy Brigade commanded by Col. de Grey has moved upon Sta. Marta (on the Seville road) to look out and gain intelligence on the side of Fuente del Mestro, and a Brigade of Infantry with 2 squadrons of Cavalry are gone to occupy the village of Talavera on the road from Badajoz to Merida. Badajoz is thus invested, or rather blockaded, and I suppose when everything is ready, we shall proceed to retake it, and thus complete the reconquest of this part of Spanish Estremadura.
　It now remains for me to comment upon our operations. Altho this expedition (if I may call it so) has been in contemplation for upwards of six weeks, no kind of preparation beyond that of collecting the troops appears to have been made. No magazine of provisions assembled. No pontoons or boats to make a bridge secured. No artillery de siège prepared, no engineering tools provided! Our supply of bread has been from day to day from hand to mouth, and often the Troops have wanted it altogether. The Cavalry have been subsisted in many instances on half a ration of barley only (6 lbs per diem) and even this scanty provision irregularly procured and supplied.

The consequence is we are parading about since 25th ult. with 20,000 men doing nothing, or rather setting about doing *something* that under a system of more activity and foresight ought to have been accomplished in a few days, and might have entailed consequences upon the Enemy of a most unfavorable description. I know not where the fault lies, nor is it my business to enquire. But one cannot help seeing with regret the army detained on the banks of the Guadiana for days wanting a bridge to pass it, whilst the Tagus is groaning under the weight of our naval means; that same army calling out in vain for bread whilst a store of flour equal to 8 months consumption is at this moment formed in Lisbon, and an insignificant Town garrisoned by 300 men detaining 5,000 men before it for days in consequence of the want of Artillery and this in sight of Elvas, which is the strongest fortified town in Portugal, and where, from its importance in a military point of view, an Arsenal has been established and should not, I presume, have been quite empty at such a moment as this.

Such is and has been the state of things with us, and volumes written on the subject could not give you more information.

Luckily for us, the weather has generally been fine, prodigiously so for the last three days, or the sufferings of the Army would have been great, and its sickness I presume corresponding.

We are now in the midst almost of interminable plains where much Spanish blood has been vainly and lamentably spilled. The Enemy, however, is driven completely from Portugal, and if some gross errors are not committed, it will take them more than one campaign to recover the ground they have lost. I should suppose their loss in men during the retreat can fall little short of 5,000, but the most prominent advantage to us consists in the practice which the Portuguese have had in co-operating with the British in their daily manoeuvres and conflicts to dislodge the Enemy from post to post, and the opportunity thus given them of looking at that Enemy with indifference and of becoming daily more *aguerried* and conversant in military movements and of course feeling more confidence in their own strength.

The Enemy on the contrary must from the nature of things be discouraged. They are further removed than ever from the object they fondly anticipated the possession of. They have been met and discomfited by soldiers they were taught to despise, their most celebrated generals yielding ground before a British Commander. Is not all this flattering, and, if the Spaniards would but do their duty, must not the result be universal success?

I begin to hope that our resources will improve as we go on. The Spaniards have concealed under ground large magazines of corn, which British cash or credit will soon bring again to light. Two of this description were made known to me at Valverde. I immediately agreed with the Proprietor and 3000 rations of excellent barley are now on the road to our camp, taken from one single pit which I employed the Dragoons to open. All this is well. If we had but force to occupy Merida and take a position near Zafra where in conjunction with Ballasteros we might shut the tri-coloured gentlemen up beyond the defile of El Monasterio, the French Army in Andalusia would be in an awkward situation. Something of this kind I suppose to be in contemplation, but I have doubts about the adequacy of our force for its perfect accomplishment.

I have had my command increased by the addition of two Spanish guns drawn by six mules each. They cannot be so rapid as I wish, but still they are *something*, and had they been with us the other day at Campo Mayor, the fate of the gentlemen who opposed us on that day would have been very different indeed. The *Marshal* has, I think, behaved *very unhandsomely to us all* upon the memorable occasion alluded to, and *his* report to Lord Wellington has been such as to draw down perfect silence on the part of his Lordship, as far as concerns me, but decided reprimands to the Troops engaged, for their (certainly indiscreet but) gallant pursuit. Whilst the Heavy Dragoons and Col. Grey have received his particular thanks for having, under the Marshal's personal directions, done nothing but *look on*, and *suffer* that Enemy to escape unmolested from their swords who in ten minutes might have been annihilated! Such is the reward of zeal on the part of the world, and the effects will be visible enough on the next occasion when the services of the Troops, disgusted by such treatment, shall be called for. They will look on, too, in the hope of thereby meriting the Commander in Chief's approbation. It is too bad, and shews the *curse* of secret influence. You will scarcely believe that an English General *could* be so inconsistent and unjust as to give his thanks to two *Portuguese* squadrons for disobeying orders, and extolling their gallantry to the skies, whilst no notice was taken of the 13th Dragoons, who charged and beat the Enemy so brilliantly; and to wind up the absurdity a report of the whole affair seems to have been made in such a language and in such a temper as to require that Lord Wellington's displeasure should be recorded almost in the same page, where the Marshal's approbation has been previously inserted. The Portuguese themselves are quite thunderstruck, and asked me "Qu' est ce que cela veut dire?" I referred them to the Marshal as he is a better linguist than myself, and only observed that not being English I could not understand it, but I dared to say it was all right. This unsuccessful attempt to flatter the Portuguese at the expense of British soldiers is not *d'après mon goût*. I do not like it.

Sir Stapleton Cotton[1] has joined again, and if General Fane should resume his command, some new arrangement must take place. I shall be perfectly satisfied to see my command reduced to two British Regiments, for the Portuguese Cavalry is so bad I wish not to have any concern with them.

Cavalry Affair at Los Santos

TO C. B. LONG

Los Santos, near the road from Almendralejo to Zafra, border of Estremadura

Weds., 17 April, 1811

I wrote you a letter, my ever dear Bro., on the 13th inst. from our Bivouac near Albuera. I proceed in my Journal:—

14 April

Remained in the Bivouac near Albuera.

15 April

Marched at 9 o'clock A.M. to a Bivouac near Santa Marta on the high road from Badajoz to Seville.

16 April

Marched again at 2 o'clock A.M. towards Zafra. We reached the neighbourhood of Los Santos about 12 o'clock at noon, and whilst the reconnoitring Parties were out halted on the road and grazed our horses.

Intelligence was soon brought that 5 or 600 French Cavalry were advancing, and had actually entered Los Santos. We put the Column of Cavalry in motion, turned the village by the left, and just as we passed it I observed them in Column of Squadrons quite close to me, about 300 yards off, and just as they saw the head of my Column, the 13th Light Dragoons, they put a part of their force in motion to attack it. The Marshal was in front with all his Staff, who on the approach of this attack fled, and created some confusion to the 13th Dragoons; and they were scarcely formed when the Enemy charged them. They did it however in so frigid a manner that they were soon turned to the right about. The Marshal desired me to dispose of the Enemy, who with the 13th Dragoons were rallied.

[1] Major-General Sir Stapleton Cotton (1773–1865) commanded a cavalry division in the Peninsula from 1808 to 1812. He was later, as Lord Combermere, to be Governor of Barbados, and Commander-in-Chief, India, 1825–30. Twenty-five years later he reached the rank of field-marshal.

I therefore directed the Portuguese to form in line behind the 13th to support them, sent the two heavy regiments to turn and try to cut off the Enemy's retreat, whilst the 13th hung upon their rear. The Enemy immediately commenced his retreat, which by our rapid advance became a complete rout on their part, and a chase on ours, for about 10 miles. We pursued them at such rate as enabled us to preserve something like order, and at the same time pressed them so hard by pursuers that as their horses were passed, blown, or left behind we came up and secured them. Never was there such a fox chase, but I did not enjoy it, because I knew that the *ignorans* expected us to take every man of them, which I knew was impossible, without disbanding every soldier I had in pursuit; and *this*, after the thanks I experienced at Campo Mayor, I did not feel inclined to do. Had I had my will, I should have detached a Corps to the left by a road which intercepted the line of the Enemy's retreat, and would infallibly have been fatal to them. But here again I was over-ruled. Thus success is not left at my disposal, but I shall be made amply responsible for all failures. I know not what number of prisoners some Spaniards carried off with them, but we killed one Captain and some men, and took 107 prisoners and two lieutenants. The loss of the Enemy altogether I should place at 150 men and horses, and this without any loss on our side.

We are awaiting the arrival of another English Division, and then I believe in conjunction with General Ballesteros' Corps, which when collected may be estimated at 6 or 8,000 men, and I hear a force from Cadiz, we shall proceed to dislodge the Enemy if possible from Seville. The result of this interesting operation cannot be foreseen but sincerely do I pray that it may be successful, and if so Spain will be saved, and I hope England satisfied with her sons in this part of the world.

I have this day received your letters of the 24th March and 2nd April. Thanks for settling the business about the stolen horse so comfortably. My note, left with Christmas, was decidedly written under his *positive declaration* that the *Animal was stolen*, and claimed as such by him out of my stable.

The weather here for the past 10 days has been beautifully fine, and as hot almost as in the dog days in England. I cannot bear a waistcoat, and only clothe in a loose great-coat. My horses have all joined, Palafox excepted; but they are not in fox-hunting order, and therefore when I expect a *brush*, I ride a very clever troop mare lent me by the 13th Lt. Dragoons.

I have escaped all blows and shots hitherto, though, at Campo Mayor, I was on all sides surrounded and in the midst of the Enemy for some time; but they took no notice of me, and very fortunately, for I was ashamed to think of my own security in presence of men who were running away and whom I was trying to bring back to their duty, and shew a good face to the Enemy. From every appearance the Enemy are almost as afraid of us as the Spaniards of them; but notwithstanding, they have been uniformly the first to advance to the attack, which, however, properly given, they will never stand.

It is not less astonishing than true, that in yesterday's chase, the Horses of the Heavy Dragoons decidedly beat those of the Light Dragoons, from their superior strength. Eleven horses however, of the 4th Dragoons, chiefly the black beasts drafted from the 3rd Dragoons in England, died at night in consequence of fatigue, and many were on their sides in the field before we halted. And all this upon grass, with very short allowance of barley, not a grain of which they have for this day's consumption; and have often been put upon half-allowance, about 5 lbs per diem. If this system is continued, we shall have very few left in 6 weeks or two months.

I hope Lord Rivers will do the handsome by you, as I am doing by his son, whom I like very much. I have besides two Portuguese aid-de-camps, an Adjutant and Quarter Master General to feed, in all six persons. Sad work for the pocket, but I do not feel it yet. I shall continue to write you whenever I can, and I do beg you will as soon as possible after the receipt of my letter transmit it to our dear Pater with my best love. It is tiresome to write a story twice over, even had I time. A short extract of the substance to be forwarded to Mrs. Nesbitt, and when it talks of battles, an outline to be forwarded to Major Wright.

I saw General Beresford's account of the Campo Mayor business in the Lisbon Gazette, which I think a very unfair one. His measures were never calculated to accomplish what he professes to have been his intention, and as I had completely cut off and surrounded the Enemy a word only from him was wanting to ensure their capture and secure 15 pieces of artillery.

Mortier is gone back to Paris, and La Tour Maubourg now commands his Division, stationed near us at Llerena. Ballesteros is near Zafra, but with not above 2,500 men; he expects more daily. Part of Castaños'[1] Corps at Villa Franca on the Almendralejo road is about 1500. These Gentlemen, from their accurate knowledge of the country, will be very useful to us. All we want is another Regiment of Light Dragoons, and a Brigade of flying artillery. It was as absurd as cruel to send us into these plains without the latter assistance.

And now, my Dearest Brother, if in this contest I am doomed to fall I shall die contented with the best love of my relatives, and *I hope*

[1] Xavier Castaños had recently been appointed Captain-General of Estremadura.

with the deserved regret of those I am endeavouring and anxious to serve—I mean my Countrymen. I hope I do not want zeal, talent I cannot command, and I have had but little practice in this way before the Enemy.

If I am to be gratified at seeing you all again, it will be double pleasure from having been not an idle spectator of the interesting events now passing.

Comments on Beresford's Report of Campo Mayor
TO HIS SISTER, ELIZABETH HOWARD

Los Santos
22nd April, 1811

Your letter of the 12th March is now before me, and I offer no apology for its remaining so long unacknowledged, because we are campaigning and that is no time for gossip of any description. It is as much, or rather more than I can do conveniently, to send to one of my Beloveds a hasty sketch of our movements, etc., in a moment of hurry, in order that you may not be quite in the dark respecting poor Bobus, who hitherto has had the mortification to find disappointment even in constant success, so much are we at the mercy of those who possessing the power to carry everything their own way and represent it as best suits their own interests. In short, it is a sad thing for a Cavalry Officer to be under the judgment of an Infantry General.

Our début at Campo Mayor was most brilliant, and but for the untimely interference of others would have been attended with perfect success and little loss. . . .

Now for other matters. Your nice little friend Mrs. Dalbiac[1] is always by the side of her husband, whether lying under the canopy of Heaven or enjoying the blessings and shelter of a roof. I am surprised how she has been able to stand the trial without injury to her health, but really, of the two, she is the stoutest. I wished to do almost more than is in my power to lighten the burden her affection has imposed upon her, but no, she is inexorable, and rejects prayer, petition or remonstrance. Sincerely do I wish them both a safe return to their own fireside to enjoy as they ought the inestimable reward of such fidelity and attachment!

Trifles from those we love are acceptable. St. Cuthbert has been hospitably received, but I have no confidence or trust in the virtues of such saints. The prayers of the Angels around you would in my opinion be more efficacious and infinitely more gratifying. Lose no

---

[1] Wife of the Colonel of the 4th Dragoons, who accompanied her husband in his campaigns, and even on to the field of battle at Salamanca.

time therefore in getting them upon their knees. If they cannot preserve me in this world their good wishes and intercession will be my best and only passport to a better. I am ready for either, and feel grateful for any dispensation that may await me. The Charlottes, the Harriets, and the Arabellas are all delightful torments to *young* men, but I am getting old very fast indeed, and when they cease to disturb the constitutional fires that Sir Walter has so long declared to be raging within me, I shall enjoy the society of the loves if possible more than our dear Pater, than whom no one knows better how to appreciate Beauty, whether of the mind or person, in those around him. . . .

And now, my dearest Eliz, I take my leave, wishing you and your babes many years perfect enjoyment of all the blessings of this life. Lane[1] (that good soul) has promised his guardianship of our beloved pater. You are his tutelary Angel, and between you both I confidently hope for another opportunity of kissing his revered cheek.

Best love to your Lord, and kindest remembrance to all friends.

[1] Lane was Edward Long's doctor in Arundel. The family gave him a piece of plate as a reward for his efforts to keep E.L. in good shape. At this date E.L. was approaching his seventy-seventh birthday.

IV

Albuera

Acting under very clear and definite instructions from Wellington, who had ridden south from the Northern Army for a few days' personal visit, Beresford opened the siege of Badajoz, hoping to conclude it before Marshal Soult could collect a relieving force. The town was completely invested on May 6, 1811, but the opening attempts to capture the main fort of San Cristobal proved unsuccessful and costly. Beresford's siege material was as inadequate as his artillery was antiquated—some of the cannon used were two hundred years old and most of the others dated from the early eighteenth century.

During this period Long with his cavalry remained round Los Santos and Villafranca, some forty miles south-east of Badajoz, covering the preparations and siege, and observing the enemy, who remained behind a screen of pickets and prepared for a swift advance northward under Soult to relieve the town. As soon as news reached Beresford that the French had moved out of Seville, he raised the siege of Badajoz on May 12. Long occupied himself in writing many detailed accounts of his exploits to his friends at home, all decrying Beresford. He also amused himself by carrying on a paper war against his chief, asking for meticulous instructions to govern his actions. One of his scouts and liaison officers at this time was William Light, of the 4th Dragoons, later to be the founder, in 1836, of Adelaide, South Australia, where he was surveyor-general.

Long also repaired the defects of his wardrobe and equipage due to his hasty departure from England by giving extensive orders to brother Charles to fulfil. Ankle-boots, watches, dressing-gowns, and books were soon travelling to him. He found life passed agreeably enough in his little private circle of three aides-de-camp, the Brigade Major, and administrative officers. To add English variety to ration issues he sent home, attached to his descriptions of the new scenes about him, requests for cheeses, tongues, portable soups, a supply of good tea, and other appropriate seasonings.

A Pause for Reflection

TO C. B. LONG

Los Santos, near Zafra

24th April, 1811

... General Blake is expected with a considerable force (8 or 10,000 men from Cadiz) to join Ballesteros and defend the Southern Frontier of Estremadura. His arrival in the intended position will perfectly secure Lord W.'s position and render his Lordship's whole force disposable for such operations as he may judge necessary to undertake. But after what has passed I should be inclined to doubt his inclination to co-operate again with Spaniards on Spanish ground. They are so little to be trusted, and their assistance in arms so contemptible, that Lord W. will probably be satisfied in securing the integrity of Portugal keeping his Army in a menacing attitude on the frontier ready to take any advantage the Enemy may offer him, or at all accounts keeping in check a very large French force which otherwise might be applied in completing the subjugation of more distant Provinces. The siege of Badajoz is the first consideration and its recapture forms the principal object of present concern. I can scarcely think the Enemy to be in sufficient force to oppose externally any resistance to this undertaking, but I suspect from the description of force left to defend it, and the strength of the works, quantity of artillery, etc., it will not be a bloodless concern or one of a few days.... We are dreadfully slow in our operations south of the Tagus. It is now nearly three weeks since we passed the Guadiana and nearly 10 or 12 weeks since the retaking of Badajoz has been in contemplation. I know not to what extent the preparations have been carried, but still we are only *preparing*. I know no more of what is passing at Headquarters or in my rear, than you do. Never was there an Army kept more completely in the dark, upon every subject; so much so that all interest about it nearly vanishes and we think only of ourselves.

All the Spanish Troops I see are of a most despicable description; neither clothed, paid, disciplined or even organised, and but precariously fed. They resemble more a motley Banditti than Battalions of Infantry, and their great Generals have scarcely more than lieutenant colonel's commands. The Spanish Government appears to be doing nothing in a military point of view, satisfied, I suppose, that the seat of their residence and deliberations is sufficiently secured from insult by a British force. General Castaños was with me yesterday; he seems to be a perfect old woman, whose sole occupation is powdering his hair, and patrolling about his country with a suite of servants and soldiers from 50 to 60 in number, at which the common people gaze with admiration and cry out 'Viva!' The General's hat is uncovered, and on he proceeds to enjoy the same gratification in other villages thro' which his operations are conducted. Ballesteros is the best soldier among them, and the most tractable Spaniard, and the only one who makes la petite guerre upon a system which has hitherto given his enemies great annoyance, and enabled him to maintain himself against all attempts to exterminate his force. The People, alternately in the power of Friends and Foes, shew indifference to both. They cannot take a part without danger to themselves; they prefer consequently personal security to a display of unseasonable loyalty or patriotism. In their hearts I believe they hate the French, but they have at the same time no great love for us; and their pride revolts at the idea of Spain being assisted, even in her struggle, by British blood. . . .

On the 28th March I sent you a bill of exchange on the Treasury for £147. 1s., which I requested you to transmit to Greenwood and Cox to be placed to my account.

I now enclose the duplicate, and beg you will forward it also to Greenwood. I did not endorse the first, thinking it unnecessary. I have endorsed the enclosed to anticipate every objection. I likewise begged you to procure and send me a ten guinea watch made by a man who lives in St. Martin's Lane, and who I hear is famous for watches of that price. I do not wish for a more valuable one for it is ten to one but I lose it according to custom.

All my stud are doing well except 2 invalids left at Elvas, Palafox and the Bât horse. I have heard no news of them but they are in trusty hands. The two I purchased in London will I hope turn out well, but they are very shy, and not sufficiently formed for the field. The horse of an orderly Dragoon which I have hitherto rode in action will continue to be preferred for such duties; I have therefore nothing to regret. My establishment is rather too large: viz. 3 aides du camp, 1 adjutant general and one Q.M. General. We get on, however, in a humble way. I do not expect that my present command will be continued to me, if all the other senior officers join, nor do I care one farthing about it. A Brigade will satisfy me, for I hate responsibility, and the Portuguese mar all my projects.

Dinner-table Scandal

H. HOWARD TO C. B. LONG

Arundel Park
April 28th, 1811

I went to Town last Wednesday and returned again last night. I heard the news. I was disappointed in seeing Brownrigg on Friday, but I saw Mrs. Brownrigg and had a good deal of conversation with her. She told me a curious anecdote, which she assured me was perfectly true, and as such ought to be related in justice to Col. Vickers.[1] Sometime ago at a dinner where the Duke of Cumberland was he said to Colonel Vickers, "Long has been made a Brigadier

[1] Colonel Vicars had succeeded Long in command of the Queen's Bays, and it was with Vicars that the protracted quarrel over regimental accounts was waged.

G

General, and sent to Portugal. I don't care where they send him if they would take him out my regiment." Vickers answered, "It might be as easy to take your Royal Highness out of the Regiment as him. These things cannot be done in this country." I am very much astonished that Vickers should have made such an answer, but she assured me that it was true, and that the Duke afterwards invited him to tea with him on the Sunday following.

Marshal Beresford has not certainly done our General the justice he was entitled to, but he could not say a great deal more without throwing so much blame upon himself, as one can hardly expect anyone would.

I saw Addenbrooke in town. He told me that he had had a long detail from the General[1] and that he had read it to Lady Pitt and Mrs. Howe;[2] and the latter will make it known at Windsor. I also understood from him that he had made Lord Harrington[3] and the Duke of Richmond[4] acquainted with it.

Life on the Spanish Plains (I)

TO C. B. LONG

Villafranca

1st May, 1811

On the 28th ult. I removed my quarters to this place in consequence of the Head Quarters of the Army being transferred from Olivenza to Almendralejo. There is a strange kind of fatuity in our proceedings that I cannot comprehend.

The preparations for the siege of Badajoz are going on, but when they will be sufficiently advanced to enable us to commence operations is more than I can say. We have now spent more time in contemplating and preparing for the primary object of our campaign than the Enemy employed in possessing themselves of it.

The farfamed partisan L'Empecinado made a good haul the other day. An Aide-de-camp of Berthier[5] (a Count le Jeune) had been sent from Paris with dispatches to Soult at Seville, and was on his return with Soult's answers, escorted by 40 dragoons. On approaching

---

[1] That is, Robert Long.
[2] Lady Pitt, the widow of Long's previous chief, Sir William Augustus Pitt, was a warm personal friend of Long's; on her death, in 1819, she left £4000 to Addenbrooke. Mrs Howe was one of her sisters-in-law.
[3] Charles Stanhope, third Earl Harrington (1753-1829), General. Colonel of 1st Life Guards, Commander-in-Chief in Ireland 1805-12. He was a personal friend of both George III and George IV, and his wife, Lady Harrington, a favourite of Queen Charlotte.
[4] Charles Lennox, fourth Duke of Richmond (1764-1819), gave the eve of Waterloo Ball in Brussels.
[5] Louis-Alexandre Berthier, Prince de Wagram (1753-1815).

Madrid the guide was desired to shew the officers the spot where a similar surprise had before taken place, and whilst the Frenchmen were surveying the ground, out rushed L'Empecinado, put the whole escort to the sword, and took the officers prisoners. The despatches were found sewn up in the clothes of one of the servants, and I understand are very interesting, as detailing the exact situation and circumstances of the Enemy. L'Empecinado would not permit the officers to dine at *his* table, but sent them to mess with the servants. This equality savouring treatment was not at all relished, but the Count was satisfied to escape with his life.

An officer of ours, Colonel Waters,[1] a sharp clever fellow, was taken prisoner whilst reconnoitring one day, and remained some time with Masséna's Army. He would not accept the parole offered him and as he was indulged with a horse, with two Gendarmes as his escort, he planned his escape. Under pretence of getting his boots repaired at Cuidad Rodrigo, he bribed the men to put a good pair of rowels to them, and thus provided he availed himself of a favorable moment to profit by them, and effected his escape. He reports Masséna's Army to be in a most shattered state, afflicted with the scurvy, and what is worse with the panic-anglicaine. The Light Division[2] of Lord W.'s Army has trimmed them so constantly and incessantly, that they have a perfect horror of them.

I am doing all I can to procure you a good Spanish pointer to cross your breed with. I fear the *most* difficult part of the business will be the getting it conveyed to England. They have also an abundance of greyhounds at this place, but I do not discover anything about them superior to our own. In my life I never saw such a country for sporting, and such a quantity of game as we found in the woods and immense plains surrounding our bivouacs near Albuera. There were likewise wolves in great abundance, and alarmed by our fires at night they made a most pitiable howling. The country thereabouts is such a desert that they will long continue in the undisturbed sovereignty of it.

There is also a curious sight out of my window. The church is close by and on the steeple is an assembly of storks, *hawks* and *pigeons*, all living and nestling together in perfect amity.

Palafox has not yet joined me and James Lynch I am sorry to say has had a severe return of his old complaint. Brewer, the Dragoon of the 15th, is an excellent servant, and will be I hope an excellent

---

[1] Waters, of the Portuguese staff, was captured on the Coa by outposts of Marshal Ney's 6th Corps.

[2] The Light Division at this time consisted of the 43rd and 52nd Foot (now the 1st and 2nd Battalions of the Oxfordshire and Buckinghamshire Light Infantry) and the 95th (now the Rifle Brigade), with some Portuguese light infantry. They were commanded by Major-General R. Crauford.

substitute for Risborough on some future occasion. I am perfectly satisfied with Dean my Aide-de-camp. He is a steady fond creature, and it is much to be lamented that his papa did not sooner take him by the hand, and assist by a superior education the natural strength of a good mind and a willing disposition.

Lord W. has done his business well. He has been fairly pitted against Bonaparte's Marshals and has beaten them all.[1] What will Cobbett[2] *now* say of the Wellesleys? I believe he might be King of Portugal whenever he pleased, were his ambition equal to his popularity. He is certainly a fine creature, but at the same time never was a British Commander possessed of such powers, and above all of such a command of money. The expenses of this Army are incredible, but the arrangements which occasion it indispensable to its preservation and efficiency. Everything is carried on mules which are brigaded, and for each mule is paid one dollar per diem, besides a ration for the muleteer and ½ ration of forage for his beast. Some Spaniards have 50 mules of their own thus employed, and as they are fed chiefly in the fields, they absolutely realise per diem a better salary than the Commander in Chief himself receives; and the best of it is, that their pay is constantly kept in arrears, so that their own interest insures their fidelity. The spare ammunition for the Troops is conveyed in this manner, and follows the columns, and I have seen these fellows always at their post regardless of the Enemy or his fire. I think an observation I heard the other day not a very unjust one—that the Spanish muleteers ought to be the nobility of Spain, and all the Nobility muleteers.

My landlord is a decided Frenchman in his heart, I know not from nature principle or predilection. Marshal Soult preceded me in this quarter and I suppose he bit him. I give him a daily fit of bile by dwelling on our successes, and the disgraces of his friends.

Will you beg Windeler to make me another pair of blue worsted-stocking overalls, lined with leather, etc., and Gordon (in Cockspur St.) a pair of his ancle-boots like the last. Send Windeler a coloured calico dressing gown that you will find in the bureau near the bed, and also a Spanish grammar and dictionary in the book-case near it; and if you can your hands upon it, 6 volumes of a military work written by Capt. Rocheaymont, with a book of plates. There are two sets of it, one bound but covered with white paper not belonging to me, the other purchased just before I left town. Either may be sent.

---

[1] Junot, Soult, Jourdan, Masséna.
[2] William Cobbett (1762–1835), the author of *Rural Rides* (1830), had founded the *Weekly Political Register* in 1802, and as a Radical was a vehement opponent of the Tory Ministry.

Have the whole packed up together in a box well secured from wet, and forwarded to me, to the care of

>Senor Jose Antonio Pereira
>Moradora Jenellas
>Verdes No. 13
>a Lisboa.

I also request you will be good enough to pay the accompanying bill for me by draft on Greenwoods. I hope you have received the bills of exchange I sent you to be forwarded to Cray's Court.

Life on the Spanish Plains (II)
TO C. B. LONG

>*Villafranca*
>*7th May,* 1811

Our Headquarters moved yesterday to Talavera on the Guadiana to be à portée to Badajoz, which place was invested by the allied troops on Saturday or Sunday last.[1] The preparations for the seige indicate an expectation of vigorous resistance, altho' the Garrison does not consist of more than 2000 Infantry and 100 cavalry; but they are good and will probably do their duty....

After solemnly declaring to me that there was not a grain of barley in this village to be had for love or money, I caught 3 cart-loads last night which they had secreted and sent out of the town. Of course I confiscated the whole, but still it proves their apathy to our welfare. The Spaniards appear to be collecting their runaways into corps, which corps will when assembled form Armies and which Armies will again go in search of the Enemy and get beaten. Their whole system is defective. All these untrained, unarmed, unclothed Banditti should be marched off for Cadiz and there be officered, organised and instructed. Thence they should be sent, when fit and effective, to join the forces in the field. All *actions* to be avoided, merely a guerrilla warfare established to train and accustom their troops to fire on the enemy.

The pause has been most favorable to the Cavalry. They are now in as good condition as I could wish to see them, and I hope within ten days to receive a remount of horses that has arrived from England, which will very much strengthen our force. I shall then expect to see my Division nearly 2000 Cavalry, with 4 pieces of English horse artillery, which I shall be happy to shew to the enemy whenever and wherever they may please to take a look at them. I can hardly expect,

---

[1] Badajoz was invested on May 5. On this day Wellington defeated Masséna at Fuentes de Oñoro, one hundred and thirty miles to the north.

however, to retain this command, whilst senior officers are only at the head of Brigades. I am indifferent about it, and this is no good sign, but a certain indication that I am not satisfied with my chief, who I think has but ill-requited the services he has received from us.

Two deserters came in the other day (both French) and they declared that the French Army were never worse off than at present; that whilst their officers were living sumptuously, the men are frequently without bread, and very seldom get wine or spirits. Their horses are fed upon green forage exclusively. They begin to feel a little more respect than before for the British land forces. One of them said, "Nos officiers nous disent toujours que l'armée anglaise ne vaut rien, qu'ils ne sont pas soldats. Ils se sont diablement trompés, et chaque jour les démentira bien. Allez vous en chez vous et il ne faudroit pas beaucoup de temps pour arranger M. les Espagnols." They certainly have a most contemptible opinion of the Dons, for when I asked them how they could be so absurd and rash as to attack us as they did at Los Santos, their answer was "C'est que les Espagnols nous ont gâtés!" I hope, whilst at it, we shall continue to dissipate their illusion, and shew them that afloat or ashore British blood is the same. Within the past two months the leopard has made the imperial eagle fly before it, and the Massénas of the age have yielded to the Wellingtons of the day.

All here is approaching to harvest time. In ten days the barley will be cut, the wheat next month. The latter is not secured in barns, but when the corn is thrashed or trodden out of the ear it is placed in large pits dug in the ground, and there kept for years in perfect preservation. No art is employed in constructing these pits, the earth having sufficient tenacity without it. Straw is placed round the sides, and the mouth of the pit then secured with a stone and covered over with dirt. These pits are on rising ground. They make no use of the harrow but plough in the grain and then leave it. If the winter is likely to be very dry, they roll the surface to preserve, as they say, the humidity; otherwise it is left without this operation. The corn appears well sown, clean and in great abundance. This province is best for the merino sheep; the finest are found near Serena on the Guadiana. They have two descriptions of them: the Tras os Montes and the Estranles. The former are the richest and best, and are those which are sent annually about this time of the year to the mountains of Leon and Gallicia, and are thence called Tras os Montes. They hereby escape the heat and drought which prevail in Estremadura during the summer months, and they feed during the same period upon the rich cool grass which they find in more elevated situations. The Estranles are the portion of them that do not benefit by the above process. They wander about during the night to feed on the uncultivated lands, and during the day are taken to the banks of rivulets where they remain during the meridian heat. In the autumn and winter months they are penned up together to manure the ground, and these pens are formed by nets, such as you catch rabbits with, only the meshes larger, and they are so fine and being of a brown colour are scarcely visible on the ground. Their plough, a very simple piece of machinery, consists merely of the shaft with the iron shape, without wheels or other appendages. It is worked by two mules, asses or oxen. The man holds the shaft and directs the plough with one hand, whilst the other holds a long pike, which serves as a whip to drive the animals, and is a kind of hoe to clean the plough share of weeds, etc, as he goes on. The arms, legs and faces of the peasants are as black as Moors, to whom in affinity and dress they bear a strong resemblance.

I do not know what time I may have for reading, but to anticipate the possibility of leisure, I wish in addition to what I requested in my last, that you would send me Swinburne's[1] "Travels in Spain," with a view to guide one's attention and observation to what might otherwise be overlooked. I should likewise be glad to run the risk of getting a small supply of eatables from England viz. some Wiltshire cheeses, tongues, portable soup, vermicelli for soup, vegetable powder for ditto, some bottles of best burgundy, vinegar and a supply of good tea. Mind, I do not wish for a *magazine* of these articles, which would spoil before they could be received or consumed. Have them packed in two boxes of nearly equal weight, and some person deputed at Portsmouth to take charge of and forward them to Lisbon. I likewise beg you will procure me 2 boxes of Wayle's white tooth powder and 2 sets of Smyth's tooth brushes to be sent with the overalls, etc. I forgot to beg a *small thermometer* to let you know what are called dog days in Spain. From what we experience at this moment they must be dreadful! Tell Robin I have nothing but *flies* to send him, and if he knows what a blister is, he will not desire such a present from Spain.

By May 12 the French move forward was affecting the Allied positions. The Count Penne Villemur, a French émigré commanding some Spanish horse, fell back before the enemy's advance, and Long, still demanding exact instructions, also retired northward, reporting to Beresford the daily progress of the French. At half-past seven A.M. on May 15 D'Urban,[2] Beres-

[1] Henry Swinburne (1743–1803) had visited Spain in 1774–76, and three years later published *Travels through Spain*.
[2] Benjamin D'Urban (1777–1849) entered the 2nd Dragoon Guards in 1793, and served with Beresford and the Portuguese Army throughout the war. After being Governor of Antigua and other Colonies he was appointed to Cape Colony in 1834, and he was in charge, during the abolition of slavery, the establishment of a legislative council, and the Great Trek. Durban, in Natal, is named after him.

ford's Adjutant-General, gave Long definite instructions to march immediately to Albuera, a dozen miles south-east of Badajoz. No time was lost in doing this, for it was quite clear that Soult meant business. Beresford was hastily gathering about him all the forces he could; Blake and 14,000 Spaniards were arriving; and British troops, hurriedly withdrawn from before Badajoz, were also marching towards Albuera, an advantageous field of battle exactly foreseen by Wellington in his original orders to Beresford concerning the siege of Badajoz.

Long reached the village of Albuera in the afternoon of May 15. In the subsequent recriminations he was accused of coming unexpectedly and in great confusion, causing much delay at the bridge, and abandoning the whole right bank of the Albuera stream to the enemy. On the other hand, it is perfectly plain that Long had definite instructions to report at Albuera village, which is on the left bank; it also appears that a staff officer conducted the cavalry over the bridge. The French, with whom Long had conducted a skirmishing retreat, were close at his heels.

Throughout the night of May 15-16 troops were closing on Albuera from all sides, and being posted, as far as the Allies were concerned, wherever fancy seized their commanders. Beresford in fact seems to have little notion as to how the battle was to be fought or even whether a battle was to be fought at all. It seems certain that the 4th Dragoons were told to forage early on the morning of the 16th, and ordered to the rear at that moment when the French were about to launch their almost triumphant assault on Beresford's right. Long posted the cavalry, expressed surprise at the way the Allied position was held, and himself discovered that the French had crossed the stream and were forming to attack. He at once sent word about this to Beresford, who was at breakfast.

The Marshal then played his winning ace in his personal struggle with this obstinate and critical Brigadier. Long, among other queries no doubt calculated to annoy his commander, had raised the point as to the command of the Spanish, Portuguese, and British cavalry, indicating that some of the Spaniards were much senior in rank. At the very moment of the battle beginning Beresford placed Major-General William Lumley, who had been commanding an infantry brigade of the 2nd Division, in command of all the Allied cavalry, and for the rest of the day Long cantered about the field at Lumley's elbow, a mere cypher.

The British cavalry at Albuera was hardly in action at all, though at one time the 3rd Dragoon Guards and 13th Light Dragoons pushed back some French horse which had crossed near the unroofed and shattered village. The enemy was a body of lancers, in action against the British in Spain for the first time. Long refers to them as "Pikemen."

Albuera was primarily an infantry fight, and, in proportion to the number of troops engaged, the most bloody of the whole Peninsular War. In four hours the British and Portuguese suffered four thousand five hundred casualties, the French almost six thousand. Beresford fought a personal duel with a Polish lancer, but exercised little direct influence on the struggle. At times he thought the battle lost, and even next day expected a renewal of the French attack.

In the subsequent pamphlet war between Napier, historian of the Peninsular War, and Marshal Beresford the latter plainly showed the hatred of General Long which he felt at the time of the battle. Long was a sensitive man, and observed, resented, and returned this strong dislike. His own faults of obstinacy and grudge-bearing prompted his pen to use strong and biting terms about Beresford's deficiencies. Nor was he the only critic in the Army. Albuera became a threadbare subject, and one which could hardly be mentioned in Beresford's presence.

The view of the private soldier is well expressed in the snatch of conversation reported by a fusilier sergeant. "Whore's or Arthur?" "I don't know, I don't see him." "Aw wish he wor here." So did they all.

First Notes on Albuera

TO C. B. LONG

*Bivouac near Solano, about
2 leagues from Almendralejo
22nd May, 1811*

Our situation does not permit me to enter into those details of our late interesting proceedings which led to the Battle of Albuera on the 16th Inst., a battle which we ought to have lost, but which the unconquerable spirits of the Troops secured to their fortunate commander. The fault committed by us was not occupying the *proper* position, and what indeed was the key of it. The French saw our error, took advantage of it, and we had to recover by deadly exertion the ground which if disputed originally as it ought to have been done, would have cost our Enemies rivers of blood and saved our own. However, as it was, enough has been shed. Our loss amounts to more than 5,000 men, that of the Enemy killed and wounded I would state as being very short of the mark if estimated at 7,000. We buried upward of 2,500 in the field. An intercepted letter from one of the état major to Soult states the amount of wounded with *his* column at 4,000, and wherever we have followed them, hundreds are abandoned, and their positions strewed with dead. We have followed, or rather kept them in sight only, ever since, and we hope this night to be at Almendralejo, as I just learn that they have abandoned Azeuchal. Had the whole Army been put in motion to follow up the victory I can have no hesitation in asserting that the greater part of Soult's Corps must have been destroyed, all his wounded and prisoners taken, his artillery and baggage and in short everything which constitutes an Army. But it has been deemed more prudent to offer him the golden bridge to retreat by, and our Troops have resumed the investment of Badajoz.

This Cavalry was so much superior to ours both in quality and members that our services during the day of action were limited to keeping them in check, and counter-acting their attempt to gain our flanks, and deprive the Infantry of our support. We only came in contact with them, partially, twice, but our Artillery made considerable havoc among them. I never, in any instance in my life, saw such a scene of carnage in the same space of ground. The field of battle was a human slaughter house.

In consequence of the union of the Spanish Cavalry, and to prevent disputes about rank, General Beresford directed Major General Lumley to take the command of the whole Cavalry, and, in my opinion, rather indelicately, permitted this command to be assumed after the action had commenced, and whilst I was manoeuvring the Troops. *This* I can never forgive and thus has fortune deprived me again of what I am free to think and hope might have been my hard-earned reward. Though deeply hurt, I did not abate my zeal and endeavours to promote the Marshal's glory, and my perfect knowledge of the ground, which I had reconnoitred the night before, enabled me I believe to be of assistance to the officer who thus superseded me.

It is odd enough that the evening before the action I pointed out, to the Adjutant General the defect of our position as then taken up, and foretold the consequences; had I obeyed the orders I received in the morning to move with all the Cavalry to the position intended for us in rear of the British line, the consequences might have been fatal. The Quarter Master General had himself marched off with one of the Regiments and not half an hour afterwards down came a strong column of Cavalry opposite the ground they had occupied, and endeavoured to force the passage of the River; which a portion of them actually accomplished, but were driven back by a charge of the 3rd Dragoon Guards, which Regiment and the 13th Dragoons (foreseeing the danger) I had detained near the village of Albuera to counteract any such attempt. Had my advice been followed as to a further part of the disposition I think the fatal advantage taken of our Infantry by the French Cavalry would not have occurred. I pointed out the certainty of this happening, recommended a Regiment to be placed in column on the very spot where it happened, and even placed a Spanish Corps in reserve there; but which Corps, when the French attack upon our Infantry by their Cavalry took place, never moved one yard in advance to their assistance. The only difference in what afterwards happened between what General Lumley did and I should have done, was his not availing himself of a favorable opportunity to attack the Enemy's Cavalry during their retreat, and at a time when their Infantry was flying in all directions. By shaking their covering force at such a moment we should have been put in a situation to cut off a great part of the runaways. The events of the battle rested entirely on the Cavalry preserving their ground. Had they been beaten, the Infantry would have been annihilated. But tho' dreadfully weakened by separation on different points, our countenance was so firm and imposing, that the whole French force (upwards of 3,000) attempted, and appeared to wish, but dared not carry into effect the *duty* of attacking us. But as I purpose giving you in detail the whole of our proceedings on the first favorable opportunity I shall add no more at present to what the Gazette will make you acquainted with. I escaped unhurt. Captain Dean had a hard knock on the shoulder blade, which however being a grazing shot only incommoded him for the moment. He was riding by my side when it took place. I heard it strike him, and after a short exclamation he begged me to look and see if the shot had gone through him. At the first view of his coat, I really thought it had, but told him not, and sent him to the rear to have his wound dressed. In ten minutes, to my utter surprise, he returned to me all alive and well, only a little sickened with the blow.

I this moment learn that the Marshal is in full march with his Infantry to follow our steps, and hasten the retreat of his Enemy. He is too late. Had this been done two days ago, I am not clear but that Soult's whole force might have been cut off from the Sierra Morena altogether. At all events the fruits of the pursuit would have doubled those hitherto gained by the battle.

Now, my dearest C. as I have been talking a great deal of *myself* and my thoughts in this letter, I beg what I have said may be confined to my belongings. I shall always speak the truth to *them*, both for and against myself. Where I commit a fault I shall acknowledge; where I feel myself right in thought or action I shall declare it. We have now been 8 days and nights without any cover whatever but the sky, but with the exception of 2 days and nights cold wet weather we have been fortunate. Thank God I preserve my health, and hope it will continue. My next letter will I trust be written on a table and under a roof, when you may expect a *bumper*.

The rain which fell during the battle of Albuera continued on the day after, and not until the morning of May 18 did the Allied army move forward after the shattered French.

Wellington had been kept in the north during the first days of May 1811 because of an effort by Masséna to restore the French position. The British commander, intent on Badajoz, which he regarded as vital, suddenly found himself attacked. The battle of Fuentes de Oñoro had to be fought and perilously won before Wellington could get down to restore the position. He arrived at Beresford's Headquarters on May 19, 1811. Soult was pushed back out of harm's way to the south, and the siege of Badajoz was once again taken up.

On May 25 a spirited cavalry action took place at Usagre, where once more the French cavalry was overthrown and ridden down with considerable loss. The British Commander in the field was still Major-General Lumley, but Long played a prominent part; well over 100 of the enemy were killed or captured. At the end of the month Sir William Erskine took over the command of the Allied horse, Lumley returned to the infantry, and Long was once again in charge of British cavalry. Another, and for the Army and for Long a much more important change, was that the Southern Army was taken over by General Rowland Hill, and Beresford returned to Lisbon.

Cavalry Action at Usagre

TO C. B. LONG

Villafranca
Wednesday, 29 May, 1811

If the Enemy leave us in peace and quietness for three days more I shall try to fulfill the promise made in my last letter of sending you a bumper, viz.: a Journal of our proceedings since my last. The period is so long and has been so interesting that it is a formidable task to undertake and one I could not accomplish until I am a little recovered from the fatigue of fourteen as hard days and nights work as ever I experienced in my life.

My present object is merely to tell you that having followed the Enemy's retrograde movements from Albuera, and keeping quite close to them, we advanced on the 24th inst. to Usagre (in the direction of Llerena) where we found one Regiment of Cavalry which was very soon dislodged from the Village, and they at the same time evacuated Benvenida. The next day, however, they returned with all their force of Cavalry, and six pieces of artillery, to recover the ground. At first M. General Lumley had determined to meet them on the other side of the Village. I strongly advised him against it as from the nature of the ground if beaten, the greater part of our force could scarcely escape destruction; and I can never put reliance on any other than the British Troops, which in point of numbers are scarcely one third of the Enemy.

Accordingly, having ordered back our only 3 Regiments, the whole retired across the defile as the Enemy advanced. They established themselves on the heights on the opposite side of a deep ravine, and likewise took possession of the village. They then formed their guns into a battery and opened a cannonade which we answered. Soon after they pushed 3 Regiments of Dragoons thro' the village to attack our right. Two of them formed in Columns of attack, the other deployed. This took place in front of the 4th Dragoons and 3rd Dragoon Guards. General Lumley was with the latter Regiment, and not observing the enemy, was actually making a change of position during the time they were advancing. From the badness of the ground which the 3rd Dragoons Guards had to move their column over, I observed them broken and apparently in confusion, the Enemy within 200 yards. To rescue them from this critical state, I immediately directed the 4th Dragoons, supported by the 13th Dragoons to attack, and proceeded to the charge. Scarcely had I advanced 50 yards, when I observed the 3rd Dragoon Guards wheel into line and also move forward to the attack, which in consequence was made simultaneously by both Regiments, and as well as if the whole had been preconcerted and arranged. The Enemy received us, were overset, and having a wall and defile to their rear, were completely broken and beaten with the loss of about 30 to 40 killed (we counted 30 on the ground, the rest were killed in the village) and 78 taken prisoners. Among the latter one Colonel, one Major and 2 Lieutenants; one officer besides killed.[1] The number of horses about 60, exclusive of those seized and carried off by the Spaniards, when delivered over to them in the rear. Our loss not above 3 killed and four wounded.

This so damped their spirits that they did not renew the attack but in the evening brought up an additional number of 9-pounders which from their superior metal we could not answer, and they obliged us to take up a new position out of their range. Both parties remained looking at each other all the following day (25th) but as we had no means of foraging our horses and the duty itself was so harassing to both men and horses, who from morning till night were under arms, without food or shelter from a burning sun, on the following day, or rather night of that day, General Lumley determined to fall back and resume the occupation of these cantonments. I remained with the rear guards, and returned at day break on the morning of the 28th inst. without molestation, or their knowledge even of our movements.

This little affair has been brilliant, and, from being almost bloodless on our part, gratifying. But what to me is most gratifying are the acknowledgments made by General Lumley both in his letter to Marshal Beresford, and in his orders, as a tribute of approbation for the humble part I lent in seconding him upon the above occasion. This is all the reward I ask for, and I am perfectly and amply remunerated. Our object was to drive the Enemy if possible from Llerena, but as Soult with 12,000 men was there, the attempt was impracticable. I think we were wrong in making it by any force incompetent to the execution. I shall not be surprised to see them advance again in consequence of this insult, and return it by driving us from our present quarters, which would be a very easy task.

[1] Long underestimated the French losses, which were over three hundred all told.

For 14 days, my dear C., we have now been working under a scorching sun by day and heavy dews by night, without any other covering than the canopy of heaven, and often without food; and as far as I am concerned, without a change even of linen. My eyes have suffered dreadfully, but 2 or 3 days of repose will set all to rights again. I consider the Campaign is only commencing, and if the Enemy is reinforced to any degree, the issue will be doubtful, for our losses have been most severe also.

The greater part of our men taken prisoners in the battle of Albuera have escaped by the mountains. The enemy openly acknowledge that had they been pursued by any considerable force of our Troops after the battle, their Army was in such a state that annihilation must have ensued, and that a few of their Cavalry only could have escaped. I am decidedly of the same opinion, but good and perhaps great reasons interposed to save them, and therefore they consider the whole as a triumph, particularly when adverting to the trophies they snatched from our hands in guns and colours. Lord W. is now at Elvas, the siege of Badajoz renewed, and everything appears to be waiting the result of the second attempt. We have been strengthened, however, by 2 British Divisions drawn from the Army of the North. I only wish our Cavalry force could be augmented in a similar proportion. We are lamentably deficient in this arm, a most important one in such a Country as Spain. The Enemy's Cavalry opposed to us consist of upwards of 13 different Regiments, all cut down to 2, 3 or 400 men each, but still their aggregate force outflanks us considerably, and they are all good and wellfound Troops. Our miserable allies serve for show and nothing else. There is one Corps however (the Count of Penne Villemur's[1]) that forms an exception, and as *Guerrillas* are most excellent. Ballesteros is at Zafra, Blake at Sta Marta, General Stewart with 8000 men in our rear at Almendralejo, occupying also Azeuchal and Villalba. We are cantoned in Los Santos, Villafranca and Ribera. Sir Wm. Erskine is coming to command the Cavalry. General Lumley was appointed to do away with the claims of the Spanish Brigadiers, who were my seniors. I retain at present the same command as before—Heavy Brigade, 13 Dragoons and Portuguese Brigade. No time to say more!

PS. I have rec'd the watch and yr. letters of the 8 April and 5th May.

[1] Commanding the Spanish cavalry under General Castaños.

V

Retreat from Badajoz

Long remained in the hot plains south of Badajoz, feeding on ration soup badly cooked, and bad wine made worse by heat and fermentation, until the second siege was given up, and a slow retreat to the Guadiana took place. They passed Albuera, blackened and still, littered with the remains of the dead who had been burnt in heaps. At one point Long's guideless wanderings in a dark pine-forest looking for a ford across the Guadiana brought his cavalry under the guns of Badajoz. It was during this retreat that Long was appointed major-general. Long's Brigade now consisted of the 11th Light Dragoons and two squadrons of the 2nd Hussars (King's German Legion).

On June 22 Long's command was involved in another scrape when a whole picquet of the 11th Light Dragoons was cut off and captured. It seems that the squadron was placed in a bend of the river, Long declared by Sir Stapleton Cotton's orders. Soult pushed forward a strong reconnaissance towards Elvas, and Long's German Hussars, making a fighting retreat, were pushed back. The French got almost within gunshot of Elvas, but then returning by another route, having accomplished little, came down upon the rear of the 11th's picquet, commanded by Captain Lutyens. Lutyens, who had not been warned by the Germans, at first thought them to be Portuguese, but discovered his error when the French were only a hundred yards away, and tried to charge. However, the French were not only in great strength, but well informed through a deserter of Lutyens's exact position, and over one hundred men were lost. D'Urban, who as Beresford's chief staff officer always stood by his chief's actions, and hated his chief's enemies, blamed Long not Cotton. Wellington was angry about this loss, and sent a curt note of instructions to Long through Erskine. It was an added misfortune that Lutyens, who had just arrived in Spain, had been specially recommended to Wellington as "an intelligent clever young man" by the Duke of York, whose private secretary he had once been.

Notes from Quarters

TO C. B. LONG

Villafranca

3rd June, 1811

Altho' our post will not take its departure until the day after to-morrow I must avail myself of a favorable moment of leisure when it occurs to acknowledge the receipt of your letter of the 12th May.

Those previously received were dated 8, 21, 30 April and one of 5th May.

I am concerned to say that I have been obliged to send James Lynch to the rear. His headaches and rheumatic affections having increased to a degree that obliged him to relinquish his duty. I scarcely expect to see him again, for he appears rather faint-hearted upon the subject, and will I think return back to England. Brewer, too, has been ill with a bowel-complaint arising from the extreme heat and drinking perhaps bad wine and water. These are all little rubs that produce inconvenience for the moment, but will, I hope, occasion no very great embarrassments to me. I continue well, thank God, myself, and these few days of repose have restored all my organs to their proper tone. We have suffered exceedingly from the heat, and have the happiness to be told that it is nothing compared with what is yet to come. The Barley is now cutting, and you would call it beautiful harvest weather, only with the heat of the dog days. . . .

One of our greatest neglects appears to be an inadequate Artillery. Our horses are as able to drag a nine-pounder as a six. The Enemy brings constantly heavier metal than ourselves into the field, and its effects are too evident to need description. Hundreds of lives would be saved by correcting this evil. It is lamentable likewise to see the miserable state of equipment of the Spanish Army. They are clothed in whatever dress they can pick up from friend or foe; many of them, indeed the greater part, in French clothing, and several in British. The consequence is that it is scarcely possible to distinguish them from the Enemy, and in the recent instance of Albuera they were fired upon by our Infantry. Is England so poor that she cannot provide a few thousand jackets and pairs of overalls to remedy this deficiency?

Desertion appears to be gaining ground in the French Army. Several have come in to us since the affair at Usagre, and the last of them declared that nearly 200 had gone off in the direction of Zafra, taking the direction of the mountains to escape pursuit. . . .

Siege of Badajoz to be raised

TO C. B. LONG

Villafranca
11th June, 1811

I believe my last was addressed to you on the 29th ult., since which nothing of any consequence worth relating has occurred; but I am concerned to say that by the accounts received this morning from Badajoz it appears that our affairs in that Quarter are going on very badly indeed. So much so that there exist grounds for believing that Lord W. has directed the siege to be raised. It is at least certain that last night an order was issued to remove the guns from the batteries. Two unsuccessful attempts have been made to storm Fort St. Christopher, and these failures have depressed the spirits of our people as much as they have exalted those of the Enemy. Still I cannot bring myself to believe that Lord W. will, upon light grounds, abandon so important an object. His Lordship may be influenced by the receipt of intelligence as to the reputed march of Drouet from the North, and may find it necessary to take measures to frustrate the proposed junction of it.[1] A letter was intercepted the other day from Soult, addressed to the officer commanding Drouet's advanced guard, pressing the march of that Corps, and the importance of saving Badajoz, the fall of which was represented as entailing the most serious Consequences upon the French Armies. This letter was to be forwarded to the bridge of Almaraz or Archobispo on the Tagus, but we got hold of it at Hornaches. He therein expressed besides his intention of moving forward again in a few days and having lately reviewed his troops at Llerena, Villa Garcia and Usagre, and provided them with several days provisions, such precautions should indicate the approaching execution of his projects. The Deserters (we have had 5 within the last 24 hours) say that the Army expected to move about the 15th or 16th.

Since writing to you last Sir Stapleton Cotton has arrived and assumed the command of Generals; therefore we have at present a super-abundance and I wish the Broth may not in consequence be spoiled. Two squadrons of German Hussars have also been added to our Strength, and at present they, with the 13th Light Dragoons, are put under my care; but it is expected that my Brigade when all things are arranged will consist of the 11th and 13th Lt. Dragoons and if so I am as well off as my neighbours, tho' indeed I am perfectly indifferent upon the subject.

The heat is really insupportable. The flies too are a perfect nuisance, worse than Frenchmen, tho' much resembling them in their spirit of persevering annoyance. I do not recollect that I ever was what I call disturbed by them before. I have just been reading a wise treatise recommending the use of sugar for feeding, fattening, propagating and improving animals and fowls of all descriptions. I am convinced by the arguments and the wisest thing you West Indians[2] can do is to consult your own interests by practising the experiments which the

---

[1] This information was correct. The second British siege of Badajoz was abandoned on June 11, 1811.
[2] A reference to the family connexion with Jamaica.

author recommends, for if you will not be at the trouble to set the example who should?

Not a dollar to be had for love or money, and Cobbett has taken care to give the Spaniards a good idea of our paper currency. So that between the two we shall be compelled to adopt the French system and live by forced contributions. Ration soup badly cooked, and bad wine made worse by heat and fermentation are all I have to offer my guests, and they partake of it with good grace. You do not know the luxury of such privations, for after all when things change for the better they really become such, by a kind of substitution or improvement which otherwise would not be perceived.

Ribera. 12th June

This small town being exceedingly exposed, we are quite on the alert. I have brought nothing with me but a couple of horses and 2 small packets of provisions. We make night of our days, and days of our nights, and at this season of the year it is no unpleasant change. The wheat is ripening very fast and before the end of this month the harvest ought to be over. Poor devils, between French and English they little know for whom they sow. How I shall envy you your sea breeze and dip in July. Dripping is our portion and we have enough of it.

The watch goes famously; but the glass broke on the journey and you should have sent two keys to replace loss and fractures.

We hear the Duke of York *is* certainly Commander in Chief.[1] The information is gratifying to us. Anything better than the "*Old Object.*"[2]

In Retreat

TO C. B. LONG

Elvas

20 June, 1811

Your letters of the 19th and 27th May are now before me, the former received on the 14th inst. when in Bivouac on the river Guadagira between Solana and Azeuchal. The latter I had the pleasure of getting sight of this morning. The date of my present communication will shew you that my advice not to be too sanguine in your

[1] On February 5, 1811, the Prince of Wales became Regent after the final relapse of George III into insanity. One of his early changes was the reappointment of his brother, the Duke of York, as Commander-in-Chief at the Horse Guards, in June 1811.

[2] Sir David Dundas (1735–1820), "Old Pivot," then aged seventy-six. He was Commander-in-Chief from 1809 to 1811. While a colonel he had written *Principles of Military Movements, chiefly applicable to Infantry* (1788), and several drill-books. Hence his nickname.

expectations at home, was not ill-judged. Instead of driving the Enemy behind the Ebro, they have contrived to make us raise the siege of Badajoz, a second time, and post ourselves behind the Guadiana. This event, in every point of view is much to be lamented. . . .

A fresh arrangement has been made of the Cavalry. They form two Divisions; one commanded by Sir Stapleton Cotton (the Northern) the other (Southern) by Sir Wm. Erskine. The 11th Light Dragoons and 2 Squadrons of Germans form my Brigade, and as both are very effective, they are considered as composing as strong a Brigade as any in the field. At all events I am satisfied, tho' I regret the loss of my Spanish Friends, under Count de Penne Villemur, with whom I have been doing the outpost duty with great concord, ever since I last wrote to you from Villafranca on the 11th Inst. . . .

Having but a few minutes to spare before Post departs, I shall proceed as usual to the Journal of our proceedings. . . .

16th June

Retired in the morning to Corte de Peleas, and about noon the same day to the wood of Albuera where bivouacked for the night. That memorable spot had all the appearance and gloomy stillness of the dead under its bosom. Everything had been burned, by accident or on purpose, so that it was a black dreary waste, the remains of heaps of dead who had been burned still disgusting the Eye, whilst our intention to relinquish, without a struggle, this memorable scene of contest, made the heart sigh to think how fruitless had been the sacrifices of blood there spilled.

17th June

We retired across the river at Albuera, and having halted 2 hours to collect all stragglers, proceeded to cross the Guadiana, and continued our movement to this place, where we were received with one of the heaviest Thunderstorms I have ever witnessed, and the night was a repetition, in a greater degree, of this unwelcome reception.

Before reaching the Guadiana, you come to an extensive and thick pine forest, intersected by numerous roads, where I was taught to expect a Guide to conduct us to a Ford. None, however, appeared, in consequence of which we wandered about misled by those who had preceded us till I found myself under the guns of Badajoz. At last I made a cast, and having found a Ford about 2 miles below the Town, crossed the River, formed, and halted for 2 hours to collect stragglers, bringing off about a dozen of the Infantry Gents whom I picked up in different parts of the wood. The Enemy sent a picquet to observe us, but kept at a respectable distance. As we left the Guadiana we observed a considerable dust in the wood, and afterwards learned that it was a detachment of 50 horse that fell in with a Portuguese commissary, who took some bullocks from him, and murdered all the peasants accompanying them. They had also been straggling about the wood in search of the right road out of fifty.

In the afternoon I retired to this place, bivouacked in front of it, and found the greater part of the Army collected round the Town. . . .

Thank God I am very well tho' moving noon and night in a stewing pan, and do not despair of seeing better times for this Army and myself. The Enemy is said to be extending to his right. Both Parties will probably be in Cantonments before the expiration of a fortnight, tho' I believe the British would rather fight it out now than postpone the conflict. Lord W. seemed in very good spirits, and the sunshine on his brow will dispel all clouds from ours.

Some Comments for a Brother-in-Law
TO COLONEL HENRY HOWARD, M.P.

Bivouac near the Village, Vicente,

26 June, 1811

A thousand thanks to you my dearest Colonel, for your last and all your former epistles. When I write to Charles, I consider myself as writing to you, and therefore I limit punctuality of correspondence to him exclusively. The histories I have to record are so egoistical that I have some pain in writing them *once* over, to do it twice would be a tax upon my patience that I should be unable to encounter. . . .

I augur, with you, no good from the increasing influence of the Arch-Intriguer, the Duke of C., at Carlton House. We have been taught from our earliest Infancy "Principibus nulla fides" but it is reserved for our old age to discover the truth and wisdom of this remark. You have all been faithful adherents, we shall see the Reward which Royalty prepares for Fidelity.

The step recently given to me makes it a matter of perfect indifference to me in which Regiment I am now placed. My only Regimental concern from this time forth will be to draw my Regimental pay as Lt.-Col., and which, when not actually serving on the Staff, is the full extent of remuneration I have to look forward to from the Service till dust returns to dust. Rank without the means of supporting it can have no charms for me ergo the late Brevet has not added one inch to my stature, or excited one ray of hope or of prospective good beyond what I before enjoyed. If it enables me better to meet the expenses incurred by the Service, I am satisfied, and this of course it will do. . . .

I shall attack your portable soup the moment it arrives and by a mental delusion fancy myself feasting at Park House. But the Climate here is so furnace-like I doubt the possibility of its reaching me in a state to eat; at all events the Soup will be ready for the Tureen the moment it reaches my Quarters. General Hill[1] is too much esteemed in the Army not to have already secured my prepossession in his favor. The Cavalry, however, being a distinct Arm, we have little to do with Infantry Generals, and to speak the truth I have been constantly so much advanced, and always at the outposts, that, except at Albuera, I have scarcely seen an Infantry Regiment for these two months. . . .

Report speaks highly of your new shrubberies, pommeries, etc., etc. You cannot better employ your time than in devoting your mind to increase your own comforts and those of your Friends. I always thought your walks too straight for comfortable flirtations. Love delights in winding ways, prepare them therefore for my next interviews with the Harriets, Charlottes, Carolines, Louisas, etc., etc., of immortal memory.

So then, to you, and all chez vous I beg the tender of my affectionate and best regards, and tell my Pater that to hear of his again being upon his legs stout and strong, would be more gratifying to me than a baton de Maréchal. I hope he will exert himself to give me this happiness!

God bless you, my Dearest Colonel, and grant you everything my heart wishes.

More Thoughts on Beresford; and a Mishap to the 11th Dragoons

TO C. B. LONG

Bivouac near Vicente

26 June, 1811

I had yesterday the happiness to receive your letters of the 4th and 11th Inst., and I hope you will, ere this, have also been put in possession of a very long detail I sent from Villafranca containing the Journal of our operations in Estremadura. I do not pretend to perfect accuracy in my description of what relates to others, but when I narrate what I personally witnessed, you may rely, I hope, not only on my veracity but my impartiality. I am of opinion that Marshal Beresford never deserved at my hands the zeal with which I served him, and endeavoured to merit his good opinion. But unfortunately the business at Campo Mayor, added to the collisions which arose out of the circumstance of a Portuguese Brigade of despicable Cavalry having

---

[1] Rowland Hill, affectionately known as "Daddy Hill," commanded the Anglo-Portuguese army of the south.

been placed under my command, produced, perhaps, an alienation that he could not easily get over. To ensure his good graces I had nothing to do but to *swear* by the Portuguese part of my command as being everything perfect. But this I could not exactly reconcile to my conscience, and separation in such a cause is death.

With regard to General Lumley's appointment it certainly arose out of an *act of my own*. I had written from Sta. Marta to state the awkward circumstance arising out of the union of the Spanish Brigadiers with the force under my command, and I *there* received a notification that General Lumley would be appointed to do away the difficulty. He did not arrive, however, nor did he assume the command till after I had manoeuvred the Cavalry for a considerable time against the Enemy on the 16th May, and was in the act of placing them in that position in which they afterwards defied, under General Lumley, the efforts of a superior Enemy. Notwithstanding the mortification I experienced on that occasion, it did not lessen my exertion in *his* cause, and you have seen the reward I have received for it. The action having begun I still think it was most indelicate to take the command out of my hands, for under the existing circumstances I knew that both the Spanish Generals would have most cordially co-operated with me. One of them had been serving with me in perfect harmony for several days previous to, and during the whole retreat through Estremadura, and the other, throughout the day, uniformly applied to me for instructions for his guidance, therefore there was no absolute necessity for the supersession, and delicacy, as I said before, would under such circumstances have had some consideration for my situation. That is all I have to complain of, for certainly I had no pretensions to a command of that magnitude, still less to assume, or exercise any control over officers (Spanish) senior to myself.

I have just received the Marshal's account, and he has written it with more prudence than was shewn in preparing for the contest. The whole sum and substance is comprised in the words "As the heights which the Enemy had gained (by our having neglected to occupy them, he might have added) *raked and entirely commanded our whole position*, it became necessary to make every effort to retake and maintain them." Here is a just description of the position *as it was taken up*, and the cause of that bloodshed that was so profusely spilled in the attempt to retrieve the error. The Marshal has here stated the fact, and by his own confession my observations, as to accuracy of narration, may be appreciated. I have never said *half* as much against him as I hear from others, very high in authority indeed, and therefore I am convinced that the battle of Albuera will for ever be to General Beresford the most unfortunate day for his military reputation that ever he encountered! You will doubtless have seen, read or heard of various other private accounts of this memorable day, and I only beg that you will abide in your opinion by that which appears the most favorable and at the same time the most impartial.

With the exception of a reconnaissance on the 22nd Inst. made by the Enemy against our advanced posts, everything has remained perfectly quiet since my last. The business of the 22nd. however, unfortunately cost me 134 men and horses of my Brigade, a whole picquet of the 11th Dragoons with its Captain (Lutyens) and another officer, having to a man been cut off. All having been reported quiet in the morning I had rode out to wait upon Sir Wm. Erskine, who commanded en chef, at the time the posts were attacked, and therefore I did not see what passed nor was it in my power to prevent it. Had my orders been obeyed, it probably would not have occurred, but when young officers first come out with young men, they have not always their wits about them, and think only of shewing their *spunk* instead of their *judgment*. The post occupied by Capt. Lutyens was certainly an unpleasant and indeed an extremely dangerous one; so much so that I had warned all the officers of the Picquet I first placed there, by Sir Stapleton Cotton's orders, of their situation, and pointed out vigilance as their only security. I indicated the point by which I considered a retreat alone practicable. Lutyens had, unfortunately, but just relieved the post, when he was attacked, without having had time to prepare and look about him, and I understand the cause of his disaster arose from his mistaking the Enemy for his friends, and leading his men in consequence into their very clutches. The loss at this time is to be lamented, but it will do good in the end.

We know not what the Enemy are about and they I believe know as little of our situation and intentions. I suspect they are busily employed in revictualling Badajoz, and putting everything in order for its security under protection of Marmont's[1] force, and that a portion of Soult's army has already fallen back upon Seville to oppose Blake and the Spaniards from Murcia. I further am inclined to think that he will not commence at present any offensive operations against us, and in this case both Armies may before many days are past, retire into Cantonments for the dog days....

You must therefore expect little of interest more in this quarter for some time at least to come, and I have only to hope that the North of Europe may in the meantime furnish you with sufficient matter to

---

[1] Marmont (1774-1852), Maréchal de France and Duc de Raguse, who had fought at Austerlitz in 1806, and was to be present at the battle of Leipzig in 1813, succeeded Masséna on May 10, 1811.

speculate upon, in the suspension of further triumphs in this part of the world.

I receive your congratulations on the step recently given me in all humility of spirit. I have not ambition enough to feel as I ought on such an occasion, and I think I may safely say that this step will place me, with many others, on the shelf, where I shall continue till covered with the dust from whence I sprang. I was not cast in the mould that secures fortune by acts of servility and sycophancy, and I am not blessed with the ability to command her graces by personal endowments. I must be satisfied to relinquish the theatre of glory to more aspiring candidates for favor, satisfied if my conscience and my friends accuse me of no dereliction of duty, in discharging the debt I owe to my Country.

A thousand thanks to you for your kind attentions, I hope soon to announce the departure from Lisbon of a cargo of segars sufficient to last you throughout the next winter's campaign.

When next you go to Town send me a couple of the Scotch wooden snuff-boxes. General B.[1] will be good enough to frank them as he did the watch and then my comforts will be complete. I lost my old companion in the gallop on the 22nd Inst., and now am compelled to have recourse to the tin canister.

By the bye, I have just received a note from Mr. Greenwood, dated 25 May, in which he says he has not yet received the bill I transmitted to him by you.

[1] General Brownrigg.

VI

A Spanish Summer, 1811

During the spring and summer of 1811 matters in Spain had quietened down after an exciting opening near Cadiz. Barrosa near by had been fought and won by General Sir Thomas Graham on March 5, practically as Long arrived at Lisbon. After the fall of Badajoz, two unsuccessful sieges, the battle of Albuera, and the various cavalry engagements which Long witnessed, the Southern Army paused in its operations and kept an eye upon the enemy forces to the south and in the east of Spain. The Spanish troops were obliged to surrender Figueras and Tarragona, in Catalonia, both after hard fighting, both in circumstances of horror and disaster.

Wellington and the Northern Army had a livelier time than the southern detachment. No sooner had the battle of Fuentes de Oñoro marked the end of the pursuit of Masséna from in front of the Lines of Torres Vedras than Wellington proceeded to blockade Ciudad Rodrigo after a brisk exchange of manœuvre and mutual threats with Marshals Soult and Marmont. During September two combats were fought, one at El Bodon, the other at Aldea da Ponte, and other small engagements kept our troops in activity.

The French were too busy elsewhere in Spain to be able to give their full attention to the British Army. There were Spanish troops to be defeated to the north, in Galicia, and in Murcia, to the south. And even though the Spaniards might never win more than a minor success they were indefatigable in gathering together, and insatiable for defeat. The French rolls of victories, of captured towns, of guns, colours, and prisoners taken, impressive as they are, denote little more than the measure of their failure. And this French failure to accomplish anything decisive during 1811 was to mean their ultimate collapse.

Meanwhile, in July, tormented by flies, the Army went into cantonments. Rumours, several minor changes in command, gossip, wolf-hunts, horse-racing—this included mules and donkeys—and speculation passed the time. Uniform alterations ordered by the Prince Regent caused much ordering and reordering, and a measure of justified criticism. Sickness depleted the ranks. A comet-like star became a much discussed subject.

From a staff officer named Heathcote, who was with the Northern Army, Long received vivid and accurate accounts of their operations, in particular of El Bodon, fought at the end of September. Robert Long's personal diary reveals other facts which have their interest. He usually noted down the dates of all letters sent and received. Brother Carolus, his father, and his friend Addenbrooke take the lead. But others appear too: "A.W.," "Lady Arabella W.," and "Arabella Ward." On June 23, 1811, is the entry: "A.W. brought to bed of a boy, reputed to be my son, named Charles Henry Hopkins." This is followed on August 10 by: "Arabella Ward married to Mr Wolstenholme of Bixington, Dorset."

Quiet Times before the Enemy
TO C. B. LONG

Camp near Vicente
3rd July, 1811

... I received the other day the gracious thanks of our pure and honorable Parliament communicated officially by the Marshal. I have bequeathed the precious documents to our Pater, who, if they have any value attached, will best know how to appreciate and be pleased to receive them. I anxiously wish that anything I could do might gladden, for a moment, his unequalled heart, and therefore I was pleased to be able to send him a record, such as it is, that his son was considered as having deserved well of his Country.

The Prince seems determined to make Honor and Ornament go hand in hand. The recent promotions have been very extensive, and the hats of the Generals amazingly bedizened. It is a pity His Royal Highness possesses not the power of improving the blocks under the hats, tho', if he did, some risk would be run that wiser heads would not be fools enough to follow soldiering. . . .

Our weather recently has been quite delightful, very different from the roastings we experienced in Estremadura—days invariably fine, with cool western breezes, but the nights are very cold and dewy, and this it is, that cuts up the Troops, exposed as they are in bivouac to the effects of both. They talk of placing us in Cantonments, and I wish they may, for I can see no good we can now do by continuing in the field. We must nurse up our strength for a fresh day of trial when circumstances render it necessary. The Spaniards, I take for granted, will complain bitterly of our inactivity; we shall have to hold them out a looking-glass and bid them see what is passing at home! I much fear they will end in becoming the adopted children of our Enemy. Mr. Perceval himself seems not to extend his hopes beyond the spinning out of the war here for another year. More sanguine expectations in the North would have rendered such a sentiment high treason. Time alone can clear up these matters, and we must have patience.

I believe I mentioned in my last that Greenwood had written the word that the bill I sent him per your worship had not been received. Make enquiry and set this to rights. He behaved so handsomely I am anxious to show him that I am not insensible of it.

A Major-General's Ambition

TO C. B. LONG   Camp near Vicente
9th July, 1811

I received the watch on the field of battle at Usagre, and acknowledged its arrival, and my perfect satisfaction. It was just what I wanted, and as far as I can judge is a very good one.

Tho' desirous of standing well with all, I know that the thing is impossible. I limit therefore my concern to those most dear to me, and if *they* are satisfied *I* am contented. I know well in my own mind how to estimate and appreciate the approbation of my superiors. I wish no-one to commit an injustice for my sake; and am equally desirous not to be spared when the rod should fall. General Lumley's account was rather underdone, for he forgot to blazon forth his trophies. No mention was made of the officers and horses killed and taken, tho' among the former one Colonel, one Major and two others of inferior rank, besides one killed, graced our triumph, and the horses captured were nearly in amount with the men. He was wrong too in fancying the Enemy did not see the 3rd Dr. Gds. My only apprehension was they saw them too well and that in a state to have insured their defeat had the Enemy been more active and quick in his formations. It was to anticipate so fatal a result that I put the 4th Dragoons in motion, and this was done before ever the 3rd Dr. Gds had formed line.

The battle of Albuera has in its consequences been certainly a victory to our Enemies. But Soult might have stated the truth without much diminution of his own reputation. The conduct of his troops, to be sure, would not stand the test of very minute inquiry for never did Raggamuffins make better use of their legs, and never were despersion and déroute more complete.

As long as the Enemy maintains his ground, the balance will be in his favor. With Ciudad Rodrigo and Badajoz he holds the keys to Madrid; and in his hands (as we shall see) they will not be easily surrendered. All we can do is to protract the contest as much as possible, waiting the occurrence of events yet unforeseen by man, and the accomplishment of designs only known to the Supreme Controller of our destinies. At present both Armies are lying upon their oars, in this neighbourhood at least.

Nothing but blows and hard ones too, will make the Leopard crouch beneath the Imperial Eagle, and the feathers recently plucked from the wing of the latter,

> May make him fly an ordinary height,
> Who else would soar above the reach of men,
> And help us all in servile fearfulness.[1]

[1] Adapted from *Julius Cæsar*, Act I, Scene 1.

Let the conscripts march, and when they join their veteran ranks, let them listen if they like it to the funeral dirges composed at Fuentes de Honoro [sic] and Albuera,[1] and prepare for fresh glories! Let them buckle on the armour of the "Legion of Honour," and see if it is proof against the British bayonet!

I have just received a letter from Le Marchant announcing to me his displacement from the Lt. Governorship of the College[2] over whose interests he has so long and faithfully presided, and in whose establishment he was so instrumental. I wish to God I could see in such an act *recompense for public services*, a mark indicating that it arose from patriotism and a sense of the public interests, rather than from that spirit of intrigue, jobbing and persecution which mark the abuse of power, and strike at the root of all zeal of fidelity in the servant. But the day of retribution must come, and the intermediate hours will serve but to swell the triumphs of the oppressed.

I also hear of great expected changes at the Horse Guards. I never was enamoured of that pile, even when it contained the friends I value most. How it will appear when big with frowns and haughtiness instead of smiles and condescension, I leave you to judge. There is room enough, thank God! both in front and rear of it, to *turn a horse about*, and I must practise mine to expertness in this manoeuvre. Neither beggary nor wooden shoes shall ever make me a Courtier, therefore prepare your cabbage seeds and when these squabbles are over I will bury all ambition (should a remnant remain) in the Bay of Biscay, and prepare to cultivate them for you. The thanks of Parliament, recently bestowed, shall be folded up with the Parchment Roll of Family Pedigree, and indexed

        Thanks of the Country
                to
          Robert Long
Major General and Cabbage Planter
Who had luck enough to do his public duty
Sense enough to know when he had done it,
               and
Wisdom enough to prefer Cabbage-planting
                to
Dependence upon Princes or Power
               for
More substantial happiness
Bello finito
Requiescat in pace!

---

[1] Oman gives the French losses as 2844 at Fuentes d'Oñoro and over 6000 at Albuera.
[2] The Royal Military College at High Wycombe.

I have just received an invitation to dine at Head Quarters to meet the Prince of Orange,[1] who has just arrived to take a lesson in the art of human butchery. Adieu till tomorrow.

July 10*th*

Well, this said Prince of Orange is an amiable looking youth, and his countenance denotes peace and benignity. His profile is exactly that of your neighbour the Hon. and Rev. Mr. Grey, whom he resembles exceedingly in every point of view.

I entrusted to Capt. Leggatt, A.D.C. to General Lumley, who is going to England, a box containing 108 parcels of your favorite cigars. It was addressed to Addenbrooke at Strathfieldsaye, and the supply is to be equally divided between you and Lord Rivers. Should it arrive safe I hope there will be enough to last you for a 12 month at least. Had we succeeded in taking Badajoz, where they are manufactured, you might have had a shipload.

I fear my stud will require an increase before the end of Autumn. Keep a look out, and if anything very clever and reasonable falls in your way secure it for me. I think mares stand service better if anything than horses. The sex is therefore indifferent.

I wish likewise you would procure me a letter of recommendation from some of your friends in the city to some house at Lisbon, to which I might have addressed any articles coming for me from England, and in whose hands I could lodge sums of money from time to time to discharge bills at Lisbon, as we are occasionally obliged to send there for supplies of different kinds, and I find it the awkwardest thing in the world to be without a correspondent there.

In Cantonments

TO C. B. LONG

Redonado
28*th July*, 1811

... From the lamentable issue of the recent campaign south of the Tagus, and the probable effects of it upon the minds of the Spaniards, I am not disposed to augur very favorably of our future operations. They may be said to be in the true sense of the word a disunited people, without a head or authority to control and regulate their movements. The Gallician Army will do nothing because the Enemy is no longer in that Province, the Valencian Army the same; they are therefore acting like so many separate Kingdoms or independent Provinces, without political or military union. General weakness is the result.

[1] William VI (1772–1843), later to become first King of the Netherlands.

In the meantime the French are getting on in Catalonia, the only Province where vigorous hostility has never ceased to exist, tho' the efforts of the brave Catalans have been miserably supported by the Government. Tarragona is said to have fallen; nothing further remains to be accomplished there but the recovery of Figueras.[1]

In looking back to the part *we* have acted since taking the field, I fear the impartial historian will have little less to put upon record than the grossest errors, and a system of mismanagement which have terminated the most brilliant prospects that ever flattered the hopes of an Army, with complete discomfiture and disappointment. . . .

I believe it is now six weeks since any Pacquet has arrived from England. You may imagine the state of despondency in which this circumstance has placed one whose every happiness and enjoyment are derived from communications with you. It is quite a blank in life to be exposed to such a privation, at a time too when want of occupation makes minutes hours, and days years. I can scarcely help looking with an envious eye at those who are about to convert this season of inactivity into a Holyday time, and "lash the lingering moments into speed" by a pleasant excursion across the Bay of Biscay. The list of truants is pretty large, but the greater part on the score of health. It is reported in the Army that Lord W. himself contemplates a few weeks absence, but this I do not credit.

They have taken the 11th Dragoons from me and given me the 14th in their stead. The latter are the more expert and experienced Corps, but the former in point of conduct and efficiency everything I could desire. I am sorry to say that your old acquaintance Cummings[2] does not draw well with his officers. All parties, as usual, to blame, but I fear the breach is irreparable.

Rumours in Cantonments

TO C. B. LONG

Borba, near Villa Viçoza
2nd August, 1811

. . . On my arrival here I was overwhelmed with rumours. To account for the long suspension of intercourse between this County and England, a Packet was said to have been dismantled and put into Scilly. A General Embargo was likewise reported to have been laid

---

[1] Tarragona was finally stormed and sacked on June 28, 1811. Figueras fell on August 19, 1811.
[2] Henry John Cumming was Lieutenant-Colonel of the 11th Light Dragoons and served in the Peninsula from June 1811 until January 1812 and from May 1812 to April 1813. He survived until 1856.

on all shipping in the English ports, and on all Americans in the Tagus, in consequence of war being declared against the latter power.[1] The death of our poor King was announced as a fact, and lastly it was confidently assumed that the Spanish Cortes had made proposals of peace to Joseph. Upon these rumours we must live till the mystery is cleared up.

Kenneth Howard[2] is here commanding, in the absence of Generals Stewart and Lumley, the 2nd Division of Infantry. His own Brigade is a beautiful one, and I believe him deserving of the honor. The weather is cruelly hot, and agues increasing. The officer commanding the 2nd Hussars in my Brigade went off very suddenly the other day in consequence of a coup de soleil, and a Portuguese officer of the 2nd Division shared a similar fate here the day before yesterday in an equally rapid manner. A few days rain would do us a great deal of good, but really I do not think I have seen above *three* showers since my arrival in the country.

This vicinity is reckoned the Garden of Alemtejo, and very beautiful and productive it is. The wine is the best, to my taste, I have met in Portugal, and the fruits are good and abundant. The villages are neat, clean and inhabited by people in the full enjoyment of their usual comforts and prosperity. What a perfect contrast to the scene north of the Tagus! They are the perfect representations of Peace and War! ...

More Gossip
TO C. B. LONG

Borba
14*th August,* 1811

... Our Marshal here is, I find, busily employed in refitting and recruiting the Portuguese Levies, which have lamentably decreased during the last 3 or 4 months. If we could carry our force up to 80,000 effectives of both nations, I think we might bid defiance to Napoleon and his thunder-bolts.

I sympathise in your feelings at the state of our poor King, and wish his case terminated one way or the other. This is a bad time for sickness to be at the head of affairs. I do not like that *Prussian* propensity which the Prince has displayed in his recent regulations about dress. We are here all fighting in true blue, and thinking of what is more

---

[1] Unrest between the U.S. and the United Kingdom resulted from the various attempts by Napoleon to interrupt British trade. Although acts of war were committed before official hostilities began, the "1812" war did not start until June 1812.
[2] Howard normally led a brigade of the 1st Division.

essential. The Drum majors were happy with their feathers, the Generals satisfied without them. Why rob the former to lay an additional tax upon the latter in favor of Messrs. Cater? Better would H.R.H.'s time and strength be imployed in rousing the spirit of his countrymen and thereby procuring the *materials* to *dress* his Enemies.

I have received a letter from Le Marchant acquainting me with his destination and that he had applied for Seelinger[1] as his Brigade Major, but the Duke had refused. To me this is quite unaccountable since the information I received of his (Seelinger) positively being on the eve of exchanging from the 15 Dragoons into the 4th West India Regt. This additional sacrifice, therefore, might it should seem have well been spared to him. Oh, what a curse is power in the hands of unfeeling tyranny!

Still More Gossip
TO C. B. LONG

Portalegre
17th Sept., 1811

... With regard to our *operations* in the north they continue to puzzle all the Speculators. A letter which I received dated the 12th inst. says, "I am quite ignorant of what is going on in the front, but I should guess that something will take place soon, as the battering train has arrived at Pirchel, and the reinforcement which is now not even supposed to have left France."

The rains are stated as generally setting in about the beginning of October, and when they do come the mountain torrents are regenerated, the Tagus and Guadiana cease to be fordable, and many of the roads practicable. Such a season is, therefore, but badly adapted to offensive operations on either side, and least of all for sieges.

In the meantime I am sorry to say our own sick list is formidable, and we have lately lost several officers. The Enemy I take for granted are not better off in this respect, and consequently if the odds are not changed in this respect, the operations on both sides may be neutralised. The Commanding Officers of the two Light Dragoon Regiments last arrived[2] (the 9th and 12th) are on the non-effective list. Col. Ponsonby has gone to England and Vicomte de Chabot will I believe soon follow. A most melancholy circumstance, the recent death of his wife, will likewise deprive us of the services of my friend Le Marchant,[3]

---

[1] John Joseph Seelinger was a captain in the 15th Hussars and had served in the Coruña Campaign. He died in February 1820, still a captain.
[2] From England.
[3] Le Marchant was commanding a cavalry brigade with Stapleton Cotton's 1st Division, whereas Long's brigade was with Erskine's 2nd Cavalry Division.

from whom I yesterday received a sad epistle annoucing his misfortune. I have no doubt but she fell a prey to distress of mind arising from the cruel treatment which he I think has lately experienced at home, and the whole of which, in my eyes, has originated in the intrigues of those who were *his* Enemies, because he was too vigilant a Guardian of the public rights he was officially appointed to protect. He is thus left the sole prop of a Family of nine children half of whom are very young, and the whole dependant upon his fate for future existence. Thus circumstanced, I have advised his not returning to this Country, to risk an existence so important and essential to his Family, for an ungrateful ——! Should he, however, return, it will be a good opportunity of sending the things I wrote for in my last from Windeler, and to which may be added 4 pairs of *strong* calico *drawers* made like the last: viz to reach to the ancle, and a couple of pounds of good windsor soap, and *2* calico under-waistcoats.

Our curiosity has been for some time past awakened by the extraordinary appearance of one of the stars, which tho' resembling a comet, still I believe is not one. We have observed it for nearly a fortnight past, and I think you must have done the same in England. The star itself appears like a globe of lights, with a long train of a radiated and luminous appearance extending upwards as it were towards the North Star. Its situation is just under the Ursa Major, as it appears at *present*:

The Star as it appeared just under Ursa Major, and as sketched by Robert Long.

I

I have not observed that its situation has been changed and this it is which puzzles me. We see it best about 8 o'clock P.M., but as it verges towards the horizon (about 10 o'clock P.M.) its luminous appearance ceases. Let me know if it has struck your attention.

Tomorrow is the day fixed upon for the Portalegre races and other amusements intended for the gratification of the Damsels of this place. A mile course has been marked out, stewards appointed, and the whole conducted under the patronage of our Chief, whose greatest happiness appears to consist in promoting the pleasure of others. The shew of cattle will not be very brilliant, but mules, donkies and foot races make up the deficiencies. My stud is too small and too precious to be risked. I shall therefore be an unconcerned spectator of the sports.

My Aide de Camp, Dean, is now at Lisbon doing some commissions for me, and I hear that the 5th Dragoon Guards have arrived and landed, and the Transports ordered back instantly to Ireland to receive the 6th and 7th Dragoons. Had half this vigour been shewn before the recent campaign opened, both this Army and Spain might have had good cause to bless such foresight. At present unless circumstances open an opportunity of employing this force *beyond* the frontiers, it will be perfectly useless, and I see no chance of advancing under the reduced state of the Spanish Armies and of Spanish spirit.

If everything should promise a prospect of quiet winter quarters, I propose making a trip to Cadiz, embarking at the mouth of the Guadiana. I am anxious to see that celebrated City and Port, and the measures adopted for its protection. I am *told* the Isla de Leon is a second Gibraltar, and that nothing but treachery could wrest it from Spanish dominion. . . .

Another Move

TO C. B. LONG

*Portalegre
Sunday, 22nd Sept., 1811*

As I depart from this place tomorrow to take charge of the advanced posts, and our regular post day being Tuesday, I may not have leisure to write to you and therefore I avail myself of a favorable moment to announce the safe arrival of your letters of the 26th August and 2nd inst. . . .

I have this morning sent off for Lisbon a poor fellow (Capt. Barrett of the 11th Dragoons) who, if any man ever shook hands with death without accompanying him home, has done so. The moment he began to recover his senses I cheered him with the hope of soon seeing again old England, and I am convinced the prospect gave his very blood an impulse that vivified and reanimated the whole man—a sovereign medicine I have never exhibited without good effect! I have embarked to his care a small box of preserved pears presented to me this morning, and have directed it to you at Langley. Not having tasted the dish I know not if they will prove eatable or worthy of your acceptance, but good or bad it will be a Portuguese bon bon for the little ones.

As soon as the actual operations are over I suppose we shall go into what may be considered Winter Quarters: that is, the enjoyment of dismal, wet, cold weather, in houses without glass windows, and rooms without fireplaces. Think of this when November comes, and relish your social blaze as you ought. I shall know hereafter, perhaps, how to value it more than I have hitherto done, and, released from the shackles of persecuting Dukes and doubtful Protectors, make up my mind to a steady pursuit of happiness in my own way and according to my own fancy.

I know not exactly never having seen how the cigars are manufactured, but both Spaniards and Portuguese make them up with paper almost in the same way, often without any other instrument than a knife to make the first fold compact. The cigars I sent you should be used with a glass tube, I think, for the smoke from the straw envelope persecutes terribly the *eyes*, and this you very likely may have observed. They are made chiefly, if not altogether, in Spain, and Badajoz I am told exports them largely. Is not this consideration enough to make you bewail our ill-success there? I might, under a proper tuition, have become a manufacturer myself, and have supplied the whole Craven Hunt!

A Wolf Hunt
TO C. B. LONG

Portalegre

30th Sept., 1811

... I am at this moment occupied by a General Court Martial,[1] which employing us all day, leaves me but the night as it were to myself. I fear it will be a tedious sitting altogether which nothing but Soult's advance can suspend. Yesterday, however, being Sunday in all countries, but not a day of great austerity in this, I went out to see a wolf-hunt by the Peasants, several officers joining the party. The former are regularly summoned to the duty by a Magistrate, and the

---

[1] From September 26 to October 16, 1811, Long was President of a General Court Martial at Portalegre. Two officers were tried: Captain Candler of the 50th, acquitted of embargoing mules in the public service; and Lieutenant Hunt of the 57th, found guilty of going to Lisbon without leave, and publicly and severely reprimanded.

whole plan of operations consists in enveloping a portion of the country with chasseurs, or caçadores as they are called here, and then with the assistance of other Peasants driving everything towards them. The result of the chasse was only one poor fox slain, a beautiful creature that would have made your mouth water to look at, and with a brush that would have authorised any degree of neck-breaking to have carried off triumphantly. On my way, however, in company with 2 officers to the scene of action we overtook on the road a young lupus, about 22 inches high, but so dreadfully emaciated and in so weak a state as scarcely to be able to make a run of it. We immediately charged him, upon which he crept into a Vine-yard. One of the officers with me dismounted and pursued, whilst I rode round to cut off his retreat from a thick cover close by; and thus we succeeded in catching the hero, and he was sent back in captivity to this place, where he will meet with such hospitality as will shortly enable him to take vengeance, and probably effect his escape, this having generally happened to his predecessors in such a situation. Lord Tweeddale having brought over a pack of Foxhounds he may possibly be reserved for a day's sport before them. Thus you see we are not to be left without recreation of some sort, and indeed if circumstances permit it, General Hill himself being a great Courser, with ample means to engage in such sports, if within reach of him, I shall have my field days of this description as well as you. Considering the precarious tenure under which soldiers hold their existence, I am decidedly for their enjoying it to the best of their power to the last, and I should apply to General Philippon[1] [sic] for security against all hindrance or molestation in such pursuits, to which he and his garrison might come if they pleased. This would be conducting our quarrel upon gentlemanly terms, and the best policy for those to pursue who cut each other's throats to please others and not themselves. I fear however our Enemies are not so sociably inclined, tho' they did, it is true, invite our officers to their theatrical representations at Santarem....

More Cantonment Gossip

TO C. B. LONG

Portalegre
8th October, 1811

I am most happy that the adjournment of the Court Martial for a day gives me an opportunity to resume my confab with you....

...I maintain that unless some very great change occurs, such a one as I cannot at this moment foresee or expect the game in this

[1] General Armand Phillipon commanded the French garrison at Badajoz.

Country is verging fast to its close. "The Beloved Ferdinand"[1] has no longer charms to please a Spaniard's ear; they must have something better to fight for than the shadow of a shade. They want freedom and a good government, if England would let them have either. But so long as we support the Rulers *they* despise, and who have placed themselves beyond their reach, so long will they contue to increase in indifference as to the result of the contest. The monks still rule the roost among the Cortes, and the People can have nothing to hope from them. In this state of affairs few things would please me more than to hear of Cadiz being in an uproar, and the Regency set afloat. But whilst the British Leopard is there to watch over their safety this can hardly be expected!

If Soult and Marmont are satisfied with their recent exploits, the Campaign for this year may be considered as at an end. The weather, it is true, continues beautifully fine, but everyday brings us nearer to that kind of change which must produce a cessation of hostilities. We are not, however, quite certain about Soult. Some accounts represent him to be in motion towards Estremadura, others that Drouet is to assume the command on this part of the frontier, and Soult is about to repair to Madrid to become K. Joseph's Lieutenant. We are striving in consequence to increase our numbers, and I think no force under 15 or 20,000 men would be permitted to dislodge us. Altho' the Alemtejo is considered the most unhealthy Province in Portugal, our sick at this moment bear a very small proportion to those of the Army of the North. With the exception of the 71st Regt.[2] I should be disposed to say we were as healthy as we could expect to be. Nothing can be more delicious than the climate we at present experience, and our cantonments are the best in the country.

The fox-hounds commenced their operations yesterday and had, I am told, a very pretty run, but the earths and places of refuge are represented to be so numerous and the difficulty of stopping so great, I am inclined to think a pack of harriers would have afforded more sport. I likewise think that the wolves, when they are met with, will occasion such dismay and desolation as to produce a serious loss of hounds, and make our casualties beyond the reach of reparation in this country. Two packs have come over; one belonging to General Hill's brother forms the Corps de Chasse south of the Tagus; the other, the property of the Marquis of Tweeddale,[3] is attached to the

---

[1] Ferdinand VII came to the throne of Spain in 1808, but was immediately deposed by Napoleon in favour of Joseph Bonaparte, King of Naples, who was King of Spain until 1813.

[2] The Highland Light Infantry.

[3] George Hay, eighth Marquis of Tweeddale (1787–1876), served in the Peninsula from 1807 to 1813. In later life he became Governor of Madras and a field-marshal.

army of the North, and placed under the immediate command of Lord Wellington. Is not this doing the thing in style? Nor is the spirit of rivalry confined to arms, horses and hounds. The very cooks are put in competition for trials of skill and I have been summoned as an umpire to decide between the culinary talents of two Professors in this art in the service of Sir Wm. Erskine and Lord Tweeddale, a bet of five guineas being staked upon each dish. Unless an oath is administered in furtherance of Justice I am determined to make it a drawn battle, and propose a fresh trial. Thus you see we are determined to live all the days of our lives, and I hope the Enemy will get the wind of these proceedings, as I am told that nothing annoys them so much as the indifference which the British show upon all occasions—even where they calculate that we have no right to feel at our ease. Such philosophy is to them perfectly insupportable. They know of no law or practice which authorises such insolence. It is an invasion of their just prerogative to frighten the world out of its senses, insulting to their power, injurious to their rights, degrading to the Napoleon system: in short, "c'est une étourderie détestable. Je n'y comprends rien, moi."

James Lynch has at length joined me in a convalescent state, having submitted to a regular course of salivation. He now and then gets a letter with the Newbury postmark, and I always dread a relapse when they arrive. He tells me however that your gardener is his correspondent, and tho' the handwriting is not so straight as his lines of cabbages, there is nothing crooked going on between them.

Dean joins me on Sunday next with my stores from England etc. and after a three weeks dissipation at Lisbon. I understand Houston is not expected out again. He cannot keep his health out of reach of the rays of the rising sun. He is right! and Lady Jane will think so too. Everyone in his turn, glory ought not to be monopolised. Nothing more fair than a regular roster for broken heads, particularly when one gets little else for one's pains.

I hope my turn will also come, sooner or later, and enable me to enjoy the future without regretting the past.

Various Reports and Additions

TO C. B. LONG

Portalegre
14*th October*, 1811

By this mail, in addition to this letter, I forward to you a pacquet containing a more detailed statement of the recent affairs in the North. Attention to the contents of these documents will prove to you, incontestably, that Lord W. has not much to boast of on the score of his proceedings, and that nothing but the bravery of his Troops, added to the influence of his belle étoile, as Marmont calls it, saved him from a severe and unnecessary loss, and very great disgrace....

The French officers were I understand very unreserved in their communications to Major Gordon,[1] Lord W.'s ADC when he went with a flag of truce to Rodrigo, and was detained there three days among them. They expressed their disgust of the war, and ventured to think that if the Spaniards persevered Napoleon would never succeed. Give me that *if*, and I think so too. They acknowledged themselves not in sufficient strength at present to re-enter Portugal, but thought that a fresh attempt would be made next year, or the following one at latest. They paid high compliments to Lord W. and the British Army, and what they have since observed at El Bodon and Aldea de Ponte[2] will not lessen their respect. They talked of certain propositions for peace being on the tapis, which were to surrender to the French that part of Spain north of the Ebro, the British to have Portugal and Cadiz, and the Prince Regent to be raised to the throne of Spain and have the remainder. Of course such propositions are only circulated to increase distrust between the Alliance and weaken the bonds of connexion between them....

Tell young Carolus and Henry that I was once in Spain and of course saw some Spanish butterflies, but when such an opportunity will *again* occur is more than I can speculate upon, but I shall be heartily rejoiced to find myself in a situation which enables me to execute their commission.

I am grieved to hear that Caroline Swinburne should be so offended at my beautiful letter to her, which really cost me more trouble to dish up than anything I have composed from this country; and I thought it impossible to mistake anything, for I took every pains to make it unintelligible; but I did not, it appears, sufficiently appreciate the cleverness of the intellect to which it was submitted. I have a delightful knack at offending young ladies, both by speeches and letters. I must confine myself, hereafter, to pawing them, and see what that will produce. Next time you see her tell her to specify the crime and its extent, shew her the article of her creed under which it comes, and then I will take the opinion of the Bishop here as to the extent of the penance it requires from me. This done we will kiss and be friends again. If this is not a Christian proposal I know not the characteristics of Christianity, and must apply to her for better information. I was certainly rather naughty towards her sister Elizabeth, because she is

---

[1] Later Sir Alexander Gordon (1786–1815). He was killed at Waterloo.
[2] Two engagements fought on September 25 and 27 respectively.

an old married woman, and does not regard such trifles, but nothing did I say which could the least alarm the virgin delicacy of the beautiful Caroline. Let her take out her dictionary and read again. If there is even a crooked word in the whole epistle I will consent to swallow the whole sheet, tho' I should never be straight afterwards!

Tell your little Mary I congratulate her on being shipped from her cradle, and launched into the pool of public education to acquire all the pretty little arts of fascination. And I make no doubt but Mrs Renouard will teach her how to charm the dolphins that sooner or later will be playing round her during her cruises on the more boisterous element of the world, and perhaps accomplish her so far as to bewilder the brain of that odd fish her uncle, Old Bat. But tell her that as he grows old he grows nice and squeamish and nothing but a petticoat of perfection can penetrate his tough hide. Without this condition

> Her bugle eye-balls nor her cheek of cream
> Will ever tame my spirit to her fancy.[1]

You must make Villebois acquainted with the gallant conduct of his friend Col. Cumming and his brave associates. Let her Honor be paid to whom it was due. They were beginning to frown upon the 11th, but I cut the serpent's head off, and they have nobly repaid my confidence.

My poor broken-hearted friend Le Marchant[2] has joined Lord W. and by doing so has increased the sources from whence I hope hereafter to be put au fait in all their proceedings.

Pray procure and send me under a frank from Calvert a pocket Journal book for the year 1812, as soon as they are out. Peacock's is what I bought for this year, but they are pretty much alike. . . .

[1] Very freely adapted and obviously quoted from memory: *As You Like It*, Act III, Scene 5.
[2] After the death of his wife Le Marchant was able to make arrangements for the care of his family, and so remained in the service, contrary to Long's expectation.

VII

Arroyo dos Molinos

This period of inactivity was interrupted at the end of October when Hill executed a rapid and most successful thrust against a French force under General Girard. Two columns moved off, Long having command of a Portuguese brigade, three Portuguese six-pounders, and the 13th Light Dragoons. After much hard marching over wild country in bitter, drenching weather a complete surprise was effected on the enemy at Arroyo dos Molinos. Long's cavalry, which now consisted of the 9th and 13th Light Dragoons and the 2nd Hussars of the King's German Legion, pursued the French troops, who escaped from the village; Long in person, at Hill's request, chased and captured the enemy guns, and although, during his absence, the French scattered and escaped without being charged many prisoners were taken. The dash and spirit with which Hill handled this brilliant and exciting exploit were only exceeded by the humiliation of the French and the annoyance felt by Napoleon at such a display of Gallic élan from the British. The French loss of some 1500 all told included two generals and three guns.

It was unfortunate that even this brilliant little success had to involve Long in another personal quarrel. This time it concerned an aide-de-camp, and a great favourite of Hill's—a certain Captain Currie,[1] of the 90th Foot (Cameronians)—and a rumour said to be circulating in Lisbon about Long's conduct of the cavalry at Arroyo dos Molinos. It would have been best to ignore tittle-tattle, which almost certainly originated in the general gossip concerning the over-all criticism of British cavalry in the Peninsular campaigns. Currie made a dignified reply, and the matter came to a stop so far as letter-writing went; but, as Long had proceeded to gather some evidence in writing, it is unlikely that the rumour itself died. Long, who had, it appears, a most sincere liking for his divisional commander, could hardly expect to go on quarrelling in this fashion without serious repercussions upon his own future.

Journal at Arroyo dos Molinos

Monforte

27th October   4th Nov., 1811

... The 2nd Hussars marched at day break for Aldea del Cano and the Casa de Don Antonio. Not finding the Enemy at either, they

[1] Mrs Currie accompanied her husband in the field. She used to make tea for Hill and the 2nd Division staff and held little receptions wherever the division settled down in its billets for a few days.

pushed on to Alcuescar, patrolling into Alvala, where they met the Enemy. The Enemy still make no Patrole or reconnaissance to their front, altho' Alcuescar is not above 3 miles from Arroyo Molinos, where they were collected. It was impossible to account for such negligence, but every information received confirming their ignorance of our proximity it was determined to attempt surprising them in the morning or at all events to attack, and try to cut off their retreat upon Merida and Medellin. Dispositions were made to this effect, and every precaution taken to prevent discovery. It rained hard during the early part of the night. The Troops were bivouacked but not allowed to make fires.

28th October

The Column was formed in readiness to march at 2 o'clock A.M. The morning was dreadfully dark, and the rain came on in torrents, so much so that with two great-coats and an oil-skin cloak over all, I was nevertheless drenched to the skin. One of the guns which I followed was upset in a ravine which crossed the road, and there being a high wall on the left and a deep and impassible ditch on the right, we were blocked up and our progress delayed for nearly 1½ hours. As soon as it could be extricated I pursued my march, but did not reach the British Columns till the village had been carried, the Enemy formed in solid Columns of retreat, and General Howard's Brigade moving round their right flank to cut them off from the line of retreat. The weather so distressing to the men, was most favorable to the success of the Enterprise. They were completely surprised in the Village, but having intended to march early that morning, a part of the Troops were already under Arms prepared for the purpose. I detached, by order, two Squadrons to the right to assist the Spaniards, which meeting a portion of the Enemy's Cavalry on their way, charged them most gallantly, almost annihilated them, and took the French General Brunn prisoner. Left on the left with 4 Squadrons I first put them in a situation to cover the left flank and rear of General Howard's Column which I thought exposed, but afterwards perceiving the difficulty he had in gaining upon the Enemy, I determined to throw myself on their opposite flank (the left) and front, and endeavour to check their advance, and at the same time get between them and the mountains. Whilst in motion for this purpose I received an order from General Hill to press upon them. I thought the doing so injudicious, but immediately formed a Column of Squadrons and advanced, as if to attack upon their rear. They halted—what I wanted. I did the same—they then got in motion. I repeated the feint, they halted a second time. At this moment an Aide de Camp brought the word that General

Howard was going to charge. I prepared to join in it, and immediately detached two of the 4 Squadrons with me to attack the front and left flank of the Column, whilst I did the same upon their rear, and General Howard upon their right flank. The Enemy edged away from General Howard, and he did not accomplish the charge. On seeing this, and observing their approach to a small rocky height which was separated by a small road only from the great Sierra where they took refuge, I marched off with the two squadrons remaining with me intending still to get between the Enemy's Column and the mountain and check their advance. Whilst moving to this point and for this purpose, General Hill rode up, and told me their guns were all getting off, and entreated me to pursue and take them. I therefore left one squadron to pursue my original intention, and with the other I made after the guns, which I overtook and secured. This accomplished, I returned back to the scene of deeper interest, and to my mortification observed the Enemy had passed the road and had gained the Sierra. Had I been here sooner, I could certainly, by charging them in the act of passing the road, have checked their advance, and given time to General Howard's Brigade to close upon their rear. This was neglected, and General Hill lamented the circumstance as much as I did, but I could not be everywhere at once. The British followed them up the mountain, and I galloped off with the Cavalry and placed them in a situation to prevent their escaping on the opposite side. About 1,000 surrendered to the pursuers, but Girard, the great object of our wishes, still remained with about 400 men whom he had collected. Had the pursuit continued, and the Cavalry remained where I had posted them, his escape was impossible. Unfortunately it appeared desirable to lose no time in proceeding to Merida, consequently all the Troops which were on the mountain or surrounding it were too quickly withdrawn, and the pursuit left to some Spaniards under Murillo. Girard observed this, descended, and passed the plain rapidly where I had taken post, and gained a wood, the Spaniards being unable or unwilling to prevent it, tho' supported by ½ squadron of Cavalry which was detached to assist them. I then proceeded with 3 squadrons and a Brigade of Infantry towards San Pedro, but the Infantry was so fatigued, I was obliged to halt where the road we were marching upon intersects the high road to Merida and Truxillo. Towards the latter place I placed a small picquet in ambush, and in the course of an hour surprised a Captain of the 27th Chasseurs and about 24 Hussars who were trying to reach Merida, and took the whole prisoners. In the course of the Evening I took about 8 or 10 more, chiefly infantry. I detached ½ squadron to San Pedro, and at 2 P.M. on the following day (29th Oct.) I proceeded with the Column by San Pedro to Merida, which we reached about 5 o'clock P.M. Count de Penne had entered it at 12, the Enemy having retired during the night.

30th October

The Army halted at Merida and on the 31st retired to Montijo, continuing their retreat without loss or interruption, on the following day to Campo Mayor. Halted there the 2nd Nov., and yesterday (the 3rd) marched off for their respective Cantonments.

Such is the result of this "marche militaire," which by French negligence, confidence or presumption, has enabled us to strike the most brilliant blow against them that has been achieved, almost without bloodshed, this year. As such I hail the lucky star which dictated and directed it, for otherwise nothing but a most harassing and distressing march would have been our reward without a single object, worth the sacrifice, being acquired. As it is, the official despatches will detail to you what we have lost, and what we have gained, and the comparison will gladden your heart, and induce you to fill a bumper to the Army of the Alemtejo.

I fear I shall not have the credit I might have gained had I let my dogs loose and charged them vigorously, which in the state their musquets were in I could have done without risk or loss, but I foresaw the doing so would only tend to accelerate their dispersion and more rapid flight to the mountains and thereby defeat the object proposed to be gained by General Howard's column.

I regret that I was not present at the time they gained the Sierra, for a charge *at that moment* could have done no injury, and must have produced some degree of delay which would have favoured the closing of our Infantry upon them. But above all I lament the message which counteracted my first intentions, the prosecution of which would in my opinion have been decisive.

Such is the true and faithful narrative of our proceedings as far as they came under my observation. Many things occur afterwards which if carried into effect, would have improved the business, and it is in this manner that the wise young-heads reason. But everything considered, enough, I think, was done, and 20 times more than, upon my calculation, however sanguine, we had every right to expect. This Division of Girard may be said almost to be placed hors de combat, and the humiliation which Gallic Pride has sustained will not readily be forgotten or forgiven. It will teach them to be more circumspect in dealing with the British, and exalt our character beyond the limits they have hither to prescribed to our pretensions.

We suffered a good deal from the severity of the weather, and incessant fatigue, and our horses, being for nearly three days without hay or straw, are not the better for it. A fortnight's tranquillity will set all this to rights, and prepare us, I trust, for the day of revenge which they have graciously promised us.

No mail has arrived from England since I wrote last, and it is reported that one of the Packets has foundered in the Bay—God forbid such a misfortune!

I remove tomorrow my Headquarters to Cabeca de Vide and my Brigade will be stationed as follows: Monforte—13th Light Dragoons; Cabeca de Vide—2nd Hussars;[1] Alten de Chao—9th Light Dragoons.

The 9th and Germans covered themselves with glory. Their conduct could not be surpassed.

More of Arroyo dos Molinos, Prisoners, and Orders

TO C. B. LONG

Cabeca de Vide[2]
12th November, 1811

Nothing has occurred in the way of news, but as I met several of the French officers at Portalegre the other day, and had a good deal of conversation with them, amongst others the Duke of Aremberg, General Brunn [*sic*][3] and Col. Verral of the 40th Inf., I wish to lay before you what appeared to me to be their opinion respecting the present state of affairs.

It required little difficulty to knock down at once all their arguments or attempts tending to justify their proceedings in this country, therefore the question was reduced to the simple proposition of how far they were likely to succeed. In this they appeared to be nearly unanimous, and say that the Spaniards are so panic-struck that they can never again be brought into the field, and that such has [*sic*] been during this war their severe losses in men, that even the population of the Country is unequal to the wants of the Government. *They* say that scarcely a young man is now to be seen in any of the villages of Spain, and that they are so completely sickened by disaster as to be almost universally desirous to peace upon any terms. They consider Valencia is on the eve of subjugation and, this accomplished, the efforts of their whole Army will be turned against us, and altho' they do not

---

[1] The Hussars of the King's German Legion were perhaps the finest light cavalry in the Peninsula, their horse management in particular being extremely good.

[2] This hamlet was to be Long's most permanent quarters from November 1811 till the final advance, at the end of April 1813. It lies some eighteen miles S.W. by S. from Portalegre.

[3] Prosper, Prince of Arenberg, Colonel of the 27th Chasseurs, and General Bron, commanding the cavalry, had both been captured at Arroyo dos Molinos.

deny the difficulty of the undertaking they consider the British Government is not inclined to risk even the fate of such an Army merely to preserve Portugal. Consequently that when adequate means are prepared, and the invasion renewed with system and method, we shall decamp. They consider a Russian War as almost certain, but say that it will not effect the contest here, which will be carried on with reinforcements furnished by Austria, the Troops of which nation they teach us to expect to see in this country before the lapse of five months. They acknowledge the great difficulty they have to subsist in Spain, and say that notwithstanding the contributions imposed on the Country they are obliged to have recourse to France for the greater part of their supplies in money, clothes and equipments of every kind. They consider peace with England as impossible until it can be dictated by France, and this can only take place when her maritime means are equal to our own. They speak with confidence of the approach of this day, and altho' they call the invasion of England a chimera they think that Ireland presents a theater where the interests of Great Britain will receive sooner or later a severe wound at their hands. From the manner in which the Emperor treats those who have the misfortune to be made prisoners, they consider their military prospects as blasted for ever by their recent disaster, and they have a perfect horror of the interminable captivity they are about to experience altho' aware of the humane treatment they receive in England. They idolise their Emperor too much to think it possible he can do wrong, but still they acknowledge that the war in Spain was a malheureuse aventure. They have a high opinion of Suchet, and say D'Orsenne[1] is a most promising officer. They are unanimous in their abuse of Masséna. Albuera was a sore subject, and I was not displeased to find my own opinion confirmed by them, that had we followed up the blow there, the Army of the South would have ceased to exist, and Andalusia would have been ours almost without a further struggle. Badajoz would then have fallen without a shot being fired. Sad mistake of the Great Marshal Beresford! General Brunn told me that he narrowly escaped becoming our prisoner at Usagre; being well mounted he was able to leap a wall and got away in this manner. He says the attack was a *bêtise* of General La Tour Maubourg, and as the surprise at Arroyo Molinos was also a betise of Giral,[2] I think these gentlemen might as well acknowledge at once that some of their Generals, at least, are bien bêtes. Brunn's Dragoons are however the finest in their service and as they have twice tried their hands with us, and have been terribly punished on both occasions, I think the British may without

[1] Marshal Suchet commanded the Army of Aragon, Dorsenne the Army of the North.
[2] This should be Girard.

arrogance claim a decided superiority. The Colonel of the 40th Infantry (Verrol, I think his name is) is a fine fellow, and as he behaved particularly well to some British Prisoners, I gave him a letter to our Minister at Lisbon, Stewart, and another to Capt. Boyle of the Transport Board, and if you have an opportunity I wish you would urge the latter to do all in his power to favor his return to France on his parole, his exchange or to ameliorate his situation whilst detained in England. It is not ungratifying to see that whilst Napoleon threatens tears to English mothers, his French children can feel as well as ourselves the miseries attendant on warfare. The enclosed note [not to be found] I received this morning from the Captain of the 27 Chasseurs whom we took on our road to Merida, and you will see the distress which threatens to overwhelm his Family by his capture. The poor creature has half lost his senses, and the first thing he shewed me on being taken was his wife's picture hanging round his neck, stating at the same time that her existence and that of six children depended solely on his exertions, and that their ruin would be consummated by his detention. I have done all I can to procure his release, but Lord Wellington is so offended with Masséna at a breach of faith which occurred in a negociation between them for the exchange of his A.D.C. Captain Percy, that he swears he will not listen to any proposal whatever of the kind until this injury is repaired.

It is reported that the Army of the North is again in movement towards Ciudad Rodrigo, with the view probably to bring back Marmont into the field, as it is suspected he is co-operating with Suchet in Valencia. This is right enough, but as the sickness of our Army in the North is still very great, I fear these renewed operations at this late season of the year will not diminish the evil. The 4th Dragoons have lost upwards of 30 men and have now 170 in hospital. Of the two Armies that of the Alemtejo is I think the healthier, in the teeth of common calculation.

Had the weather been fine our late tour in Estremadura would have been pleasant enough. It gave me an opportunity of seeing Merida for the first time, and to a lover of antiquity a short residence there must be delightful. There is the most perfect Roman amphitheatre I suppose in existence; a Temple of Mars which the Spaniards have dedicated anew to Alma Maria; a Triumphal Arch; the Bridge; and a most beautiful tho' mutilated statue of Cleopatra, which I suspect the French are preparing to carry off. A thousand other relics, equally interesting, are found in different parts of the Town and neighbourhood. We only halted there, however, one day. My researches therefore could not be very minute.

One of the finest plains I ever saw extends almost from Merida by

Montanches to within a league of the Guadiana. The soil is as rich as that at Walcheren, and lying low on the right bank of the Guadiana, the water stagnates, and the smell is precisely the same. I suspect therefore the whole of that tract to be very unwholesome. It is a noble coursing country, and from its high state of cultivation abounds with hares. I picked up a brace of Greyhounds at Montijo, and three more since my arrival here. I have been out only four times and have brought home $5\frac{1}{2}$ brace of hares. This answers my purpose exceedingly well, for I am obliged to consider the *pot* as well as the pleasure of filling it. One of the brutes is a dead hand. He yesterday made as good a *point* at a hare as any pointer you could have done. We then started her, and off he set *full cry*. He finished by killing her very handsomely single handed. I think he unites, beautifully, the qualities of the hound, Greyhound and pointer in tolerable perfection, a great desideratum for service. I shall re-baptise him, and instead of Gavillon (his Spanish name) call him Caterer.

I am delighted with Cabeca de Vide. I have a good house (but nothing in it but a few chairs) in a beautiful situation, and a fine sporting country in every direction; and it is exactly in the center of my Brigade; Portalegre about 18 miles off. I pray we may not stir from it till we take the field again for good.

I must now send you some commissions which you will have executed for me as well as you can. First of all I am much distressed for plates and dishes, my canteen holding only half a dozen of rusty tin ones. Now I think you might procure me a small set of the cheapest Wedgewood, sufficient let us say for 12 persons; viz:

$1\frac{1}{2}$ dozen soup plates;
4 ,, meat ,, ;
a Soup tureen;
4 *Medium* sized dishes for joints of meat;
10 or 12 small side dishes for made dishes, vegetables, etc.;
2 Butter boats;
1 dozen good sized tea cups;
1 ,, saucers;
A good Wedgewood teapot and milk jug and slop dish.

The whole of the above to be neatly, equally and securely packed in two baskets covered with oil cloth or horse skin, so as to be quickly and easily put up and taken out, to be as nearly as possible of the same weight, and a small space to be left in each basket for table clothes. In general plates travel best when arranged edges upwards. I wish the whole to go in the smallest possible space consistent with security and celerity in packing. Now the sooner the above could be procured and sent the better. Let them be plain but neat, and strapped round with canteen straps and brass padlocks. When ready they may be sent to Portsmouth to the care of Lt. General Whetham, the Lt. Governor, to whom I will write, addressed to me as follows;

> M. General Long,
> Portugal,
> To the care of Captain Brayman (King's German Legion)
> Town Major's Office,
> Lisbon.

Pay for them by a draft on Greenwood and Cox. Likewise wish Windeler to send me a new plain undress Major General's coat, for I am in rags. I believe I begged a hat in a former letter. I think you will find in the drawer in my room bureau, some very good tablecloths. Send a few with the baskets, and let Windeler enclose in the box he forwards (addressed as above) a pair of calico sheets, which I think are also to be found in the same bureau.

Captain Hill is gone home with the despatches of his Brother.[1] In case he should go to the bottom you may like to know that our spoils at Arroyo Molinos were about 1,500 men in K., W.,[2] and taken; 3 pieces of artillery, 6 ammunition waggons with six mules to each; about 40 or 50 officers, including 2 Generals (Duke of Aremberg and Brunn) and 2 or 3 Colonels; the Military Chest, but I know not as yet how many thousand dollars it contained, and probably about 4 or 500 horses, with an immensity of baggage, most of which the Spaniards secured to themselves, leaving us the honorable task of fighting for it, and taking it from the Enemy. A few Ladies likewise graced, as captives, our triumph. I wish Giral [sic] had been of the party, and he escaped only by our premature relinquishment of the pursuit. Soult was at dinner when he heard of the disaster, and his crockery and wine bottles suffered most severely in the first paroxysms of his rage. How delightful to annoy the rascals in this manner, or indeed in any other! They richly deserve it.

A mail from England has arrived since that which brought your letter dated 22nd Sept. I fear some accident has befallen one or more of the packets. They are hunting away in the north, and several officers of high rank have been made to bite the dust, among others the Q.M. General, Murray,[3] broke his collar bone. In the south the fox-hunting campaign is just opening, but they will have no sport unless they come here.

---

[1] General Rowland Hill.   [2] Killed and wounded.
[3] Sir George Murray (1772–1846) later held the varied appointments of Governor of Canada, Governor of the Royal Military College, Sandhurst, Colonial Secretary, and Master-General of the Ordnance.

VIII

A Quarrel with Beresford

THE end of the year passed for Long partly in letter-writing, racing, serving on courts-martial, greyhound coursing with immense success, and partly in another vexatious and disagreeable personal quarrel. This was with Beresford, who had written to Wellington and accused Long of taking without permission two Portuguese officers for his aides-de-camp, and of giving them sick-leave and other leave of absence in complete indifference to their regimental duties. This attack, made so that the Commander of the Forces himself was involved, and implying unworthy motives, drove Long to some most violent and forceful remarks, and to a very long and involved correspondence through Hill. Hill, one of the kindest and most considerate of men, was troubled by this business, and tried to quieten Long down; the care he took is shown by the much amended and corrected draft (to be found in the Hill MSS. in the British Museum) of a letter of November 18, 1811, in Long's collection (in which he suggested Long might modify his furious defence). Even if Beresford's attack were launched through personal animosity and based on flimsy evidence Long certainly showed ill judgment in his manner of dealing with it.

A Hurried Note

TO C. B. LONG

Cabeca de Vide
18th Nov., 1811

After being nearly two months without any intelligence from England, last night brought me the following letters, which I have not yet had time to read, but beg to acknowledge the receipt of: yours dated 30th Sept., Oct. 7th (enclosing one from Pater), 14, 21; one from Eliza without date under Frank from Calvert dated 4th Oct; one from Howard dated 6th Oct. The post going again within an hour, I must leave the perusal of the whole for a period of greater leisure, but the next mail will I hope convey my replies.

I intended devoting several hours to you yesterday, but was attacked early in the morning with severe spasmodic pains in my bowels, which confined me to the bed all day; arising I suspect from getting cold by some means or other. I am almost well this morning, but not quite the thing.

I am at this moment engaged in an unpleasant correspondence produced by that Ruffian in mind and manners, my friend Marshal Beresford, the result of which is still to be ascertained, but I shall forward to you by the next mail what has passed upon this subject, and which has set him and me at complete daggers drawn.[1]

I have had no bulletins of the success of the fox hounds in this neighbourhood, but as they are coming over here next Sunday I shall know more about their proceedings. I believe the game to be too plentiful to admit of much sport.

My Greyhounds kill every thing they see, but still they are not of a description that would do credit to your kennel.

If not too late I wish Windeler would send me a good Kerseymere waistcoat made fully long, with the other things.

Commissions for a Brother

TO C. B. LONG

Cabeca de Vide

25th Nov. 1811

I am inclined to think that the complete subjugation of the western and southern provinces of Spain will first be accomplished before they proceed to the last grand undertaking that will not be attempted without a very great superiority of numbers indeed, for the French are really beginning to dread a conflict with our Troops, and I do not think they will ever hazard one upon equal terms. Our recent treatment of their prisoners has quite turned their hearts. They say they always esteemed, but now they love their generous Enemies. Young Ahremberg (the Prince's[2] brother) told an officer of the 2nd Hussars on his return to Campo Mayor that he wished to God he could exchange services, "qu'il n'avait jamais rencontré des gens comme les Anglais;" their bravery was only equalled by their generous hospitality; I hope this sentiment will gain ground, and civilise in the end the system of warfare between us. But in truth they have so many savages fighting under their standard, whose sanguinary inclinations are not easily controlled that the bayonet, after all, is the only weapon that can be employed to tame them with effect. I suspect your Brest and Boulogne bustle[3] is only to paralyse our arm in this country by inducing you to set limits to your reinforcements. The winter months are not the period for maritime operations.

[1] Long sent home all the papers concerning his quarrel with Beresford over the Portuguese aides-de-camp.

[2] Prosper, Prince of Arenberg, who had been taken prisoner at Arroyo dos Molinos.

[3] One of the periodic refurbishings of Napoleon's mouldering fleet of 'invasion' barges.

I rather differ in opinion with you about Paddy's land. I think they shewed in 1798 that they can act as well as menace, and the intimate union of Protestant and Catholic now established is for other purposes than mere Catholic emancipation. Repeal of the Union, and Irish Independence will be the next watch-words. They are a troublesome race and will be always a millstone round our neck, and Napoleon's best ally.

The General Court Martial of which I was President prevented my attending the second Portalegre races, and the last were suspended by the news from Caceres, the principal Turf General having been despatched upon duty to Castaños—Capt. Churchill, A.D.C. to General Hill; Capt. Battersby, A.D.C. to Kenneth Howard, and Capt. Handley of the 9th Dragoons were the great rival competitors.

You ask me what is the amount of Lord W.'s force? I should not be inclined to estimate what he had with him at Rodrigo at more than 40,000 men, including everything. I do not estimate the British force at more than 35,000, the Portuguese at 15,000; and we had 10,000 of them in this province. The sickness has been very great in the North, and I suspect the mortality not inconsiderable. . . .

My sporting campaign leaves you far behind. Caterer and his yelping comrades have already procured me 12 brace of hares, and I have been feasting upon them daily. One of the Spanish purchases shows blood, and really runs beautifully. They kill, as you see, and that is all I want. I am in daily expectation however of being removed from this delightful cantonment, which I like better than any other I have seen, and hoped to occupy throughout the winter. The 2nd Hussars, who were here, marched yesterday for Cordeciera near Albuquerque, in consequence of the unfounded report of the arrival of 4 squadrons (French) at Badajoz. A deserter came from that place yesterday and assured me they were trembling there from an apprehension of our renewing the investment of it, and that the few cavalry there are almost starved. I shall therefore try to get the Hussars back for their sakes as well as my own.

I transmit you herewith the correspondence alluded to in my last, and which is not yet terminated. What do you think of the great Marshal now? Does he not shew his elevation in the true potatoe style? Read his infamous report again and again, then reading my explanation of it, say I have been too severe upon him. He will not keep me in terror, as he does his Portuguese, by his dungeons at Fort Bougie,[1] and the day may come when I shall be able to tell him my mind in very different language and manner. At present, I shall not be astonished at their pushing matters to the utmost extremity,

---

[1] Fort Bugio is a small island, used then as a prison, in the mouth of the Tagus.

but I am "in utrumque paratus," and bid them defiance. I despise their power as much as I detest their motives.

I have received the packages from Mackay, but his Vermicelli and mustard were both musty, for which he ought to be scolded. I have no objection to receive a fresh supply of some hams, vermicelli, curry powder, mustard, pepper, spices, and pickles, in sauces. They make a bad ration go down wonderfully. Colonial products such as tea, sugar and coffee, are procured easily here. Another supply of medicated brandy (one bottle) and a few yards of flannel to repair waistcoats and make a pair of drawers would be acceptable, as would also a few brass padlocks with keys; a bottle or two of Vancouver's glue, and if they can be procured, two or three cock-locks for tapping and drawing off with keys any liquor from barrels. The horse commission may be postponed, but it would a great treat to order a paper (The Times[1]) to be regularly transmitted to me with Cobbett[2] and the Edinburgh Review[3] as they come out. I see no news but what some kind friend favors me with a sight of.

I was quite indignant at the unchristianlike conduct of a certain lady in Sussex. I will have nothing more to say to her. She had a fine opportunity for ingratiating herself with the neighbourhood. She appears to have held such a consideration cheap, and I hope they will punish her as she deserves. Oh! that I was there to be the Champion of such a cause! Poor Charlotte Montagu should not stand in need of an avenger.

I have now a more troublesome commission for you than any I have yet bored you with. Mons. Ifland[4] is becoming so intolerable in manners and temper that a separation must take place. I have (not foreseeing this circumstance) left all his books and papers of accounts behind, I believe in the black leather box, the blue portfolio, or my writing desk, perhaps in each. These I shall want to enable me to discharge him, as also the red morocco pocket books for the years 1809 and 1810, both of which I believe are to be found in one of the above places, or else in the oak box in your library (the largest at least of the two.) But this will not be sufficient. Mr. Ifland must be replaced, and I think a young healthy man of good character for honesty, sobriety, and temper, not objecting to come abroad, nor to serve as groom and valet, would be the thing. Will you look out and try to procure one? I care not about wages, but he should know that he will be fed here. Should you meet with one he might be charged to bear

---

[1] Founded in 1785 under the title of *Daily Universal Register*. This was changed to *The Times* in 1788.
[2] *Weekly Political Register.*   [3] Quarterly periodical founded in October 1802.
[4] Long's manservant.

the accounts, taking a memorandum of them in case of accidents, with the sums that appear in my pocket books as paid to him. Col. Gordon,[1] the Q.M. General, will I am sure on your application procure him an order on the Transport Board for a passage; and on his arrival at Lisbon he has only to wait on the Town Major there for further directions. This is a sad job for you, but I cannot avoid it. Should the procuring of such an animal be difficult, then any man as a butler and valet will do, and a foreigner of good character be preferred. He must be apprised he will not always repose on a bed of down. He must be satisfied with what I can procure for him, and take his chance with the rest.

Tell dear Robin his best wishes will suit me equally as well as his beads. The progress of innocence may have more charms than holy stones.

By a letter from the North it appears that Lord W. is making a fresh attempt to intercept a convoy destined for Rodrigo. I wish it may be more fortunate than the last.

Capt. Dean had a sad accident the other day coursing. His horse fell and he had the misfortune to break his collar bone. He is doing well.

Sundry Notes and Jottings
TO C. B. LONG

Cabeca de Vide
3rd Dec., 1811

Now you have got back to your winter quarters, I can pretty well accompany you in your daily occupations. For the sake of field sports, I wish you were here. Everytime I go out I see woodcocks in abundance, and on Friday last I had four very good courses and brought all smugly home. The country is however very rocky and stony, and therefore bad for the feet of horses and dogs both of which suffer in consequence. I coursed a fox the other day for about two miles, but only one dog being up he escaped into the crevice of a rock before I could secure him, which I wished to do. The hounds, I understand, have had some good runs, but no blood. This *must* be the case where the country is unknown, and stopping impossible. They were to have come over here last Sunday sennight but the

---

[1] James Willoughby Gordon (1773–1851), after serving as military secretary to the Duke of York when Commander-in-Chief, was Quartermaster-General to Wellington from 1811 to 1812, succeeding George Murray, much to Wellington's annoyance. His frequent blunders and incompetence were only surpassed by his disloyal conduct in sending home confidential reports from Wellington's headquarters to the Whig Opposition. Gordon was recalled, and George Murray returned to the Peninsula.

continued dry weather has put an end to their field days. The foxes are beside too plentiful for sport, the hounds are eternally dividing in every direction, and confusion ensues. Addenbrooke writes me word that Lord Rivers has lost 45 Greyhounds and was unable to run for the Swaffham Cup. I think this visitation will nearly exterminate the race of Rolla, and sicken his Lordship to such a degree as to put an end to his favorite pursuit. As soon as the weather changes, and I am allowed a participation in the sport, you shall have regular bulletins of our proceedings. In the meantime I am concerned at your diminished stud, and really advise you to make a bold effort, to re-establish it in glory. Do not trouble yourself about horses for me. Those I have will, barring accidents, suffice for the war in Spain, and if misfortune of any kind intervenes money will always tempt some poor devil to dismount and replace my casualties. In short, I could have bought a very useful mare belonging to the French General Giral [sic], and which he rode at Arroyo Molinos. He was sold for £50, but I did not like to bid against the man who purchased her.

Nothing further has transpired between the great Marshal and myself, my letters I suppose having been sent to him at Lisbon by Lord W. Things come out by degrees. Col. Colborne,[1] who is just arrived from England and passed thro' Lisbon, told my Brigade Major that he had heard at the latter place that Marshal B's pretensions to the glories of Albuera had fallen very much in the opinion of the Horse Guards, from several communications received there from different General Officers, among whom my name was mentioned; that this circumstance had come to the Marshal's knowledge, and he was excessively indignant. This will account very satisfactorily for his late proceedings and conduct towards me. I thought he was too great a Hero to wish to shine under fake colours; but it appears that the simple narrative of truth makes him writhe, and if so I cannot be astonished at his predilection for misrepresentation. I have likewise since learned that this very man who reported to his sovereign that the conduct of the Cavalry at Campo Mayor had prevented his capturing most certainly the Enemy's Corps with his Infantry was himself the cause that the Infantry did not accomplish what was within their power to have done. The same Col. Colborne told me that he was detached round the Town, and observing the Enemy with the baggage etc., was quitting it, he sent back word to beg he might be supported and that he was in a situation to cut them all off. The answer he received was a positive order to halt, in consequence of which the opportunity

---

[1] Colonel John Colborne had commanded a brigade of the 2nd Division at Albuera; he was to be wounded, on January 19, 1812, in the capture of Ciudad Rodrigo. Later he was raised to the peerage and became a field-marshal.

was lost, and could not be again recovered. Compare this account of fact with the Marshal's despatch, and tell me what you think of the Hero who could sit down and commit to paper for public inspection so disgraceful a falsehood. Can I be astonished that all his thoughts and writings should savour of the same ingredient!

At Campo Mayor we were blamed for doing everything ourselves, and not giving time to the Infantry to act. At Arroyo Molinos we are blamed, the Infantry being up and within musquet shot, for not doing everything ourselves. Tho', observe, the only fighting that took place that day was between the Cavalry of the contending forces. There is no pleasing these gentlemen. Strike high, strike low, their backs are never hit in the right place; and yet if anything goes wrong it has arisen thro' their interference. They direct you what to do, and then abuse you for the insufficiencies of their own acts. Such is the misfortune which Cavalry are exposed to when subjected to the orders of Infantry Officers. . . .

More Cantonment Small-talk
TO C. B. LONG
Cabeca de Vide

9 Dec., 1811

I am obliged to scribble to you a day sooner than was necessary, as I purpose going over to Portalegre tomorrow to take leave of Sir Wm. Erskine, who is about to take his departure for England.

Since my last letter Lord W. has returned my letters to Lt. Gen. Hill dated 17 and 19 Nov., stating that he would not become the channel of an acrimonious correspondence between the Great Marshal and me, and therefore requesting that I would confine my reply to the facts stated by Marshal B. without references to his reflections, "which might as well have been omitted." His Lordship being in possession of my opinion upon the subject, I have therefore limited my answer to direct contradiction of the Marshal's facts, and pointing out their want of veracity. I must however observe that Justice in this world seems to be playing odd pranks. A Marshal is permitted to deal out his insulting insinuations against an officer of inferior rank, to whom they are communicated, and when animadversion on the part of the injured follows, all redress is arrested by a refusal to become the channel of an acrimonious correspondence. With whom did this acrimony originate? Who received and encouraged its introduction? Had Lord W. been guided by sound principles of Justice, he would have returned the Marshal's letter for amendment, and have waited for my reply to any statement he strove to make out, before he formed any opinion upon the subject himself. I shall not lose sight however of this conduct, and Major General Beresford will not be a Marshal all his life.

On Wednesday last I went over to Alter de Chao to take a day's coursing there, but was surprised on entering the village to meet the Foxhounds going to throw off with General Hill at their head. I immediately turned about and having found, we were amused with a very pretty run for about an hour, when Renard sought refuge in a rabbit burrow, whence he was quickly dragged out and mercilessly delivered over to his Persecutors.

On the following day we coursed but had no sport.

On Thursday the foxhounds tried again, but a cold northerly wind added to our chase being confined to dreadfully thick gum cistus, and a frequent change of foxes, we experienced a very hard day, but without much amusement. The horses suffered a good deal. I could scarcely get my old horse back to the Stable, and a very nice creature rode by my Brigade Major died during the night. In truth bad barley and straw are not ingredients to prepare a horse for severe exertion, and I foresee this amusement will cost too dearly to be indulged in frequently. I have therefore had enough of it, as it will not do to find myself dismounted at the opening of the ensuing Campaign. . . .

I have received a letter from the old veteran Leighton[1] dated from Canterbury. He states his having seen our dear Pater, but not in the good looks he left him. I suppose his story will improve by repetition and lengthen with his years. Give him time and it will last out a pretty long visit at Arundel. He is a good-hearted well-meaning honorable creature, and I wish half of those he has left behind in the service may be as punctillious as himself in the discharge of their duty. He did wisely however to take off his sombrero, to look for happiness where it is to be found, and to enjoy it before his sun sets.

I do not believe a word about a certain General returning at the express request of the Prince Regent. The truth is the work of favor and patronage had been completed by former assiduity and every object attained, why should he volunteer further and uncalled-for sacrifices? No, no! Indisposition in such cases is always at hand to help a lame dog over the style, and the Campaign at Brighton under a royal eye will be more brilliant and efficacious than fagging here. Ambition in some cases is made of very pliant stuff, the glory it aspires to being a comfortable berth at home. We see many instances of it here, and hear much more of its effects; but it requires a mind and a backbone of a particular cast to pursue with success and effect. I

---

[1] Major Burgh Leighton, of the 4th Dragoons, was an old friend of Long's. He was in the Peninsula from April 1809 until August 1811, when he retired from the service.

am grown stiff and rheumatic; it does not suit my infirmities and unbending disposition. And à propos of rheumatism, the weather for the last 3 days has been of so shivery a description as to make my bones ache, and from every appearance the long expected change is about to take place. The late Estremadura soakings and bivouacs have renewed all my old aitches; and I am now as lissom as Botheran and as much in want of a doctor. I think I should have escaped pretty well, but for the separation of my baggage on the 28th., which deprived me of a change of clothes and my bear skin, and obliged me to make the most of a well drenched shirt and a well soaked bed of earth during the succeeding cold night, which was followed by a fresh ducking next morning. Old age cannot stand such visitations. These miserable houses, too, with doors and windows in every direction and without fireplaces, leave us no remedy for such evils. Langley is bad enough but a candle would burn there where a flambeau would be extinguished here. However, if the rascally frog eaters get the rheumatism too, and remain quiet, I shall contrive ways and means to introduce a little more of "the genial power of nature" than we are at present blessed with, and thus to give your next communication a warmer reception than the last received.

The Portuguese, like sensible people, who do not understand the use of fire and fireplaces, go to bed when the shivering fit comes on; and if they should have the good fortune to discover in a century more that the keeping on a shirt in bed is more comfortable than being without it, I think they will have made great progress in the science of enjoyment.

I have entrusted to the care of Capt. Donnopp of the 2nd Hussars, now on his return to England, a box of Cork tree acorns for you to experiment with. I think they would grow at Hampton Lodge. At all events there will be no harm in making the trial; and I beg that a small portion may be sown on the 25th March next to record Marshal B.'s glorious achievements at Campo Mayor, and the memorable "Halt!" that stamped them with immortality. And you may christen them the "Beresford bunch." Place another clump upon some eminence and call it Cork Hill in honor of the general of that name and take care that it is in a situation to look down upon the bunch, over which it must always stand pre-eminent. Give me the Hill and the Marshal may go to the bottom. Sink he must in spite of all his Portuguese Valerosos. Praevalebit Veritas![1]

I am concerned for Lord River's loss and yours. You should keep your kennels well purified with lime and lime-water. Tainted ground, I am persuaded, will generate epidemics.

[1] "Truth will prevail."

Nothing to report
TO C. B. LONG
Cabeca de Vide
Monday, 16 Dec., 1811

... I mentioned to you in a former letter that I had sent you by Captain Donnopp of the 2nd Hussars a box of the cork tree acorns. I shall forward by another opportunity a supply of what is called the sweet acorn. The oak is an evergreen, and the acorns are as sweet as chestnuts, and eaten by man and pigs. Perhaps the Duke of Norfolk might like to have some of each. If so, send Howard quantum suff. I know that the cork tree will grow in England, for there was a very fine one in a garden at Harrow, which is a cold bleak situation.

The fox-hunting goes on brilliantly. They have had some good runs near Gafete, and have killed several nags; more horses, indeed, than foxes. The northern pack is said to have occasioned similar devastation. They tell me however some awkward stories of the latter viz.: that they had a noble burst one day and after running principally upon a road for several miles the hounds threw up at a cart, and they discovered that they had been running a cargo of bacalhao, or salt fish, which of course made an excellent drag. We have not had as yet any sporting of the above description, but if foxes should become scarce, the hint will not be lost.

Sir Wm. Erskine is gone home for a couple of months, and if things are likely to proceed gaily will probably return; otherwise an earnest request of the Prince Regent, or urgent business, may induce the wiser step of remaining north of the Tweed.

My friend Le Marchant is planning great doings with his Brigade, but he will soon discover that good or bad luck, as it turns out, will be the Tactician that "decides."

The expected change of weather has not taken place. It is however, as cold as I wish it to be. The roasting last summer makes us feel it. The Infantry of Portalegre have all got stoves and fire-places. We suffer our shiverings with patient resignation.

A Soldier's Duty
TO C. B. LONG
Cabeca de Vide
23rd Dec., 1811

The success which attended the Expedition into Estremadura does not alter the original idea entertained upon the subject. Such a result no man in his senses ever could foresee or expect and had the surprise not occurred in addition to the distress brought upon the Troops by such a march in such weather, my opinion is that we could not have retreated again back to our cantonments without loss, as the Enemy would not have failed to hang heavily upon our rearguard, and then we should have got our labour and our losses for our pain. What occurred only proves how much good or bad luck influences the circumstances of war. With respect to the affair itself, it was too insignificant to merit much comment one way or another. The only fighting that took place was between the Cavalry: that is 2 squadrons of my Brigade under Major Bussche and the Enemy's Dragoons under General Brunn. The charges were brilliant and their success complete, tho' I doubt if much notice will be taken of it. Had I not feared to do mischief by dispersing prematurely the Enemy's Column of Infantry which General Howard was momentarily expected to cut off and surround, I should have charged too, and I *now* almost wish I had, because the credit would have been mine, and the Infantry might have abused us for doing too much rather than too little, with less regret to ourselves. But battles are so admirably fought after everything is over, and the science of afterthought is so overwhelming that there is no standing against it. I therefore content myself on all occasions to act to the best of my own judgment, and where I am not interfered with I take upon myself all the responsibility. But when such interference takes place, I have only to execute the duty prescribed in my best manner. Was the affair of Arroyo Molinos to occur again, I should proceed exactly as I did then, with this difference: from recent experience, that it is sometimes wiser to think more of oneself than of others. As matters turned out the Expedition has been a most happy one. It completely disorganised a whole Division of the Enemy's Troops, disgraced their reputation, occasioned them a serious loss, and secured the Cantonments of the Spaniards. All this has been the effect of chance; or, as Marmont says, of Lord Wellington's lucky star.

If the French account of Blake's action be true I cannot see how much valor could have been displayed by the Troops of the latter, for it is impossible to fancy that his resistance could have been very great where the loss on either side was so dissimilar. The fact is the Spaniards are led into action, but not easily kept to the bloody work. They are mistrustful of themselves, have a terror of the Enemy, no confidence in the talents of their own officers, and not sufficient discipline or steadiness to secure themselves against disaster. They are led like sheep to the slaughter house; the French look upon them in this light, and once broken they are exterminated without mercy because no resistance is offered to check the ardor or insolence of pursuit. They lose a third or a half of their army in these attempts go back, recruit, and prepare for fresh disasters of the same description. Their vanity is incurable. They are not calculated for an offensive system of warfare. They should take a leaf out of Lord Wellington's book, and never give battle but where every conceivable circumstance of ground, etc is in their favor. They should avoid the plains and stick more to the heights and enclosures, where if unsuccessful the Enemy's Cavalry cannot get at them. Theirs should be a campaign of incessant resistance in favorable situations, and a constant harassing of the enemy's line of operations by active detachments under able officers. . . .

Liberty I feel to be so dear a blessing, and despotism such a curse that the very tyranny of subordination tho' necessary for arms is odious to me. I fully coincide in your opinions upon this subject, and believe the best bulwark for a country's safety and independence will be found in free hearts satisfied with their Government or Rulers. The People, as Cobbett says, should have something to fight for, without an object that is dear to their hearts, fighting can have but little attraction to the generality of men. I confess I see no end to this struggle but in the downfall of the universal subjugation. His purposes are firmly resolved upon, war is the high road to them, and war we shall have to the end of the chapter till his career is stopped or we are subdued.

The Alemtejo hounds are hunting this day at Monforte two leagues from hence. I preferred chatting with you, but if they remain there (or rather General Hill) I shall go over and join the party on Wednesday or Thursday next. Holydays in this country do not interfere with field sports, Sunday is believed to be as favorable as any other day in the week and by the Inhabitants generally preferred. The extermination of the Cattle appears however to have checked the ardor of the sportsmen, and their fields are woefully thinned!

I wish you would send me a red book for the year 1812, and get Calvert to frank it to me. I should prefer one that is as copious as possible, with an almanac in it. I find there is a parcel for me arrived at Lisbon, but I know not what it is.

I have scarcely seen 9 days rain during the 9 months I have been in the country; the fact is scarcely credible. I shall be happy to hear how your little Mary stands schooling, and how Robin is going on.

I am satisfied with my little Brigade. They are getting again into good order, and will I trust be as ready and able to do their duty as the favorites of the north. I never torment them, and we are very good friends.

General Hill's staff appear highly delighted with Cobbett's approbation. You see the rascal can please when he tickles! How much do we lose in the world by not practising the art more assiduously.

IX

Observations on War by an Unwilling Warrior

In the last days of 1811 General Sir Rowland Hill issued orders which took his troops off on yet another excursion against the French, but this time with less success than at Arroyo dos Molinos. The French were driven from Las Navas de Membrillo and Merida, but Long and his cavalry failed against a very steady and well-managed party of hostile infantry, who were surprised while moving back to join their main body on December 29. Some three hundred Voltigeurs and a few hussars in a cork-wood showed a steadfast front, beat off five cavalry charges by the 13th Light Dragoons and 2nd Hussars, and then withdrew for nearly five miles in complete order. Though they lost some men to the fire of four nine-pounders, they succeeded in carrying off their wounded, and they received a warm tribute from all who saw them for their cool discipline and courage.

Long's conduct came in for criticism from Hill's staff and certain regimental officers. He was said to have been indecisive, and to have lost over twenty men—about as many as the enemy. The tone of his letters home shows that, with fog, mud, and broken, rocky, wooded country to work over, he was in fact most doubtful about the wisdom of Hill's orders to press cavalry attacks home against steady and unbroken infantry.

In another skirmish on New Year's Day 1812 some of Long's cavalry, dispatched on a flying column under a Major-General Abercrombie, met and routed two squadrons of the French 26th Dragoons. The admirable behaviour of forty-two men of a Portuguese squadron, whom the French contemptuously summoned to surrender, was a source of encouragement in this affair. And though Hill's account of the first of these two actions shows a very cool attitude towards the cavalry he praised the second with enthusiasm. The British troops, somewhat cut up by their marches in the winter mud, then withdrew to their quarters.

This raid of Hill's had been designed with two main objects: to alarm and annoy Soult, and possibly thereby to cause him to raise the siege of Tarifa; and to draw attention to the south of Spain while Wellington himself prepared a swift strike against Ciudad Rodrigo. So long as that town and Badajoz remained in French possession Wellington dared not move far from his Portuguese base. With the capture of Valencia by Suchet, and the destruction of yet another Spanish army (this time under General Blake), there was no saying what the French might do if they were left alone.

Tarifa, in fact, had been so bitterly defended that the French had abandoned their attempt to besiege it even before Hill's operations brought any noticeable effects. But Wellington's lightning move against Ciudad Rodrigo, and his savage, expensive assault there, took the enemy off balance. By January 19 the town had been taken. If the French were appalled Hill's forces were overjoyed to hear of its capture. Only a little later they were shaken to their depths by the arrival of the first examples of the new uniforms, which the Light Dragoons pronounced "quite shocking." Long himself was "not a little disgusted by the spectacle."

Early in March Hill's men were again on the move, this time towards Merida to cover the impending siege of Badajoz. Long took the 13th Light Dragoons across the Guadiana by a ford, whereupon the French bolted. The British troops took up the pursuit, and Merida, with its lovely broken Roman bridge, fell into our hands. On the night of April 6 Wellington stormed Badajoz; the musket-flashes from the ramparts could be seen from the old position at Albuera, where most of Hill's command were then stationed. Long stood upon the dreadful breach on the morrow of the attack, and, like all who saw that terrible sight, was overwhelmed by its horror. The British had lost close on three thousand in killed and wounded in the efforts to storm the town.

During this period, while Wellington hoped for great things, Long was despondent about the campaign's prospects; he found it impossible to believe that the French could be evicted from Spain. Unless Napoleon took some utterly senseless step, such as invading Russia, Long could see no real chance of ultimate freedom for the Peninsula. For himself, he paints a clear self-portrait. He hated war and its attendant misery. His own future he saw plainly: entertaining as he did but slender hope of ever obtaining the full colonelcy of a regiment, with all the emoluments which then accompanied that appointment, he looked forward to a bleak financial prospect. His quarrels with senior officers were bound to harm his personal career. Yet, so long as he satisfied himself and his family, Robert Long cared not a fig for anyone else.

Servants and Horses

TO C. B. LONG

Merida

12 Jan., 1812

Many thanks for all your troubles on my account, but had I been nearer I should have recommended your taking no Servant for me who has served either in the Hompesch or 2nd Hussars. Good men are not discharged for some disability, and the former of these Corps was not celebrated for its materials in point of moral qualifications.

With regard to the horse, stallions are certainly not the most desirable, but still everything is turned to account. Any clever horse would be acceptable, if an opportunity offered to send one, for I am reduced to two only that are serviceable in the field, and one of these is not to be depended upon. The bat and forage allowance becomes due in March, and then I shall be rich enough to repay you the cost of the animal.

I believe I mentioned that the pocket book for 1812 sent me is useless. There is no room for memorandums.

You see how we have been disappointed in our expectations of quiet Winter Quarters. I fear this expedition[1] will cut us up for the Spring Campaign. At present we have a sharpish frost, which makes the nights cold and the Guadiana fall.

I am still of the same opinion about Spanish affairs, and shall be happy to see the day when I can change it for the better. Our offensive attitudes are mere demonstrations against a weak point. We gain no ground permanently, and very little credit. This is a sad up-hill kind of warfare that is not encouraging.

Ciudad Rodrigo besieged
TO C. B. LONG
Cabeça de Vide,
20 Jan., 1812

My last to you was I think dated 12th inst. from Merida....

I shall continue to enjoy myself at this place, which I prefer to any other in the Alemtejo. When at Montijo I added another Greyhound to my kennel. Captain Dean took him out yesterday and says he promises very fairly. My stupid servant lost me a prize at Villafranca. Since I retreated from that Town I have been told that a most beautiful creature, belonging to the French, was left in my quarters, and the ass had not sense enough to secure it for me, or to say a word upon the subject. I shall avail myself of the first opportunity to send you a brace, though I do not think they will be worth your acceptance.

We have had some sharp frosts during the last eight days, but never was anything more beautifully fine or delightful than the weather. Still, we must expect the rains as the Spring approaches, and if they should be severe our military operations will be probably suspended till they are over, or towards March, though Lord W. may and will be naturally anxious to follow up any advantage he may obtain by his present operations. Had we made ourselves masters of Badajoz last year what a difference would it not have produced in our favor! The rascals are now fortifying Merida, and we left it without destroying their works which were more than half-finished. They will think us strange beings! I have not heard when they reoccupied the Town, but I suppose on the 14th....

[1] Hill's drive to Merida.

Ciudad Rodrigo falls

CAPTAIN HEATHCOTE[1] TO ROBERT LONG

Gallegos

21 Jan., 1812

I am happy to inform you that Ciudad Rodrigo is ours. On the evening of the 19th two practicable breaches having been effected, the 3rd and Light Divisions stormed and carried the place, which was pillaged and sacked in the most complete style. The Garrison, consisting of about 1500 men, being put into confusion by the different points which were attacked at the same time, made but a bad defence. Our loss however is not inconsiderable. General M'Kinnon[2] was blown up by the explosion of a magazine and killed on the spot; General Crauford[3] was shot through the lung and his life is despaired of; Lt. Col. Colborne[4] was shot in the shoulder and the ball having lodged in the joint whence it cannot be extracted, his case is pronounced desperate. Major Napier[5] has lost an arm, and many a poor fellow of less note his life. Our loss is put at 250, mostly killed. The Enemy sprung no mines, but three magazines exploded; their loss was chiefly owing to this cause.

All things considered, this siege is I believe one of Ld. W.'s most brilliant achievements. It was undertaken contrary to the opinion of every military man, and entirely was directed by him. Marmont now is not expected to advance, and we I hope shall go into Winter Quarters as soon as his Army has left the frontier. The weather was most favorable, and "la belle Etoile de Mylord" comes in for her share of our success. The Enemy was 40 days before the place, and we only eleven.

---

[1] Captain Ralph Heathcote was on Wellington's staff during the last years of the war. He corresponded regularly with Long, and gave him accurate information about the operations of the Northern Army.

[2] Major-General Henry Mackinnon was the senior brigade commander of Picton's 3rd Division.

[3] Major-General Robert Craufurd (1764-1812), commander of the famous Light Division trained by Sir John Moore, was shot through the spine and lingered for four days before he died.

[4] Lieutenant-Colonel John Colborne commanded the 52nd Foot. He recovered from his wounds.

[5] Major George Napier (1784-1855), of the 52nd (Oxfordshire and Buckinghamshire Light Infantry), had led a party of three hundred volunteers in an assault on one of the breaches in the defences. A brother of Sir Charles Napier, the conqueror of Sind, and of Sir William Napier, historian of the Peninsular War, he later became Governor of the Cape of Good Hope, 1837-43.

After the Capture of Ciudad Rodrigo

TO C. B. LONG

Alssalhao
29 Jan., 1812

This very day 12 months I embarked at Portsmouth on board the "Victory," for this country. I consider myself therefore as having been already one year absent from all I care about in the world. To say that I wish for the continuance of such a sacrifice would not be the truth. On the contrary heartily shall I rejoice when the hour of emancipation arrives. Despairing as I do of any permanent advantage or reward to be derived from my services, I do my duty like a common labourer, with the exception that he may be more attached to his ploughshare than I to my sword. Although embarked in a thing I dislike, I shall, whether prosperously or otherwise, nevertheless endeavour to fulfil my duty, to the best of my ability, praying most sincerely for the arrival of the day when

> The world shut out to rural scenes I fly,
> And in retirement taste tranquillity.

Since my last General Hill's Corps has been put in motion towards the Tagus to support Lord W.'s operations, and considerable part of it including the 2nd Hussars have crossed the River. General Howard with his Brigade is at Castel Branco. Ciudad Rodrigo, however, having fallen, we suppose Lord W. to be waiting only to restore the defences of the place, and to see how Marmont chews the cud of disappointment, when he will return to his former Cantonment, after the most brilliant achievement he has performed, and the success of which does him great credit.

The particulars you will see in the despatches that have been sent home, and therefore I forbear to speak of them. The enterprise cannot fail to disconcert the Enemy's intended operations for the opening of the campaign, and to place Lord W. in a more secure, and indeed offensive, attitude. To counterbalance the advantage on our side, however, the Spaniards have lost everything in Valencia and the Army of Blake,[1] according to what I have heard, has nearly ceased to exist. This circumstance is seriously to be lamented, because it tends to place one of the finest Provinces in Spain in the Enemy's possession, and disengages another French Army.

---

[1] Joaquim Blake, Spanish Commander-in-Chief in Valencia; here Blake capitulated with his troops to the French under Suchet on January 9, 1812, and Blake was imprisoned by Napoleon at Vincennes.

If Lord W.'s views should be directed against Badajoz, he will never take that place without standing the brunt of a general action, which will decide the respective pretensions of the chiefs. If the Enemy are determined on the conquest of Spain, never will they surrender Badajoz whilst they have a force in the country to prevent it. The question therefore appears to rest on Lord W.'s ability to meet them in the field, and this he will never do without calculating the consequences of even a victory too dearly purchased. Had half the energy and precautions been shown and taken before Badajoz last year, that have been displayed before Rodrigo *this*, that fortress too would as certainly have been ours, and Soult would have had a hard time of it in Andalusia.

The recent expedition into Estremadura has cut up my Brigade so much that I despair of seeing it in a state of strength and efficiency for renewed services, by the time it will again be required to take the field. The bivouac and starving system is bad for man and beast, and I am only surprised how they get on as they do.

The day before I quitted Cabeca de Vide I received a box which Howard must have sent about June last, containing portable soup in a fine liquid and high-scented state, and a small thermometer. Do acknowledge the receipt of both for me, with my apprehensions that the soup speculation will never answer. We experience sad difficulty in getting up things from Lisbon, all for the want of some general arrangement for the accommodation of officers in this particular. The distance is so great, and our movements so uncertain that we are afraid to detach transport to fetch up articles from Lisbon. My box of saddlery however I hear has reached Abrantes, and I have received a note from Dr. McGregor[1] stating his having brought over for me and left at Lisbon another box, I suppose of clothes, which by the Prince's recent regulations will not be conformable to order.

I do not know if you attended to my request to have newspapers sent to me? *None* have ever been received.

We have had continued frosts until yesterday, when the weather broke, and we are now deluged with rain. Gafete, in the neighbourhood of this place, is the fox-hunting Headquarters, and their best country. My Greyhounds however appear to do more mischief among them than their more regular bred enemies. The coursing likewise is good, so much so, that the lurchers are uniformly beaten, and we can no longer bear from the field the spoils we have been accustomed to do. I regret not having commissioned you to send out my gun and apparatus by the servant you may have hired for me. If ever a favorable

---

[1] Sir James McGrigor became Wellington's principal Medical Officer, and was a very capable and much-trusted man. He knew Long through the Walcheren Expedition.

opportunity should occur, forward it with a stock of flints, and the charges, etc. I despair of reaching the Ebro, consequently the defending of Portugal only will require something to drive away ennui.

Your great Berkshire Hero, Colonel Bunbury,[1] does not shine in the opinion of the Army here, as he has made his friends at home believe. They tell odd stories about his conduct at the Talavera business, and ask how the first Lt.-Col. of the Buffs[2] can consent to command a second Battalion at home, and leave a junior officer to command the first Battalion of his Regiment on service, and this question, I confess, is an awkward one to answer.

I see there is nothing like a wife to make the Army a comfortable profession. Let us see—

General Houston transferred to Home Service—nuptus.
    Wm. Stewart[3] ,, ,, ,, ,, — ,,
    Hawkins ,, ,, ,, ,, — ,,
    Grey ,, ,, ,, ,, — ,,

Do get me a wife and I may hope to eat my next Xmas dinner at Langley. No chance without. The married Colonels and Lt. Colonels absent from their Corps to comfort their wives at home—*numberless*. Therefore with a wife in one hand, and a sword in the other, is the true way of making war—*comfortably*. Be assured of this. Colonel Cumming has left us, indisposed; I hope you will see him. He is a fine fellow, notwithstanding his wife. She too is at Weymouth.

Badajoz again?

TO C. B. LONG

Cabeca de Vide

10 *Feb.*, 1812

... I returned to this place yesterday and my Brigade has resumed its former cantonments. But their sojournment in them will I expect be but of very short duration. Lord W.'s success at Rodrigo has inspired the hope of doing something against Badajoz, and active preparations are now making for that undertaking. In the most happy view I can take of it, I consider it an operation more of a defensive than of an offensive description. It is to strengthen our line of defence in Portugal rather than to offer any means of conquest beyond the

---

[1] Not a good soldier. He was 'allowed to resign' after his conduct at the battle of St Pierre, December 1813, had aroused grave criticism.

[2] The 3rd Foot (East Kent Regiment).

[3] Here Long did Stewart an injustice, for he returned to the Peninsula in November 1812, and in March 1813 he was appointed to command the 2nd Division "under Hill's direction." The other three did not return.

frontier, though of course its possession would tend to facilitate incursion into Estremadura, and give us in some measure possession of that Province. . . .

What is going on at Cadiz is nothing more or less than a battle between the French and English Parties. The *People* there, I believe, are with us, the Aristocracy on the side of the Enemy, and the free press they have established has armed them both in their respective causes. The loss of Valencia must make a great sensation there, and as the defending of Portugal is not the reconquest of Spain, the spirits of the loyal will be proportionately depressed.

It is now going on hard upon seven weeks since I have heard from you, my dearest C., and this is a long deprivation of happiness, particularly for one who can see nothing consoling before him, and therefore whose enjoyments must all come from the rear. I feel too anxious about our Pater, Eliza and indeed all of you, not to be a little disconcerted at any unusual interruptions of the bulletins. Like a good Christian I throw all the blame upon the winds, but they listen to me not.

After eight days of continued rain, fine weather has again returned, but we expect another deluge before the end of this month. A report has reached us that in one of the recent storms several of the boats which were to have transported the garrison of Rodrigo from Abrantes to Lisbon, foundered in the Tagus, and all on board perished. The Escort being considerable too are sufferers by this disaster, but I have not yet heard to what amount.

By the arrival of some officers of the 9th Dragoons from England, we have been favored (not gratified) with a sight of the new projected dress for the Dragoons, and I confess I was not a little disgusted by the spectacle. To see the British Army denationalised as it were in appearance to pay a compliment to French taste, is what my English blood cannot brook. What a silly race of beings are ——! But such courtship will not avail. The Tyrant will still continue to hate us, and despise the mind that prefers the livery of the monkey to the leopard's skin.

James Lynch's *aitches* I am concerned to state have returned with increased force and completely crippled him. I know not what to do, but if they continue, I fear the only alternative is keeping him as living lumber here, or sending him back to England. If the latter, I am apprehensive the contagion may spread and lameness and rheumatism will infect the whole establishment. The home-sickness is a difficult complaint to cure, and the high and low are equally subject to it. If I dared to be an open traitor to the cause I should tell them, "Wait a little and you will soon be gratified." . . .

I transmit to you a bit of a newspaper[1] sent me by old Malagrey, and which records the triumphs of his Boys. It is a flattering document and too grateful a one to a Father not to be proud of. He has been boring me to apply for the vacant places of Adjutant General or Quarter Master General in Ireland. I have answered him by stating that although *his* sons are rising *my* sun has set, and that the utmost I can look to, if I survive this contest in Spain, is not to be tormented again in England. I have nothing to expect from the favor of Princes, and I have no right so to do, for I like them not.

We are "high and dry" for subjects to write upon, and have our eyes steadily fixed upon Carlton House[2] and St. Stephens[3] for the development of our future concerns and expectations.

Some General Reflections

TO C. B. LONG

Cabeca de Vide
Monday, 17 Feb., 1812

Since my last letter dated 10 inst I have been amply gratified and repaid for past privations by the receipt of a monthly contribution from you under the respective dates of 5, 13, 19 and 27 ult. . . .

With respect to your question about officers being obliged to leave their horses behind in this country when returning to England themselves, I have heard the fact stated, but know not the authority on which it rests. I cannot bring myself to believe that so odious a Tyranny would be exercised in any other manner than by throwing difficulties in the way and this perhaps is done. For instance Transports returning home are not allowed to take back horses, the Packets do not receive them; how then, without freighting a vessel, is an officer to get such property away? . . .

I received a letter yesterday from Captain Barnett, to whom I entrusted the cadeau of preserves, accounting for its long detention. The Custom House officers probably have a tooth for the "dulcis" as well as Robin, and have paid themselves the duty in kind. I send you Barnett's letter to be forwarded, if you think proper, to my friend the D—— of Cumberland, to shew him how much pleasanter a thing it is to receive the thanks of gratitude for humane attentions, than to

---

[1] This cutting is not to be found.
[2] The residence of the Prince of Wales, who, since February 4, 1811, had acted as Regent, George III having finally lapsed into insanity. Built in 1709, Carlton House was pulled down in 1826.
[3] The present St Stephen's Hall occupies the site of old St Stephen's Chapel, in which the House of Commons met from 1547 until the destruction by fire of Westminster Palace in 1834.

peruse the "stubborn facts" of revenge, engendered by the actions of an unfeeling heart.

The Spaniards have lost their Colonies, as they will their Mother Country, by their pride, stupidity and obstinacy. Too infatuated to concede and too weak to command, they provoke the storm in which they are doomed to perish. It signifies not one penny who is at the head of the Government whilst the French have got possessed of the heart and body of the country. The Spanish Army does not deserve the name of soldiers. They are assembled, it is true; march towards the Enemy; pretend to fight; retire in a panic; take shelter in a Town, and march out with Honors of War, Prisoners to their Enemies. Such was the fate of Romana's[1] Army last year near Badajoz; such has been the fate of Blake's this year in Valencia. The arms we furnish them with are for the Enemy's use more than their own, and it is a cheap and easy way to recruit Napoleon's forces, for nearly the whole of them, be assured, will enter the French service, and under French officers will fight his battles in Germany or elsewhere.

With respect to our noble selves, the preparations I before mentioned, and which indicate an attack on Badajoz, are in train, and it is supposed everything will be ready by the beginning of March. Lord W. has certainly his "lucky Star." It remains to be seen how far it will avail him on the approaching occasion.

I see the "Canopus"[2] is again on her element. Had you an opportunity of shaking hands with the young fish, Edward Pocock,[3] and how does he get on—promisingly? I hope our worthy brother, Howard, will contrive to realise the arrears of his long parliamentary labours by hook or by crook, and that his happiness may be completed by another chip of the old block of the right sex. He ought to be successful in this and various other undertakings, for he strives to deserve it. . . .

I have received the saddlery from Gibson safe and sound; also a box from Windeler with the most splendid hat I ever saw—intended I suppose for Madrid—sad mistake!

I hope our dear Pater is going on prosperously. I should not recommend his abandonment of the Terraces. He then gets his stroll as inclination suits and sunshine permits.

When the hunting is over you must vote yourself young to be

---

[1] José Caro, Marquis of La Romana, Captain-General of the Spanish Army, had died of a heart disease on January 23, 1811, near Badajoz. It was his successor, Mendizabal, whose army was largely destroyed by Soult.

[2] H.M.S. *Canopus* (ex-*Franklin*) had been taken from the French at Aboukir in 1798. She had a distinguished career under British colours.

[3] Son of a brother-in-law, Admiral George Pocock, created a Baronet in 1821. Edward Pocock at this date was a midshipman.

Robin's play-fellow. He will never grow without a little stretching.

God bless you. Nothing more to say but peace and prosperity to you all, for I am sick of this eternal and blackguard War. Nothing but a long Peace can restore it to a gentlemanly complexion.

Some Thoughts on Military Men
TO C. B. LONG
Cabeca de Vide
24 Feb., 1812

... My friend Le Marchant is coming to the Alemtejo with his Brigade, and I confess the prospect of having him near to me is very gratifying. By a note I received from him yesterday he says, "My last accounts from England contradict the unfavorable reports I sent you respecting affairs in the North of Europe. By the last packet it appears that matters have again taken a favorable turn in that quarter." God grant they may, for on the realisation of such a hope does the cause of this Country materially depend! A powerful diversion in the North of Europe must diminish the pressure here, and by keeping up the hope that all Europe has not yet yielded to the pretensions of the Enemy, may inspire fresh expectations of successful resistance to them. The French Armies themselves in the Peninsula are heartily sick as it is of the contest, and the severer the task imposed upon them, the more will this alienation increase. I believe they have as great personal dread of a British Soldier, as the browbeaten Nations have hitherto had of *them*. They feel they are no longer invincible and acknowledge it. Their contempt of the Spaniards has only increased their respect for more regular troops, and this difference often leads to dismay and panic.

I am told that the Prince Regent is at variance with his friends Lord Moira[1] and Hutchinson[2] upon Irish politics. If so, it is not a pleasing augury for the future.

Since my last General Hill has been my guest on a fox-hunting excursion for three days. We had one good run, and, in the whole, killed 2 brace of foxes. We had besides 2 days coursing but only brought home 2½ brace of hares. The sport was, however, tolerable. He has some handsome dogs, but mine I think are as good both in nose and foot, and yelp as harmoniously.

---

[1] Francis Rawdon-Hastings, second Earl of Moira (1754–1826), was a soldier, serving with distinction in America, at Bunker Hill and other places. He was a close friend of the Prince of Wales, and an advocate of Catholic Emancipation. He later became Governor-General of Bengal.

[2] Richard Hely-Hutchinson (1756–1825), first Earl of Conoughmore, was a strong champion of Catholic Emancipation.

I beg to remind you that I do not at all want my correspondence to be communicated out of the Family Circle, and more particularly so to Military Officers, such as General Houston. *Favor-hunting* men are *never* to be trusted. Everything with them is sacrificed to personal interests and considerations. Besides, they have not all sense enough to know what may with propriety be retailed, and what not; and the love of gabbling is too predominant, generally, to admit of such discrimination. Therefore the safest course is *not to trust them.*

I am well pleased to hear that our Pater is satisfied with the result of the Marshal Controversy.[1] I should have told you that the second letter to General Hill which you deemed superfluous was written at *his* request and suggestion, to do away the offensiveness of a direct contradiction to a positive assertion. He, General Hill, felt as much as anyone could do, the malice of the whole proceeding, and did not disguise his opinion. He is a man who offends no one. On the contrary, the affection and respect for him are unbounded, and the contrast between the two characters forms no small cause for triumph to General Hill's friends. But I have seen few such men in the world as he is, so much benignity of mind and heart, and such equality of temper! As a character I think him *perfect,* and everyone enjoys the Honors *he* receives. I wish I could say as much of the other.

I fear my communications will continue to be uninteresting until the bloody work of butchery again commences. But the people of England love a battle, and I think they are very likely to be soon gratified with one. Badajoz at least will hardly be ours without one such a trial, which, wherever it takes place, will I trust be *decisive*. The "Lords of human kind" will not mind a hard knock or two to get possession of that key to their Cantonments, and Count Vimiero[2] is not deficient in nerves. It is an omlet, however, that will require a good many eggs to make. Let us hope it may not be spoiled in the cooking.

God bless you, and may your pleasures continue to be extracted from the sugar-cane rather than from the blood of your fellow-creatures.

New Preparations for Badajoz

TO C. B. LONG

Cabeca de Vide

1st March, 1812

At present my chief object is to acquaint you that I have been under the necessity of deciding upon James Lynch's case, and he appears so

---

[1] The quarrel over the Portuguese aides-de-camp is here referred to.
[2] Lord Wellington had been made Count of Vimiero, in Portugal, after his victory over the French there on August 21, 1808.

thoroughly crippled that I have determined on sending him back to England, to endeavour under your protection to obtain some relief from his sufferings, if not the complete re-establishment of his health; and for this purpose I could wish he might have Chilver's advice, when an opportunity may enable you to get him up to Town for this purpose. I enclose you a memorandum of his accounts for the last year which you will be good enough to take care of, and having given him 20 dollars to meet his expenses 2 and at Lisbon, and a draft on Greenwood for £10, to be made use of on his arrival in England, I trust he will experience no difficulty in reaching Langley without further trouble.

I have confided to his care a brace of Greyhounds, the first I purchased at Montijo, both being Spanish. Should they arrive safe I recommend your endeavouring to get from the Lady one litter of genuine Spaniards for trial, after which you may make experiments by crosses, etc. The Lady shews and possesses blood, the Gentleman, though strong, not so much. Both I fear will prove very inferior to what you at present possess, but they are a novelty and will serve as a keepsake. The name of the dog is Gavillon, that of the bitch Corceira. I have seen her run beautifully when having the lead, and single handed. She does not exert herself so much when others get the start, whether from timidity or bashfulness I know not. She is delicate and poor; I attribute the latter to worms. I hope they may arrive safe, though not in time perhaps this year to give you a yelping exhibition of their merits.

I have also entrusted to James's care 2 packets of papers, that may be useful to me for future reference, but the transporting of which infringe too much on the small space prescribed to my portmanteaux. Also an old great-coat as a pattern for Windeler, in case I should wish to have one like it sent out from England. He will tell you he left me in good health, and in the best spirits that our prospects can give.

The Northern Division of our Army are advancing progressively on our right by Fronteira towards Estremoz and Villa Vicosa. Lord W., I believe, is expected shortly, and when everything is prepared the curtain will probably rise. I remove from this tomorrow or next day to Monforte, at which place and Azumar the whole of my Brigade will be then concentrated. On the arrival of a superior officer I shall resign command of the *Division*, i.e., the Portuguese Brigade under Col. Campbell.[1] . . .

---

[1] Colonel John Campbell (1780–1863) commanded a brigade of Portuguese horse. He was knighted in 1815 and for four years acted as military adviser to the Portuguese Government. Like Long, he was an Old Harrovian.

Monday, 2nd March

From Portalegre I have received a letter stating that on the 4th inst. the whole of General Hill's Corps is to vacate their present Cantonments, and to be concentrated at Albuquerque, Campo Mayor, St. Olaia and Arronches, and it is proposed to send my Brigade in advance towards Merida, at Villar del Rey. These arrangements sufficiently indicate the intention of our taking in a very few days the field for good.

As Sir Stapleton Cotton, who commands all the Cavalry, is to arrive *here* tomorrow, I take for granted the greater part of the command is following his steps, and that even the Lord himself is at this moment, at no great distance from Portalegre. My friend Le Marchant I hear will arrive at Alter de Chao (a league from hence) this day, and I purpose riding over there to meet him.

You must not be surprised if I should occasionally fail in my accustomed regularity in writing to you. I shall transmit, when circumstances permit, my Journal in the old manner, and forward it by every opportunity that offers.

Tuesday, 3rd March

I am about to depart immediately for Azumar. Tomorrow I march to Condeceira, and on the 5th inst. to Villar del Rey, a small village between Albuquerque and Montijo in the midst of an endless wood and an ocean of gum cistus, the very worst cantonment and post for Cavalry, the very best for Infantry; so that military maxims are now unattended to. I missed seeing Le Marchant yesterday, and therefore shall not expect this happiness till I shake hands with him in Philippi. I understand the impression in the minds of the Northern Army is that Lord W. will carry Badajoz without a general action, Marmont's Corps not being in a condition to meet him. Everything Lord W. can muster will be collected upon the present occasion, and whatever his force may be, a finer I believe is not to be found in the Peninsula, or one that will take more beating. His Lordship is not yet arrived, but relays of horses are ready for him, and when put in motion he will fly like a whirlwind to direct the storm. The works of Badajoz have been considerably strengthened, since last year's attack, and I should suppose the place could not be taken under a month.

An Unwilling Soldier

TO C. B. LONG

Villar del Rey
14 *March,* 1812

Not knowing when the order for moving may arrive, I avail myself of a leisure moment to prepare my usual dispatch, and in doing so I have the pleasure to acknowledge the receipt of your letters of the 9th, 17th and 23rd ult. That of the 2nd inst. alluded to has not yet arrived, and indeed the mail of that date has not yet made its appearance. The papers, however, have cleared up all our doubts about the future, and I confess that although I think the interests of the country will be kept consulted by avoiding all change in the Government at so momentous a period, nevertheless, the discontents in Ireland, the threatening aspect of America, etc., with so formidable an opposition in Parliament, will give rise to fearful difficulties to contend against. I do not exactly admire the manner in which the Prince has settled his determination, for after the previous refusal of Lords Grey and Grenville[1] to unite his present administration, it was little short of an insult to repeat such an offer. It has been a fine lesson for the blue and buffs,[2] and they ought not to forget it. . . .

I have read with the feelings of affection that my nature cherishes your kind remarks and advice in your letter of the 23rd inst. Was I, what I am not, and never have been, a soldier in my heart, the reflexions that called them forth would never have been offered. Those who follow a military life from natural predilection and preference, are, in the very execution of their duty, prosecuting their sweetest pleasures. To some its attractions are paramount to those of any other calling. They know no greater happiness than when thus following the bent of their inclinations. To minds not formed in the same mould, the feelings are widely different. To me the day of Cateau[3] was one of mourning, that of Albuera of deep affliction. I felt pain where others found pleasure. Their joys were to me tears, their sunshine darkness, their happiness misery. I dislike butchery in all its forms and shapes, and of all kinds of butchery that of the human species is to me the most odious. No ambition, no love of reputation can conquer this feeling. A Profession that is at constant war with one's feelings cannot be an agreeable one; Lord W. talks of *expending* such and such Battalions in such and such affairs, as you would talk of expending so much shot and powder on the 1st Sept. To him, War must have every charm that can fascinate a man's heart. He is a *thorough-bred* soldier. I make a distinction between the duty that summons every man to the field to defend his own country and rights; but Armies which are formed for other purposes (and all of them are) should be made up of Volunteers, those who adopt the profession from preference and predilection, who love War as a trade, in all its forms and features, and follow what they like. I say honestly that *I* have no business among *this* class of men, for I dislike the thing, and always have. You cannot, therefore, be surprised at my anxiety to see an end

[1] Two Whig leaders. [2] The Whig colours. [3] The cavalry fight on April 26, 1794.

to what I abhor, and more particularly so when I feel as assured of the future recompense that avails my toils and sacrifices, as I do of your being my well beloved brother. I have really nothing to hope for or look to but what you call the bubble reputation, which with us, is, nine times out of ten, the *gift of fortune*, and, generally speaking, as easy to be lost as acquired. Ambition should be made of sterner stuff than any I possess, therefore I discard it from my heart, and in all humility seek the only consolation I ever can enjoy, that of living and dying, unmolested, among those who are most dear to me. In the meantime, and waiting this most desirable consummation, we will endeavour to discharge a painful duty to the best of our abilities, in the hope of deriving from this reflexion, hereafter, a comfort that even Princes cannot deprive us of.

Everything remains here in statu quo. Lord W. arrived at Elvas on the 11th inst. and on the following day summoned General Hill to be invested with the red ribbon.[1] I did not like to quit my post, and therefore did not attend. I strongly suspect that his Lordship is not serious in his present menace against Badajoz, though much will depend upon the movements of his adversaries, and particularly of Marmont. . . .

Capture of Badajoz

TO C. B. LONG

Bivouac near Talavera Real

9 April, 1812

Only time for three words. We left Merida on the 6th inst. for Arroyo de St. Servan, blowing up the Bridge at the former place. On the 7th marched to Lobon and on the 8th to this bivouac. On the night of the 6th Inst. Lord Wellington stormed Badajoz and took it. Never was man more lucky. Our loss dreadfully severe, but not so much so as it might have been. The assault at the breaches failed and in my opinion never could have been carried. The Town fell by two escalades under Generals Picton[2] and Leith[3] which succeeded. The

---

[1] The K.B.

[2] Sir Thomas Picton (1758–1815) commanded the 3rd Division. Guedalla refers to him as leading his infantry into action "in a cloud of blasphemy and a top-hat." Wellington described him as "a rough, foul-mouthed devil as ever lived"; and it was characteristic that Picton, wearing a blue coat and a top-hat, should send his men into action at Vittoria with the words: "Come on, ye rascals! Come on, ye fighting villains!" An eyewitness at Cuidad Rodrigo described how "the voice of Sir Thomas Picton, with the power of twenty trumpets, proclaimed damnation to everybody." He was wounded at Quatre Bras, and killed at Waterloo. Wellington broke down and wept on reading the casualty list which included Picton's name.

[3] James Leith (1763–1816) commanded the 5th Division.

carnage at the points of attack woeful, and only second to Albuera. Lord W. expected Soult would attack him on the 7th and 8th and our forces were concentrated at Albuera and this place to give him battle. He appears however to be retiring again, and probably the fall of Badajoz will induce him to give up his intention, unless he has some sly plan in his head.

I must refer you to Lord W.'s despatches for the details of the siege and attack. Suffice it to say, never was British valour more conspicuous and persevering. Marmont is said to be besieging Rodrigo, and if so he will probably take it. He would have been better employed in taking Badajoz, which he might have done.

Some Thoughts on War to a Brother
TO HIS BROTHER EDWARD BECKFORD LONG

Ribera
20 April, 1812

I do not recollect having received either of the two letters you allude to, but I am happy to acknowledge the safe arrival of your last dated 12th March. Could I easily discharge the debt which the leisure and kindness of my friends might impose upon me, I should covet and solicit their regular contributions to my comfort. But the little I send to Charles, as circular and for your general information, must shew you that both my time and materials are very scanty, and do not admit of that latitude of intercourse, which otherwise would be most grateful to me. . . .

The state of affairs both abroad and at home appears so far from encouraging, that it is with reluctance one proceeds to a contemplation of it. The Era which might have been opening with smiles, hope and promise is ushered in upon us with frowns of fearful discontent, disunion and dread. The infirmities of human nature have triumphed over those patriotic wishes which all encouraged because they thought them possible, through the firmness and exertion of a great mind, discarding selfish considerations, and looking only to the general good. Fate has willed it otherwise, and therefore I seek refuge in the fiat of a superior power that directs the storm, and to which, if so decreed, even the British oak must bow its sturdy head. If it is essential for some wise purpose, that all the world should be covered with bloodshed and misery, so be it. *We* shall suffer, but those who follow will probably be the wiser and better for our transgressions and misfortunes. Those above us are not perhaps the most to be envied. They will be the first to feel the blow, and the higher they stand, the harder will it be given, and the severer will be their fall. Five feet four inches is quite altitude enough in these ticklish times. It is a pity that Henry has passed that mark.

For myself I have been taught a lesson that must reconcile me to any lot. For me no exchange can be for the worse. They only know the blessing of *security* who are constantly exposed to danger. It matters not how large may be the cabin or what its situation. Can we lay down in it in peace, and take our rest? An affirmative to this query should constitute the sum of every reasonable man's happiness, and so it will with them, who, if not attached to life, can scarcely value any inferior consideration. All the world, my dear Edward, should feel and know the curses of warfare, and they would appreciate very differently from what they do, the value of domestic peace and security. Those whose faces will gladden at the capture of Badajoz, and direct the merry peal to announce it to others, should have stood on the breach the day after the assault, and have contemplated the scene of desolation that will occasion so much joy. Had they hearts they would feel for the bravest of the brave, and curse the spirit that consigns them, with so profuse a band, to premature annihilation.

As I passed along this scene of death, I observed a poor fellow scraping with his hand some dust, and throwing it over the body of a comrade. I rebuked him for this slovenly operation, and desired him to get a party and bury the man properly. He burst into tears, and asked me what he could do? It was his brother, and he could not bear to see him lying thus exposed. I would to God that every Tyrant could have witnessed this scene, but had they hearts to feel it, they would not be what I have called them. But the age of philanthropy is gone, that of selfishness has succeeded, and we care not who lies in the ditch of honor provided we are not there ourselves.

The picture you have drawn of your domestic cares is not lost upon me. Like others, too, I have had my embarrassments, but fortunately they are diminishing daily, and when surmounted will enable me to assist in extricating others. Happy shall I be so to do, and to share with my friends the bounty I receive.

The breeze that is freshening in the north will I fear blow Alexander out of his cradle before he can get his night-cap off! What fools are ———! I begin almost to take pleasure in their misfortunes, and should do so sincerely were they alone the sufferers. The Imperial eagle has for some time been preparing his iron pinions for a distant flight, his eye steadily fixed on his prey, and he will not quit till he has devoured his victim. The Bear may growl and feel sore, but the injustice he was practising on the Turk will revert, with tenfold force, upon himself—a well-merited retribution! Napoleon will endeavour to retrieve in Poland the honour he has lost in Spain, and if he stakes his person on the die, be assured he has well calculated the chances of the game. Submission or Victory will equally fulfil his objects, and I suspect that Alexander will chuse the lesser evil.

Your accounts from Park House are a cordial to my soul. God grant a continuance of such sunshine. It is the only kind I enjoy and bask in. My prayers are anxiously put up for the happiness of embracing you all again, but whether granted or denied, I remain in this, as I shall in the next world, your always affectionately,

R.L.

Army Gossip
TO C. B. LONG

Ribera
28 *April,* 1812

Since writing to you yesterday, M. Leon[1] has given me in his accounts, and they have alarmed me so much, that I must request you will send me immediately a copy of the agreement entered into with him.

What think you of the following items?

London	Coach hire		3 0
	Stage to Portsmouth	1	15 0
	Luggage		16 0
	Coachment Guard		5 0
Portsmouth	Porter		3 0
	Boat		8 0
	Letters		1 6
	Boat		3 0
	Lodgings	1	4 0
	Paid muleteers to bring me from Abrantes	1	10 0
	This Account Book		2 6
	From Jan. 7 to April 21 is 15 weeks board wages at 5/– per diem	26	5 0
		32	16 0

What think you of the above for a commencement? Board wages five shillings per diem? Was there any stipulation upon this subject? The Gent. has alarmed me so much with his *first* account that I shall not be very anxious to see a *second.* . . .

[1] M. Leon was the body-servant asked for in a previous letter.

I am going to purchase a Merino Ram and a couple of Ewes to accompany my goats, and, when an opportunity offers, to send to you. It is with great difficulty, however, such intentions can be carried into effect.

How does your young colt come on? If I had any advice to give the striplings Henry and Charles, it would be to follow those professions which at the same time that they offer the means of distinction, secure also the best prospects of personal happiness in this fleeting life—viz., the Church or the Law. Diplomacy, I fear, is beyond the reach of family influence. At all events, I am not an advocate for the Army, unless where there are a great many cubs that can be spared and killed off without any injury to the old stock. Let them wait a few years, and then see what I shall have got for my pains. Slender powers of arithmetic will bring them to their senses upon this subject. I believe the old York Hussar sword will be my greatest prize if any Jew could be found to give me for it half what it originally cost. I calculate that the siege of Badajoz, alone, will put nearly 400 English Families into mourning, and if we proceed for a few years, at the same rate, the true blue of England will soon be succeeded by a national colour of a darker description.

The Divisions of the Army have all their respective titles, viz.—

Light Division	..	..	..	*The Division*
1st	,,	(Guards, etc.)	..	The Gentlemen's Sons.
2nd	,,	..	..	General Hill's Lambs or the Corps de lit (d'élite).
3rd	,,	..	..	The Fighters.
4th	,,	..	..	The Observers.
5th	,,	..	..	The Dirty Division.
6th	,,	..	..	(forget the name)
7th	,,	..	..	The Invisible, or often heard of but never seen.

Sir Stapleton Cotton is styled The Lion d'or (from his finery) and his Adjutant-General, Colonel Elley,[1] "The great dog of war," Slade might, with equal propriety, be called the Lion Noire [*sic*], Marshal Beresford the Lion blue [*sic*], Sir Wm. Erskine Lion rouge, Le Marchant the Lion jaune and your honourable servant Lion blanc, and thus we are all of a family. A soldier disputing about Lord Wellington swore it was him for he knew him by his d——d snipe nose. "Old Snipe," therefore, stands for his Lordship. By the bye, Cobbett seems to have forgotten his old friend Talavera and the Douro

---

[1] Later Sir John Elley, he fought at Waterloo, was M.P. for Windsor in 1835, and died four years later.

wars. I think the opening of this campaign will puzzle even his ingenuity for a lick at the Snipe. It has certainly been most brilliant, lead to what it may.

Some General Reflections
TO HIS FATHER, EDWARD LONG

Ribera
1 *May*, 1812

Your letter of the 10th is now before me, and I am infinitely obliged to the fair Emanuensis by whose assistance this comfort has been afforded to me. I must however scold you for two sentences, viz., the one which announces Charles's promise of "sending, for your perusal, my last dispatch, as he had kindly favored you with the sight of the preceding ones." The other misdemeanour is that which declares your "expectation that I will not take the trouble of writing an answer to you but merely intimate to Carolus the receipt of your letter." Now with regard to the *first*, my letters to Charles are intended for you, and written under that stipulation; secondly, I can never permit it to be considered as a trouble to me to acknowledge direct the happiness conferred upon me by your communications.

These points arranged I have to congratulate you that the fate of Badajoz was settled without any *general action*, thanks to the disunion probably of the French Generals. It has occasioned us a lamentable loss, but success qualifies our regrets, and more particularly so, when we recollect that our loss last year, was, in toto, greater, though attended with final discomfiture.

Though we are not yet in a *starving* condition, our supplies are not so flourishing as heretofore, and of course they cannot fail to feel the influence of that scarcity which appears to exist in England, Ireland and France. A war between Russia and France will exclude the hopes of assistance from Poland, and a squabble with the Americans will settle our prospects in that quarter. Much misery certainly exists in *this* Province from the pressure of French exactions, and in many towns the poor are literally starving and dying in the streets. British humanity does all it can for their relief by subscriptions to procure rice, and giving up the heads, feet, etc. of slaughtered cattle, with which soup is made and distributed to these wretched objects. From the nature of things this assistance is precarious and uncertain, and can only be considered as a small mitigation of a great evil. Still however it is to be apprehended that Famine, with its dreadful consequences, may be the portion of this unfortunate country by a continuance of the war, for when men have sown their all and reaped nothing, the land will be left uncultivated, and a great quantity is already in that state.

I have already expressed my intention, should circumstances permit, of revisiting you towards the end of the year. Not upon any consideration of "Sat vixi gloria," but because I prefer the happiness of embracing you, my dearest Pater, again, to *any* honors glory could confer upon me. I have never felt much of this ardor for glory; first because I am not ambitious, and secondly because I have witnessed too often the sacrifices required for its attainment. Not a drop of blood do I wish to see spilled to obtain for *me* the greatest honors. If in the performance of an unavoidable duty, the correct execution of it merits approbation, I am satisfied. With such ideas, I shall always make a sorry soldier, but I think, if I live, that my remaining days will not be, on this account, less bright or happy. . . .

I understand the Government at Cadiz can scarcely raise the means of paying its Civil Officers, the Cortes, etc. The Military are obliged to shift and live as they can from hand to mouth, without pay, clothing, or equipments, and when bread fails they disperse to avoid starvation. The only wonder is how they can get people to serve at all under such a system, but it is perfectly clear that increased numbers must only produce increased embarrassments. The English Army could not subsist here without the Port of Lisbon, and the further they go from it, the greater become their difficulties. The French only live by dispersing their armies over an immense surface, the resources of which they command by the effect of terror, for every village knows the consequence of resisting their demands. This instrument of power we do not possess, and nothing but good and prompt payment can draw forth *for us*, those supplies which the Enemy commands by a stroke of the pen. Money is not superabundant, and therefore we are often obliged to live upon Portugal, when we might be husbanding these resources, and deriving our subsistance from the country we occupy.

Could Great Britain, in contemplation of a Russian war, have strained every nerve in favor of Spain this year, it is possible that by such an effort the French might have been compelled to concentrate perhaps behind the Ebro. If we are unequal to such exertion, and if as the "Times" newspaper very sensibly observes, "Napoleon can keep Spain down with the pressure of one of his fingers whilst he is crushing the Russian Power with the strength of his other arm," then indeed must the contest here be considered as hopeless; and the moment it ceases to be a diversion in favor of Europe, that moment I think it would be wise to give it up, for whether population or expense be considered, it will always be a losing game to us. People may call it a Spanish war, but it is nothing more than a British contest with

France on Spanish ground; or rather with Europe, for we have the contributions of almost every nation to fight against.

I am delighted to hear of Eliza's well being, although disappointed at her obstinate adherence to old practices in producing nothing but girls.[1] The times require a different system. But seeing a petticoat Government established at home, perhaps Eliza is of a contrary opinion. Well! I wait to see what wonders "the good mutton cutlets and strong curacoa" will produce, though the former dish, unless corrected by the latter, should lead one would think, to very *sheepy* measures. ...

General Slade is at Fuente del Maestro. He wished I believe to come to the south in the hope of getting Sir Wm. Erskine's command, thinking the Baronet would not return so speedily, if at all. In this he has been disappointed. He expects when General Garth dies to get the Royals (his Regiment.) In this he will also be disappointed. He is likewise a candidate for Sarum. In this he will be for a third time disappointed; so that in a short time he will look blacker than ever. ...

Thoughts on the French and the Legion of Honour

TO C. B. LONG

Palomas
4 May, 1812

Since my last the Enemy before in our front have made a flank movement by their right and thrown themselves into the Serena. Their object is I believe to exhaust the Serena as much as possible, presuming that the period is approaching when they must take at least a temporary leave of that fertile valley. We shall as usual wait till they have done all the injury they can, and then put ourselves in motion to protect the plundered inhabitants.

If we are to do anything and can do anything, now should appear to be the time for it, when the French and Russians are settling by the pen or the sword their northern difficulties. It appears to me that Napoleon is meditating the re-establishment of Poland. The doing so would give him a great command over Austria and Russia, and furnish him with great resources in men and horses for forming a new and strong army, as the advance guard which will secure to him the tranquil possession of and dominion over Germany. The Poles would not forget the favor and would become his best ally. Austria by this measure would be paralysed, Prussia and Saxony kept completely in the Trammels of Napoleon, and thus his universal continental preponderance could be effected.

---

[1] This refers to the birth of Elizabeth Howard's daughter Juliana Barbara, the fifth and last child, and the fourth daughter, only the eldest child being a son.

The direct intercourse opened with France will I trust be beneficial to *your* interests, and may, in its prosecution and results, tend to diminish the asperity existing between the two countries, and bring them, sooner or later, to a dispassionate consideration of their true interests. This must be the work of time, and I fear a pretty long time too. But the task of conciliation must have a beginning.

That "Legion of Honor," that morceau we affected to turn into ridicule, has proved a fruitful source of evil.[1] It has aroused that military spirit and love of distinction that keeps alive the French Army. The French officers appear to me to think and dream of nothing but the "croix d'honneur," and they would sooner be stripped to the skin than part with the bauble. The Army is the road to its attainment, consequently it will never want officers. War gives it effect, consequently it will never want advocates. And war is the key-stone of Napoleon's Crown, the main-spring of his power. Let no-one, therefore, laugh at the "Legion of Honor," which begot, and *may* accomplish, the project of conquering the world. Our commemoration tokens are a precious kind of substitute! But still, with all their defects, they, even they, have not failed to do good.

There is a blue book of mine somewhere, either in the black leather box or one of the oak boxes, or in the writing desk or case, called, I think, "March's Register," and if I recollect aright I had begun the entries in it of some pecuniary payments to my servants, but discontinued it. If you can find it in a leisure moment, and without much trouble, I wish you would see if there are any entries against Ifland, and transmit to me the copies of such memoranda.

---

[1] The Legion of Honour was instituted by Napoleon on May 19, 1802, when he was First Consul.

X

The Bridge of Almaraz, and the Operations of May–July 1812

In May Wellington employed Hill once more on one of the detached expeditions which aided the general objects of his plans. The French had a floating bridge over the Tagus at Almaraz, and this was to be destroyed; the plan was first suggested on February 1, but not until May 29 was the attempt made. It was entirely successful. Long was not much employed, his column being used merely to demonstrate against a pass defended by an old but refurbished castle and some small forts; however, with great skill and impetuosity the outworks of the bridge were carried by the infantry, and the bridge itself, a most elaborate and imposing affair, was completely ruined. Hill withdrew his force without any trouble, carrying off nearly three hundred prisoners; the Allied loss was 177, two-thirds being in the 50th Foot (Royal West Kent Regiment). The cavalry had no losses, nor in fact did Long's command suffer at all. The forlorn hope went forward, and scaling-ladders were ready to assault the defences of the pass; but when the enemy opened a cannonade and it became obvious there was to be no surprise the left and centre columns did not engage.

The breaking of French communications across the Tagus was part of Wellington's plan, which finally led to the great victory at Salamanca; but before that happened another disaster to the British took place in a cavalry brush. This time Long was not involved; it was his friend Jack Slade and the heavy cavalry who lost 160 men near Llera, and incurred a stinging rebuke from Wellington.

In June Hill and his men were once more back on the old Albuera position, which they strengthened with a redoubt—on the famous hill which had seen the Fusiliers' victory—and breastworks elsewhere; it is a grim comment that so luxuriant had the grass grown over the old battlefield that it had to be burnt off to clear the field of fire.

Long and his cavalry were out in front, in broiling heat and wild heaths, with no shade save that to be found in improvised huts. The French pushed forward. A few scuffles among the outposts were followed by a slow British move southward over the familiar ground of Santa Marta and Usagre, culminating in a smart action at Ribera on July 24. The French General Lallemand occupied the town, only to be driven off in handsome manner by the 9th and 13th Light Dragoons and some Portuguese cavalry, supported by horse artillery. The French force of three regiments, beaten in fair fight, retired in haste, was pursued by Long for over six miles, and incurred some sixty casualties. As Lallemand was the commander who had defeated Slade much satisfaction in the Army was felt at this affair, which cost one Portuguese trooper killed, and ten men wounded and missing.

Preparations for Almaraz
TO C. B. LONG

Palomas
9 May, 1812

As I expect to move in a day or two upon a secret expedition with General Hill, I avail myself of the present moment of leisure to prepare my weekly bulletin, and to apprise you of the probability of some interruption occurring to the punctual transmission of the next. . . .

The Enemy are *squeezing* the *Serena* most lovingly, and I argue from this their expectations of bidding it a speedy adieu!

I am favored with your letter of the 20th ult., and papers to the 21st ult. Your queries about the vineyards and expected vintage this year I cannot satisfactorily answer, but as the Port you drink comes principally from the Douro, which has not been the scene of much warfare, I should be inclined to suspect that scarcity or dearness of wine in England must arise from two circumstances: viz. the quantity consumed by this Army, and the increase of price arising out of the uncertain state of the country. With respect to the prospect of the next crop, no opinion can be formed at this moment, the season being too early; but of this you may be assured, that if the Army continues in Portugal, *their* demands will not be diminished either by success or adversity. In the former case there will be much to be celebrated plenis poculis; in the latter, much required to drive dull care away. Should our operations be transferred to Andalusia, then indeed the resources of that province, with Malaga, Grenada, etc., will come in aid of a few pints to be spared for your consumption. But if the immortal juice goes on increasing in price in the way you have stated, you must have recourse to your gooseberrys, currants, etc., and apply to your friend Bacon, or old Dame Herring (Addenbrooke's love) for the necessary receipts to turn out choice champagne, sherry, etc.; or broach your oldest cask of negro juice (rum), and do as we do, when straitened for Falernian. But as Napoleon is, to o'er-flowing, full, and has consented to exchange his superfluities for yours, I hope Barsac, Frontignac, etc., will make the Douro tremble, and lower its pretension in your favor. . . .

I suspect your British scarcity is to be ascribed more to the Contractors and Country Banks, than to the soil or season. The knowing ones foresee the improbability of importations from France, and keep back their supplies to increase the price of the article. America pacified and will be soon right again. We want money more than corn. The Spaniards do not relish slips of paper payable in Lisbon. They do not understand the nature of *credit* and *paper money*, unhappy souls! They can only clearly discern the value of the metals, and prompt payment. Sad ignorance! But so it must continue until Messrs. Perceval and Co. can enlighten them on these interesting subjects.

I see most of the opposition—Loyalists are measuring the breadth of St. Stephen's floor, and adjusting their —— to new seats. They appear to be much like the Spanish Juramentados (as they are called) whose oath of fidelity to the Enemy only binds them to the cause during French dominion, but when fortune favors *us*, off they come again to share the blessings of success.

I shall leave this letter open for General Wynyard's[1] perusal, that he may know what the "Invincibles" are about.

[Endorsed on cover] 5 June, 12. Your brother writes in excellent spirits, at which I am delighted. The business to which he alludes[2] has been done very satisfactorily by Sir R. Hill's Division. The particulars not yet received. W.W.

The Bridge of Almaraz Operations

TO C. B. LONG

Truxillo
23 *May*, 1812

My last to you was I think dated on the 10th Inst. and announced our intention on the part of General Hill to make an attempt upon the Bridge of Almaraz. I am now to announce the complete success of the expedition as far as fulfilling to the very letter the instructions conveyed for General Hill's guidance. . . .

It was intended to attempt the surprise and attack of the Fort of Miravete which commands the pass of that name and without which artillery could not be carried forward. Also to attempt the surprise and attack of the Enemy's works on the Tagus, which cover the Bridge of Almaraz.

For this purpose the Corps was divided into three Columns. The Right under General Hill, consisting of Kenneth Howard's brigade was to traverse the mountains and gain a road which passing by Romangordo, turns the pass of Miravete, and leads down directly to the Bridge and the works which cover it. The Left Column under Lt.

---

[1] Wynyard was a family friend, in office at the Horse Guards, through whose hands most of Long's letters home passed. This was the type of occurrence which made Wellington (and Beresford) extremely angry.

[2] The breaking of the French bridge of boats across the Tagus at Almaraz.

General Chowne was to proceed along the high road to within 2 miles of the Castle of Miravete and then to strike off to the left, and try to gain the mountain on which the Castle stands and carry it by escalade before daybreak.

The Centre Column under my own Command consisting of the Cavalry, Artillery and Brigade of Portuguese Infantry, was to form the reserve to support both attacks, if the Castle should be taken to push through the pass down to the Bridge. Otherwise to take up such a position as should secure the communication between the right and left columns, and cover the retreat of either if necessary.

For the above purpose the Columns marched at the prescribed hours between 7 and 10 o'clock the same evening to their destination, but the object completely failed, the right column from the difficulty of passing the mountains could not reach Romangordo, and the left column, misled by the guide, did not reach its destination till long after daylight, and of course until the Enemy had discovered, and was prepared to resist the assault.

They therefore remained in position about $1\frac{1}{2}$ mile from the Fort of Miravete, and reconnoitring parties were sent on to obtain a knowledge of the country, and the situation and strength of the Enemy's works.

It appears that the pass of Miravete was so exceedingly strong as to be almost unassailable. The Enemy had fortified an old Moorish Castle on the top of the Sierra which commands the whole country round, and this work supported by others lower down the mountain completely command the road.

On the Tagus near the Bridge, and on this bank of it, they had likewise thrown up a considerable flanked Redoubt, having a fortified Moorish Castle in the centre, and connected by a covered way (or double sap) with a small village at the head of the Bridge, every house of which was fortified. Beyond the Bridge on the right bank was another Fort of the same kind called Ragusa. General Hill's instructions were to destroy the Bridge, and not to trouble himself with Forts and Castles beyond what the necessity of the case should require.

He therefore determined to mask Miravete and attempt the attack of the works covering the Bridge and the Bridge itself by the Infantry unassisted by the artillery. For this purpose he marched early in the night of the 29th Inst. with General Howard's Brigade and one Regiment of Portuguese, with scaling ladders, etc., by the road of Roman Gordo, intending to attack the moment they should arrive at their destination. The difficulty of the country (requiring 5 hours to march 1 mile) was such that the Column did not arrive in front of Fort Napoleon till nearly 6 o'clock A.M. after marching the whole night to traverse not more than a league of road, or rather goat-track. Just before daylight we made a feint-attack upon the Castle of Miravete to engage the attention of the Enemy. At 7 o'clock A.M. the columns of attack being prepared, they advanced in the most regular and determined manner against Fort Napoleon, and the Village, with ladders, etc., and in 15 minutes carried the whole. As soon as the rampart was gained the Enemy fled in confusion, and some of them having cut away the boats, all on this side of the river were killed, wounded or taken prisoners. The Troops pushed over the Bridge, re-established the passage, and the Enemy fled also from Fort Ragusa, without attempting a further resistance, leaving us completely masters of every object of our wishes. No time was lost in destroying the guns, the bridge, the Castles in the redoubts and the fortified houses, and this accomplished they retired on the following morning to their respective positions and thence to this place.

A great deal of good luck, as usual, has attended this enterprise. Had the works been better manned or more vigorously defended, our loss would have been enormous and success problematical. Or had the Enemy, aware of his weakness, retired from Fort Napoleon (as he might and ought to have done), spiking the guns, and thrown himself into Fort Ragusa, removing the bridge to the opposite bank, our failure would have been complete. Another instance was that at this time Count d'Erlon[1] concentrated his troops near Medellin and threatened our communications and rear. Had General Hill received the report of this circumstance sooner, he would have abandoned his project, but luckily it did not arrive till after the attack had been made, and the bridge having been destroyed we felt perfectly indifferent about Count d'Erlon's movements.

Our loss has been 3 officers killed, 8 or 10 wounded and about 160 Rank and file killed or wounded, most of the latter severely. Howard had a shot through his hat, which of course was going as near as any General Officer could desire. Thank God he is safe and well, and thus a good officer, and as fine a Brigade as any in the Army, are, with little loss, preserved for future glories. Two Battalions had been sent from Talarea de la Reyna, but arrived too late. The loss of the Enemy was about 10 or 12 officers and 300 men. I confess it grieved me to leave Miravete still in their possession and the works not destroyed. Two or three days more might have accomplished everything in the most perfect manner, and had a Division been pushed from Portalegre to occupy this Town during the operations, no risk could have been run, or impediment offered, and such an end would have gone far towards preventing a wish on their part to re-occupy this part of the County,

[1] Drouet.

whereas at present, they have only to procure boats, and this done, everything can soon be established as before. Nothing could be more perfect than their establishment. The Bridge a beautiful Pontoon one, with carriages, cordage, etc., in abundance, and provisions for several months. The blow as struck will annoy them confounded, and had Wellington's object thus accomplished, paves the way for any further operations he may have in contemplation, and to which this was considered as a preliminary. . . .

An order has this day been received to enlist 100 Spaniards into each British Regiment preparatory I conjecture to an organisation of them into Battalions under British officers. This may, therefore, be considered as a new era for Spain, if it unfortunately should not have occurred too late. The Regency and Spaniards in good humor at our recent successes may be inclined to think less of themselves, and more of us, and if they do, a road to better policy may be opened, and lead to more permanent advantages.

Of course the state of the war in this country must and will be considerably influenced by the result of affairs in the North of Europe. But as things stand at present, we have so much strengthened the frontier of Portugal by the capture of Rodrigo and Badajoz, that the contest there may be considered, by these events, as being prolonged for at least another year, that is if means can be found to subsist the Army required for its defence, and this I should think will depend a good deal on the result of your negociations with America. The Regent's declaration respecting the Orders in Council is a masterstroke of policy, and it is only to be lamented that it has been so long delayed. France must now speak, or America must forever hold her tongue about her impartiality, tho I perceive a fresh spark for mischief engendered by the discovery of Sir J. Craig's[1] intrigue, which, upon the face of it, does not seem a very honorable transaction, tho justified, perhaps, by the practices of national policy.

The result of the Catholic debate appears to me a prelude to their final success. Much is certainly to be said on both sides of the question, and with equal justice, and in this case a compromise should appear to be the wisest step. At all events, if it is made a Party Question (which it ought not to be) many serious consequences may ensue. The Ministers have gained another year's reprieve and much may turn up in the course of events, before the renewal of the discussion. The

[1] Sir James Craig (1748–1812) had an interesting career in the Netherlands, South Africa, India, the Mediterranean, and Canada, where he was Captain-General and Governor-General from 1807 to October 1811, when he resigned. He managed to avoid open warfare with the United States during his term of office. Bunbury called him a "pocket Hercules."

campaign at St. Stephen's may be considered as nearly terminated, and the interval between this and the next, will doubtless be judiciously employed in weakening the adversary's ranks by *the usual means*. It is about time too that our operations should be suspended till the return of cooler weathers.

The heat is becoming oppressive, and the Guadiana will soon reign in all its feverish terrors. Nevertheless the mountains on the other side of the Tagus called the Sierra de Placente are covered with snow, and their influence extends even to this place, which is a considerable Town, and an old Roman Station, having a Castle built by Julius Cæsar, which the French commenced fortifying, but have since abandoned. The Spaniards have destroyed their works. It is besides the birthplace and was the seat of residence of the renowned Pizarro,[1] whose house is in the Square, and with several others, was converted into a Barrack. A descendant, the Marquis of Conquisya, lives in the neighbourhood. The very first thing the Frenchmen did on entering the town was to enquire after the burialplace of two of Pizarro's brothers and to destroy their sepulchral momuments. Such are the Vandals of the present day!

We have just received the order to march tomorrow morning at 4 o'clock and I grieve to learn that some of our wounded here must be left behind. Should Foy[2] continue to advance, even as far as Deleztoa, I fear they will fall into his hands. There are no troops in the Country except a Guerilla Corps under a ci-devant Goat-herd of the name of Cuesta, who has about 150 mounted men. He is enterprising and had harassed them a good deal. So much so that the communications between Miravete and the Bridge was completely interrupted by him, and he once had the boldness to attempt the destruction of the Bridge by swimming the Tagus at night and cutting the cables. They lost a few boats on that occasion. We have given him a good supply of French ammunition of which I trust he will make an advantageous use.

Count D'Erlon has been driving in all our outposts from Usagre to Palomas inclusive. All this "fanfonnerie" is merely to alarm us, hasten our retreat, and cover Soult's advance upon Tariffa. We have halted here two days, and most likely shall return via Medellin, in which case he will be very well disposed to measure back his steps upon Castuara and Zalanca, and console himself with having accomplished—nothing.

We have to lament the loss of an excellent officer here—Major

---

[1] Pizarro, Spanish adventurer (1475–1541), was the conqueror of Peru.
[2] General Maximilien-Sébastien Foy (1775–1825) commanded the 1st French Division of Marmont's Army of Portugal.

Squire of the Engineers, whose name you will see mentioned in Lord W.'s dispatch. The fatigues he was exposed to at Badajoz brought on, it is supposed, a Paralytic stroke which terminated fatally in a couple of days. We were looking over the Castle here together the day of our advance, and he lies buried in the spot which excited his curiosity.

Such is the precarious tenure of a soldier's life. He well merited every honor that could be bestowed upon him, but he died unencumbered with a single token bespeaking the approbation of his Sovereign or Country. I wish we were as lavish of our honors as we are of our blood. England would not be the worse, and the friends of the fallen would have their best consolation bestowed on them.

I have received your letter of the 28 ult. With respect to your query about the cultivation of Spain, you must be aware that, for our misfortune, we have not had much opportunity of seeing a great way into the Country. The cultivation is very partial. The best I have seen is in the immediate neighbourhood of the Serena, about Don Benito, Villa Nuera and la Guarama. The country about Villafranca and Zafra has likewise a promise of abundance. But in these respects, everything is a dreary uncultivated waste fed off by flocks of sheep and goats. Between this and Merida the prospect is equally famishing. La Mancha, Andalusia and the Castilles probably present a very different appearance. But with a diminished population, and incessant exactions, famine will soon press hard upon both friends and foes. The poor are daily victims to want, and perish in the streets almost without pity or observation, death under such circumstances being considered rather as an alleviation of their misery. War, be assured, is the greatest of national curses, and Englishmen may be grateful for the exemption they have so long experienced from such evils. The Enemy's bayonets are taxgatherers they are yet to become acquainted with. As soon as they know them a little better you will hear no more murmurs about the appearance of Excise Officers, etc., etc. But I trust with Lord Liverpool[1] that this Army will prove a shield impenetrable to the Gauls, and that as long as it exists England runs no risk ever of being insulted. The French have been taught the respect due to the red coats, and this borders nearly upon hating and fearing the sight of them. I trust the impression will long continue, even after the sword is sheathed, of which the prospect appears distant enough even for the most bloodthirsty.

I leave this open for General Wynyard's perusal, and having nothing more to say bid you farewell with every affectionate wish.

---

[1] Lord Liverpool was Prime Minister from 1812 to 1827.

Army Gossip and Reports

TO C. B. LONG

Merida
1 *June*, 1812

My last hastily written dispatch announced to you our successful excursion to the Bridge of Almaraz, in the operations however I had but little share, the column placed under my own immediate command being intended to act as a reserve. As Lord W. has judged it of sufficient importance to send home the official dispatches upon this subject by one of General Hill's Aides de Camp, of course you will see the worthy Chief's unaffected narrative of his operations, and I can only add to them that nothing could exceed the brilliancy of the exploit, be more fortunate than its issue, more creditable to himself, and more honorable to his Troops.

The day before we left Truxillo Baron la Foy with his whole Division arrived at Miravete, and followed our route as far as Santa Cruz, whence he has retrograded by Deleztosa to the Bridge of Arzobispo. General Hill has transferred his Head Quarters to Almendralejo, leaving Kenneth Howard's Brigade and the 13th Dragoons here. The Enemy has re-occupied Don Benito and Medellin, and continue in possession of the whole Serena, and of the frontier of this province beyond Usagre, Llera, etc., and this in the teeth of 12 or 15,000 men. I have always lamented this forbearance, which I think equal to the Spaniards and impolitic in ourselves. But nothing is done without orders from the Chief of Chiefs, and he has not yet thought proper to occupy the whole of this Province. Thus you see you were right in your speculation about Almaraz, but I strongly doubt your being equally fortunate respecting our march to Madrid. To read the English papers, indeed, and their absurd comments, we ought by this time to have reached the Ebro, and sent Soult with his Army prisoners to Lisbon. We are far from thinking ourselves able to do either the one or the other, and every day will increase the difficulty. Much must depend upon the state of affairs in the North of Europe, and I might now add in England and Ireland, for if the discontents at home should by any unfortunate fatality assume a serious aspect, the Army must be recalled to fight pro aris et focis.[1]

As far as my poor commonsense can go, I do not think the history of England does not bear upon record such acts of impolicy, as have within the last few months engendered all the mischief that now disgraces the country. What effect the recent melancholy catastrophe at St. Stephen's may produce I know not, but we need not have waited

[1] "For altars and hearths" (the gods and ourselves).

till the present moment to ascertain with impunity. Sooner or later it must and will make itself be heard in a peal of thunder, the crashing drift of which no arm but the sword can impede the progress. Then commences the battle between pride and despair, hatred and revenge, and this is followed by the usual train of crime, persecution and ultimate oppression.

It now remains to be seen what changes poor Perceval's fate[1] will produce, a partial or a general one. It is odd that almost all the papers of the 12th ult. containing the account of Perceval's assassination have been stopped in England. Howard is the only person who has received one. My papers are generally a week in arrear, I know not why, but suppose from some irregularity or delay in putting them into the post office. I have not yet seen the horrid particulars, and am indeed almost ashamed to see them, for it is a national disgrace.

Since my last I have had the pleasure to receive your communications of the 4th and 11th ult. and also one from Edward Dawkins[2] at Cadiz, who has had the good fortune to be appointed Under Secretary of Legation to Sir H. Wellesley.[3] He has been born under a lucky star, and his parents may banish all anxiety about his future interest. Your query about the acorns is easily answered. The box *not* marked contained those of the *Cork* tree, the others marked were from the Spanish oak producing the sweet acorns. Both are evergreens, and handsome trees, and would I think thrive in the neighbourhood of the sandpit, in sheltered situation with a southern aspect. At all events you may try the experiment.

The heat here is now becoming very oppressive. The other day the thermometer was 86° in the shade, and 96° in a tent. The marches were in consequence laborious and the wounded suffered severely. We have this morning buried with military honors the French Governor of the Forts on the Tagus, who died of his wounds. He was most highly spoken of for his skill and bravery, and his body showed ample marks of determined resistance. It is reported that the Governor of Fort Ragusa, with nine men, have been condemned to be shot for misbehaviour, and they deserve it, for their conduct was most dastardly.

I purpose removing in a day or two to Fuente del Maestro (near Villafranca) to join the other Regts. of my Brigade, which I hear have been harassed a good deal lately, and have suffered proportionately in appearance and condition. The Cavalry under d'Erlon have been

---

[1] The Prime Minister, Spencer Perceval.
[2] Edward Dawkins was a nephew in the Diplomatic Service. He was later British Minister at Athens.
[3] Sir Henry Wellesley (1773–1847), a younger brother of the Duke of Wellington, was Ambassador to Spain from 1809 to 1822.

quite upon the alert during our absence, driving in our outposts in every direction, attempting surprises, etc. Quite gay and alive. The destruction of the bridge of Almaraz is a receipt in full for all we owe them, and I hope they will be satisfied with it.

I think you treat my old friend Addenbrooke and his matchless Dame in a very uncourteous manner. So often as you visit his domains you never condescend to break his bread, drink his ale, or kiss his better half. I make it a rule to practise all three of these hospitable attentions whenever opportunity offers, nor will two years growth of beard more on the venerable chin of the hostess diminish the fervor of my embraces when we meet again. She must contrive to totter, as well as she can, under the weight of my affection.

I am not at all surprised to hear of the frequent breaches of parole among the French officers in England. The state of public feeling and opinion will always determine upon the point of honor. When a Government connives at such proceedings, and the individual guilty of such conduct is received into the bosom of society without experience, the parole of honor, depending as it does for all its worth upon sentiment, becomes a mockery, ceases to be a pledge, and binds only the conscientious, whose ideas are elevated above the rank of society they live in. Bonaparte has never shewn much regard for morality, and I believe he cares very little about any other source of honor than that which induces his officers to do their duty, when in the ranks. I have heard that he has made a kind of compact with our smugglers by which the importation of a French prisoner is allowed to cover and licence the illicit traffic. True or not, it is very Napoleon-like. How long Providence will permit him to scourge the earth I know not.

I see a Pamphlet published by an Adjutant of the Guards professing to be the Campaigns of 1810 and 1811 in this country. If it is worth perusal I should like to have it. But in truth not an atom of anything you have sent from England (except what Leon brought) have I yet received. There is a sad inattention to the comfort of officers in this respect, here. By the bye, Leon is an admirable fellow and fully answers your expectations of him. He is willing, active and intelligent.

Count de Penne is not a Portuguese but a Frenchman, and his countrymen are very indignant at his condescending to command a Banditti. I am sorry to say he is becoming rather unpopular with the Army, and they begin to call him a Humbug. On his return from near Seville Lord W. directed him to place himself under the orders of General Hill, who in consequence wished him to go with his Corps to cover the Serena. But the Count thought Zafra, where he could "passer tranquillement, sans souci, sans affairs, la nuit à bien dormir et le jour à bien faire," was a better quarter, and refused to go, in consequence of which General Hill would have nothing more to say to him. I have not seen him since the Arroyo Molinos business, but when I do, I shall not fail to take him to task for all his misdemeanors.

A proclamation has been published by the Duke of *Rodrigo*[1] inviting the Spaniards to enter our service, but as it has not been accompanied by any official document and recommendation from the Government, they appear to suspect its validity. The Alcalde here says there are no men available for such a service, the few young ones met with being either deserters from some Spanish Corps, or else the sole support of large families, who must perish without their assistance. I think we should try what effect an appeal to the Spanish Juramentados in the French service might have, and invite the Peasantry to assist their escape.

Another Pause before Action

TO C. B. LONG

Villafranca
8 *June,* 1812

All we hear of at present is that Lord W. is in full march for Salamanca, and that Castaños with some of the Gallician levies is at hand near the Douro to cooperate with him. Still however his Lordship's force is not of that magnitude to induce any sanguine hopes or opinion. At first it struck me that he might be desirous of opening a direct communication with Gallicia by taking Zamora, as a point of appui for the Spaniards; or as the harvest is beginning he may wish to appropriate to his own use the supplies west of the Tormes; or he may have some object in view by obliging Marmont to concentrate; prevent him perhaps from re-establishing the Bridge at Almaraz.

The report this day is that Soult is also concentrating at Seville. It is not impossible or improbable that when he hears of Lord W.'s movement in the North, he may be desirous of profiting by it himself, and of dislodging *us* from the south bank of the Guadiana, to enable him to carry off this year's grain to his magazines in Andalusia; or if it is intended to station Suchet and his Corps in Andalusia, I think Soult would be advantageously posted on the Tagus.

Perhaps both Parties are waiting for the development of Politics in the North of Europe. If a determined contest takes place there, we may be inclined to push our exertions here to the utmost.

The Army sees with regret the loss of our late Quarter Master General, M. General Murray, who is appointed to be head of that

[1] Wellington had been made Duke of Ciudad Rodrigo by the Spanish Cortes.

Department in Ireland. It will not be very easy to *replace* him. It is rumored that Colonel Gordon is coming out. No one can doubt his intelligence, but he cannot possess his predecessor's local knowledge, and this is a great point.

The recent excursion to Almaraz excited some bustle, but that having subsided, we are as quiet again as in profound peace. The increasing heat of the weather indisposes much to exertion, and if made on either side will be productive of indisposition. In a fortnight more we shall be completely salamandered.

Our Headquarters at present are transferred to Fuente del Maestro. My Brigade is divided between Villafranca, Los Santos and Fuente del Maestro. Slade with the 3rd Dragoon Gds. and Royals is at Ribeira. The Infantry are cantoned in Villafranca, Fuente del Maestro, Villalba, Azeuchal and Almendralejo; Count de Penne with Murillo at Zafra. The whole of this force may be estimated at 14 or 15,000 Infantry and about 2,000 Cavalry. I reckon Lord W.'s force at about 30,000 Inf. and 3,000 Cavalry. Soult's whole force if collected cannot be short of 30,000; and Marmont's I reckon between 40 and 50,000. If this approximates to anything near the truth, the prospect does not appear very flattering, for it does not include Suchet, the Army of the Centre, nor the French forces north of the Elrro.

You have heard a good deal of the famous Empecinado, the Guerrilla Partisan in Castille. I enclose, as a curiosity, one of his passports, in which he makes himself a man of greater consequence than his Enemies will be inclined to admit; and I suppose to *blister their vanity* as much as he could he has adorned his passport with a vigrette emblematic of the treatment which the Imperial Eagle is to receive from the Spanish Lion. Such a representation ought to be highly amusing to the Duke of Aremburg, for instance, who thought the French Army disgraced by employing any other weapons than *sticks* against these said Spaniards.

I see the papers have already disposed of Sir J. Molyneux's place in the event of his decease. It is a pity that the arrangement you alluded to some time ago could not have been carried into effect two or three years back. I have always understood Sir Francis to be a close narrow-minded man, and if such be the case I should place but little reliance on his post-obit intentions towards Howard. Men are not always rewarded for their attentions in this world. Old Craig (of the 13th Dns.) died the other day, and General Bolton, who transacted almost all his wordly concerns for him, and appeared to be his chosen friend, found himself disappointed with the legacy of a mourning ring, the whole property (a very large one) having been bequeathed to Lord Harrington's family. Happy the man, say I, who expecteth nothing —*he cannot* be disappointed!

I suppose you are now planning *your* summer campaign, and about the time you move, we shall march too. This has occurred several times. On the 12th ult. you were to start for Park House, and on that day I marched from Palomas for the Almaraz expedition. Well! I would sooner be doing something or anything to remaining idle, and as the Spaniards at Zafra, who know everything by anticipation, insist upon it that we shall march shortly for Seville, I hope, ere long, to announce a movement in that direction.

British Cavalry in a Scrape
TO C. B. LONG

Los Santos

16 June, 1812

Since my last we have had some movements, the object of which was to try to get Drouet's Corps a little further from us, but with the exception of obliging them to evacuate the Serena in order to concentrate on our front, I do not think we have succeeded.

It so happened on the morning of the 11th inst., General Slade being in the neighbourhood of Llera fell in with General Lallemand's Brigade of French Dragoons, which was attacked with the greatest gallantry and success, but, as is usual with British Dragoons vying with each other for distinction, they broke away into such a rapid and disorderly pursuit, that a reserve of the Enemy's Troops brought up at this moment turned the side of victory, and it ended in our complete discomfiture with severe losses.[1] I was made acquainted with the circumstance on my arrival at Usagre on the 11th inst. and having heard the same night that the Enemy had left 15 of our wounded men at Maguilla (intending I suppose to send for them the next day) I detached the same night a squadron and brought off 12 of them, the other three having died. A detachment of Heavy Dragoons was directed on the 12th inst. to patrole to Maguilla for the above purpose, not aware that I had secured the object, and on their arrival there fell

---

[1] This skirmish at Maguilla is described by Oman as "the most unlucky combat that was ever fought by the British cavalry during the Peninsular War." When General Lallemand's dragoons turned to fight, their line was broken by Slade's first charge with his 1st Royals and 3rd Dragoon Guards, and one hundred French prisoners taken. But the British cavalry pursued so recklessly over several miles that they were taken in the flank by Lallemand's reserve squadron, and fled in disorder. Slade lost one hundred and sixty-six men in killed, wounded, and prisoners.

Wellington commented in a letter to Sir Rowland Hill: "I have never been more annoyed than by Slade's affair.... It is occasioned entirely by the trick our officers of cavalry have acquired, of galloping at every thing, and their galloping back as fast as they gallop on the enemy. They never consider their situation, never think of manœuvring before an enemy—so little that one would think they cannot manœuvre except on Wimbledon Common: and when they use their arm as it ought to be used, viz., offensively, they never keep nor provide for a reserve...."

in with a superior force of the Enemy, who was charged, routed, and one officer and 18 men and horses taken. On these two occasions General Lallemand lost his two Aides-de-Camp taken prisoners, but as he took two officers from us, a mutual exchange will take place.

The Enemy is represented to have suffered severely on the 11th inst., but as they succeeded in rescuing most of their prisoners, the prize remaining in our hands has been inconsiderable. This circumstance compared with what we have lost has of course created some regret, and will give rise, I doubt not, to much malicious remark and insinuation. The failure is, in my opinion, decidedly to be attributed to the indiscreet manner in which the reserve or supporting body was conducted, for they cease to fulfil that character the moment they join in the attack or pursuit of an Enemy's rear-guard, and in doing so advance so far and with such speed, as to destroy all order, blow their horses, and necessarily become the prey of fresh Troops brought against them. General Slade it appears observed this error, and endeavoured to provide against the consequences by directing a squadron on the right of his line to halt and stand fast, but by some fatality the order was not complied with, and consequently the men, when obliged to turn about, found nothing to rally upon, and therefore continued their flight to what may be considered an unfortunate and perhaps disgraceful distance. Thus you see how much depends with us upon the Chapter of Accidents, and how much we are the creatures of chance. A day that promised to be a brilliant one, and if successful would have established Slade's fame for ever, has turned against him, and left only recollections of the most painful description.

I know from experience how difficult it is to contain a British victorious Cavalry in sight of a fugitive Enemy, and I know equally well how much better the Enemy has his men under his hands than we. Knowing this, although I must lament with others the result of this unfortunate day, I do not see what Slade could do more to prevent it than he did, for in all such affairs, which are more or less extensive, one man cannot be everywhere to control every individual, and of course something must be left to, and depend upon, the discretion of others. . . .

Back on the Albuera Position

TO C. B. LONG

Bivouac near Corte Peleas

22 June, 1812

. . . Soult, either to assist Count d'Erlon, to put him in possession of the harvest of the province, to strike a blow against us as a diversion in favor of Marmont, or some other good reason has advanced from Seville with we believe about 10,000 Infantry and some Cavalry, which united with D'Erlon's Corps make up an Army of 16, or 17,000 Infantry and about 3,000 Cavalry. They give out that they have 30,000 but this, unless Suchet has previously joined him in Andalusia, we know to be impossible.

Well, Sir R. Hill has concentrated his Army (about 17,000 infantry and near 3,000 Cavalry including Spaniards and Portuguese) with the intention of offering battle on the old ground, and we consider to-morrow as the likely day for a trial of strength. But up to this hour they do not appear to be very rapid in the execution of their intentions, their advance not having passed Almendralejo and Azeuchal. It is doubtful to me, when he becomes acquainted with our determination whether Soult will attack with his present force, but if he does, I confidently trust in a happy result to our arms. The French give out they are come to fight us. If so, a battle they will have at Albuera.

I am not satisfied that Albuera is the best fighting ground we could have selected, and should be almost inclined to prefer Valverde. The latter is stronger, better flanked, offers more shade and better comforts for the Troops, in case of disaster it is more secure, (as Cavalry could do nothing against Infantry in the woods,) and our left flank is well secured by Badajoz. Albuera is the reverse of all this. If defeated, the result would be terrible to us. On the contrary, the Enemy, beat at Albuera, are secured from the greatest evil they have to dread, by the wood near it which they would occupy, and which is strong. It conceals all their movements and manœuvres, and above all they are masters of the ground. At Valverde they have to traverse an immense plain to attack or retire over, would find no wood or water, and they have never fought over that ground before. However the Chiefs must be the best Judges, and the result of battles is in the hands of Providence, who will direct everything for the best, whatever may be our opinion upon the subject. . . .

The last news I have heard from the North was that Lord W. had entered Salamanca, Marmont retiring to Valladolid. A short time will disclose the result of this important operation. At present I cannot foresee it unless it leads to the destruction of their magazines on the Douro, and gives King Joseph the *calenture* (the fever of the country). I consider General Hill as strictly on the defensive, and it will I think be unwise to act upon any other system. If the State of Andalusia recalls Soult, D'Erlon must break ground. If he remains, we keep him in check. But unfortunately Ballesteros received a check in the beginning of the month, and is now I am told at Gibraltar; the very moment when he might do something. Thus all combination is thwarted.

Rumours from the Salamanca Front
TO C. B. LONG
Bivouac near Albuera Wood
28 June, 1812

Tomorrow being post day, and our situation being one of extreme uncertainty, I must prepare my weekly dispatch for your information.

The Enemy continues in the same position in our front as when I last wrote. He appears from the accounts of the Deserters that the force sent from Seville consisted of 8 Battalions, 3 Regts. of Cavalry and 6 pieces of artillery, and it appears to be the general belief that they have not more than 12,000 Infantry, 2,000 Cavalry, and about 18 pieces of artillery altogether. Under these circumstances it is much to be regretted that we ever abandoned to them the strong position of Zafra and Los Santos. Still, there is one Division of Infantry unaccounted for, and if so, I suspect it is gone to the Serena or Tagus.

Being in possession of all the corn growing part of the Province, they are busily employed in collecting it for their immediate use, and this appears to be the principal object of their expedition, tho' it is given out that their advance was to keep Genl. Hill's Corps in check and prevent his detaching to Lord Wellington's assistance. We are waiting for instructions to direct our future movements.

In the meantime his Lordship has advanced to Salamanca, and Marmont retired to Toro, but shortly reappeared and took post within 3 miles of his Lordship's position. Some skirmishes have taken place, and the Proximity of the Armies, estimated nearly at the same force (about 35,000 men) naturally excited the expectation of a battle, and which letters from the North taught us to expect about the 23rd or 24th inst. Not a communication was received by yesterday's mail, but two rumours are afloat. The one (British) represents Marmont as having again retreated after surveying Lord W.'s force; the other (French) expects an action to have taken, and that Marmont had the worst of it. All we know for a certainty is that the Enemy having fortified the Convent of St. Vincente at Salamanca left 600 men to defend it. This work Lord W. attacked, but was obliged for want of ammunition to suspend his proceedings and withdraw the guns, having lost about 200 men in the attempt. We are all in doubt as to the exact object his Lordship has in view.

I must remark in confirmation of a former opinion respecting the feelings of the Spaniards in *this* Province, that since D'Erlon's last advance not a Soul, with one exception, has shown any anxiety to transmit to us intelligence of the Enemy's force and movements, whilst last year I received hourly and unsolicited bulletins from all directions. Is not this a change, and of a most unpromising description too? The best informed people in this Province have assured me, repeatedly, that the Spanish Government might, if it pleased, recruit 10,000 men in this Province. Well! Murillo has been trying to increase his Corps without effect. The British have issued proclamations inviting them to enlist in British Corps; still, all will not do. Not 50 men have been obtained. What then has become of Spanish zeal and spirit? Both are exhausted and subdued! They have no objection to *our* fighting the battle for them, provided there is a chance of success; but if not, they would prefer closing the sufferings and miseries of war upon any terms rather than see it prolonged. They received Lord Wellington with "Vivas" at Salamanca. So will they Marmont when Lord W. retires. This is no criterion for your judgment. You have to calculate in your mind the chances of a recovery of this country by British means alone, (for I leave Spanish co-operation out of the Question) and, comparing our resources with those of France, form your opinion.

Of course the result of the Russian struggle will influence materially matters here.

We are here bivouacked on a wild heath, with nothing but shrubs, and without a single tree. In the shade of my hut the thermometer for two days was at 94. In the sun (in which we have been sufficiently exposed of late) it could not be less than from 110 to 120. Enviable existence for a gentleman!

The 4th Dragoon Guards have joined us, I had the pleasure of meeting an old acquaintance in Colonel Sherlock, who appears to have been a good deal at York, and spoke in the most friendly terms of Sympson and his family. There are pleasant occurrences, which come now and then to relieve our weary work, and remind us of endearments that we only enjoy in imagination.

We live, however, in the hope of relief sooner or later; and whenever it comes, it will be an oblivion of the past. . . .

Reconnaissance and Skirmish in the Spanish Summer Heat

TO C. B. LONG

Bivouac between Bienvenida and Usagre

6 July, 1812

I believe my last was dated on the 29 or 30 June. Since then we have been moving, and generally speaking so harassed that I have had not time even to make a memorandum of the daily occurrences. To the best of my recollection however, it was on the 1st inst. that the Enemy's Cavalry reconnoitred us in force on the two points of Corte de Peleas and Sta. Marta, driving back the Portuguese from the former and chastising properly the Spaniards under Count Penne near the latter. Having advanced about 8 o'clock A.M. with my Brigade to the assistance of the former, the Enemy retired immediately on my appearance to Almendralejo and Azeuchal. Scarcely had I got back to Albuera wood about 2 or 3 o'clock P.M. and unsaddled, when a report came that the Spaniards were all driven in at a gallop, that the Enemy was already in Albuera wood, and within a short distance of my Bivouac. Out we turned again, but on our reaching the edge of the wood, found the Enemy had been met at its entrance by the 3rd Dragoon Guards posted to support the point, had been charged by one Squadron of them, and had immediately retired. The Spaniards lost 8 or 10 men killed and I believe from 150 to 200 taken prisoners. This Coup de main was accomplished by Lallemand's Brigade (*Slade's friend.*) It was all the Count de Penne's fault. He refused to listen to the reports of his officers that the Enemy was advancing, conceiving that having retired on the right, they did not intend to stand on his left. Consequently he advanced towards them till within reach, when they made a dash upon him, and pursued so vigorously that his people were soon in disorder, and the rear of his column was overtaken and bagged.

I returned to the wood at ½ past 10 P.M. and received immediately an order to march again at 1 A.M. on the 2nd inst., on which day the whole Army advanced to Sta. Marta to act on the offensive. There appears to have been a great deal of indecision how the operations should be conducted, and I believe the Plan having been changed three times was finally decided on the morning of the 3rd July. It was that the right column under General Hill should proceed to Los Santos, and the left under Sir Wm. Erskine consisting of one Division of Infantry, my Brigade and the Portuguese Cavalry should direct itself upon Villalba, to dislodge the Enemy from that point, and endeavour to join Sir Rowland Hill at Los Santos by Fuente del Maestro. You will observe that the Enemy's whole Force, Cavalry, Artillery and Infantry, was supposed to be concentrated between Fuente del Maestro and Villafranca, consequently Sir William's column was to run the risk of encountering and being engaged with the whole French Army.

We came upon them very suddenly at Villalba (the Lancers) and they retired in great haste upon the heights above Azeuchal, where we soon perceived 3 other columns of their Cavalry. We then moved by our right along the river to the spot where the direct road from Sta. Marta to Fuente del Maestro crosses the stream, where we halted. We soon after learned that General Hill had again changed his intention, and had halted near Ferea, and he proposed the next morning to attack Fuente del Maestro. This was taking the bull by the horns with a vengeance had the Enemy determined on resistance. Their Cavalry appeared very soon on the left and front of our Bivouac, and kept me so much on the alert, as nearly to starve both horse and man.

The next day at 3 o'clock A.M. (4th July) we were under arms for the purpose of attacking Fuente. They had retired 2 Regiments during the night from our left, and the Lancers alone remained to watch our motions. We remained under arms in the sun till nearly 1 P.M. waiting the moving of the Column under Sir Rowland. About 2 P.M. the information received was that he had again altered his mind, and was in motion for Los Santos, whither we were to follow him leaving the Division of Infantry and Portuguese Cavalry near Feria to observe Fuente del Maestro. We marched accordingly about 4 P.M. The horses had nothing to eat the whole of the day, so that being obliged to forage on the road I could not reach the Army at Los Santos till ½ past 10 o'clock at night. I then received an order to be ready to march at 3 o'clock A.M. the following day (5th July) with the whole Army (one Division excepted) upon Bienvenida. We had got about halfway, when information was received that the Enemy occupied Usagre. The Cavalry therefore were turned in that direction, with the Horse Artillery and one Brigade of Infantry. On arriving there we found Count de Penne's Corps skirmishing briskly about a mile from the Village, and on the heights in the rear were five Regiments of Cavalry commanded by young Soult. Not observing us approach he had crossed the Ravine with one Regiment to attack the Spaniards, and had I been aware of this circumstance I could have annihilated them. But pursuing the line of march directed for me, they got sight of the Brigade, and retired rapidly to their position. I made a flank movement to threaten their left, and on perceiving our force they retired without resistance upon Valencia de los Torres. Count D'Erlon had fallen back the same day upon Maguilla by the route of Ribeira and Llera, covered by Lallemand's Brigade of Cavalry.

13th July, Villa Garcia

This letter tho' commenced as you see on the 6th inst. and intended for the post on the following day could not be finished in time. An alarm at the outposts prevented my doing so at the moment, and ever since we have been so harassed and employed that for 2 hours in the 24 I have not been able to get an uninterrupted nap. In fact both my Brigade and myself are nearly, from fatigue, want of rest and exposure to insupportable heat, done up, and a few more days continuance of our recent fatigue will finish our powers of campaigning. The mischief has been that all our movements appear to have arisen from the impulse of the moment, and the order for them delayed till the hour when we were laying down to sleep, so that 3 hours rest has neither been permitted nor could be taken. Constant exposure to the rays of the sun when the heat in the shade has been at 96 and 100 has been enough to subdue the stoutest constitution. But I proceed in my Journal.

7 July

The Army marched at daybreak in two Columns from Bienvenida and Usagre by Villa Garcia to Llerena. The left column halted at Villa Garcia, the right proceeded to its destination.

10 July

The Army marched in two columns upon Berlangen, where the Enemy's Cavalry with some artillery were posted. After an insignificant cannonade they retired to Azuaga.

11 July

The Army returned in two Columns to their former stations at Llerena and Villa Garcia. On this night for the first time for a month past, I ordered my bed to be made in the hope of taking a treat, that of undressing, and going regularly to bed in a house. Scarcely had I closed my eyes, when in came an order to march at the dawn of day again to Berlangen to make a reconnaissance.

12 July

Marched to Berlangen, found three Regiments of the Enemy's Cavalry there, which retired on our appearance. Halted a few hours at Azllores and marched at 8 P.M. on our return to Villa Garcia where we arrived at 1 A.M. this morning.

Of all the days I ever experienced I think the 11th inst. was the severest I ever passed. The whole atmosphere was black with heat, and a distressing sirocco wind prevailed, which passing over the burning fallow ground felt to the hand, when extended, like burning steam. The hilt of my sword became so hot, that I literally could not grasp it for any length of time, and the heat of the stirrup irons was not less annoying. Such weather you may well conceive is ill adapted to taking or keeping the field, and the scarcity of water completes the quantum of suffering. Count D'Erlon, supposing we intended merely to resume our old cantonments, went himself with the greater part of his Corps to Zalamea, for the purpose I suppose, of securing the supplies from the Serena. The whole of the Cavalry with a Division of Infantry fell back to Azuaga and La Granja. But conceiving us to have some further object in view, I hear he has now assembled the whole at the latter place. Let our station be what it may, I do not think it will interfere much in his prospects upon the part of the harvest of Estremadura. He has had a tolerably good share already, and I am convinced the best slice (the Serena) will be his also. If they feel us troublesome, another detachment from Seville upon Monasterio and Fuente de Cantos will soon conduct us back to Zafra and Los Santos, if not further still.

Our news from the north is of an uncertain description. . . . They say the Enemy has lost in the North in Prisoners and Deserters upwards of 2,000 men since Lord W. crossed the Agueda. Our old friends the Lancers have shewn symptoms to change sides also. We had five came in yesterday, in addition to many more before. But, considered upon the grand scale, all this is nothing. The French will not starve for some months to come, and if we have not bayonets enough to clear the provinces, nothing else will do it.

I have received your letters of the 9 and 16 June. I cannot feel regret at our poor Aunt's[1] departure from a theatre where every enjoyment in life had ceased. I shall receive her bequest with the same grateful remembrance I should have done had it been ten times the amount.

Howard's good fortune, however, is a source of unalloyed joy to me. To be independent in life is I think the summum bonum, and I hope he will never let politics so far blind his faculties as to risk that independence in a cause which experience must now shew him to be the most baseless fabric, that short-sighted mortal ever speculated upon. Everything he can rationally desire is now within his reach, let him endeavour to live long, and as long as he does live to enjoy life to the utmost. The change which those circumstances may produce in our domestic concerns will be an interesting subject of contemplation for me, and one upon which I shall be happy to see you enlarge in your future epistles. I have no hesitation in pronouncing my opinion that our Pater should not be induced by any circumstance to abandon his beach, or the sheet anchor (Lane) that has kept him there so safely at his moorings. Every consideration sinks before that of prolonged existence, and this, whether we consult his welfare or our own. . . .

I have received Edward's last letter, and also a joint epistle from the Harrovians.

The articles so long sent out to me are still detained at Lisbon, as I possess no means of getting them from that place. I am reduced to a threadbare condition in every respect, but the dogdays have arrived opportunely to do away with the inconvenience of rags.

I bid you adieu! And must apologise for a scrawl written at intervals as they occurred, in a dusty, dirty bivouac.

---

[1] Catherine Maria Long, Robert Long's aunt, was born in 1727 and died at Taplow on June 5, 1812. She married Sir Henry Moore in 1751. St Catherine's Peak, near Newcastle, Jamaica, is called after her because she was the first white woman to climb to its summit.

Some General Reflections on the War and the Government
TO C. B. LONG

Villa Garcia

18 *July*, 1812

I had yesterday the pleasure of receiving your letter of the 30th ult., and papers to the same date. Since my last, written I believe on the 14th inst., I have been assailed with one of the usual attacks of the season, but three days of confinement and discipline have nearly put everything to rights again, and I hope to be the better for it during the remainder of the ordeal. In fact men and horses are suffering equally, and the Spaniards themselves say they scarcely recollect a more trying time. Luckily we are at this moment in a state of repose, the Enemy in his cantonments, and we partially in ours, and I hope a further respite will be accorded to us, to restore everything to serviceable order at least.

I have not received a single scrap of news from the north. . . . I am surprised at Soult's inactivity.[1] It appears to me that without risking anything in Andalusia he might strike a blow against this Army, or at at all cost dislodge us easily from our advanced position, which, if reinforcements are expected in the South, we ought not to be allowed to keep. I can only account for it by his being busily employed in the harvest, and establishing in his rear those Magazines which will give him greater security and increase our difficulties. The frequent desertions from their Light Cavalry have induced D'Erlon to remove them to the rear. The evil will recommence the moment they are again brought to the front. I suspect the Lancers have been offended at their not having been permitted to return to Poland, and also from their having changed the number of the Regiment from the 1st to the 7th Regiment. The knowledge of this Russian war has certainly dispirited the French Army, because they have sense enough to perceive that the weight of the conflict here will be doubled upon them and they feel themselves left to their fate as a kind of forlorn hope. If such a moment, so favorable to Spain and ourselves, is not duly appreciated, or cannot be properly turned to account, the business had best be closed, and let us be satisfied with what our means *can* sustain. I know not what effect upon Spanish hope and feeling Lord W.'s advance may have produced in Castile, but everything here is as torpid as death. No rising, no expression of joy, no voluntary offers to join our standards; and as far as any measures or proclamation of the Government at this

---

[1] Oman declares that Soult's flagrant disobedience of orders at this juncture was prompted by self-interest and hatred of Napoleon's brother, "King" Joseph.

interesting crisis, tending to reanimate the people, and excite them to renewed exertion, if any such have existence, I do not learn that they have passed the walls of Cadiz. They seem to think that they have done enough, and the rest must be left to Lord W. and their allies. Perhaps they are waiting the news from the North, as a Convict expects the warrant which is to pronounce a respite or speedy dissolution. If Russia engages heartily in the struggle, and with a spirit that promises perseverance, I shall not be astonished to see the whole French Army drawn behind the Ebro by order, thus occupying the gates of the Country till more favorable times enable them to resume their locust-like invasions upon the largest scale. But still all reasoning must be defective without that information which perhaps Lord W. alone possesses. A thousand springs may be in motion at this moment of which we are not aware, and that time will develope. We hear of reinforcements expected from England, Sicily, Gibraltar, etc., of expeditions from the Tagus. In short a campaign is not the work of a day. We must await patiently the result, and then reason upon the past rather than anticipate the future.

Lord W. will I think experience a severe loss in his representative, Sir Thos. Graham,[1] who has been obliged to leave us, nor do I clearly see how he can be replaced. Such is the misfortune of having our greatest General low in the Army List. Those above him are necessarily superseded, and those below are unequal to tread in his footsteps. Such men are born and begotten, not erected; for no experience will alone make them what he is. . . .

20 *July*

This being post day I must bring my scribbledum to a conclusion. General Hill is gradually withdrawing his Troops to the rear, and I shall not be surprised at seeing his headquarters ere long established on or near the Guadiana. We intercepted some letters yesterday from Madrid to Soult, but being written in cipher could not unravel them. We have likewise intercepted some billet-doux from some Ladies of Llerena to the French officers. They say "the beastly English are still there, that they have been trying to make themselves amiable, but have completely failed." Fine consolation for the Ball-givers and petits Maitres of Head Quarters, who think themselves irresistible! Should Lord W. retreat again, re infecta, he will have some difficulty in atoning for his neglect to attack Marmont at Salamanca, at a time when our force of every arm was infinitely superior, and the latter General committed his Troops so indiscreetly. But I have often observed that

---

[1] Graham had been invalided home for expert medical attention. For some time his eyes had been seriously affected, and he was threatened with blindness.

Lord W.'s taste is rather for defence than attack, and I suspect he was deceived by the hope that Marmont intended to become the assailant, and thus lost a glorious opportunity of crushing him for the whole Campaign. But without accomplishing such a blow, as a successful battle could alone give, I really do not see what advantages (permanent ones) Lord W. could gain had Marmont retired before him even to the Ebro. If the latter can subsist in his present situation Lord W.'s career is nearly finished, and he has received a checkmate. I very much apprehend that my former opinions upon this and other subjects will not prove far from the mark.

Pray do not trouble yourself any more about *horses*. I shall go on very well with those I have.

Cavalry Action at Ribera
TO C. B. LONG

Villafranca

26 July, 1812

Tomorrow is the regular post day, but as the Enemy is on the alert, one knows not what may happen from cup to lip, I therefore avail myself of the present leisure moment to acquaint you that on the 21st Inst. (the day succeeding that on which I last wrote) we retired from Villa Garcia, and on the 22nd to this place. Our retrograde movement was the signal for the Enemy's return upon us, consequently on the 23rd they advanced and drove in our posts from Usagre, Llera, and Bienvenida. On the 24th General Lallemand (Slade's friend) marched with three Regiments of Cavalry (10th Chasseurs, 17th & 27th Dragoons) direct upon Ribera by Hinogosa, and dislodged the Portuguese there stationed before I could reach the place to prevent it. Unable to ascertain their exact force, which was represented to be from eight squadrons to four Regiments, and having three Troops of my Brigade absent, and as they occupied the strong ground on this side of Ribera, and from the appearance of their baggage in the rear, indicated an intention of continuing there, and disputing the point with me, I thought it advisable to collect all my force before I marched against them, and as a security against disaster, to obtain the support of the 3rd Dragoons Guards stationed at Fuente del Maestro. Some time elapsed before my absentees joined, during which I concealed my people, and indicated no offensive intention. They employed this interval in regaling themselves at the expense of their Ribera friends. At length my people having joined, and as it was growing late, I determined not to wait the arrival of the 3rd Dragoon Guards, but put my troops in motion in three columns and moved rapidly upon them.

Contrary to my expectations they relinquished, without disputing, the high ground they occupied and passed the River. This enabled me to bring up and post advantageously the Horse Artillery which opened upon them with great effect, and covered my passage of the river. I had directed Col. Campbell with 4 squadrons of Portuguese to manoeuvre upon my left, and to dispose of two squadrons of theirs detached in that direction. Had Col. Campbell not been impeded by the difficulties of the ground, and been at hand to support an attack upon them by one squadron of the 2nd Hussars sent round their rear, the whole of these two squadrons would have been taken. I hung upon them, however, for five or six miles till I got them fairly beyond the defile of Hinogosa, where from the lateness of the hour (nearly sunset) and the fatigue of the troops, I thought it prudent to halt, and desist from further pursuit. The ground occupied by Lallemand was so favourable to him in every respect, that I was astonished to see him hurry away as he did, without a struggle. The two squadrons alluded to went off in the most scattered and disorderly manner, but the ground was so broken and rocky I could not avail myself of the circumstance without the risk of throwing my own people into as bad a state. The result however of the whole affair is a loss to the Enemy of thirty-five found dead between Ribera and Hinogosa, and eleven Prisoners. I estimate their loss of horses at more than this number, tho' from the number taken by the Peasantry, left dead or mutilated in the field, and brought off by us, it is impossible to ascertain the exact amount. They entered Llera in a very distressed state, many driving their horses before them, and from the shots heard after our pursuit ceased, I am inclined to think they destroyed, themselves, such horses as were too fatigued to be carried off. They had besides a good number of wounded.

My casualties were only seven men and seven horses wounded, and one Portuguese killed and three taken Prisoners, two of whom have since escaped.

Thus I think M. Lallemand has paid dearly for his luncheon at Ribera, and he will not be satisfied till he has taken his revenge.

Yesterday at 1 P.M. 1500 of their Infantry and 250 Cavalry entered Hornaches, where I believe they still remain. That place is only two leagues from Ribera and three from this place, consequently they keep me on the Qui Vive. I suspect they are moving a Column thro' the Serena upon the Guadiana, either to induce us to break ground still further to the rear, or else to get a start for the Tagus, and unite with any Corps in that direction for the purpose of co-operating for the relief of Marmont. Whilst they are displaying these symptoms of restlessness, I am rather surprised to see our force dispersed in Cantonments over half the Province. But, however, this is not my affair, and therefore I must not trouble myself about it.

I have just received a note containing the report of the Officer left at Hinogosa to observe the Enemy. It says, "Sir, Cpl. Payne reports to me that the road from his picquet to Llera was actually covered with baggage, a great number of trunks with blank returns, etc., and a number of others that had been plundered by the peasants. A quantity of saddles and five horses, and some bodies were also seen on the road. By all accounts he received, they were much distressed."

I have no doubt from this circumstance of their bringing their baggage with them that Lallemand intended to remain at Ribera during the night to cover, probably, the movement of the column that entered Hornaches, yesterday, and where they still remain. I am inclined to suspect another visit from them this evening at Ribera, but if Head Quarters does its duty, their reign there will be of short duration.

The heat is our bitterest antagonist, but the Enemy suffers equally from it. The Prisoners say they have been "parfaitement grillés." From all appearance we shall have a restless summer of it, but this will be of little consequence, if the result should prove favorable to the cause. But here I feel, I confess, a little sceptical. We receive no letters from the North. One would suppose that the Earl had suspended all intercourse, or embargoed all the pens and paper. The last I heard of him was that Marmont was extending to his right down the Douro, and his Lordship was making the corresponding movement to his left. How long this state of things will continue I cannot divine, but unless it leads to the evacuation of Andalusia (of which I observe no symptoms as yet) nothing good can be derived from it. Andalusia is the key to the recovery of the Peninsula, and so long as the Enemy holds it, our cause cannot be expected to prosper in any great degree.

27th July

All quiet but I have obtained information that the Enemy have 3 or 4,000 Infantry collected at Valencia de las Terras with 600 Cavalry and some Artillery. They also occupy Llera with a Battalion of Infantry and three squadrons of Cavalry. I know not what this means, but it makes this Cantonment an advanced post, and keeps me in hot water. I am ordered to fight it out with them near this Town, if they come forward, and with the blessing of God I must do so to the last.

I had yesterday the happiness to receive yours of the 7th ult. The opportunity of Transport will determine the period for sending off the nags, and I certainly wish James, if able, to accompany them. He must bring a new plain saddle and bridle from Gibson's, and if practicable a couple of new Bat saddles, for baggage complete. I likewise want a supply of a dozen new shirts, and the same number of worsted ancle stockings. I forget the chemise-maker's name, but he lives at 3, Tavistock St., Covent Garden. Draw upon Greenwood for the expenses incurred.

I suspect Napoleon himself is at the bottom of all these breaches of Parole. His officers would not dare to do it without his approving sanction. He wants *hands*, and he cares not how they are procured. If they have Honor enough to fight well for him in the field, it is all he cares about. Morality he has long disclaimed. It imposes a difficult task upon our Government, but the best preventative would be good rewards for apprehension, and severe punishment to the aiders and abettors of these dishonoured fugitives. When caught a Jail should be their portion, and all exchanges refused.

The Lisbon Gazette announces peace between Turkey and Russia, and a kind of defensive Treaty.[1] If this be true, the Emperor may pluck up courage enough to meet the coming storms, and means to arrest its career. But the Poles will join Napoleon to a man, and increase fearfully his resources. A protracted warfare there would be the best hope for Spain. Such however are the miseries attendant on this scourge of the earth, that heartily do I pray to Providence, for humanity's sake, to terminate the bloody work. Europe has suffered sufficiently to expiate almost any offences. It is time to have mercy upon the human race.

I do envy you indeed, my Dear Bro., your salt water walks and sea breezes. We must continue to pine on for two months longer, and the trial is a severe one. I never submitted to a greater. It is an incessant evaporation of one's substance and strength, and debilitates, even to a state of nervousness. Drinking is all one desires, and this cannot be indulged in with impunity. However, everything will have an end one way or the other, and on this must our hopes be fixed.

[1] On May 28, 1812, a treaty of peace was signed between Russian and Turkey at Bucharest. The two countries had been at war since 1808. The treaty enabled the Emperor Alexander to turn all his strength against Napoleon's invading armies.

XI

Salamanca and Victory: Madrid and Retreat

THE dominating fact of the summer of 1812 in the Peninsula was Wellington's victory on July 22 at Salamanca, where Marmont's army was overturned, and "forty thousand French men beaten in forty minutes." The really distressing outcome of the battle, from a French point of view, was the indubitable proof that Wellington could attack as well as defend, and could manœuvre on equal terms with the best French commanders.

July and August were, for Robert Long, filled with constant skirmishing, threats of charging, gallops, exchanges of carbine shots, and rapidly changing bivouacs. His opponent, Lallemand, was a courteous foe, who exchanged civil notes with Long. On one occasion, having captured two German hussars who had been surprised while watering their horses near Ribera, he returned them, as a mark of respect.

The final results of Salamanca and the summer's manœuvring were that an advance was made on Madrid, the long investment of Cadiz was raised, and the French abandoned southern Spain. A tremendous change now took place in the complexion of the Spanish war. Long's ragged brigade passed over the bleached plains of Talavera, and took station to the south of Madrid, which Long seized the chance to visit. The Spanish inhabitants were warm-hearted and friendly, though Long held the usual opinion of his kind about the fighting qualities of the Spanish Army.

Though by now the main strength of France was deeply engaged in Russia, there were, as Long realized, still plenty of French troops in Spain. While he optimistically asked his brother to send out maps of the Pyrenees he was also aware that a fresh enemy concentration might well cause Madrid to be abandoned once more. And this happened. Wellington failed in his threat against Burgos in the north, where his brusque assault was as unsuccessful as his earlier attacks on strong-points had been triumphant. In October Long found himself once again commanding a rear-guard, as Rowland Hill's men withdrew from the south of Madrid and through the capital to meet Wellington, who was drawing sullenly down from Burgos with the French following cautiously.

Like most of our retreats in Spain, this was a bitter and heart-breaking affair, beset with straggling, pillage, and disorder that were only to be exceeded when in November Wellington had to withdraw his entire force towards the south. Long's pickets were driven in by the French at Alba de Tormes, right at the beginning of this further retreat. Then followed ten terrible days of rain and weariness, of hurrying back in disorder and deep fatigue, of hunger and misery. Long's brigade was left exhausted, having lost 150 horses within a month; the 13th Light Dragoons were brought down to an effective strength of 180 men.

Luckily the French were equally worn out, and our Army was left to lick its wounds, to retire to winter quarters, and to brood over the scathing, and in certain cases unjust, memorandum of November 28, in which Wellington severely criticized the relaxation of discipline, and attributed the straggling disorder, the outrages, and the losses of the retreat to the "habitual inattention of the officers of the regiments to their duty."

Results of the Salamanca Victory
TO C. B. LONG
Villafranca
2 Aug., 1812

Lord Wellington's dispatches which will probably have arrived in England before the receipt of this letter will also have put you in possession of the details of one of the most brilliant actions which have graced his military career, and in which as usual his "belle étoile" has shone conspicuous. . . .

All accounts agree in representing the Enemy's loss in killed and wounded and prisoners at near 12,000 men, 2 eagles and some other colours, and about 12 pieces of artillery;[1] several General Officers killed, wounded and taken, and Marmont himself represented as dead of his wounds.[2] Our loss has likewise been severe, but reinforcements having joined Lord W. a day or two before the action, he is nearly as stout as before, tho' he must feel I should think the absence of such General Officers (who have been disabled on this occasion) as Marshal Beresford, Sir Stapleton Cotton, Generals Leith, Cole and Le Marchant,[3] the latter of whom was the only General Officer on our side killed outright. Thus has fate put the seal to the misfortunes of his numerous and helpless Family by cutting off, in one short year, both their parents. Unable to secure the provision he wished for in and deserved from his country, he opened a new career in this, and Providence has very soon released him from all worldly cares and anxieties. Poor fellow, he was one of the few faithful and esteemed military friends left me, but as they continue to quit the stage my desire to remain upon it diminishes, and a short time, perhaps, will bring us all together again. I have

[1] Oman reckons that the French lost over 14,000, two eagles, and twenty guns.
[2] Marmont was severely wounded when a shell burst near him as he was mounting his horse.
[3] Le Marchant, having led his brigade against the French battalions in a successful charge that wrecked the enemy's left wing, was shot dead by a ball that broke his spine. Oman described him as "one of the few scientific soldiers in the cavalry arm whom the British Army owned," as an able executive commander in the field, a born commander of cavalry, an admirable artist in water-colours, and "a man of lofty and religious spirit, ill to be spared by his country."

written to his son offering him an asylum near me, if he chooses to accept it, as extra A.D.C., until an opportunity shall occur for placing him in a more advantageous situation. What will become of his poor ten orphans, I know not. They have only God and a few friends left for their protection. I hear my lamented friend and his brigade behaved nobly, and the Cavalry throughout have merited and received Lord W.'s highest applause and admiration.

Well, what will be the result of all this? Ought you not to believe that all Spain would become intoxicated, that a fresh impetus would be given to their former hopes and spirits, that they would flock to their own standards if not to ours, and rise in awful majesty against their oppressors? I know not what may be going on in the North, but *here* in Estremadura the news seems to have produced a general palsy. No rejoicings, no congratulations, no symptom of internal or external satisfaction—does not this confirm the opinion I long ago hazarded as to the complete change I observed in the feelings and disposition of the people of this Province?

It is an interesting moment, and had we the means at hand that I have so long called for the result might be most auspicious, but I still think our inferiority will be manifest more and more every day, as the Enemy unites his strength, and that the sanguine will be ultimately disappointed. I must continue firm in *this* belief, so long as I see French Armies of such force in existence as are yet to become disposable.

If glory beams upon the Troops in the North, incessant harassing and fatigue are the companions of those in the South, and I would venture to say that my poor little diminished and diminishing Brigade has had severer duty within the last two months, than all the Cavalry of the North within the last six. . . .

Madrid, tho' a most interesting point, is very awkwardly situated for us with an Enemy on the Douro, and another that may concentrate on the Tagus. The supplies of an Army so situated must be precarious, and its position not the most eligible. The setting free however such a population as Madrid contains, and dislodging the intrusive Government from its seat, are events that ought to produce a very great impression in the country, and also upon the French Armies. But I persevere in my opinion that until Andalusia is liberated, there can be no hope for Spain.

Campaigns are more or less "glorious" things, but the "à quoi bon?" must be determined by the result. Spain is a large chess-board, the Kings, Queens and Castles are still in existence, and there is no want of Bishops and pawns. In such a game as this the Knights should be of some consequence, and here, I think, we have the superiority. King Joe I apprehend has never been so incommoded since he mounted the throne as at this moment, and I should like to see the countenances of his renegade Spaniard subjects. If Madrid puts on an angry or satisfied look, both will be equally alarming, and require the jealous superintendence of his Corps de Garde, of which the majority are Spanish Juramentados.[1] If any French General *can* retrieve their misfortunes it will be Soult; he has the best head and the best heart among them, and I believe his Army participates in his feelings and spirit. But still they are Frenchmen, and the British bayonet is not rendered less impressive by success.

This Victory will naturally put you all on the tiptoe of expectation as to the results to which it may lead. Lord Wellington is wise in concealing his intentions in a masterly manner, and few can penetrate them. He appears to be born for the age in which he shines, and destined to support the name and glory of his country against French pretensions. May the end of his career be equal in good fortune and merit to its commencement and progress, and, what is a better wish, may he not want a Successor worthy to tread in his shoes!

To the list of *wants* in my last I must add the very great one of a couple of Hussar sword belts, embroidered or stitched with gold. Hawkes of Piccadilly is the man, write to him to forward to me a brace by the *first* opportunity.

August 3rd

We still remain quiet and in statu quo here, but we are preparing for a start. We are too weak by 20,000 men at least, and I fear the result of the Campaign will prove it to your conviction.

Yesterday evening another mail arrived from England bringing me your letter of the 13th July. By the paper I see the die is cast between Russia and France, and all my apprehensions arise from the *Government* of the former. Spain may be said to have had no Government, and has fought on courageously to the last inch of ground they could secure. Had King Ferdinand been at the head of affairs, I doubt if he would have submitted to so long an incarceration of Cadiz, or have stemmed so perseveringly the torrent of mishaps that Spain has experienced. If Alexander is determined to fight his way back to Siberia, rather than yield, he will be successful; but if the loss of a battle makes him despair of the Country, he is already subdued, and the war there will not continue six, nor, in this country, 12 months longer.

I do not recollect if I requested you in my last to send me a *nest* (as it is called) of best double block-tin kettles, with handles to take off and on, and kettles and handles to be marked with a corresponding and similar number.

[1] Those who had sworn allegiance to Joseph.

Whilst you envy us our constant stewing, I envy you your occasional respites, your cool breezes and showers, things we rarely see. One thing however characteristic of this climate is the total absence of all *coughs* and *colds*, and their attendant consumption. No such thing as a cough to be heard in the country, in church or out of it. This is really a blessing.

I see America is growing very angry.[1] I am pleased we gave in before the gauntlet of defiance was thrown down. We cannot live here without her, therefore peace, I say, with her upon almost any terms.

You cannot for a moment doubt about the pleasure I shall feel in shewing every attention in my power to a son of Bacon's,[2] and I am perfectly certain that Slade will do everything towards him that a Father can desire. A short residence at the Depôt, however, in England, to learn something of his business, would appear an advisable preliminary to his departure for this country.

The Spaniards, the Army, and the War
TO C. B. LONG

Villafranca
Sunday, 9 Aug., 1812

Since my last to you on the 4th inst., we have received accounts from the North which represent Lord W. as having advanced with a part of his force as far as Valladolid where they took 700 sick prisoners, some stores, and I believe 17 pieces of heavy artillery. Marmont has been represented as marching to Arande de Douro, and subsequently to Burgos; I know not which statement is correct. Lord W., however, moved with his main body upon Cuellar, where he was on the 3rd inst. 12,000 Spaniards had arrived at Medina del Campo (near Arevola) and were directing their march upon the Guadarrama Pass. Our numbers have been a good deal diminished by fatigue, but the Army is said to be healthy in other respects. This is the trying month for them, not only on account of the heat, and scarcity and badness of the water, but the dangers arising from eating unripe or even ripe fruit to excess, which it is difficult to prevent. There is also a *report* that the Sicilian and Spanish forces from Majorca have landed in Catalonia.[3] . . .

---

[1] Although on June 23, 1812, Great Britain repealed the Orders in Council which had caused so much friction with the United States, President Madison had signed a declaration of war five days earlier; so that when Long wrote open warfare had been waged for more than six weeks.

[2] Anthony Bacon, a cornet in the 16th Light Dragoons, served in the Peninsula from August 1813 to the end. The Bacons were Berkshire friends of the Longs.

[3] General Thomas Maitland landed on August 7, 1812, at Alicante, with 14,000 troops. Although Maitland left in October 1812, the troops remained on the east coast throughout 1813 and early 1814, doing very little good.

The Northern accounts represent the minds of the people of Valladolid to be completely subdued, and no good is expected from them. The Peasantry in general are firm, but they have no persons of distinction in authority to call them, by example, into action. The people of Madrid are said to be well-disposed, and only wait a favorable opportunity for declaring themselves. If Soult *continues* in a state of inactivity it will shew, at the same time, the importance he attaches to the maintenance of Andalusia, and also his opinion that the North is in possession of sufficient means to retrieve its own affairs. But he has lately been making a great bustle towards Cadiz, Gibraltar and Tariffa, and this *looks* very like an intention of concentrating his forces near the Guadalquiver for some northern expedition. The Northern Gents expect great things from us, perfectly forgetting that Soult's Army is more than double our force, one third only of which is British and the rest Portuguese. With fair play and the same terms upon which they have fought, we have no apprehensions of being outrivalled, though the Lord's "belle étoile" is not near to guide our destinies. Had Marmont been less vain and anxious for *personal* distinction, Lord W.'s campaign would have been of short duration, and the glories of the 22nd ult. would never have been reaped. Soult will play a wiser game, and he and his Army must be looked upon as the sheet anchor of the French cause in the Peninsula. Nevertheless, I am almost tired of this Estremadura work. I prefer going with the stream that carries everything before it. Your Observation Corps[1] have much labour and little profit.

I am told the movements of the two hostile Armies between the 18th and 22 July were perfectly beautiful as well as interesting, resembling a well-contested race between two high bred coursers, running neck and neck for the plate. The Lord however kept the whip hand of his antagonist, and the French jockey was dismounted, and lost the use of his bridle arm. The Frenchmen were terribly distressed, and the superior condition and blood of the British were conspicuous. I lamented to see among the lists of sufferers poor Lady Arabella Ward's son-in-law, Captain Osborne of the 5th Dragoon Guards. He was an exceedingly fine young man, and the pride of her domestic circle.

> But wherefore grieve! His lot is that of all.
> The friend who mourns must yield to Nature's law,
> Like him must sink, and o'er each darkening fall
> Will death's cold hand the eternal curtains draw!

---

[1] C. B. Long's private source of information, and a play on the term Observation Corps, which was sometimes used to designate Sir Rowland Hill's force in Estremadura.

Many others must expect the same fate before this bloody trial is terminated, and I only hope the future generation will profit by the sacrifices imposed upon the present. He has left a widow and I believe four or five young children to the care of God and their country.

I heard from Edward Dawkins[1] the other day. He says Soult is bombarding them most unmercifully, and I am told from other quarters that the citizens of Cadiz no longer relish such serenades. Lord W. will not be thanked for giving precedence in his visits to the pseudo King at Madrid, rather than to the "constituted authorities of the Cortes, legitimately assembled by, and under the authority of the beloved Ferdinand." Sad mistake!

The difference between us seems to hang upon so slender a thread, that I am decidedly for proposing to Joseph and Ferdinand the settlement of the dispute by *their own* swords, and let the victor bear away the crown. All competition would then cease, and the lives of many "braver far although untitled wretches" would be saved to the country. I do not think either the French or British Army would oppose a veto to this proposition, for one is about as much attached to Ferdinand as the other is to King Joe. The Spaniards would receive it with acclamation, and pretty nearly for the same reason.

Thank God we are getting on towards September and of course towards October, when our broiling miseries will cease. I never stir out in the sun if I can avoid it, and latterly there has been little or no necessity for so doing. The thermometer is now down in my room to 82, although it rises towards the afternoon. The fact is we want some good soaking showers to cool the ground, which is red hot to some feet deep and of course affects every breath of air that passes over it. They have had a storm or two in the north, but no such blessing ever visits us. The "Father Abrahams," too, in this Province, (the fountains) are not very liberal in their donations—all as dry as the eye of unfeeling indifference. . . .

Should you receive this letter in time, let James bring my gun out with him. We hope for relaxation at some period or another, and as I lost all my greyhounds on the last march to Los Santos, I have no caterer for the pot.

We suspect that Sir Stapleton Cotton's wound and his expectation, perhaps, of a red ribbon as having been second in command on the 22nd will send him home, and although Sir Wm. Erskine should be his natural successor, M. General Ch. Stewart's pretensions, supported as they will be by a powerful influence at home, are considered sufficient to trip up Sir Billy's heels, in which case both Sir William and Slade may have a throat-cutting reprieve, and return to their shelves. I

---

[1] A nephew, son of Robert Long's sister Jane.

really am of opinion that a regular relief should take place every two or three years, and if some such measure be not adopted, I shall commission you to get me a wife and post her off to the Horse Guards on my behalf. Never did woman plead there in vain, and how can they, when certain of support from such petticoat-eaters as my friend General Wynyard? The frame of a ship may be sound, but to keep it so you give her now and then a new *planking*. Even so do unto us. Let us regain the flesh we have lost, and then to sea again for a fresh cruise. I am for giving all the "Gentlemen's Sons" a little practice in their turn. The old boys should not be kept eternally in the *third* form. *Fagging* is not the *prerogative* of grey hairs. Sad treason this, but as I have nothing to lose I dare speak out, a liberty not permitted to *expectancy*. Such language as this would horrify my friend Slade, and make every hair stand more on end than would the spectre of his rival, General Lallemand; who, by the bye, is always civil enough to make kind enquiries after *him*, and which I am equally attentive in communicating.

The French are driven from Southern Spain
TO C. B. LONG
Villa Garcia
29th Aug., 1812

As I predicted here we are in movement, but I confess I cannot, as yet, discover why we are steering South. The Enemy broke up from Hornaches on the 27th and have made a fairly rapid retreat upon Azuega and La Granja. We quitted Villafranca on the 28th. It is reported this day that Col. Skerrett, who landed at Moguer from Cadiz, has entered Seville, and as we had heard that the Enemy was actively employed in destroying at that place, what could not be carried off, the report in question is credited. . . .

Having prepared this much I shall continue to add the daily news and occurrences until the post takes its departure. I ought to mention, however, the safe arrival of the things you sent from England. There were some fractures among the cups and dishes, but Vancouver's recipe was immediately applied with the desired success. The supply of boots will be sufficient for this war at least, and to that of the books I shall look for many an hour's recreation.

Berlangen, 30th Aug., 1812

As the post goes off from hence this evening, I must finish my say. The Enemy evacuated this place at 4 P.M. yesterday. We advanced to it this morning. I know not what is cut out for tomorrow. . . .

The Enemy has abandoned everything in Andalusia in a manner that proves how slight are their hopes of ever returning there. Their depots of grain, etc., at Belalcazal, Constantina and other places have fallen into our hands. They have been prevented destroying several works and forts they intended to demolish, nor was a man left in the lines before Cadiz to prolong their defence and arrest if possible the garrison of that place from pursuit. Fear and precipitation mark their flight, and to me they certainly indicate a probability that that flight, if assisted by corresponding movements on our part, may be carried to the Ebro. I now entertain sanguine hopes that the Peninsula will be recovered. But still this will depend upon the Russian Contest, and I am inclined to hope that the communication at Petersburgh of what is passing here will determine the Emperor to follow his example of consistency and perseverance shown in the South, as the best security he can have for ultimate success in the North. The prolongation of the Russian Contest will enable us to clear Spain, and the greater the degree in which this be done, and the nearer our Arms can be carried to the French Frontier, the greater will be the diversion in favour of the War in the North.

The Spaniards appear thunderstruck with this miraculous change in their affairs, and they begin to think Lord W. is really a General, and, as they are piously given, call him an Angel. But the apparent loss of the French cause has struck a deep wound into the breast of thousands who, having from fear, inclination, or their supposed interests, abandoned their Country and allied themselves with its Enemies, justly apprehend a severe visitation for their offence. Wherever the French have been long stationed as in Andalusia and this province, the more extensive has been this prostitution of public virtue, and this sufficiently accounts for the dismal and even angry countenances we observe wherever we go. Not a "Viva" have I heard from anyone since this glorious, and, to proper minds, intoxicating change has taken place, and notwithstanding all you will read and hear of the reception of the troops at Seville, and demonstrations of Joy displayed etc., I have seen a private letter from the best authority, which states that at a ball given at Seville after its capture, not the slightest attention was paid to any *British* or *Portuguese* officer. But in a country where "All is noble, save nobility," this will not excite your astonishment. The poor despised Peasantry, the soul and pride of the Country, certainly betray different sentiments, except in those instances where they have French adherents for their Tutors. I am told that *they* did not hesitate rushing, in the midst of the fire, to carry assistance to the Troops to enable them to pass the Bridge, and tho' the action continued through the streets, they absolutely impeded the march of our Troops by flocking round them to congratulate their deliverers, and several, of course, fell victim to their Patriotism. Such are the lower orders of Spain, and the reflection makes one join almost in the wish of seeing the muleteers and nobles exchange places in the State. God forbid that I should witness a bloody proscription as the companion of our triumph, but still some severe examples should be made to determine, hereafter, the calculations of the speculators. Now is the time for the Spanish Government to display all its energies, to provide without delay against future contingencies, and to make the country an Armed Nation. They should feel as though a new war were about to commence, and prepare accordingly. Establish the conscription in its fullest extent, organise, first an Army, and then support it with an Armed Militia. One year will suffice for this purpose, and once accomplished, let Napoleon try, when he pleases, the re-conquest of this soil. They should hasten to free the British Army for other operations, by putting themselves in anattitude to defend their own cause. But without proportionate means and the infusion of a little British activity into their measures, they will not be more advanced a year hence than they are now. . . .

No foresight could have calculated upon such results as this Campaign has already produced, and I am not aware that blunders or disasters will improve the French Generals, or render their soldiers more formidable. They are now reproaching Soult with not having advanced against us to operate a diversion in favour of Marmont. I hope their differences of opinion will never cease to exist, and produce corresponding jealousies and animosities. There appears to me to be a *reaction* in everything. To make Generals, Bonaparte rewarded military success with the Honours of Nobility. To support this rank they were permitted to plunder and amass wealth ad libitum. This shook the morale and discipline of the French Army, and paved the way for its disgrace. The Generals, having rank and fortune, *wish to live* and enjoy both. The soldier, no longer animated by his examples of former times, has lost *his* greatest incentive to exertion. This creates mutual displeasure and distrust and neither do their duty. If the Russians are tough, and things continue to go on prosperously here, Napoleon will lose his temper, and then folly not wisdom will be the ruling power of his Government.

Campanano, Sept. 6th

The letter alluded to from Lord W. was 13 days on its route, and brought an order for our immediate march to Talavera de la Regna, whither we are now proceeding. This march as far as Almaraz will not be very interesting to me and others who have been over the ground before, but I shall enjoy myself at Talavera[1] (where so much British blood was unprofitably spilled) in witnessing that scene of glory. This poor village (Campanano) has made up in loyal demonstrations for all the former deficiencies. The poor creatures, men, women and children, received us with cheers, and what is better with the sincerity of a flood of tears. They have been full three years under the iron grip of Frenchmen, and at length are taught to breathe, and are flattered with the hope of future liberty. God grant they may not be disappointed, and that constancy under affliction may meet its reward!

I now enclose Lallemand's love letter. I little thought that whilst I was complimenting him on his *humanity*, he was in the act of directing the execution of two poor wretches at Hornaches, one on the *suspicion* (but without foundation) of being a spy in our pay, the other for robbing one of his men. He will receive no more billet doux from me —the Murderer![2] ...

March across the Tagus

TO C. B. LONG

Mesa de Ibor

18 Sept., 1812

As I think it likely that General Hill's Head Quarters will be at Oropesa on the 20th Inst. and that the mail will be despatched from that place on that day, I shall prepare accordingly, as we are now on our route to Talavera de la Regna, and shall not halt until we reach it. We have had continued thunderstorms from the 10th to the 16th. inst inclusive. All is now clear and fine again, but the Tagus was rendered unfordable, and as the boats for the Bridge will only arrive near Almaraz this day, the progress of the Troops has been in consequence impeded. My Brigade received orders to march by this route which is through the mountains, and the one by which the British and Spanish troops retreated in the year 1809. The two most formidable ridges of mountains to pass lie between this village (which is in ruins) and Daleztosa, and great indeed must have been the difficulty in getting

---

[1] The battle of Talavera was fought on July 27-28, 1809. British losses were approximately 6,000 men.

[2] This refers to the return of the two capturred Hussars mentioned in the introduction to this chapter. Lallemand's letter is not transcribed. According to the *History of the King's German Legion* (N. L. Beamish; Vol. II, pp. 129-130), two Hussars of the 2nd Hussars, King's German Legion (then in Long's brigade), sent from Ribera with dispatches, were taken while watering their horses. Lallemand, when the capture was reported to him, gave the prisoners permission to depart and to take their arms and horses with them. " It gave him great pleasure," he declared, " to show his respect for the German Hussars."

the Artillery over them. From the summit of the nearest ridge (a league from hence) you get sight of the whole valley of the Tagus almost as far as Talavera de la Regna. The valley is bounded on the north by the formidable Sierra de Bejar, which are the highest chain of mountains I have seen in this country.

Having halted one day at Daleztosa I rode over to Miravete, and felt very happy that no serious attempt had been made upon the forts there. They were very formidable and would have cost us a river of blood to carry, even had the doing so been within our power. From the Castle you have the most extensive view, I suppose in Spain, nearly over the whole province of Estremadura, both sides of the Tagus. It was really magnificent. After passing the Tagus the tameness of the scene is only relieved by the Bejar mountains.

On the 20th inst. I shall reach Puente Arcobispo, where Cuesta's Army was defeated, and on the 21st the classic ground of Talavera de la Regna. There for the present the Cavalry are to halt, and the Infantry at Oropesa. This situation inclines me still more to the belief that our ultimate destination may be the Douro, particularly if Soult goes to Valencia. At all events the Great Lord (as he is called) has left Madrid for Valladolid to drive the Enemy back from that place, and it is conjectured that he will push him across the Ebro whilst he is about it. He will hardly stop short of Burgos, the possession of which alone can enable us to cover the province of Leon. In three days more we may consider ourselves ready for any enterprise, and this approximation to the Northern Army gives me infinite pleasure. The nearer we get to the "belle étoile" the more confidence we feel and the better the prospect before us.

I am this day going to feast upon wild boar, which the Cacadores (hunters) very opportunely brought in as I reached the village, and without which it would have been "jour maigre" with me.

Puente Arcobispo, 20 Sept. 1812

I am this moment arrived here, and letters are going off immediately. The gratification of being north of the Tagus is so great, that even the miserable state of the Villages we have passed, and of this town, does not influence my feelings on this occasion. The prospect as to supplies I hear is so bad, that Slade's Brigade, which was ordered to join us at Talavera de la Regna, has been countermanded, and is to remain in some cantonment more to the rear. This town is as nearly destroyed as a town can be, and before their Gallic Friends left it, they took care to relieve the poor inhabitants from all such encumbrances as tables, chairs, etc. Consequently we found the bare walls with here and there a roof. The Guerrillas appear to have kept them in a state of anxiety to judge at least by the pains taken to secure the Troops posted here. Here is a perfect specimen of the blessings of warfare, and the advocates might take a lesson to improve their feelings of humility. Tomorrow we march to Talavera (six leagues) when a few days halt will be necessary to restore our condition. . . .

All the remounts for the Light Cavalry have arrived at Lisbon, but I have heard nothing of Mr. James.[1] As he knows the country and will hear of our route I think it hardly necesary to write about him. I am prepared to expect a return of his aitches. Servants are not very well off here, and they can scarcely be blamed for wishing that kind of life that common sense and experience have taught them to be the best. I am only surprised at so many of them persevering as they do. They have enough to dishearten them without a love left in England.

Alarms and Excursions

TO HIS FATHER, EDWARD LONG

Puebla Nueva, South of Tagus
near Talavera
25 *Sept.,* 1812

I am at length enabled, my Dearest Father, to acknowledge and thank you for your kind and affectionate communication of the 17th and 23rd ult. I believe such a Family Party as you describe has seldom or ever been assembled for the gratification of domestic feelings, and perfectly sure I am that the contemplation of so *many* descendants was less a subject of joy to you than the impression arising out of the conviction of that union and sympathetic affection which, thank God, have hither to bound the whole circle together in concord and amity. To have felt yourself, at the age of 78, still to be the object of their greatest love, anxiety and interest, was the best recompense that could be tendered to the heart that produced so many social blessings. I will not despair of witnessing a recurrence of such interesting scenes, tho' I cannot conceive that the prospects of doing so is considerably diminished.

Lord W. ("nil actum reputans dum quid superesset agendum"[2]) *must* go on. He is now too deeply embarked, as a Principal, to admit of an alternative. The struggle has gloriously commenced, but the coup de grace remains to be given. He has stormed and carried the outworks, but the Citadel still remains to be attacked.

From the moment war was declared against Russia, the French in this country were placed on the defensive. Their object was to main-

---
[1] James Lynch, Long's groom.
[2] "Thinking that nothing was really done so long as anything remained to do."

tain the footing they possessed, and to risk nothing. If Joseph has reason to expect strong reinforcements, Soult will probably maintain himself in Valencia till their arrival, and then combine his movements with the Army of the Douro for the recovery of the ground lost.

If the deliverance of Spain be our object, I see no respite for British exertion, but in the termination of the Russian struggle; which, if successful, may give peace and independence to the Peninsula; if otherwise, will seal its subjection to the Common Conqueror. Such are my views, right or wrong, of the present and prospective state of this country. Its interior resources have been lamentably curtailed by French rapine and desolation, its exterior hopes are blasted by the revolt of her Colonies. The Plains of Talavera, still bleached with the remains of the victims of that struggle, remind us of that memorable struggle, remind of us of the frail tenure by which the possessions even of success are held. Such lessons are well calculated at least to excite circumspection in our military calculations. . . .

In Quarters beyond Madrid

TO C. B. LONG

Madridejos, 11 leagues south of Aranjuez

4 Oct., 1812

I write this at a venture, as I know nothing of the day or hour fixed upon for the departure of the English mail from Aranjuez, where the Headquarters of General Hill are now established. My last letter was dated from Puebla Nueva. On the 20th ult. we left that place for Navalmoral, near the mountains of Toledo. On the 29th marched to Galuez in the direction of Toledo. Thence to Sonieca on the 1st Oct. On the 2nd of this month we removed to Yevenes, in a southerly direction, and yesterday the 3rd inst. we reached this Cantonment, occupying also Consuegra and Urda. General Slade is to be stationed to our left at Camuna, Villafranca and Herencia. To his left comes Count de Penne and Murillo, and at Belmonte are the Headquarters of the Murcian Army under General Ellio.[1] The Infantry are upon the Tagus between Toledo and Aranjuez inclusively. Two British Divisions occupy Madrid, and the 1st Hussars and 14th Dragoons are within a league of the Capital.

Thus we scouts have had no opportunity of seeing the most interesting objects near us, Toledo and Aranjuez. Those who have been at the former speak in the highest terms of admiration of the general

---

[1] General Francisco Elio commanded the Spanish Second Army.

appearance of the Town, and the magnificence and beauty of the Cathedral in particular. The Infantry have by far the advantage of us. They occupy, always, the best towns, and live in something like a civilised state of society. We are associated constantly with the *Boors* of the village and the beasts of the mountains and fields. Nevertheless our passage from Talavera de la Regna has improved the scene very much. We have been, and now are, in one of the finest plains I ever saw, richly cultivated and thickly inhabited. In former times of peace these plains were appropriated, and very judiciously, for the Cantoning of all the Spanish Cavalry.

Our last accounts of the Enemy represented them as traversing Murcia in the direction of Valencia and marching in three columns. The king and Suchet are likewise said to be still in the latter province; when the whole have united, their future intentions will be developed.

The Spaniards are calling in the larger Guerrilla Parties, and incorporating them with their Regular forces. A judicious measure, and one which has already added to the Army of Murcia one of the finest Cavalry Corps (that of Chalsca) which they possess. A conscription for 50,000 men (it ought to be 100,000) is now on foot, and the only requisite wanting to turn them to good account will be *time* for disciplining, and money for clothing and arming them. Never will the proper degree of confidence be re-established in the Spanish Army till these two points are attained, and without confidence they will do nothing.

Lord W. is attacking the Castle of Burgos,[1] which has given him more trouble than he expected. He lost 300 men in carrying some advanced works, and 400 more in an unsuccessful assault upon some other point. Marmont's command is now said to have developed upon General Caffarelli.[2]

The Inhabitants in all these parts have received us with great cordiality and apparent gratitude. The landlord of my present quarters on my entering his house, threw his arms round me and burst into a flood of tears. This is right and auspicious enough, but though the debt on their part would be the same, and the sacrifices on ours increased, I doubt if these civilities would be improved by a reverse.

The immediate environs of this town present a vegetable world, and what is very rare, the potatoe lords it over his contemporaries. Abundance of wells are everywhere sunk for the purposes of daily irrigation

---

[1] Wellington's unsuccessful siege of Burgos lasted from September 19 to October 20, 1812. Inadequate siege material and cannon and a spirited defence caused final retreat, despite several desperate assaults.

[2] General Louis-Marie Caffarelli now commanded the French Army of the North.

performed by jars stuck upon a wheel which is kept in motion by an ass or mule, the water falling into a trough whence it is conducted by the husbandmen into the various channels which diffuse it over the whole surface of the ground for acres round. These wells, I understand, have been the cemetery for many hundreds of Frenchmen immolated by the peasants, and thrown into these receptacles.

It would be curious to see a correct return of the casualties that have occurred on either side since the commencement of this Sanguinary Contest, and having ascertained it, I should like to inscribe the totals in letters of blood on the walls of every room occupied by the Demon who has occasioned such human devastation. Though he would only grin, perhaps, with ferocious delight.

We are here in the neighbourhood of Don Quixote's fictitious exploits, and the Inn where poor Sancho got his drubbing is only three leagues from hence. How easily can a good author give consequence, though delusive, to places and things that have nothing else to recommend them!

Do send me a map of the Northern Theatre of war. You will find one I believe in a flat box where all my maps are, as also Arrowsmith's[1] map of the Pyrenees, which I should also like to have. In the drawer of the upper green-painted bureau, you will find a case of instruments, and a small box with a pocket sextant. These articles I am in want of. Add to them "The Spirit of English and Irish Wit" for an occasional laugh, and La Borde's view of Spain for instruction, and my commissions will cease.

If the Duke of York consents, Le Marchant's eldest son will join me as an extra aide-de-camp.

The Spanish People: Some Shopping Commissions

TO C. B. LONG

Corral de Almaguer

10 *Oct.*, 1812

My last letter was dated I think from Madridejos, which place we quitted on the 6th inst. for Villacanas and on the 7th arrived here. This movement was occasioned by an advance of some of the Enemy's Cavalry from Alvacete in the direction of Roda.

The latest accounts I have seen represent Soult's Army as having effected its junction with Suchet's on the frontier of Murcia and Valencia. . . .

We want 20,000 men more, my dear C., at this moment, to secure to Lord W. the advantages he has acquired, and it will not astonish me

[1] Aaron Arrowsmith (1750–1823), a map-maker in London.

P

to see the greater part of those advantages lost from this deficiency of his means. The present I do consider as the most critical moment he has experienced, and if he gets well through it, he will be greater than ever.

The Spaniards here have a most contemptible opinion of their countrymen in arms, and their only anxiety arises from the apprehension that the British Force, exclusively, will be found incompetent to contend against the united masses of the Enemy, which in the South East alone they estimate at 70,000 men. I fear our Spanish Allies, in their present state of discipline, will be more for show than use.

With respect to the effect to be produced by the promises of liberty held forth in their new constitution, and by its publication, I have been rather surprised at the little emotion betrayed on this occasion. My present host, who is a sensible man, has elucidated the subject by a simple explanation, viz. that the more powerful part of the nation who can read and understand the propositions, do not relish them, feudal servility being more consonant to their wishes; that the lower orders are so ignorant that they know not the meaning of the word liberty, and if it was susceptible of explanation to their understandings, so confirmed are their habits of slavery and submission to their superiors, that they would be incapable of casting them off. For which reason says he, "You will see Spaniards opening their breasts with courageous indignation to the menacing bayonets of the Enemy, unappalled and regardless of life, and those same men crouch to the earth with terror and servility before a countryman of superior rank and power." He therefore thinks that, incapable of appreciating the blessing intended for them, the prize has no importance in their eyes, and they will be easily deprived of it. In the absence however of this general principle to incitement and exertion, we have certainly no mean substitute in the deep-rooted and inextinguishable hatred of the peasantry to the very name of Frenchman. In peace or war they will omit no opportunity of indulging this passion, and many are the thousands of Frenchmen who have fallen victims to it, and are still doomed to perish in the same way.

The French know and acknowledge this truth. They state, unreservedly, that their arms may subjugate the soil, but that the power of France will never conquer the *hearts* of the Spaniards. The sovereignty of such a country cannot be a very enviable gift, to a Frenchman; I am not therefore surprised that Joseph should feel disposed to renounce the honor. But however, here they are, and here they must remain to the last man, unless they wish to see the seat of war transferred from the Peninsula to the south of France, a sufficient guarantee for their most determined resistance. Believe not, therefore, the visionary speculations of those who think the liberation of this country at hand, and that a hop, skip and jump will place Lord W. in triumphant array on the utmost verge of the Pyrenees. This day of éclat is yet far distant, and until it arrives, there can be no safety for Spain.

We have had recently some wet, and the cold has increased very sensibly, to Estremadura habits. We must look forward to a winter campaign, and this prospect reminds me of some further wants which I shall enumerate towards the close of this letter.

We hear nothing of the Great Lord, and I believe the Madrid Gazeteer is forbidden to speak of him or his proceedings. It was rumoured that he had attempted the reduction of the Castle of Burgos, with inadequate means, which had occasioned a considerable loss of men and time. I feel anxious for his return to the South, considering as I do that this is, now, the most interesting part. Under the aegis of his ability we naturally feel a confidence that no other person can inspire.

The condition of my Brigade, from the Estremadura Campaign, and subsequent marches, is so reduced, that, connected with the season of the year, I am apprehensive we shall not hold out much longer, and that a few weeks of winter-work will send us to the rear. With a Cavalry friend at Headquarters, we might have fared better, but representations are not relished, and I forbear making any. We work away to the last in distressing but silent submission. The Cavalry of the North are, I hear, in excellent plumage, a pretty strong proof of the truth of what I reported some months ago, namely, that although the glory was theirs, the preponderance in fatigue was ours. Such has been the case, and from present appearances, is likely to continue.

At the expiration of this year I wish you would do me the favor to collect any bills to be brought against me in consequence of the several demands made through you upon Windeler, Gibson, Hawkes, and the Hatter in Bond St., cum multis aliis; and pay them off by drafts upon Greenwood, transmitting to me the amount.

Commissions for Windeler

A new camlet waterproof cloak, lined throughout, with cape reaching below the elbows.
A plain blue single-breasted Greatcoat to wear over a waistcoat only.
2 white kerseymere waistcoats made longer than the last.
4 pairs of flannel drawers (my fashion).
2 white dimity waistcoats for summer use.
1 pair of blue worsted elastic pantaloons.
    (Thus for Windeler)
½ dozen pairs of cotton (cotton and thread) *ankle* stockings.

½ dozen shirts from No. 3, Tavistock St., Covent Garden.
½ „ black neck silk handkerchiefs.
½ „ washing towels.
Three or four packages of Smyth's Windsor Soap.
2 setts of Spencer's tooth brushes, and 2 or 3 nail brushes.
4 cotton night caps.

Note: to be packed up in a leather portmanteau, with oil-skin cover, name painted on it, and sent, properly directed, by the first convenient opportunity.

From Mackay
Two small hampers equal size and weight with a cargo of cheeses, spices, peppers, mustard, pickles (particularly walnut), currie, vinegar (burgundy and raspberry), hams or tongues to fill up vacancies, ad libitum. The whole carefully packed against thumps and falls and properly directed, for the service of campaign No. 3.

Whether they reach me or not is of little consequence, but there is no harm in making the experiment. A few ready-cut pens would likewise be acceptable, and an almanac and pocket-book (Kearsley's) for the year 1813 (to be sent by Windeler), and which God grant may see the end of this war, by the death of its ungovernable advocate, or the return to sanity of the idiotic Cabinets of the Continent.

Oct. 11th
The post goes off in an hour, and I must therefore proceed to a conclusion. I heard last night that the Enemy had made a sortie from the Castle of Burgos,[1] and rendered themselves masters of our works, and continued its possession sufficiently long to destroy them; the loss severe on both sides, but this event must delay our operations. . . .

. . . Money is reported so scarce at Madrid that they give 9/6 for a dollar. If so, our finances are in a bad way. The Troops are now six months in arrears instead of being according to the regulations, one month in advance. What a treat for the *Croakers*!

Never mind, let but Germany follow the example of Spain, and rise upon its oppressors, and all will soon be right. This single event would disorganise the French Armies. But alas, how different are the general results from our wishes!

May God protect old England from the miseries inflicted upon this *wretched* people!

[1] Dubreton, the Governor of Burgos, made two successful sallies, and altogether conducted the defence with great skill and energy.

Ready to retreat again
TO C. B. LONG
Corral de Almaguer
17 Oct., 1812

What I anticipated is now realising. Soult has advanced his forces upon Alvacete, and pushed forward Count D'Erlon to the Zancara. They occupied la Roda and Minaza yesterday, and as the Spaniards have retired behind the river, I take for granted the Enemy now occupy St. Clemente and Villarobleda, and as no resistance will be opposed I expect to see them here in the course of two days, and to be behind the Tagus in two or three more. They have likewise pushed a strong corps across the Hircar River upon their right, to Yriesta. General Freire, who is in advance, considers these movements as indicative of serious intentions. Upon this subject I am not competent to form an opinion. The secret lies in Soult's breast. The French are enterprising, they have a great though perhaps hazardous game to play, and it remains to be seen what election they will make of the various plans in their power to adopt. If they determine to fight us, I am inclined to believe they will recover Madrid, from my suspicion that Lord W. will not hazard so important an operation in any hands but his own, and the question at issue is the practicability of his Lordship being able to join this Corps d'Armée (being still at Burgos) before the Enemy can compel an action or retreat on our part. I should feel more confidence was the great presiding soul present to direct our energies for I do not relish the idea of seeing the Capital again in the hands of its Enemies, *which may be a consequence of his absence.* . . .

I have received an order to march tomorrow morning to Ocaña, 5½ leagues from hence to the rear, and if the Enemy continues his advance I shall probably cross the Tagus on the 20th or 21st Inst., as I think it would be a most unmilitary proceeding to attempt any stand with such a defile in our rear. There we shall pull up and wait further developments.

An officer of the 13th Dragoons returning this day to England I have entrusted to his care the watch you sent me last year. It has received two severe falls which have so deranged its mechanism that it becomes useless. I therefore wish it to be sent back to the maker, Barwise, with orders to put it to rights, or if this is impossible, to make another, and in either case to have it forwarded by the first opportunity which offers.

Leon quitted me yesterday by his own desire. I found it impossible to spare Ifland, and he could not bear a rival near the throne. I am sorry for it, but there was no remedy, and I fear his absence will put Ifland again upon his stilts and give me much trouble.

I am concerned to say our sickness is very great particularly in officers. I lost a fine stout Captain of the Hussars the other day, another is in a deplorable state, the Surgeon is dying (if not dead) and the Major gone also to the rear. Several of the British are in a similar state, and I understand are dropping very fast in the rear, many of them being compelled to sell their clothes to purchase wine prescribed for them, such is our lamentable state of poverty.

One of the finest and most promising young soldiers in the Army, Lt. Col. Cocks[1] (Lord Somers's eldest son) has been killed at Burgos, and this event is considered, generally, as a *national* loss. General Hope is likewise dead. Thus promotion and affliction go hand in hand. Sad time for the mothers!

I send you two coins found near this place and presented to me by my host, Don Vincente Ramirez Arellano; one is decidedly Roman, and the other Moorish, both in good preservation, and I hope they may prove worthy of admission in young Carolus' museum.

I understand everything was left in good order at the Palace of Madrid, and they are now busily employed in transporting the most precious of the effects to Cadiz. It is confidently said that not less than 30,000 families left that town with their French friends—so much for the highly applauded spirit and patriotism of the Madrigalejans.

My next communication (if I shall find time to write one) may perhaps be of a more interesting description, for in seven days I should think Soult's intentions will more or less be discovered.

In Retreat

TO C. B. LONG

Garcia Hermandez, 1½ *leagues in front of Alba de Tormes*

9 Nov., 1812

I know not either the date of my last communication or the place whence it was written. Suffice it to say that we have had no mail to England since, and even had this not been the case, our daily and constant marches with a lingering Rearguard would have prevented me from writing, and henceforth, indeed, until we take up winter quarters

---

[1] After Cocks's funeral Wellington said: "If Cocks had lived, which was a moral impossibility since he exposed himself too much to risks, he would have been one of the greatest generals we ever had."

or some settled position, you must not expect any regular intercourse....

The sum total of our recent operations has been to fail of success in taking the Castle of Burgos, and to have abandoned the Capital and all Castille as far as the Tormes. What is next to be done is more than I can say. If the Enemy determines on the recovery of Salamanca, and getting us back behind the Coa, Lord W. must either give them their wishes or fight for it, and I believe no-one knows which of the two he will prefer.

The result of the Campaign, hitherto, has certainly been most brilliant, the prominent advantage being the raising of the siege of Cadiz, the temporary (perhaps) liberation of the Andalusias, and the taking possession of the Capital, and all the magazines there established. That we have not been able to maintain our vantage ground is to be lamented, both for ourselves and the Country.

Our retreat generally speaking has not been very regular. The Inhabitants abandoned their homes, in consequence of which the men got at the wine, intoxicated themselves, and could not be brought on. Our loss in this manner will I conjecture turn out to be some hundreds. The amazing scarcity of wood for fuel has opened the door to a still more lamentable species of irregularity, namely the pulling down of houses for fuel. All this, with the pillaging, sacking, etc., has made our line of retreat as Vandalic as any Frenchified Spaniards could wish, and it has distressed me not a little to witness it. The poor natives have indeed abundant reason to be heartily sick of both friends and foes.

I passed through Madrid just to take a flying view of its attractions, and what I did see pleased me much. The streets are large and regular, the Prado (public walk with gardens, etc.) unique and magnificent, the fountains beautiful, and the Royal Palace the only building of the kind I have seen in Europe, deserving of the name. It is magnificent and in a fine commanding situation.

I arrived too late at the Escorial to see much of its beauties, but all I did see was a delightful situation near the mountains for a summer residence, and offering every advantage for field sports. The Palace itself is like a large Convent, and has nothing striking in its appearance but its size.

The pass of the Guadarrama mountains is magnificent—quite an Alpine scene!

The whole of this part of Castille is an open plain, thickly studded with villages, and well cultivated. The difficulty of subsisting an Army in it appears incomprehensible, for every house I see is filled with abundance of straw and all species of grain. The French cannot be expected to starve here, and they will make a very bad use of their innumerable Cavalry, which of itself is enough to command the resources of the Country. I wish we were likely to be as well off.

The Tormes is a respectable looking River, but being fordable in various places is no great line of defence. The ground on the left bank, however, is very strong and commanding. Lord W. being now at home in his geography must be expected to make the most of it. I fear his forces have been sadly diminished by the operations against Burgos, and general sickness. I should estimate the Lord's force at more than 50,000 men, the Enemy's from 60 to 70,000. This will give them a great advantage in manoeuvring, but the difference appears to me of little consequence if it comes to a general action. . . .

The remounts for my Brigade, with James, etc., were within two days march of us, but were ordered back on our retiring from the Tagus, and I have heard no more of them. I hope they will not wander into the Enemy's clutches.

My Brigade is nearly unfit for the field. The 9th and 13th Dragoons scarcely muster 400 swords, the men are naked and starving with cold, the horses upon their last legs. Nevertheless we appear to be preferred for harassing services, and in a short time more we shall cease to exist as a Brigade. Slade's Brigade destroyed near 50 horses in one day from inability to proceed. The Northern Cavalry has I am told suffered equally, and if so our force in this arm will not be very formidable. The Spanish contest is an exhausting one for both parties, and the fate of the country will not be decided by either. Alexander and Bonaparte will have the ultimate disposal of it, either for Joseph or its lawful sovereign, and I should think its destinies will be accomplished in the course of another year.

After the Retreat

TO C. B. LONG

Serradilla del Arroyo,
4 leagues S.E. of Ciudad Rodrigo
22nd Nov., 1812

Three words to say I am very well, notwithstanding some trying work in our retreat, from the extreme inclemency of the weather. I have not time at this moment to detail our operations, or to offer the reflexions that arise from them. Suffice it to say that the British United Army has been *reconducted* behind the Agueda, with a very serious loss of men and horses owing to want and fatigue and indeed in many instances to intoxication. It partly reminded me of Sir Jno. Moore's Gallician retreat. The weather has been dreadfully severe and continues so. Our second in command, Sir Edward Paget,[1] is in the Enemy's hands, with abundance of our baggage, etc. I suspect General Hill's Corps will shortly move again to the south. I am at this moment in the midst of the mountains of the Sierra de Francia—a pleasant Cavalry Cantonment!

Refer to my former letters to see if I have been too diffident in my opinion of the powers of the British Army to rescue this country!

More Details of the Retreat

TO C. B. LONG

Serradilla del Arroyo

27 Nov., 1812

The task I am about to undertake is a most painful one, but the gratification of your wishes rises superior to my personal feelings, and I proceed to a narration of our recent operations.

It appears evident to me from a variety of circumstances that Lord W.'s plans for the termination of this Campaign have failed, and this failure is due to two causes; first the ill-success of our operations against Burgos arising out of the inadequate means with which that expedition was undertaken and secondly the disobedience of Lord W.'s orders on the part of General Ballesteros, whose Army was not placed in the situation directed, and which was calculated to throw impediments in the way of the Enemy's intention of proceeding direct from Murcia upon Madrid.

It was universally expected that Soult's advance would have been resisted on the banks of the Jarama River, and the Capital covered. The ground was favorable, and our force apparently adequate. In a letter I wrote to you from Corral de Almaguer I mentioned my conviction that unless the Lord could be present himself, no battle would be fought south of Madrid. Such has proved the case, and the consequence has been the unresisted union of the whole French Army upon the Douro.

The next plan appears to have been the defence of Salamanca and the line of the Tormes, grounded probably upon the assumption that the Enemy would not cross the Tormes and risk a general action, or if he did that we were equal to the task of defeating him.

The Enemy passed the Tormes on the morning of the 14th Inst.

---

[1] Sir Edward Paget (1775–1849) was appointed second-in-command to Wellington in October 1811. He had been away from the Peninsula for three years, since he lost an arm at the Passage of the Douro, in 1809. His nominal command was the 1st Division, in succession to Thomas Graham, who had been invalided home on November 17, 1812. Paget, riding alone with his Spanish servant between two retreating brigades, was taken prisoner by a small French patrol. Years later Paget was to conduct operations in the First Burmese War of 1824–25.

opposite my picquets. I reported rapidly and regularly their proceedings and the immediate consequence was our evacuation of Alba de Tormes and the destruction of the bridge. The Enemy continued to extend himself to the left round our right and absolutely cut in upon our supplies. Had the Army been put in motion at this moment to attack that portion of the Enemy that had passed the river, their defeat was inevitable. But it was too late in the day when his Lordship came to the front to where I was posted. He saw their Cavalry within half musket shot, in spite of my reports and assurances that any of their Infantry had crossed the River, and having sent the Prince of Orange forward to reconnoitre, he was confirmed in this belief by the Prince's assurance that no Infantry was to be seen, and he did not believe that any had passed the Tormes.

Scarcely had his Lordship quitted us a quarter of an hour when a considerable column of Infantry debauched from the wood and formed an extensive line. It was then becoming late and at 6 o'clock we retired to the position of the Arapiles in expectation of a battle next morning. Soult acted more wisely. Having passed his Army over he extended away towards Tamanes and Ciudad Rodrigo, and by threatening the point of our retreat and supplies compelled us to decamp, which we did on the evening of the 15 inst. in presence of the whole French Army. This movement was beautiful and most ably executed. Unfortunately on the morning of this day the weather set in most severely. Torrents of rain rendering the country nearly impassable I was directed to make the rear guard, the flank of the column being covered by General Anson.[1] They threatened a great deal but could execute nothing. We lost only a few horses by an unavailing cannonade. We reached a bivouac at 11 o'clock at night, knee deep in water, drenched to the skin, and neither man nor horse had anything to eat. This wood was filled with pigs. Hunger breaks through stone walls, and away went everyone with his firearms to forage for himself. Such was the fire when I took up my ground, that I really expected to have lost half my Brigade. Every effort of mine to stop it was unavailing. I found I risked my own life fruitlessly and gave it up. They shot one of my mules through the body close to my bivouac, and I believe from 30 to 40 men paid with their lives the forfeit of such irregularity.

The next day the Army retired to a Position between Matilla and Villalba de los Llanos. In the Evening the Enemy's Cavalry came up with us, and after a short skirmish took post at Matilla. The next morning the Army retired behind a small river near St. Munoz. During the day the Enemy made an immense number of Prisoners

[1] Major-General George Anson commanded a brigade (11th, 12th, and 16th Light Dragoons) in the 1st Cavalry Division. He was recalled in 1813 to the home staff.

(stragglers) took a great quantity of baggage, and Sir Edward Paget. They made a rapid march, Cavalry, Infantry and Artillery, upon St. Munoz, reached it before the Troops had passed the river at some fords, and cannonaded us handsomely, continuing to do so all the evening until dusk. I lost some men and horses through their fire, but it was trifling. The weather continued bitterly severe, the ground almost impassable, and the men and horses perishing from fatigue and famine. I was directed again to make the rearguard that night and the following morning. The Columns were again in motion before daybreak; some got off, some missed their way, and the woods and roads were filled with stragglers, dead, dying and dished.

The Enemy crossed, pushed me back to Cabrilla smartly with the loss of one man and three horses, but the ground afterwards favoring me I made a stand with my rear-guard, to get off all the stragglers that could move, and then retired, by order, upon St. Espiritu, where we had another wet bivouac with nothing but leaves to give the horses. The next morning the whole army reached the environs of Rodrigo, the Enemy desisting from his pursuit.

The whole arrangements for this retreat have astonished me. Through a wooded and difficult country there has been no combination of arms. The Cavalry in insulated columns marching without Infantry through ground they could not act upon; the Infantry without Cavalry through ground where the assistance of the latter arm was indispensable; men sinking every instant under famine and fatigue and many from intoxication, where the opportunity offered; the Cavalry constantly on duty, with nothing to give to the horses for sustenance but leaves; the Enemy revelling in our losses! Such is the picture of our retreat from the Tormes.

What has been and will be the extent of our loss in men and horses I know not, but comprising everything in the retreat of the Northern Army from Burgos and of the Southern Army from the Tagus, I am certain 5,000 men will not replace the casualties. Since we left Alba de Tormes my Brigade is minus 80 horses, and 5 or 6 is still the daily average loss. They have not had a pound of grain of any kind each per diem for the last 14 days, and with all this work and fatigue have only had leaves, or a scanty bite of sour grass to support nature. Of course they are dished, and as we are kept still here *starving in the same degree*, I do not expect, in a few days more, to have a single horse that can march 10 miles. All my representations have been useless and unattended to. I have therefore washed my hands of the certain consequences, viz. the extinction of the Brigade. It, alone, has done the Cavalry duty of the Southern Army throughout the last year, and on coming to the North, have still been honored and selected for the rear-guard and advanced posts. All very well, but destruction is inevitable, and I expect to be abused *because nature* can do no more! The truth is that the Arm (Cavalry) is not understood here, or if it is, not at all considered, or its preservation attended to.

Lord W., I am told, thinks he got out of the Burgos scrape very successfully. It may be so, but the termination of the Campaign will woefully disappoint the sanguine expectations of his Lordship's friends. We are given to understand that he purposes taking the field again in a couple of months. I *doubt* it. This will depend upon the Enemy and not himself. If they divide, without receiving strong reinforcements, the old game may come again into play. But if they continue in a situation for combined operations, his Lordship, I think, will be brought to a standstill. But all the French require to checkmate us is a respectable Army of the Centre to be stationed on the Tagus, and with this they might safely re-occupy Andalusia, and resume their former ground. To take at all into calculation the exertions of the Spaniards themselves is a voluntary delusion. They have done nothing, they can do nothing, and they will do nothing. . . .

I have received your letters of the 4th, 11th, and 18th and 25th Oct., though in situations where I could with difficulty peruse and enjoy their contents. Mind and body have suffered not a little for the last month, but we hope an approaching cessation from hostilities will enable us to forget the past and provide again for the future.

James accompanied the Remounts as far as Talavera de la Regna, but as they could not join us they have retrograded to Elvas, and I am glad of it. I must have a furlough for the purpose of refitting and re-equipping and shall go to Lisbon. Things will hardly go on here above another year; that I will see out if I live, and then retire altogether from this scene of trouble and wretchedness, leaving to the younger ones the opportunity for a similar experience.

My Brigade has, since the 12th May last, marched 350 leagues. Add to this their incessant duties at the advanced posts, foraging, etc., and you have a pretty good proof of their activity during this period. Our loss in horses up to this day, since we quitted Alba de Tormes, is little short of 100, absolutely dead from starvation and fatigue.

I am concerned to say that the conduct of the Troops throughout this retreat has been most *vandalic*. The Enemy could not have behaved worse, or have done more mischief to the poor inhabitants and their dwellings. It will have its effects upon the minds of the Spaniards, and will be justified in seeking a retribution of the evils sustained.

I hope a short time will restore our intercourse to its accustomed regularity, but at present my mind is in as unsatisfactory a state as the condition of the Army—both terribly disordered!

Further Reflections on the Retreat
TO C. B. LONG
Monte Hermosa, between Coria and Placentia
6 Dec., 1812

... In the State in which this Army is at present, it would be very much the interest of the Enemy to keep us in movement, to give us no rest, and allow of no relaxation and refreshment, and if our Cavalry was obliged to take the field again immediately, it would be completely ruined in two months. For my own Brigade, they are perfectly unfit at present for any service—completely starved and exhausted. Our loss within the last month is 150 horses, and those that remain can scarcely carry their riders. The 9th Dragoons are gone off to Cabeca de Vide and Frontiera, and I am here with about 180 of the 13th Dragoons only. I do not think 1,000 horses will cover the casualties of the Cavalry during the recent retreat. Lord W. is very angry, and justly so, with the conduct of the Army. In a circular letter addressed to the General Officers[1] he says,

> The discipline of every Army after a long and active Campaign becomes in some degree relaxed, and requires the utmost attention of General and other officers to bring it back to the state in which it ought to be for service; but I am concerned to have to observe that the Army under my Command has fallen off in this respect in the late Campaign to a greater degree than any Army with which I have ever served, or of which I have read. Yet this Army has met with no disaster; it has suffered no privations, which but trifling attention on the part of the officers could not have prevented, and for which there existed no reason whatever in the nature of service. Nor has it suffered any hardships excepting those resulting from the necessity of being exposed to the inclemencies of the weather at a moment when they were most severe. It must be obvious however to every officer that from the moment the Troops commenced their retreat from the neighbourhood of Burgos on the one hand and from Madrid on the other, the officers lost all command over their men. Irregularities and outrages of all descriptions were committed with impunity, and losses have been sustained which ought never to have occurred. I have no hesitation in attributing these evils to the habitual inattention of the officers of the Regiments to their duty.

The greater part of this is correct, but not the whole. The Troops certainly in many instances did suffer considerable privations, without a possibility of remedy on their part, and when a man has been march-

[1] Dated November 28, 1812, at Freneda.

ing three days without food, fording incessantly rivers, and exposed besides day and night to the inclemencies of very severe weather, sickness and lassitude must ensue, and if means are not provided to assist those who sink under them forward they must be lost. Had I been furnished with a proportion of spare mules for this purpose, I could have saved hundreds of men. But when I see them dead and dying in numbers on the road, I am to presume there must have been a cause for it, and that notwithstanding short marches, halts, etc., the men had to sustain an effect or trial that in many instances human nature was not equal to. I likewise know that there was great derangement in the commissariat for which no Regimental officer could be responsible. But it is likewise evident that subordination was, from various causes, most dreadfuly relaxed, and no examples were made to put a stop to it. And in truth plunder and devastation is a *regular system* with a *portion* of the Portuguese Troops (as they would represent) from *necessity*, and the defect of their Commissariat. The Spaniards are worse than the Portuguese, and between both incessant examples of irregularity are presented to the eye of the British Soldiers, who love marauding as much as the Troops of any other nation. To cure the evil, subordination must be *general*, and punishment equally so. Above all, accusations must not be partial, because they become unjust, and in this case reprehension fails of its effect. A great deal of mischief arises also from the absurd mystery and secrecy observed upon occasions which produce considerable embarrassment to Executive officers, without a corresponding advantage to the service. To ask where you are to go? to halt? is high treason; consequently your ignorance upon these subjects prevents your taking such steps as might anticipate embarrassments of various descriptions. If General Officers are not entitled to some degree of confidence, they are, and must be, ciphers in the Army. The difficulties I have experienced from the above cause, in arranging the concerns of my Brigade are not to be told, and have occasioned indeed all my embarrassments. Reserve in office is most commendable and necessary, but an undistinguished and fastidious affectation of secrecy upon matters of no moment, is not less prejudicial. In addition to the above remarks I have only to observe that it has always appeared to me a very dangerous and unpolitic indulgence the having permitted the Troops that stormed Badajoz and Rodrigo to pillage and sack these Towns after carrying them. If a soldier is ever allowed to escape from the authority of his officers and to revel in robbery and murder at his leisure, the seeds for a plentiful harvest of mischief have been sown, and his taste for irregularity once imbibed is not easily restrained or subdued. A sum of money given to the Troops in lieu of liberty to plunder would have been more consonant with discipline, and more humane and generous towards the Allies, who on the above occasions suffered as much in person and property and outrage as the bitterest hostility could have inflicted.

I never saw anything more cautious than the French proceedings against us since we quitted the Tagus. When they arrived at Alba de Tormes, they made a great press, displayed their columns of attack, brought up 20 pieces of artillery, established them in batteries, and appeared determined to swallow up, at a gulp, the whole Town and Howard's Brigade which defended it. After firing away for 5 hours without opposition, back went their Artillery, back their columns. Their courage was evaporated, and they declined with all humility a collision with British bayonets. I really could not help laughing at the pantomime! Had Lord W. opposed their passage of the Tormes, or attacked them when it was partially executed, he would have added another emblem to the glories of Salamanca, and as the rains set in the day afterwards they could not have crossed at all without making a good march for it. I have regretted this point more than any other. Their joy at our departure from Arapiles, without fighting, could not be disguised. Such a chattering and noise I never heard in my life, and no effort was made even to come in contact with our rear-guard, though the opportunity was most favorable. The Lion stared him in the face with silent contempt, and that was sufficient. I never saw a cleaner or more beautiful retreat than that from the Arapiles, and I think the French Army itself must have admired it, though the day was unfavorable for such a military spectacle. It was most creditable to Lord W.'s military talents—a soldier's feast!

You wish to know the strength of the different Spanish Corps serving with us? To the best of my belief they are as follows:—

Castaños' Gallicians —	10,000 infantry.	
Ellio's Murcians —	6,000 ,,	2,000 Cavalry.
Don Carlos' Castilians	4,000 ,,	
Murillo's Estremadurans	2,500 ,,	500 and Count Penne.

Of these some of the Gallicians are good-looking and well equipped troops, Ellio's miserably bad and not to be depended upon, Don Carlos' a ragged crew, Murillo's thought to be the best before the Enemy. Their Cavalry are afraid to come in contact with their opponents, therefore cannot be depended upon. The whole want stricter discipline and organisation and better equipments. They have no commissariat but thrive and live as they can upon the poor inhabitants, who dread their appearance more than that of the French.

What with our sickness and recent losses, the Anglo-Portuguese

Army is I understand at a woefully low ebb. The British sick alone I heard estimated at 18,000, but do not answer for the truth of it. Our Cavalry can barely amount to 4,000. The mortality of the horses in this country is incredible.

I condole with you on your kennel and stable losses. Draw your purse-strings and such matters are easily set to rights. Tell Mrs. Dickson[1] I never had so useful a servant as the steel pen she presented me with. You are indebted to it for all I have hitherto said or sung. I mean this as a delicate hint for another supply.

I have only space left to offer the usual Xmas benedictions and good wishes. Distribute them to all our belongings and friends.

[1] A relative and friend, being the daughter of Sir Henry Moore, Bart., who died in 1812, leaving Robert Long £1000. Lady Moore was Edward Long's sister and Robert's aunt.

XII

The Prospect for 1813

LONG returned to the old haunts round Portalegre, where he had first met his cavalry command. There, in December 1812, he entertained Wellington, en route for Cadiz, in his rough and ready quarters, and stuffed his commander's skin full of new wine. After this flutter of excitement he occupied himself once more with speculation on the outcome of the war and on divisional matters. It is noticeable that Long had a very shrewd and immediate conception of the importance of Napoleon's Russian disasters in 1812, and that he was by this time a complete convert to admiration of Wellington as a general. Now he could see a real chance of finishing the Peninsular War successfully.

Among his cantonment gossip—accounts of new uniforms and dull days spent inspecting his regiments—Long devoted much space in his letters to forecasting possible changes in the cavalry commands in the British Army. It was as well for his peace of mind that he knew nothing of the highly confidential correspondence which Wellington was conducting at the same time with the Duke of York on this very topic; among the names of those whom Wellington wished out of his army in Spain was that of Long, for whom a staff post at home was suggested. Oman states that Wellington petitioned for the recall of five out of his seven cavalry generals, and of ten infantry divisional and brigade commanders. In Long's case the matter was held over, and he was to spend the greater part of another campaign in action.

There can be little doubt that Long's vigorous criticism of his superiors in his letters was one powerful reason for Wellington's attitude; and Beresford's influence was ever present and always hostile to Long.

By the end of March a fairly accurate rumour of what was proposed had reached Long. But he was an odd soldier in many ways. Though keen on the efficiency of his commands and assiduous in applying himself to his work, at heart the bloody business of slaughter sickened him. He was scrupulous in protecting his subordinates, yet highly critical of his superior officers. In action he was, like most generals, capable of either great success or great failure. He felt exposed to attack from England because of his Whig views, and likely to be affected through the promotion over his head of officers who possessed political or family influence. He was therefore particularly alert to notice neglect or slights.

On April 3 Long received news from his brother of a heavy personal blow: his father had died on March 13. Thus Long started the campaign with his heart full of deep sorrow, the affection he felt for his father being great and sincere.

Soon after this event the reality behind the cavalry command rumours was shown when Major-General Slade was recalled to England just as the troops were assembling for a forward move.

On his friend's behalf Long was furious, though for his own part he stated that, after two years' continuous active service, leave from the Army would be very welcome.

Dinner with Lord Wellington

TO C. B. LONG

Portalegre
20 Dec., 1812

I am now about to depart for my old quarters, Cabeca de Vide, where I hope to be left unmolested for the next six weeks or two months.

Lord W. dined with me the other day on his way to Cadiz, and his fare was but little better than what I had the honor to give to Royalty some years back at Radipole Camp,[1] with the exception that the bread, though indifferent, was positively not mouldy. I stuffed his skin full of *new* wine, and if he did not feel the effects of it within a few hours it was not my fault. I flattered myself that I had *worked* his Lordship more than ever Soult did, although the latter sent him backwards oftener than we were pleased to see.

I know nothing of the Enemy nor do I care much about him at this moment, having other things to think of. I only hope they are as quietly disposed as ourselves, and in this case we shall be good friends for the winter.

The gun is arrived at Lisbon, but Lisbon for difficulty of communication is as far off as London. I shall send Dean there in a few days to collect packages and complete my equipments. I expect to meet James and his cavalry this day, not the worse I hope for his long marches.

Lord W. told me there was good news from Russia and that Alexander had made spirited reply to an attempt of Napoleon to negociate a peace or armistice. If so all will do well, or at least it promises favourably.

The weather has been very wet and severe through our march; indeed, there has been more rain within a month past than I recollect to have seen throughout the whole time I have been in the country. The last vintage has been most abundant, more so than for three years past. Everything in Portugal is on the footing of peace, towns embellished, enriched, and commerce thriving. Would that Spain

[1] Near Weymouth; Long was there with the York Hussars and the 15th Light Dragoons.

were the same, for I prefer Spaniards and their country to all the Portugals in the world.

Tell Mrs. C. I am certainly very fond of potatoes but if her Xmas Turkey was alongside of them I should not fare the worse for it. However a fat pig to be bought this day and killed tomorrow must make up for all deficiencies.

Thoughts on Peace and the Future

TO C. B. LONG

Cabeca de Vide

Jan. 5, 1813

Since my dispatch of last week I have received your letters of the 7 and 14 ult., with papers up to the 15th ult., tho' others, two days later, have been received at Lisbon which bring the glorious tidings of the surrender of two French Corps d'Armées, viz. those of Ney and Davoust.[1] To be sure I would sooner see Platow's Daughter married upon the terms he offered, than have the whole French Army prisoners in Siberia, but he, the snake, will not be easily taken, and unless he is, the sting that has tormented Europe for so many years will still live to poison its future happiness and prosperity. The disgrace and disaster he has experienced will only render him keener for revenge, and augment his reasons for renewed hostility. But on the other hand it is not to be denied that this Campaign will have gone far towards rendering the Russian Army and nation invincible, and shaking almost to its foundations the confidence and spirit of the French soldiers, and even of their officers. The Cossacks' screech will sting their ears for years to come. The war will appear to them in its true character, that of a united nation full of patriotism and courage supporting an Army equal to their own.

I confess, turned topsy turvy as the Continent is, divided by interests and opinion, and distracted by mutual bad faith, I cannot *think* even of the nature of those terms upon which a Peace is to be made or expected. As long as Napoleon lives, the idea of entering upon a discussion of this sort appears to me impracticable. I *can* conceive that the French nation and army, worn out by this struggle, which appears identified in duration with Napoleon's life, and seeing his ambition the obstacle to peace, might discover some method of reducing him to reason or ruin. But mind me I would not make the Bourbon Dynasty for one moment an object of this war. Let them fight away with their goose quills as long as they like. The "Monster" was cradled in War,

---

[1] Louis-Nicolas Davout, Duc d'Auerstädt and Prince d'Eckmühl (1770–1823), Marshal of France.

and in War must he be wrapped up in his shroud. Such a man, and such a mind, *cannot* go to the grave in peace. I only wish the Cossacks would run him to earth, and "finish the day" handsomely.

With respect to our more immediate concerns I know of no alternation on either side since my last. Lord W. is reported to have returned from Cadiz, but I vouch not for the fact. The knowledge of these Russian successes has induced the report that of Soult having made some overtures to his Lordship; but I believe not a word of it. Napoleon will hold the Pyrenees to the last hour of the struggle, of this you may be assured. . . .

Whilst you are blowing the tips of your fingers for cold, I am now writing with every window open, enjoying a beautiful sun, and a climate as temperate as what you experience in September or October. I have not forgotten however the last *summer* nor am I quite reconciled to the idea of broiling thro' another. When your miseries are over ours will be on the eve of recommencing.

Our new clothing has arrived and I must say that never were troops more completely denationalised in appearance. At any tolerable distance it will be impossible to distinguish them from the French, and if the Spanish Peasantry continue to do their duty as heretofore, several of our brave fellows may have to lament the day which banished all outward distinction between Allies and enemies. It is a sad and vicious taste applied most unseasonably. I understand the Life Guards are sickening very fast, and resignations pouring in. They will not last out a campaign, so they might as well have remained where they were. The Blues, fresher from the plough, fare better. Your promised brigade of Hussars will scarcely do more than replace our recent losses, but we shall be happy to see anything like British Cavalry, particularly the finest we possess. But we want a large lot of them if any good is to be expected. Mere driblets will not settle the dispute and our Enemy is terribly strong in this Arm—no looking at them at all!

French Military Reports
TO C. B. LONG
Cabeca de Vide

10 *Jan.*, 1813

Yesterday's post brought me your letter of the 20th ult. Never was anything more beautifully regular than our mail, nor was motto ever more correct than "une lettre adoucit les peines de l'absence." The packet however to which we look with peculiar anxiety is the one destined to convey to us the expected Brevet of 1813, and the winding up of the Russian Campaign. In the former I am not at all interested, upon the latter point I am all anxiety. Scourged and torn to pieces as Europe is by this everlasting and barbarous war, can you wonder at the enthusiastic joy manifested at events which to the sanguine afford a *prospect* of relief from accumulated sufferings?

I see by the papers that King Joe[1] is become a great warrior, and intended "cutting us in two" at Salamanca, and of course taking the better half of the Army to himself. It is a pity his Generals threw cold water upon his great designs, and compelled him to remain satisfied with the shaving of a rear-guard or tail of a column. The result however has proved that he did wisely in listening to the "old ones," and in postponing his bisecting operations to a more favorable opportunity. Like his brother, however, he lies like a Prince of the true Corsican breed, and conjures up fogs and mists at his pleasure, for the purposes of stage effect. There was no fog at the Arapiles that prevented *our* seeing pretty clearly what *he* was about though it prevented *his* taking advantage of our unskilfulness. I believe he never was happier in his life than when his eyesight improved sufficiently to convince him that the great disturber of his slumber was fairly off, and did not intend to dispute the Arapiles a second time. The chattering and noise of his followers betrayed very clearly a similar feeling.

Your Sussex news is very satisfactory. Pater stout, and the Maidens "walked," or galloped off to the Hymeneal rest are subjects of congratulation. Women have a right to turn their talents and charms to the best account, and when their campaigners are successful, like other great Generals, they should be applauded for their skill. Their triumphs, as far as the world is concerned, are too harmless to provoke any spirit but that of hatred or envy. I like to see the dear devils matched against bloated boobies, and the latter fairly vanquished. I believe however that they are often indebted for their success to one of King Joe's "fogs," that prevents their antagonist from clearly distinguishing what they are about, and thus they turn his flank, and finally cut off the possibility of a retreat.

I was quite pleased to see the Duke of Norfolk had taken up the situation of poor Le Marchant's family, and had proposed some questions relative to a provision for them. This does the honor to his heart, and raises a monument more glorious to his fame, than any of his boroughs or his castles will produce. I expect young Le Marchant to join me tomorrow, but as he is only an *extra* Aide de Camp with me, and I have been offered a more permanent situation for him with another General Officer, it is probable his stay here will be of short duration.

I hear no news of any kind in this part of the world. The great Lord

---

[1] Joseph Bonaparte.

is I believe still a wanderer. Report has sent him to Lisbon, and places him this day at Niza, between this and the Tagus. If true he is on his return to Frenada. You will hear sooner and more largely of his proceedings than we shall.

Will you have the goodness to direct Egerton,[1] at the Military Library, Whitehall, to send me regularly the *Monthly* Army List, beginning with the present year; and when you discharge my bills do not forget the newspaper accounts.

Thoughts on Future Campaigning Prospects
TO C. B. LONG
Cabeca de Vide
31 Jan., 1813

... The weather is at this moment colder than I have experienced for a year past, owing to the prevalence of strong easterly winds. Vegetation is retarded, consequently if Lord W. takes the field very early, he will soon destroy his Cavalry, for they absolutely must exist upon such grain alone as they can transport with them, and if at all removed from our magazines, the supplies are most precarious. In addition to which they will have had less time to recover from their recent fatigues and starvation. It does not appear that we are to expect reinforcements of this Arm from England, unless perhaps the Brunswick Corps from Ireland. I therefore cannot estimate our British swords above 4000 or 4500, and if this be the case, the Enemy possessing nearly triple that force, and in a Cavalry Country, will circumscribe us confoundedly and soon worry us off our legs. It is a Spanish axiom that whoever commands in Cavalry, will command in Castille. If there be any truth in this opinion, and we apply it to ourselves, the consequence is evident. At all events we want Valencia, and must have it, before anything of importance can be accomplished.

John Ellis[2] starts on Tuesday next for Elvas, Badajoz and Merida. I have lent him a horse for this excursion. He is then to return to Cabeca de Vide, and proceed to the North. He is an amiable and sensible young man, and I am much pleased at having made his acquaintance.

Lord W. has returned to Frenada and an order has just been issued to prepare 12 days forage, corn and provisions in store. This looks like a march, but should it take place I prognosticate that it will not extend beyond the Tormes if pursued in that direction. If Soult's

---

[1] T. Egerton was the proprietor of a publishing house called the Military Library.
[2] The son of one of Long's first cousins. He was an ensign in the 61st Foot (now the 2nd Battalion, the Gloucestershire Regiment).

Army makes an offensive movement, we shall probably have to counteract him. I know not how the rest of the Cavalry is, but we are still in a most deplorable state and I look for no amendment until there is a decided change of weather. Several of our horses will never recover again, and many will not be fit for service these three months to come. We shall be cruelly abused, but suffering nature will have her own way, and I know no remedy against it. Napoleon is in a similar embarrassment, or he would not have lost, by his own confession, 30,000 horses in a few weeks. But there is no standing against fatigue, starvation, and bivouacking in bad weather. Nature sinks under the effort. Glanders and the mange get possession of the system, and they are not easily eradicated.

The American War

TO C. B. LONG

Cabeca de Vide

25 Jan., 1813

... Joseph has inserted in the Madrid Gazette his brother's arrival at Paris, having quitted Russia on account of the snow putting an end to all further operations. He will not gull the Spaniards quite so easily! I hardly know what to make of these Russian despatches. I thought from former accounts that Davoust's and Ney's Corps had been *exterminated*. The more recent intelligence however merely states the former to have been defeated and *dispersed* and the latter appears still at the head of troops fighting obstinately at different points. The want of a map creates sad confusion in one's ideas, and prevents a just comprehension of the true state of things.

I think Napoleon should have seen his poor devils safe back to Wilna, at least, before he left them; but I take for granted he thought his presence at Paris of greater consequence than with his Army. He seems, from the manner in which he sneaked back to his kennel, to have felt at least all the horrors of his fallen state, and the number of Troops assembled there pretty clearly demonstrates the fears of his Government during his absence. But they are humbugged from the first to the last; from the Conservative Senate to the poor conscripts. We shall soon see a decree requiring the oath of allegiance to his *Dynasty*, and this will be followed by a fresh demand of *victories*. The *system* is identified with his *existence*, and both will reign and fall together.

The worst of my fortunes is before me, and produces not a sigh or feeling of regret. If the present Campaign does not provide for me altogether, I see very clearly that I shall have through life the rank of a General Officer to support my vanity, and the pay of a Lt. Colonel to keep soul and body together, and my mind being made up upon this subject, no human being, thank God, can disturb it. Of course, it is most gratifying to possess the means of assisting others, but where this cannot be done, others must work out their own independence in the best way they can. A Family united in feeling, and affection, can never want friends. If it does, "there's something rotten in the state of Denmark," and let them look to it! Therefore without envying any mortal his superiority in this world, whether in rank, power or affluence, I look to the next for reducing all things to their proper level, and feel that life is much too short and too uncertain to make it worth one's while to be vexed about anything; though from the trouble taken by many people to hunt after *anxieties*, I am inclined to think they are essential to the happiness of certain dispositions. Not being one of "Ambition's, Honour's fools"[1] so liberally immortalised by Lord Byron, I look to peace, tranquillity and conscience for an ample reward for past annoyances.

Sir Stapleton Cotton is now in England, but expected back again. The truth is, the old Cavalry Generals, like their native oaks, bid defiance to age and weather, and will not die off. They bend but they will not break. One concession more on their part would give Sir Stapleton a Regiment. This obtained, he will retire, look out for another wife, and the rest of his Campaigns will be confined to her Boudoir and St. Stephen's Chapel, though I do not believe the gallant General is much of an orator. In this case Sir Wm. Erskine would become the Senior Cavalry General, but as he is as blind as a beetle I fear he would lead us into many a ditch.

These American naval triumphs[2] are mortifying to the pride of our Tars, but are they not a just retribution for the insolence with which the former have been treated? Those who exalt themselves shall be abased—id est the Navy! Those who humble themselves shall be exalted—id est the Army! To me there is something consoling in reflecting that those who can alone punish us are of the same flesh and blood. A father delights in the vigor and valour of his offspring. Great Britain should be proud of hers, even though they *have* rebelled against her. They are *naughty*, indeed, very *naughty*! The old eagles rejoice to see the young ones imitating their bold flights, and we, if we were just, should respect and not despise the power that dares to grapple with us, overgrown boobies as we are!

Captain Dean is gone to Lisbon in search of means and money for

---

[1] *Childe Harold*, Canto I, stanza 42.
[2] On October 18, 1812, the American sloop *Wasp* reduced the British sloop *Frolic* to a hulk in ten minutes; on October 25 the *United States* captured the *Macedonian*; and on December 29 the British frigate *Java* was captured by the *Constitution*.

the approaching Campaign. I hope the things you last sent may arrive whilst he is there.

Lord W. is returned to Frenada, and therefore ready to start when the time comes. He must not go very fast, or I shall never get up with him. We are still miserably meagre!

Consolations from a Brother
TO C. B. LONG

Cabeca de Vide

8 Feb., 1813

Since my last I have had (I may for the first time say) the pain of receiving your two letters of the 10th and 18th ult. . . .

. . . I honestly confess that I have strong doubts if it will be a mercy in Providence to spare Mrs. Charles's life. Her fits are evidently epileptic, and these I know from experience, though for years not endangering life, may be its frightful companions to a degree that would impose it as a wish and duty upon affection to pray for their termination. I assure you, my dear C., I dread, for your sake, *this* alternative more than the one I am prepared to receive, and which, tho' agonising to you, would be really charity to the poor sufferer. Your calling in Lane was a judicious step, and will be a consolation hereafter; but where Providence has decreed, the prescriptions and hopes of the wisest may fail, and for this you should be prepared.[1]

I have by this mail recd. a letter from Eliza and a note from Pater, the latter apparently written under a state of debility, but whether of the eyes or nerves, I know not, but am willing to hope the former. God only knows if we are destined to meet again, but if we survive this year, I have reason to expect it, as I am determined to follow the step of the *favorites*, and without forgetting my duty to my Country, perform some of those I owe to my friends. With this determination I shall enter upon the struggle of 1813, equally resolved to acquit myself to the best of my own judgment, and to reward myself afterwards by following the dictates of my feelings towards others. When or where this struggle is to commence I am still unable to say, but I believe the Army is far from being in a state to undertake it. Some of the Hussars have arrived at Lisbon, but the Cavalry before in the country are only in a state of convalescence, and any premature exertions would soon disable them for the field. The Lord will make his own calculations and act accordingly. His eyes are fixed perhaps upon a Dukedom, and he will do all in his power to realise the possession of it. This news of the defection of the Prussians is the pleasantest I have

[1] Mrs C. B. Long died on June 9, 1813, and is buried at East Barnet.

read. It will shake the confidence of France in that power, and be productive of jealousies and measures that will facilitate, admirably, our operations. If once the flame of discontent reaches the Elbe it will not be long in traversing Germany to the Rhine, and this would establish, to my mind a firmer hope of ultimate deliverance, than any steps the Rulers of the Earth may be pleased to take in the prosecution of this contest. The French are perfectly aware how much their power is upheld by their alliances, and they dread the defection of the latter more than the loss of their own Armies. I look to Silesia for the first burst and example of German spirit and indignation, and if it breaks out there it will not take much time in spreading throughout the Prussian States, and even in inoculating the Kings of Saxony and Bohemia, its neighbours. If prudently managed it will lead to a great good; otherwise much evil may be the consequence, for Rulers in general dislike the popular effervescences, tho' directed to their best interests. They fear them, therefore they should direct the storm instead of following it, and this, I hope they will do. Whether these events will lead to peace or increased and prolonged hostility time must shew; but in either case France must be expected to assume the most formidable attitude in her power, for her interests are equally concerned. If the present breeze rises to a gale of wind upon the Frontier, even the chimnies of Paris may shake with the blast; but if it subsides in languor and inactivity, the ship may soon be righted, and re-equipped, and put to sea again in as gallant trim as ever. Her stores are immense, her artificers numberless, and we must calculate accordingly. . . .

We are still annoyed by a ferocious banditti infesting this neighbourhood. They murdered two days ago a Purveyor of the Hospital at Alter de Chao, whilst out shooting, within 2 miles of this place. Two of them, afterwards, proceeding to a small village near here (Alten pedroso) entered a house to rob it, but whilst engaged in doing so, the owner, an old man, returned and perceiving what they were about knocked them both on the head and killed them, tho' furnished with fire arms. The dread of some retaliation has put all the villages on the qui vive and the inhabitants now mount regular guards for their security.

Greenwood has sent me my abstracts up to Sept. last, and I do not perceive any drafts of yours for payment for the nags. You must oblige me by calling upon him to liquidate this debt. The *Brute* is not so much so as I expected, and tho' I *could* part with him, I have now doubts of doing so. He trips and starts a good deal but is otherwise a pleasant hack. My other horses are getting into beautiful condition and have all gone thro' regular course of physic. I thank you for your offer of Tancred, but he would be of no use to me. A hard-mouthed horse is always bad for military purposes. If not very unfortunate indeed I hope to get thro' the ensuing campaign very well with what I have.

The Spaniards and their British Ally
TO C. B. LONG

Cabeca de Vide
15 Feb., 1813

On my return yesterday from visiting the Cantonments of the Brigade I had the pleasure to receive your letter of the 25th ult., with papers up to the 26th; I am happy to find that your mind is more relieved with respect to Mrs Charles's safety, but I fear you will, for a long time have to lament the consequences of her indisposition which is, unfortunately, not one of an ordinary kind, but subject more or less to relapses of an alarming nature. There is no remedy but patience and resignation. Whatever the supreme will may be, must be assented to. . . .

I am not growing rich, my Dear Carolus, as you suppose, nor will such legacies as you allude to make me so. I am satisfied to be less poor than I have hitherto been, because any state of amelioration enables me to be more useful to my friends than I otherwise could be. I thank God I am so little ambitious of wealth in this world as I am of stars, ribbands and crosses. The infatuation that assumes to itself an ideal superiority over others because folly and indiscrimination have given it a token of undeserved respect is to me a subject of compassion, not of envy.

The 15th and 18th Dragoons have landed at Lisbon, and I am well pleased to hear that my old friends are esteemed to be the best equipped and best mounted corps that has ever been seen in this country. I have sufficiently the interests of the service at heart to regret that I was not permitted to fulfil my former intentions respecting them by making them a living and recorded proof of the practicability and ease with which our system in the Cavalry could be improved. Every day's experience but confirms my conviction that half our strength is lost under the present and former management. But as I cannot make the blind see, why, let them grope their way as they can, and thank God if they escape the ditch. . . .

You have had a sad time of it, my dear C., this winter, but let us hope the next will be better. With a good house over your head, and a good library to resort to, time ought never to hang heavy on your hands. I at least think so, who am daily appreciating the blessings of *rest*.

I heard from Eliza, that is, she sent me the whole history of the

Sussex Novel, and ended with a pretty compliment to make me *quite* satisfied. In return I sent her back a Philippic against her own sex, calling them hyenas, etc. Such is the gratitude of mankind!

Changes in Command forecast

TO C. B. LONG

Cabeca de Vide
22nd Feb., 1813

My budget this week must be very scanty, for no mail has arrived since my last, nor have I heard one syllable of domestic or foreign news. I observe no symptoms, as yet, of concentration for the purpose of renewed operations, but the arrival at Lisbon of the 10, 15, and 18 Dragoons indicate at least determined appearances. Reports both from England and our Headquarters induce the supposition that it is in contemplation to draft the horses of 2 or 3 weak Regts. now here, and send them home to recruit, and among them the 9th and 13th Drs. are both mentioned. I think the plan would be very judicious, and therefore not unlikely. I have not heard who is to command the Hussar Brigade, but General Jones' name is mentioned, and if so he is a fortunate fellow, for it will be nearly the best Brigade in the Army and certainly the strongest. I suspect besides that some changes of a higher class are in contemplation. I hear Charles Stewart is returning to us with the rank of Lt. General and as we have recently lost poor Sir William Erskine by illness, one great obstacle in General Stewart's way to the Command in Chief of the Cavalry is removed, and I confess I expect to see him sooner or later in that situation. By Sir William's death General Slade succeeds to the command of this Division of the Cavalry, and if he remains they cannot dispense with dubbing him a Lt. General also. Thus it is an evil wind that blows good to no one. Sir Wm's Brother, now Sir James Erskine, will step into a brilliant income of perhaps not less than 9 or £10,000 per annum. However he will never be the man his unfortunate Brother was, whether the head or heart be consulted. These abominable fevers are worse than the sword, and they have not been idle since we returned to Winter Quarters. Besides Sir Wm. they have deprived us of two excellent Infantry officers of rank—Colonels Stewart and Wilson.

John Ellis and young Le Marchant quitted me this morning for the North. The former has been very successful in his field sports, I hope the latter may prove equally so in his present situation. They are two as fine young men as I have seen, and being both destined to the same place, will be agreeable compagnons de voyage.

Well, Carolus, where are the Russians and is it to be peace, or war ad internicinum?

> Who think that fortune cannot change her mind,
> Prepare a dreadful jest for all mankind.[1]

I am most anxious to see how the fickle Goddess will conduct herself, whether she will take the side of humanity and spare mankind, or by mixing her favors, increase the number of victims. I am fearful altho'

> Thoughts speculative their unsure hopes relate
> The certain issue blows must arbitrate.[2]

Well! be it so, until Providence has fulfilled the measure of its chastisement, and taught the world to respect its laws as well as their own, if they look for peace or happiness. The work of destruction cannot last for ever, and I trust the peace which will, sooner or later, take place, may compensate by its extended duration the long protracted afflictions of this barbarous war. . . .

We are so poor that the Staff pay is now six months in arrear and it *ought* to be one month in advance. Not a penny have I got from them since the 24th August last, and if the evil increases, I know not how we shall get one. At present we are obliged to borrow in every direction to keep the thing going. If this year does not settle the business I cannot conceive whence funds can be derived to carry on thro' another, for the debt even for transport is enormous, and we have not yet learned the secret to make war support war, as the French do.

I am most anxious to receive another bulletin from you to know the state of your poor patient. My fears about her are greater than my hopes.

My soul rejoiceth in the hope of seeing the sword once more sheathed, and if it should, I trust my career will be finished before it shall again be drawn in anger. Sat vixi Bello, and all its horrible accompaniments.

Before the Campaign Opens

TO C. B. LONG

Cabeca de Vide
1st March, 1813

. . . I pine, my dear C, for another bulletin from you, to resolve my doubt and fears about your Sposa. This is our post day and I hope before night to be relieved from this state of suspense.

[1] Adapted from Pope, Satire II, lines 123–124.
[2] Adapted from *Macbeth*, Act V, Scene 4.

Our weather is now beautifully fine. The thermometer at 60° in the shade, but the sun is becoming almost unpleasantly powerful, an earnest of his future favors. The Portuguese expect that this is a very abundant year for corn, as the last was for wine. Cultivation in order to meet our wants is daily increasing and of course the farmers grow rich. Let us keep the Enemy away from the soil, and the war will to them be the mines of Peru. The Americans have still a brisk trade with the Tagus, but this does not secure to us eatable bread. They keep the flour in store till it becomes perfectly musty, and then it is issued, and by the time it is consumed the fresh imports that replaced it are as bad as the other. Our meat too this year is considerably deteriorated, neither veal nor beef, but something between the two, and very insipid. These with adulterated wine or spirits keep bone and body together, but that is all! A good apprenticeship, however, for future times if we live to see them. . . .

Future Possibilities

TO C. B. LONG

Cabeca de Vide

8 March, 1813

Another post day, and still no accounts from England. Four mails are now due, and unless some of these have fallen into the hands of French or American privateers, the delay with the weather we have had, is quite unaccountable. Patience is indeed a virtue, and we want a good stock of it at this moment.

General Slade has been with me to inspect the Brigade, and I find from his account that we are in as good condition as any of our neighbours. Still however I have not 300 horses fit for immediate service. By the General Orders just issued, it appears that Lord W. is going to change his system and provide the Infantry with tents. Reports had apprised us of his determination not to suffer the Army to occupy Villages as heretofore, and as a Punster I immediately concluded that the ensuing Campaign would be the bloodiest we have ever had, since it was decided that the British Army would receive no quarter. This would appear to indicate a Campaign of positions and sieges, rather than of manoeuvre. Be the intention what it may the piece *ought* to open with a grand Bataille, the result of which must decide the subsequent operations.

It is announced that Soult has marched in the direction of Cuenca. If true it is to cover La Mancha, and at the same time lend an assisting hand for the defence of Valencia. They have been unusually severe in their contributions, and are determined to make a Desert of the

Country. I hear our supply of cattle for the Army is very inadequate, but whether arising from a actual scarcity or the want of money to make purchases, I know not, but salt provisions are now issued in several instances to the troops. We must make an irruption into Castille and carry on a marauding war.

I find Sir S. Cotton has wound up his good fortune by getting the Colonelcy of the 11 Lt. Dragns. In this case the door is nearly open for Charles Stewart's assuming the chief command of the Cavalry. Slade is the only impediment, but a very small bribe will settle his opposition. I therefore expect to see this arrangement carried into effect.

9th March

... I have not had time to see the papers and therefore have no data to reason upon at present. But if the *Russians* are not, at this very moment, on the banks of the Elbe, matters have not proceeded as they ought to have done, to ensure great and brilliant results. If Russia, assisted by other powers, does not settle the state of Germany (that is, recover its state of independence) this year, it will never be accomplished, and France once again in a military attitude will from experience, learn where her arms can best be carried. In fact she ought not to have broken with the Muscovites until her Spanish contest was brought to an issue, and half the Army marched to Moscow would have brought the question at issue here to a speedy conclusion. But in fact I am almost sick of reasoning upon any subject where Princes and their satellites are concerned. I look upon what is going forward as the work of Providence for some wise purpose, and it must take its course till that purpose is obtained by means and in a manner that no human mind can anticipate.

> Who knows but he whose hand the lightnings form
> Who heaves old Ocean and who wings the storm,
> Pours fierce ambition in a Caesar's mind,
> And sends young Ammon forth to scourge mankind?[1]

I have no doubt but this is the case and therefore

> Whether old age with faint but cheerful ray
> Attends to gild the evening of my day,
> Or Death's black wing already be displayed
> To wrap me in the universal shade.

Firmly relying upon the goodness and wisdom of an over-ruling power, I say amen, and let wickedness and folly take what course they

[1] Pope, *An Essay on Man*, Epistle 1, lines 157-160.

may, the career of both is pre-determined, and we shall finally be saved in spite of ourselves.

My mind is decidedly made up as the point, if I survive this year's contest, of dividing my affection between my Country and my Friends, and if my commission cannot be held upon those terms, I will make the bigwigs a present of it.

I am quite satisfied with the favorable report you make of your poor Invalid, and sincerely trust your anxieties upon the subject may be respited for years to come.

Brotherly Advice

TO HIS BROTHER EDWARD BECKFORD LONG

Cabeca de Vide

14 *March*, 1813

I have received your letter of the 13th ult. and must really accuse you of making mountains of mole-hills. Having passed the Rubicon of life myself, what greater happiness can I feel than in lending a helping hand to foster, strengthen and bring forward the young plants that are to be our pride and comfort in our last days? And why are my relatives to be excluded from a benefit which I should be ready to extend, if necessary, to strangers? I am perfectly clear that I shall have nothing to bequeath at my death, therefore my object is to do for my friends as much as I can whilst I live. I trouble myself not about the hereafter I know pretty well my wants, and how little will be necessary to satisfy them. Therefore without more ado upon the subject, I shall only say that what I offered remains at your service whenever you may feel disposed to send for it.

We are still in statu quo, altho' I hear some movements are taking place among the Troops in the North. Still I cannot believe that we shall enter the arena before next month, from the difficulty of feeding the Cavalry which at the moment is in very sorry condition. Lord W. has now a very different game to play from what he had before. The Enemy is no longer in a divided state, but all their means, physical as well as mental, are concentrated and will act from one impulse. They are laying waste the country to their utmost power, thus preparing for the worst, and you may be assured that the line between the Ebro and France will be defended to the last man. The success of the Northern war depends entirely upon the course that Austria may pursue. If she suffers herself to be *bribed* out of her senses (which is more than probable) Napoleon will redeem his losses and keep Germany in chains. The fate of Spain depends in my opinion upon that of Germany; the latter rescued from French dominion, will oblige

Napoleon to terms, and these will insure the independance of other states, but *Spain will never re-conquer itself.* It must be the work of other hands, the result of other operations. . . .

After a series of hot days equal to your July we are now all shivering with a bitter North-eastern wind that pierces to the bone. A turn of the weathercock and we shall boil again. All you have to prepare for is a screwing from Mr. Vansittart[1] to make up for last year's deficiency. How you are to get on, I know not, but as we must go on till we die, so must you, I suppose, persevere till you starve. Tell our dear Pater I intend to be with him, Deo volente, before Xmas next, and a shake of the hand will be a receipt in full for past privations.

Thoughts in Billets on Politics and the Army
TO C. B. LONG

Cabeca de Vide
14 *March,* 1813

Since my last I have yours of the 15th ultimo, but one mail (that from the 27th Jan. to 2nd Feb.) is still missing, and must, I now suppose, have experienced some mishap. Gorged as you have been with my speculations you now require some domestic accounts as you call them. What domestic concerns have I to dwell upon? Here I am with an Aide de Camp and Brigade Major, leading daily the same insipid life of rising, breakfasting, dining and then going to bed; the only variation what duty produces. The whole of this winter has been passed without any out-of-door recreations. Having lost all my dogs in Spain, I have had no materials for following up field sports, consequently, I have confined myself a good deal to the house, and have endeavoured to make the most of a perfect state of tranquillity and inaction. I am now in daily expectation of being called from my shell, and when we begin to move, shall probably be furnished with more interesting matter for communication.

Nothing has yet been settled about the Cavalry, consequently my Brigade, which report sends home, is in a state of suspense. I shrewdly suspect some great changes are in contemplation, for altho' Slade has naturally succeeded to the Command of this Division of the Cavalry, his appointment has not been confirmed in General Orders, which *looks very suspicious*! I care not one farthing what may be determined upon, nor indeed if they send *me* home with the other useless lumber. Lord G. Lennox, of the 9th Dragoons, received a letter from his

---
[1] Nicholas Vansittart (1766–1851), later Lord Bexley, was Chancellor of the Exchequer from 1812 to 1823.

R

brother[1] (who is A.D.C to Lord W.) begging to know his intentions in the event of his Regiment returning to England. This shows how the report has gained credence even at Head Quarters. I calculate that Lord W. will bring into the field this year about 5,300 British swords, which is rather an augmentation of this species of his force, but still not what it ought to be, to give him complete sovereignty in Castille. I should not think his Infantry, British or Portuguese, will exceed 65,000. I should estimate the Enemy's Armies which may be united against us (exclusive of Suchet's force) at about 90,000 including 10,000 Cavalry and a formidable Artillery.... Napoleon is making great exertions both in the Cabinet and the field, but I trust Kutusoff[2] will get the spring out of him and if he reaches the Elbe affairs will wear a promising aspect. The thing Napoleon could do (if practicable) would be to assist the Yankees against us, and threaten Canada seriously, and send Murat back to Italy to renew his menaces against Sicily, but he appears to have his Family Squabbles as well as our Regent, with this difference, that he can settle them soon and more to his own satisfaction perhaps. Jerome,[3] however must, I think, be in a little bit of a stew, and be calculating the chances of a "flank movement" from Cassel. The most politic thing Napoleon could do would be to collect the whole swarm in the hive and let them live upon the honey of France, contenting himself with security at home and peace abroad. If he can get his anointed whelp acknowledged as his legitimate successor, he will have done enough for France, himself, and his friends.

> Shall he, alone, whom rational we call
> Be pleased with nothing if not blessed with all?[4]

I should like to put this question to his imperial reason, tho' I suppose he would spit some impertinent answer in my face. But, however, he is not the only being in the world who is irrational, and before we abuse him we should correct ourselves a little nearer home, for Tyranny and Injustice are the same, whether exercised against a Wife or a Royal Cousin. Man I believe is a Tyrant by nature, but only acknowledging it, when feeling himself, instead of inflicting the sting. The despotism we ourselves exercise is all correct and proper, that we must submit to it, an infamous and outrageous imposition. So goes the world and so it will go on.

---

[1] Charles Gordon-Lennox (1791–1860) was assistant military secretary to Wellington from 1810 to 1814. He later succeeded as Duke of Richmond.
[2] Michael Koutousoff (1745–1813) was commander of the Russian armies.
[3] Jérôme Bonaparte (1784–1860), brother of Napoleon and Joseph, was King of Westphalia from 1807 to 1813.
[4] Pope, *An Essay on Man*, Epistle I, lines 187–188.

> The whole subsists by elemental strife
> And passions are the elements of life![1]

Therefore let our nails grow, and let us enjoy the delicious task of scratching and tearing each other to pieces. Between religion and politics, we shall find abundant fuel for keeping up the flame of civil discord, and a bonfire at the Bank will close the illumination. To this affairs at home seem to be rapidly approaching, tho' I know you are of a different opinion. For one, I feel satisfied to let things take their course, and what the Doctor cannot mend, must mend itself or die. In this philosophical mood I quit the subject.

The Park House arrangements are excellent and I am glad to see the old Hotel in Charles St. re-occupied. All this looks well, and shews good housewifery. Settle your difficulties with Sir Walter, and everything will then be in its proper place.

Addenbrooke writes me word that he has fitted up Park Corner (Salter's house) ready for my reception, and prefers it altogether to his old dwelling.

When you excurse to Farnham give him a call, as my representative. I see Lord Rivers is one of those arraigned before the Weymouth Committee[2] for a misdemeanour. I suspect he did not interfere but that his agent thought proper to make use of his Lordship's name to forward his own purposes. I hope my Ducal friend will get a good set down, for there is not a Being in England who meddles more with the freedom of elections than he does. How is Vansittart to make up for this terrible deficiency of £2,500,000? You will, all of you, be screwed to death! Sad time for the middle classes.

The trunk that Windeler sent arrived at Lisbon on the 5th Inst. but has not yet reached me. I have heard nothing of the other things nor of the sword waist-belts that Messrs Hawkes were to have forwarded. We shall continue to work thro' this Campaign, and if I am alive at the end of it, I hope to have the opportunity of equipping myself personally in England for a fourth trial, tho' I confess I have had enough of War and all that belongs to it, and seeing as I do, 28 Candidates above me in the Army Lists for vacant Regiments, and therefore no prospect whatever of any ultimate recompense for my labours or services, one sickens at sacrifices that promise no return. I think it is a crying injustice in the British Service that no provision is

---

[1] Adapted from Pope, *An Essay on Man*, Epistle I, lines 165-170.
[2] Complaints of corruption at the recent Weymouth election had led to a committee of inquiry in the House of Commons. It was found that the Duke of Cumberland had delayed the election in order to give the Tory Party more time to prepare for the contest, and offers of Government posts had been made in exchange for support to the Tory candidates.

made for an officer (that is, increase of pay) beyond the rank which his own money can purchase, so that unless we continue in actual employment (where the wages are pretty dearly earned) we are compelled, whatever be our rank, or length of service, to remain satisfied with the pay of Lt. Colonel to the end of our days, and this too (whether abroad or at home) chargeable with the property tax. Is this equitable, and more particularly so when you recollect that Regiments are conferred more thro' Parliamentary interest than consideration of services, so that I venture to predict that young Fitz Clarence, who entered the Army only the other day, will be Colonel of a Regiment of Cavalry long before I shall, let me live till doomsday. This is a terrible defect in our system, and as long as the purchase and sale of Commissions is permitted, the remedy will be very difficult if not impossible; that is, unless they should, at the same time, increase the number of years' service that each officer should perform in all the other gradations of rank so as to make them fairly earn (what could afterwards in several instances be the case) a sinecure for the rest of their lives. For example, if every officer was compelled to serve 5 years as Subaltern, 5 as Captain, 5 as Field Officer of Regiment, 5 as Colonel, it is evident he would have passed 20 years in the Service before he could attain the rank and increased pay of Major General, and I think he would then have earned it. If employed upon actual service, then let his pay be doubled for the time he is so employed. Such a regulation would be just, economical, and would entail very little additional expense to the Country. At present the Private Soldier is too well paid, and the officer very inadequately. And observe their inconsistency: After the unfortunate Campaign of 1808 medals were distributed (in a most injudicious manner) to officers for doing nothing. Since that, most glorious operations have been achieved, and not a token of Honor conferred. So that the famous Colonel Leigh (the Prince's Leigh) has for the only two *months* Campaign he ever made in his life, receives a reward which places him in the eyes of his Country above me (and 1000 others) who have been three times that number of *years* on foreign service! Is this sense or justice? This reminds me of the truth of Pindar's[1] remark:

> Gods! let a spent or rambling ball
> Touch but a Prince's hat or coat
>   Expanded are the hundred mouths of fame.
> Whilst braver thousands but untitled wretches
> Swept by the sword, shall fall like paltry vetches,
>   Their fate unpitied, and unheard their name!

[1] John Wolcot (1738–1819), a physician who wrote satirical verse under the name Peter Pindar.

And not a friend in Parliament to plead our cause! Why? because they have sufficient employment in providing for themselves! Aye! there's the rub!

Cavalry Arrangements in the Next Campaign
TO C. B. LONG

Cabeca de Vide
22 *March* 1813

Since my last I have been favored with your letter of the 22 and 28th ult. I have likewise recd. one from Edward dated 1st March. I trust your next will remove every particle of anxiety felt for the patients both at Park House and Langley.

I have heard no news in this part of the world except the elevation of Lord W. to a Portuguese dukedom, and Beresford to be a Marquis. The first Duque de la Vittoria, the latter Marquis de *Campo Mayor*. If is unfortunate that no *other* spot in Portugal could vouch for the Marshal's merits, the mention of which would not have recalled unpleasant recollections.

At length the Cavalry arrangements are developing. The 9 and 11 Dragns. and 4 Dragoon Guards are to have their horses drafted, and then to return to England. Nothing further is said or known, but in a letter I have recd. from Slade he transmits the following information or rather speculation:—

> Erskine, Slade and Long are the General Officers said to be relieved by Stewart, Fane and another whose name I cannot recollect, that the toil and fatigue of another Spanish Campaign should not be suffered by one Party only, but others to have their share of difficulties, privation and risk.

I know not where he got this history, or whether it be intended as a hoax, but I see nothing improbable in it, and therefore as a possible measure it may be in contemplation. The death of poor Sir Wm. has made an opening of which I have all along expected to see Stewart avail himself. To accomplish this Slade must go home, and as Fane is certainly coming out, I look to his getting the 2nd Division of Cavalry. I believe Lord W. wishes very much to give a Brigade to Lord E. Somerset,[1] and perhaps some other noble favorite is to be provided for. Therefore everything that stands in the way of these family arrangements must be disposed of, or rather, dispossessed of their situations.

For one I am perfectly indifferent upon the subject. Unambitious

[1] Lord Edward Somerset (1776-1842) served throughout the Peninsular War, and led a cavalry brigade at Waterloo.

as I am of Honors of any description, and abhorring the sacrifices by which glory, as it is called, is purchased, I shall willingly leave the field to those who take more pleasure in its sports. I consider that

> Honor and shame from no condition rise
> Act well your part—there all the Honor lies.[1]

This I have endeavoured to do to the best of my ability, and with a very quiet conscience I shall withdraw from the stage, the moment it is required of me so to do, but which I apprehend will *not* take place so soon as Slade's informant deposeth. I suspect both Stewart and Fane must by this time have reached Lisbon, and if so a very short time will put all these matters to rest. The latter seeing the red ribbon[2] flying about in all directions is of course anxious to be a candidate for such a favor, and he will succeed.

I see by the General Orders that every Regt. is directed to recruit 50 young boys. So we are come to the farthings at last, and well we may when guineas are not longer forth coming. This arrangement is to meet, I suppose, sooner or later the baby King of Rome's levies and holds forth a prospect of war being terminated ultimately, by a battle between the cradles. . . .

I have been repeatedly dunned by the Hatter, Bicknell (bottom of Bond St.) for the payment of his bill, £9 19s. 6d. I wish you would put an end to his correspondence by discharging it.

An idea has long occurred to me that in consideration of the dischargeless obligations we all owe to Lane for his kind attentions to our Pater, we should acknowledge them by some corresponding token of gratitude, by presenting him with a piece of plate to be purchased by subscription among all the members of the family including even the grandchildren. I consent to be put down for £50. . . .

Send me no more groceries. I have everything I want. Leon left his trunk here. I have forwarded it to Howard's address in Town by Captain Holmes of the 13th Light Dragoons. If you can find him out, acquaint him of this circumstance. . . .

Rumours of a French Withdrawal

TO C. B. LONG

Cabeca de Vide
12 *April*, 1813

A mail arrived on Saturday last the 10th inst. but brought neither letters nor papers for me. I therefore have not heard from you since

---

[1] Pope, *An Essay on Man*, Epistle IV, lines 193-194.
[2] The Order of the Bath.

the receipt of your fatal letter of the 14th ult. which has made the world appear almost a blank to me,[1] and unfitted my mind for pleasure or business of any kind. It is my good fortune, however, to enjoy that kind of seclusion at this moment, which is gratifying to my feelings, and as far as I can judge from appearances this state of tranquillity is not likely to be interrupted for some time to come.... The final Cavalry arrangements have not yet been made public, but I rather expect to get the 14th or 18th Dragoons in lieu of the 9th Dragoons, dismounted and sent back to England. The 11th Dragoons and 4th Dragoon Guards have shared the same fate, so that Cummings will have the pleasure of returning to his wife and family. The departure of the 9th Dragoons afforded me the opportunity of adding another very clever horse to my stud, and he is sufficiently promising to make me desirous of seeing him in your stable. The two you last sent will, in consequence, be disposed of the first opportunity.

I must beg you to draw a draft upon Greenwood for me for £10 and transmit it to be divided equally between the two Harrovians on the speech day in June next, to procure them a duck and green peas dinner, and a bumper of wine to their future prosperity. I hope the abominable Latin grammar will not spoil Robin's good humour and sweet disposition. If they stand *that*, they will last him through life.

The reports from the North say that Lord W. is much in want of meat, money, and transport, and that they are giving three shillings a pound for very bad pork.

We have been issuing *salt* meat three times a week, but I thought the measure was adopted to save the live bullocks for the field. The Guards (Howard's Brigade) have been, and still are, dreadfully sickly. They buried 630 men in three months, and had 900 more in Hospital. Quite a West Indian mortality![2] A long duration of cold easterly winds had very much retarded vegetation, but a most seasonable fall of rain the other day has dissipated the fears of the Portuguese for the ensuing crop, and they are now quite delirious with joy.

I see Providence continues to punish the arrogant both by land and water! It is all right; Englishmen, like others, should be taught moderation and humility.

---

[1] Edward Long, father of Robert Long and Charles, had died at Park House on March 13.
[2] We usually kept between 15,000 and 20,000 troops in the West Indian sugar islands, where 9 per cent. sick was a favourable proportion in the 'healthy' season. The French are thought to have lost 60,000 men through sickness in their San Domingo expedition of 1803.

Preparations for the New Campaign
TO C. B. LONG
Cabeca de Vide
18 *April*, 1813

... It does now appear that a severe contest took place in England between Generals Stewart and Cotton for the chief command of the Cavalry here, and which originated the idea of Slade's being ordered home, which must have taken place had Charles Stewart succeeded. The latter is now going to Berlin upon some diplomatic mission. It is generally reported that the Campaign is to open the beginning of next month. The Magazines are established, and a large battering train is now on its march from Abrantes to the North. The Cavalry arrangements will not be settled till Cotton's arrival. Feeling as I do very doubtful about the success of any operations this Army can undertake, my only prayer is that Providence will shew its mercy upon the poor wives and mothers, and spare as much as possible, the victims of this never ceasing war. Human nature sickens at the sacrifices already made, and at those in prospective. If the world is not to return to a state of barbarism it is high time these horrors should have an end.

The trunk sent by Windeler has reached me and the other things are also arrived at Lisbon. My wants are therefore completed, but a distressed heart and mind are bad appendages in the field. For your sakes, however, and my Country, I will endeavour to do my best, but chance after all, must give effect to this determination.

First Orders to move
TO C. B. LONG
Cabeca de Vide
23 *Ap.*, 1813

I have this morning received the order to march to Alcantara, and shall move, accordingly, on Wednesday next the 28th inst arriving there on the 3rd May. The whole Army appears to be concentrating, and of course the Campaign will open shortly. The result is beyond my powers of calculation, because I have no data for my guidance, but everything considered I cannot bring myself to believe that Lord W. will *ever* be able to liberate the Pyrenean Frontier, and we shall suffer bitterly in the attempt. I agree fully with you in the belief that far from approximating towards Peace, we are on the eve of a more bloody and extended struggle than has hitherto existed. When I see Saxony and Denmark standing aloof, and observe the undiminished confidence of the Imperial Robber (for he is nothing better) I suspect the Cabinet of Austria to be rotten at the heart, and that she meditates submission rather than resistance to Napoleon's will. If so the blood of thousands will call for vengeance on her head, and sooner or later their orisons may be heard. In the meantime the revolutionary and patriotic spirit should be let loose throughout the North of Germany, in order to produce events that must divide the heart of Germany and France. I am only apprehensive that Napoleon's rapidity will anticipate the speculations of Alexander, and stifle the means of salvation in their birth. . . .

I have now received everything I expected from England, including the sword-waist-belts, but the latter being more calculated for a Levie than a Campaign would be returned if I had the opportunity.

If General Fane cannot take upon his establishment a Lt. Webster (Lady Holland's son)[1] of the 9th Dragns., I mean to apply to Lord W. to appoint him an extra A.D.C. upon my staff, young Le Marchant being now provided with a permanent situation under General Wm. Stewart. Webster has made over to me one of two Chabraques, furnished him by Whippy, your Sadler. I wish to discharge this debt either by your enquiring of Whippy the price of each Chabraque and letting me know, or else by desiring Whippy to place it to my account instead of Lt. Webster's and when paid taking his special receipt for the latter's satisfaction and security.

James Lynch I am certain cannot stand the Campaign; therefore as soon as my stud can be reduced, I shall probably send him back to England, and on my return there (please God) I must make some final arrangement about him.

I heard the other day from Edw. Dawkins (letter dated 11th April) and he appeared well and in spirits. He gave me not a scrap of news, but did not forget to request I would destroy the document, so he is fairly inoculated. He mentions the loss of two packets taken by the Americans, and has kindly sent me a box of cigars, which I should rather were in your possession.

The maps you sent are useless. If an opportunity offers send me one of Germany (thro' Col. Foster) and I think you will find 2 or 3 among my collection in the flat deal box [endorsed in pencil "sent"].

---

[1] He served as extra A.D.C. to Long from April to August 1813, being slightly wounded at Vittoria. He was also at Waterloo as extra A.D.C. to the Prince of Orange.

A "Dirty Job" gets Slade removed

TO C. B. LONG

St. Vincente
1 *May*, 1813

I shall take my chance of this going by the Spanish post from Alcantara, which place I shall reach the day after tomorrow. At length the mystery is explained, and Slade has received orders to return to England. The whole business is a dirty job, and by the enclosed copies of the letters he recd. upon the occasion, you will perceive that they are half ashamed of it themselves. The object in view is decidedly to give General Fane the command of the Cavalry serving with Sir R. Hill's Corps; this could not be done without Slade's removal, and the latter has been brought about in the way you see. It will naturally occur to you to ask why General Clinton, a junior officer and who only came out to the Peninsula last year, should have pretensions to the local rank of Lt. General, above a senior officer who has been serving here for four years. And you will smile at the idea of its being impossible to appoint another Lt. General to the Cavalry, when you are aware that had Sir Wm. Erskine lived he would have continued in the command of the second division. However, when a point is to be carried, *justice* is not much consulted, but it would be more dignified to state the true case at once, than be sneaking about for silly reasons to justify their measures. Slade, personally speaking, is I believe glad to get back again to his numerous family after an absence of 4 years; the only drawback to his satisfaction is the recent arrival of his son in this country whom he intended taking upon his own staff, but must now leave to his fate.

I recd. a letter from Fane stating his arrival at Lisbon and as we are all upon the move he has no time to lose in repairing to his post. If my supposition respecting it be correct I shall have the pleasure to see him very soon, and I am anxious to do so, from knowing that he dined at Howard's a few days before he left London, and I want to learn all he observed about my dearly beloveds. They tell me he is very violent in his authority, but I trust experience will make him cooler.

The 13 Dragns. are going to take the field about a fortnight too soon, and if worked hard at first will soon be reduced to two squadrons. Hitherto they have not been spared, and therefore I do not expect better luck with them this year. . . .

Membrio, 2 May

I have just recd. an order to continue my march from Alcantara by Zarza le Major and Moraleja and to occupy the villages of Cazilla, Casa de Don Gomez and Calcadillia, all in the neighbourhood of Coria; whence I suppose we shall be sent to the front towards Placentia or Bejar, unless it be the intention to collect the whole Army again on the Agueda. Be kind enough to tell Edward that I recd. his last pacquet, and am concerned to see his affairs in such bad trim. Whatever I can command will always be at his service and it is not unlikely that before the end of this Campaign fate may provide me, and ease him of the burden.

Slade is gone round by Frenada to pay his obeissance to the great Lord, so that I shall not see him again, but I have commissioned him for me to shake heartily by the hand every friend of mine whom he may fall in with in England.

James is again so ill with his old complaint that I suspect he will not be able to undertake the exertions of a campaign. If he does not improve as the warm weather increases I must send him back again. It is a hard case upon us both.

I have not yet received the sword belts from Hawkes, nor any intimation of their having been forwarded. Send him a dressing.

XIII

The Campaign of Vittoria, May–June 1813

LONG'S own command, after some regiments had been reorganized, some sent home, and the horses redistributed, consisted in his last campaign of the 13th Light Dragoons alone, a mere 320 strong, and a trifling charge for a man of full Major-General's rank, particularly as a new Hussar brigade had just arrived in Spain. Also in Spain, however, was Long's old supplanter in the 15th Light Dragoons, Colquhoun Grant, who had powerful friends both in the Court and in the field. Wellington, in fact, was openly anxious to find a big command for him.

In the meantime Long took his regiment out into battle, guarded the southern and eastern flank of Hill's division crossing the Ebro to the sound of "God save the King," and finally took part in the great overthrow of the French at Vittoria, on June 21. Here the 13th Light Dragoons distinguished themselves by dispersing the baggage guard and leading the onslaught on the plunder of King Joseph's wagon-train, laden with the riches of Spain, and of carriages bearing not only gold and wine, but many of the ladies who accompanied the French Army. In truth the French at Vittoria did not fight well; they were conscious of being outmanœuvred and caught in a state of dispersion, their retreat to France was threatened, and Wellington was in the majority. Their guns were abandoned, and the whole army dispersed.

Shades of the Future

TO C. B. LONG

Casa de Don Gomez
near Coria
10 *May*, 1813

... The arrangements for the Cavalry are not yet determined, but it is certain that Fane is coming to command all the forces of that description attached to General Hill's Corps. Lord W. I am told disclaims any participation in the act that recalled Slade, and the latter, having been at Frenada, only says "that he has been scandalously treated by the Horse Guards." So *there* he must fight the battle out, and I am much mistaken if terms of pacification are not tendered and accepted within an hour after his fire commences.

I shall be very happy to see young Bacon,[1] and still more so if it

[1] A member of some friends of the family who lived at Henley Park, Surrey. One of them, John Bacon, R.A., later received £226 from Robert Long for executing the monument to Addenbrooke in the church at Esher.

should ever be in my power to be of any service to him; but I feel the debility and nervousness arising out of the last year's trial increasing daily so much, that I doubt if my strength will carry me thro' this Campaign and am pretty confident that necessity must make it the last. I want a complete year's turn to grass, and unless I can obtain it, the turf will soon be over instead of under me.

You will perceive, I fear, that my mind continues in a gloomy state and so it must remain till death do us part, or the opportunity is afforded of embracing you again, my dearest C., and which, if God should permit, I shall do from the bottom of my heart. A few months more will determine the destiny that awaits me, and God grant me health, strength and patience to see them out!

PS. *Gazan* (Soult's successor) is considered as one of the best and most shrewd officers they have. He was chief of Soult's état major.

A Cavalry General is recalled Home

MAJOR-GENERAL J. SLADE TO MAJOR-GENERAL LONG

Lisbon

15*th May*, 1813

MY DEAR LONG,

I have received both your friendly letters, and if anything could increase the regard and affection I already have for you, it would be the sentiments you have expressed in these said epistles. It is impossible, my good friend, that I ever can forget your kindness and attention.

Since it is in your commands that I should wait upon Howard, I will do so, and shall have much pleasure in it; but as it is a long time since I have seen your sister, indeed, never from the time I was quartered at Arundel, I have a sort of mauvaise about me, which will prevent my doing so, except you write to prepare them for such a visit. It is not that my conscience (good a monitor as it always is) accuses me of having done anything wrong, but I candidly confess that I acted like a damned fool, when in that neighbourhood, and for which I ought to have been well flogged.[1]

I am sorry you do not approve of my visit to Frenada. Independent of the desire I had to thank Lord W. in person for the attention he has at all times shewn me, I was very anxious to learn the cause of my *recall* home; my visit was extremely satisfactory, as I learnt the whole particulars; the detail I cannot enter into, its beyond the limits of a letter, but I will give you the substance in as few words as possible;

---

[1] Slade was an old family and military friend of the Long family. It is not known exactly what sins he had committed at Arundel in the bygone years, but the fact that Slade could act foolishly was not news.

I hope some time or other to have an opportunity of talking with you on the subject, over a Bottle of the *real Porto* in the old House in the Close.

At the end of the last Campaign, Lord W. submitted to Ministers his intention of moving in future the Army in one body and for that reason he wished the Cavalry to be in *one* Division: that there were objections to the Cavalry being in two, among the number that there was in fact no Chief, Sir Stapleton Cotton only commanding a Division. His proposal was acceded to, and had Sir William Erskine lived he was to have had a Division of *Infantry*: and your humble servant remained as before, with his Brigade.

His Lordship never dreamt of General Clinton having the rank of *Lt.-General*, that the letter of the Military Secretary was as great a surprise to him as it could have been to me. That the command that General Clinton had, had been held before by *Major* Generals, and that his increase of rank would not give him an additional soldier. His Lordship said he understood I was to be on the British Staff from the period I ceased being on that of the Peninsula, which would be the 25th June. He was particularly kind about my son. Indeed, met every wish, and desire, I made respecting him.

This is all very well, my friend, but I have been used most shamefully, and sacrificed to the Houses of Newcastle and Londonderry. As they have thought proper to order me home, I shall claim six months leave of absence, in order to attend to my private affairs.

You will have heard of the arrival of the pacquet, with papers to the 28th. Sir Stapleton is not yet come.

I will write to you again before I sail.

Ever yours, my dear Friend,

J. S.

My young soldier is a fine lad, and I think you will be pleased with him.

The New Campaign opens
TO C. B. LONG

Guijo de Corial
16 *May*, 1813
Anniversary of the Battle of Albuera

In the hope that I may have an opportunity of forwarding this tomorrow, I write you a few lines to state that we are now marching to open the Campaign. We proceed tomorrow to Azgal, the next day to La Zarga and Abadia, on the 19th to Hervas and the 20th probably to Bejar in the neighbourhood of which place will be all this Corps, consisting (if they all meet) of above 20,000 men; but I am told one of the Portuguese Divisions of Infantry cannot move for want of supplies. That is whilst we are paying 2 millions per annum for the service of 60,000 Portuguese, we never get one half of the stipulated number, and of this half starvation is to make the most it can. I have reason to believe that a column under Lord Wellington is to move direct from Ciudad Rodrigo towards Salamanca, before which place we shall take post until the operations of a third column under Sir T. Graham,[1] which is moving through the North of Portugal to turn the Douro by Miranda, shall have dislodged the Enemy from Zamora and Toro, when we shall proceed direct upon the latter Town.

Lord W.'s preparations are certainly made upon a great scale so as to meet the most favorable circumstances that Fortune may be inclined to grant him. I daresay his views extend to the siege even of Vittoria. Considerable battering trains are collected at Coruña, exclusive (I hear) of 130 pieces of field artillery, heavy and light, that accompany the Army. His Cavalry appears to be the only deficient arm he has, and I am sorry for it, because it is one the effects of which will be felt every day, and it besides secures to *us* a *Herculean* labour. I greatly fear our transport is scarcely sufficient to ensure our maintenance, and if so we shall soon fall to pieces. If we move direct upon Salamanca, we shall exchange some blows with them, probably, about the 24 or 25 inst., and as the Tormes is scarcely fordable and the bridges of Salamanca, Ledesma and Alba de Tormes in their possession, I expect to see them assembled behind Salamanca in force to welcome our first meeting in the year '13. Their old friends will appear with new faces, and I expect some compliments for the deference we have shewn to French Taylors and French taste. . . .

I hear the Lord has so high an opinion of his own Army, that he holds them very cheap, but I suspect they will make some of our hearts ache before we shall be able to dislodge them from the strong ground behind the Ebro, and have possessed ourselves of Burgos, Pancorvo, Vittoria and Pamplona. The delay attending these sieges, if made in form and in regular progression will consume so much time that we must expect to see the Enemy strongly reinforced before we can become masters of them, and if this takes place, a general action

---

[1] Sir Thomas Graham, afterwards Lord Lynedoch of Balgowan (1748–1843), had played in the first Scottish cricket match, in 1785, been Whig M.P. for Perthshire from 1794 to 1807, taken part in the capture of Minorca, in 1798, been A.D.C. to Sir John Moore at Coruña, and commanded a brigade in the Walcheren Expedition. He was the chief founder of the Senior United Service Club, in 1815. Though one of Wellington's most brilliant lieutenants, Graham did not soldier until he was forty-five. It was primarily the grief at his wife's death on the Riviera, in 1792, and despairing fury at the insults paid by Jacobins to her coffin on her last journey home, that led Graham to volunteer for service during the siege of Toulon in the following year.

will settle the points at issue. I therefore look to a bloody campaign, and I only hope it may prove a proportionately glorious and successful one.

If affairs go on prosperously in Germany at the same time, why then we may look with hope and confidence to the only legitimate object of war, an honorable peace.

All we have to solicit from you is moderation in your expectations and not to under value the difficulties we shall have to surmount. Thousands of the brave fellows now marching with glee to the field will prove by never returning from it what those difficulties are. Therefore in estimating the work, look to the sacrifices and be satisfied.

... We must exert ourselves to make this a closing campaign if possible, and if providence gives us health to fight it out, I hope the Lord will get his Dukedom and we leave to return to our own Cottage hearths. Those who fall will have bled at least in the best of causes, those who survive will have the proud recollection of their services in it. To either alternative we must make up our minds.

Will you be good enough to let me know in your next what was the price you paid for each of the two horses you purchased for me?

The Advance begins

TO C. B. LONG

Herbas, near Banos
At the foot of the Sierra de Bejar

21st May, 1813

... All the country about here being at the foot of the mountains of Francia and Bejar resembles Switzerland. The prettiest position I have seen is La Grenadilla, an old Moorish Town, with one of the handsomest castles and bridges I have beheld in Spain. The view from it is most romantic and interesting, extending to the Rena de Francia and the Sierra de Bejar, the latter covered with snow. ...

With respect to ourselves it seems to be the general belief that we shall not have much to do on the south bank of the Douro, and even that little resistance will be made till we reach the neighbourhood of Burgos, where there is a strong position for the Enemy to bring up in. The junction of our column with that under Lord W. is expected about the 25th. inst. in the environs of Salamanca. No one can say what they may or may not do.

General Fane is arrived at Headquarters, and will probably continue with the Lord till we meet. I have heard nothing of Sir Stapleton though it appears high time for him to be at his post. Slade has, I suppose, embarked before this, on his return to England, a memorable proof of the consideration shewn to the feelings, honor or character of a British General Officer. The Country has a right to the Services of its most distinguished members, nor is it any disgrace to me that another may be naturally of greater ability than myself, nor ought I to hold an employment the duties of which can be much better discharged by a new candidate. Tell me so, and I resign without a murmur. But to be intrigued or kicked out of honorable employment without meeting the spirit which does adduce the true reasons for such a proceeding, appears to me a treatment more dishonorable to the aggressors than to the aggrieved. In such times prudence would hold its tongue, and so it will. But as I prefer freedom of speech and opinion to anything power could bestow, I shall, at all hazards, continue as I have heretofore done, to have an opinion of my own, and to express it without reserve. . . .

Another month will shew us whether or not the spirit of the great Frederick[1] is again abroad. His colours, by the last account, are waving over the fields near the spot where they have been equally honored and disgraced. Rossbach[2] will remind them of what Prussians could do. Jena points out a degeneracy that must be redeemed. The bane and antidote are both before them, and I do expect to see their former glories revive. Old Blucher will not again draw his sword in vain, and D'Yorck has to justify, the steps that have humbled him in the eyes of his Enemies. Old Walmoden—*grimborn* must wash away his former sins in the waters of the Weser, and I hope the Duke of Cumberland (who is going to join him) is well acquainted with the capitulation of Closter-seven.

I enclose a letter I have just received from Slade[3] which you will communicate to Howard, and tell Eliza that as God pardons the truly penitent who confess and repent of their transgressions, I hope, as a sister, she will follow the Divine example and receive Slade as an old friend of mine, having desired him to be the Bearer of the hardest squeeze by the hand he could give.

We move forward tomorrow through the Puerto de Banos.

[1] Frederick II of Prussia ("the Great").
[2] At the battle of Rossbach, fought on November 5, 1757, during the Seven Years War, Frederick the Great defeated the French.
[3] That of May 15, 1813, printed earlier.

A Peninsular Gift for an Harrovian's Duck and Green Peas

C.B.L. TO HENRY LONG[1]

Langley
May 31st., 1813

My Dear Henry,

I have been desired by your fortis Avunculus Don Robertus to send you the enclosed bit of paper, and truly concerned am I that I cannot give it you propriis manibus. It is for a Duck and Green Peas if you can get them on Thursday next, not forgetting a Bumper to the brave followers of Lord Wellington and their speedy arrival on the Banks of the Ebro.

Charles mends but slowly. He was very much depressed yesterday with a tormenting pain in his head, but is more cheery this morning, tho' not what he ought to be, and extremely weak. We have been taking a short saunter on the Gravel Walk and he is going out in the Landau with his mother, who is a little better today. I hope nothing prevents our meeting at Harrow on the July Speech Day.

Give my best compliments to Dr. Butler[2] and believe me, in extreme haste, my dear H.

Your ever affectionate uncle,
C.B.L.

The Battle of Vittoria and its Immediate Results

TO C. B. LONG

Ocariz near Salvatierra
4 leagues north of Vittoria
23 June, 1813

You will have been disappointed and mortified at not hearing from me for so long, but we have been marching so incessantly for nearly a month without a halt, and under circumstances that have even prevented my keeping a Journal of our movements. But some day or other I hope to be able to reduce them to paper and transmit them for your information. Suffice it to say at present that a most complete defeat of the Enemy in presence of their King the day before yesterday in front of Vittoria, has put us in possession of that place, and of the whole of their Artillery, Baggage, Treasure, and Magazines. "Quos Deus vult perdere prius dementat."[3] They chose to offer battle there,

---

[1] See Robert Long's letter to C. B. Long, April 12, 1813, paragraph 2.
[2] George Butler (1774–1853), Headmaster of Harrow from 1805 till 1829.
[3] "Those whom the god wishes to destroy he first turns mad."

and confidence induced them to place the whole of their property and plunder of Spain in rear of their Position. Their Army beaten, the loss of the latter became inevitable, and the result had been the taking of at least 100 pieces of artillery, and money, jewels, etc., probably to the value of 1½ millions. They behaved very ill. Their position was strong and with common arrangements and spirit their defence might have been brilliant even in the teeth and in spite of the judicious operations concerted to dislodge them. But their infantry did not stand as I expected they would, their cavalry could be of no use from the nature of the ground, and when they saw themselves turned, a panic sieged the whole, which our rapid advance and the embarrassments they met with increased till the affair which commenced at 9 o'clock A.M. on the 21st ended at nearly the same hour in a complete déroute, and could our Cavalry have acted their loss would have been enormous. Our casualties I conjecture will be nearly 3000 and theirs about the same. I never yet witnessed such a scene. Wines, Concubines, baggage, barouches, military chests, all taken. The plunder has been enormous, and I fear the non-combatants of the Army who follow up the steps of the Troops have had the largest share. The whole of the King's property followed the fate of the rest, and he is now wandering with all his discomforts and discomfited associates to Pampeluna, where they expect to unite with Suchet, but I think they will not be in plumage to try a second rencontre.

This Campaign succeeds all former ones in brilliancy of conception and accuracy of execution, and I think I mentioned to you in a former letter that if Lord W. determined his operations by what was brilliant, he would disregard Burgos and make Vittoria his point. He has done so after a succession of judicious manoeuvres which dislodged them from Tormes, the Douro, the Pisuega and the Ebro, here we are consummating almost the liberation of the Peninsular by a Victory which has cost us little, and given a dreadful wound to the Honor of the French Army. Their robberies have met with a singular and just fate, being destined to reward the labours of the liberators.

The Cavalry have had little to do but increase the rapidity of their retreat and augment their panic. The country was so intersected with impassable ravines, ditches, etc., that our advance was broken and impeded at every step. The loss of my Brigade was only 8 men killed and wounded and 2 or 3 horses. But my extra Aide de Camp, Lt. Webster of the 9 Dragoons, had a narrow escape, a ball having penetrated his stock and wounded him in the neck, but not seriously. I have, however, been obliged to leave him at Vittoria.

We have lost a excellent officer in Col. Cadogan of the 71st Regt. That Corps of the 28th have suffered the most. The Spaniards and

Portuguese behaved admirably, which proves what was wanting before to the former—a good example and effectual support. Lord W. must now be hailed as Duke of Vittoria, and he deserves the reward, let the fate of the Campaign be what it may.

I am, thank God, better in health than ever. We have been upon such high ground that the climate is the very reverse of Estremadura —rather too cold than too hot. Here we meet with pretty nearly the November weather in England, and therefore rather unpleasant— cold winds—rain and mist—high mountains in every direction. Vittoria is a beautiful town and very rich. Their uninterrupted commerce with France has made half the inhabitants Frenchified, and although they "viva" tremendously, I doubt the sincerity of their congratulations.

XIV

The Pyrenees and the End of Long's Active Career

ROBERT LONG'S next occupation was at the blockade of Pamplona; at this time the 14th Light Dragoons were added to his brigade. Grant set off for England, and Long began to think that he would at least see the campaign to its end. Then he had the exquisite satisfaction of mounting the pass of Roncesvalles, and looking down upon the lovely land of France. The wild picturesque mountains, with their remote monasteries and snow flurries, were a fitting end-piece to the stern progress through Spain. The Pyrenees were also to be the scene of Long's last military adventures, for at the end of July Marshal Soult, once again commanding the French forces, made a desperate attempt to overthrow the Allies and to relieve Pamplona. Once more Long witnessed the bloody sights of battle, but this time as little more than a spectator, for his cavalry, being useless in the mountain fighting, were occupied in maintaining contact and communications. These duties, which Long performed with intelligence and success, and also the transport of the miserable wounded from the rocky heights and gorges to hospitals behind the lines, concluded in time to allow Long to remount the Pyrenees, and to look again upon the sweeping coast and densely cultivated fields of France. Then, on August 11, 1813, the blow fell. Long received a copy of the order for his recall from Spain to a post on the staff of the Army in Great Britain. Concluding that this was nothing but a means of veiling his dismissal from active service, he abruptly declined the proffered appointment, and paused only to collect his back pay before taking ship from Passages. Long had, in truth, approached Wellington for leave of absence at the very moment when he received official notice of his removal, and lost no time in leaving. A smart run of six days in the brig *Snap* brought him to Falmouth. He landed crippled with rheumatism, but not too ill to stop him from launching at the Horse Guards a final broadside, loaded with indignation at the way he had been treated; and he took the trouble to write a long 'Narrative' which covered the last months of his Peninsular service, and very clearly ascribed his recall to Grant's influence.

From Vittoria to Pamplona

TO C. B. LONG

Laragueta
30 *June*, 1813

I cannot commend a few observations which I have to submit upon this short but hitherto beautiful and eventful campaign better than by doing Justice to the Noble Chieftain who has displayed as much Judgment in the conception of his plan of operations as ability in their execution. This is certainly the most brilliant of his Lordship's Campaigns, and he has almost outrivalled himself.

At the same time it is necessary to say that never was the old adage of "Quem Deus vult perdere prius dementat" more fully exemplified than in the present instance. The Enemy have neither shewn head nor heart, and if they ever had any plans they either have failed in executing them, or have been most completely thwarted by the superior skill of our General, and the greater rapidity and decision of his movements.

Lord W.'s intentions have been uniform; viz. not to force in front their supposed lines of defence on the Douro or Ebro but to turn both. The first was done by the North of Portugal the second by stretching up the line of the Pisuerga, and passing the Ebro at the Puente Arena. The French have been completely surprised in both cases, and anticipated. Instead of concentrating their forces they kept them in a state of dispersion which did not permit their Junction at the point where a stand was determined upon. The consequence has been the overthrow of what was together their expulsion into France, with the exception of General Clausel's Corps (who is cut off from Pamplona, and marching towards Saragossa). They have retired to Bayonne, and a loss of upwards of 150 pieces of Artillery, 1,000 carriages, caissons, etc., and the whole of their Baggage. When they determined to halt and give battle at Vittoria two things were militarily essential to their purpose: to make the most of the strong ground they possessed and to destroy all the bridges upon the rivers to which their right was apprised, and which covered their flank and rear. Another precaution was to send to the rear all the embarrassments of baggage, carriages etc. They did neither. They suffered us to come through a pass that 5,000 men might have defended against 50,000 almost without opposition, and the greater part of our Army passed the bridges upon their flank and rear under their very noses. The whole of their Equipages were left in and about Vittoria, blocking up the different avenues and thus embarrassing the movement of their Troops; and instead of fighting as they might have done no ground was vigorously disputed, and we continued to follow them up till the déroute became general, and had the country favored our Cavalry I think they would have lost a third of their Army. To wind up the whole they had an English Prisoner, Capt. Hay, in their power whom they sent back to be exchanged the day before the action, and who being in possession of every information covering them of course imparted everything to Lord W. and determined the attack that took place. Can you conceive greater folly or infatuation, and could anyone calculate upon such extravagance? They never even occupied a single passage of the Ebro, or destroyed any of the bridges, altho' that of Arona (where we passed) might have been effectually disputed against any force by a single Brigade of Infantry! Fortune has thus favored us, and the cause we defend, and I hope the result of the Campaign will be equal to its commencement.

The present state of things is as follows: Joseph with the forces he carried off retired by Pamplona, and St. Jean Pied de Port upon Bayonne, leaving 3 or 4,000 men to garrison Pamplona, which is now invested by Sir R. Hill's Corps. Baron Foy with 2 Divisions who was on the side of Bilbao, and was prevented joining the King at Vittoria, retired upon the direct road to Bayonne by Tolosa, and has recently relinquished a very strong position he held at Dindoin, falling back before Sir Thomas Graham's Column still further upon Bayonne. Lord W. with the rest of the Army is making a rapid movement upon Saragossa to try to intercept Clausel,[1] or at least prevent his regaining France by the direct road from Saragossa and Jaca. The latter he may accomplish, but I think he will not be able to effect the former Clausel having the start, and the British Troops being exceedingly knocked up with incessant and severe marching. I have heard nothing of the celebrated Spanish Armies of the Duke de Parque[2] and O'Donnell,[3] but when they arrive, I expect a different arrangement of the Troops with the view more effectively of shutting up the avenues to this Country on the *West*.

Artillery has been sent for, and preparations ostensibly making for the siege of Pamplona. The town probably will and ought to be taken, but we shall have enough to do to take the Citadel, which is one of the strongest in Spain, and therefore I hope after the reduction of the town, that a sufficient force will be left to mask the Citadel, and occupy the passes into France, and the rest of our force carried without loss of time to the left, applying ourselves upon the sea, taking St. Sebastian and threatening the frontier of France in that direction, which appears the securest and best time we can take up. . . .

The Country we are now in, compared with Estremadura, is as different as Lapland and China. Every step we take I find my strength increasing. The Climate rather cold, moist and variable, but in the absence of rain it must be delightful. We find abundance of everything and should the Army halt here in 3 weeks we shall be fatter than ever.

[1] General Bertrand Clausel, later Marshal (1772–1842), commanded the French Army of the North, having superseded Caffarelli in January 1812.
[2] The Duque del Parque had succeeded Ballasteros in command of the Army of Andalusia.
[3] Enrique O'Donnell commanded the Reserve Spanish Army of Andalusia.

The inhabitants, like those of all mountain districts are a fine stout healthy race, showing great independence of spirit. They speak the Gascon language, which is scarcely intelligible even to a Spaniard. In short I almost feel myself in England and could I get a sight of the ocean my satisfaction would be complete. M. General Byng[1] has gone forward towards St. Jean Pied de Port with a considerable force, and the great Lord has manifested some share of vanity in directing him to place his advanced posts if possible on *French* ground; from which we are not at present distant above 8 leagues.

The excesses committed by these barbarians in their retreat are every way worthy of their Master. They have sought as usual to avenge their disgraces by murdering the poor defenceless unoffending peasantry. But the day of retribution has I trust arrived, and if France were laid in ashes to the banks of the Garonne, it would scarcely atone for her crimes in this Country. Providence appears to be redeeming the debt of Justice, and Heresy triumphs in a Catholic cause.

General Fane has lost his brother, who commanded the 59th[2] and was severely wounded by a cannon shot in the thigh. The loss appears to affect him deeply, and he is gone to the rear to give vent to his feelings and learn the sad lesson of resignation. Sir Stapleton Cotton joined us two days after the action, but as the Cavalry has no longer a field for their operations any arrangements which may ensue are become subjects of indifference. I had absolutely only $3\frac{1}{2}$ squadrons in the action of the 21st. A proper force would have enabled me more than once, to have struck an important blow. The means denied, the opportunities were lost. This will probably be my last Campaign and therefore I shall not trouble myself further upon the question.

On the 29th of April I commenced my march from Cabeca de Vide and the 29th June reached Pamplona. Who could have anticipated such progress? It will have I trust its proper effect in any negotiations which may be going forward and then the Sword will meet the recompense that is its due.

Our communications will now be thro' Bilbao, and of course more regular and frequent than they have hitherto been. We feel ourselves almost at home. There is pleasure in the approximation.

Nothing can exceed the picturesque scenery and beauty of the Banks of the Ebro near Puente Arena, nor of the valley of the Burmuda [?] from Salvatierra to Pamplona—a second Switzerland! There is one of the best roads in Spain leading from Pamplona to Bayonne by Yrurcan and Tolosa, *not marked in the map*. This will be a great advantage to

---

[1] John Byng (1772–1860), later Earl of Strafford and a field-marshal. He had commanded a brigade at Vittoria, and was to lead another at Waterloo.
[2] The East Lancashire Regiment.

us. The road from Vittoria by Salvatierra to this place till you fall into the high road at Yrurcan is almost impassable for heavy artillery and the Troops have suffered severely in marching it. Pamplona is in a rich plain bounded at unequal distances by mountains; abundance of villages but all of the smallest class. The Town looks dark and gloomy, and will cause a few headaches before we shall gain possession of it. That is, supposing the defence of it to constitute their determination, for if seriously attacked they may confine themselves to the Citadel. All the celebrated guerrilla leaders, Mina, Longa, Porlier, Don Juan, have joined and are acting with us, and shew great spirit. What are Joseph's feelings I know not, but suspect he sympathises with those of the Army, in joy at being driven into their own country. If they had not preferred France to Spain, they would have made a better business of the 21st. We lost, as it was, in all nearly 4,000 killed and wounded. A stout defence would have trebled the number.

The Blockade of Pamplona

TO C. B. LONG

Salinas de Pamplona

13 July, 1813

Since my last I have had the pleasure to receive your letter of the 7th June, and papers up to the 15th. There is so little communication between the different parts of the Army that the right hand scarcely knows what the left is doing. I only know from report that Lord Wellington's Head Quarters are at Iturea on the road from Pamplona by Lans to Bayonne, and Sir Rowland Hill's are said to be Elizondo. The 14th Dragns. are forward in that direction, and if no general movement takes place within a day or two I shall proceed to the front to join them for I am tired of staying here. . . .

The death and destruction of the combatants form but a very small part of the evils and calamities of war. Those suffer most who have the least concern in the contest, but policy never yet had anything to do with feelings or humanity, and men are as little valued as the beasts of slaughter they live upon. I only wish they would leave off canting and not invoke God's presence and assistance at their impious orgies. They really seem to think that such pastimes must be highly gratifying to the Divinity, and I am surprised he is not represented in a red cap and blue apron, with a steel to his waist and a cleave and marrow bones in his hands, a kind of "Marshal General" of the Butchers.

We hear that Joseph has written a most brilliant account of his achievements of Vittoria, dressed up for the Paris taste. He says he took 150 pieces of artillery from us, but was prevented carrying them off from the badness of the roads, and that he occasioned us a loss of 12,000 men and would have annihilated us, but for an accident sur sa droite, for which someone at least must, I should suppose, be sacrificed. He is now among the Gascons and when at Rome thinks it necessary to speak the language of the Romans. The French tailors I believe will be the part of the Nation most benefitted by the Victory of Vittoria. I should like to see the orders to them consequent upon that action from Joseph downwards. Had they left a Ramasseur General des Habits Brodés, we would have supplied them plentifully at ½ price. I must do them the justice to say their wardrobes are most magnificent, but they do not know how to take care of them.

I believe the Bâton de Maréchal of Marshal Jourdan was found among his baggage and sent home as a trophy.[1] The least return the Prince Regent can make is one of British manufacture to the Lord that presented it.

The weather here is beautiful, the climate delicious; the Harvest commenced, and probably in Estremadura finished; abundance of fruit (not very good) bread and wine; and these articles rather sinking than rising in price. The reports from the front are still more favorable, but Sir Thomas Graham has the advantage of his proximity to the coast. Under such circumstances we can no longer talk of the hardships of war. It is no more "plenty to do and little to eat," but little to do and plenty to eat. Therefore should this Campaign wind up our warlike labours, we shall return as fat and fair as ever we were. The Bronze of Estremadura is vanishing daily, and in a short time we shall scarcely have a Moreno left amongst us. This suits well with the state of your finances as it has enabled the Treasury to withhold our pay almost ad libitum. Not a sixpence have I received since Xmas last. We ought to come upon them for the interest at least, and should like to observe the vacancy of their stare at such a proposal.

Wynyard is I hear at Weymouth with his family. If you go to the coast too, my communications will have travelling enough before they reach you. Our posts are excessively irregular, and so long as the Lord is playing hide and seek among the Pyrenees this will continue to be the case.

[1] This is correct. Wellington sent Jourdan's *bâton* to the Prince Regent, who, in acknowledging this gift, wrote: "You have sent me, among the trophies of your unrivalled fame, the staff of a French Marshal, and I send you in return that of England." As no such thing existed, a *bâton* had to be specially designed.

Quiet Times on the French Frontier

TO C. B. LONG

*Larasoain, on the road
from Pamplona to Roncesvalles*

22 July, 1813

The Spaniards under O'Donnell having relieved the British Troops investing Pamplona, on the 18th inst. was directed to move the 13 Dns. into this valley, which I did on that day. Being anxious to see the celebrated Pass of Roncesvalles, I proceeded there on the 19th inst., remained there the 20th and returned here yesterday. I was much gratified by the beauty of the scenery in the immediate neighbourhood of Roncesvalles, which almost equals that of many parts of Switzerland. The village itself is very small (16 families) and having been respected by the Enemy has suffered little. It lies at the foot of that branch of the Pyrenees which forms the boundary between France and Spain. There are two roads from Roncesvalles to St. Juan Pied de Port, one by the right over a high ridge of mountain which terminates at St Juan, the other by the Valcarlos. We occupy the latter village and the defile leading to it, and on the other road our advanced picquets are between the Chateau Pignon and St. Juan, and consequently on the French frontier. The French have likewise their picquets within musquet shot of ours. These heights are so considerable that for the last 20 days they have scarcely seen the sun's rays, enveloped in cloud and darkness; and the Troops have suffered a good deal from the severity of the cold and continuous rains. I was particularly unfortunate in the weather, as you may believe when I had to face a snow storm at such an elevation on the 20th July. The view in clear weather from these mountains must be most magnificent commanding a most extensive view into France, and also the snow-clad mountains of Aragon towards Catalonia. From these points we see the British Troops posted on the summit of the Pass of Maya to the left, and they in their turn see those of Sir Thos. Graham's Column towards the sea. The celebrated Battle of Roncesvalles[1] in Charlemagne's time took place between Roncesvalles and the village of Burguete, and a cross (as a monument) was erected to commemorate the spot, but this the Vandals have destroyed. There is an establishment of Clergy there of a most respectable description, and were formerly very rich. They possessed several trophies of ancient times, which the French carried off with the exception of two instruments of

---

[1] In 778 the rearguard of Charlemagne's army was cut to pieces by the Vascons. Roland was killed.

war used in those days which they now call maces, and are merely two sticks or handles about 30 inches long to which is suspended by a chain a ball of iron like a 4 lb shot, a formidable weapon for assault in the hands of anyone possessing strength sufficient to will it with effect. The Pass of Roncesvalles is certainly strong and defensible in front, but it appears to me to be very easily assailed, and turned by Otchagavic and the Val de Salayar, and by this, if attempted, it will be accomplished. As the Pyrenees fall from the Pic du Midi towards the sea, they are by no means so formidable as I expected to see them, and indeed Artillery may pass very easily from this place to St. Juan.

Sir Rowland Hill is at Elizondo in the Val de Bastan—and as the 14th Dns are in that direction I purpose removing to Irurita the day after tomorrow, by which I shall be enabled to explore the Country in that direction and also I hope towards St. Sebastian. Lord Wellington's Head Quarters are at present at Lesaca on the Bidassoa in the Val de Leria between Sanesteban and Fuenterrabia. They are proceeding with the siege of St. Sebastian, and have taken, I understand an important outwork which will facilitate the operations against the Castle. . . .

I had written thus far when my pen was arrested by the receipt of your letter of the 22nd June, announcing the fatal event I have long anticipated.[1] I can have no hesitation in declaring my opinion that Mrs. Charles' release is an act of mercy to you both and far better it is that her life should be brought to a close, than protracted under circumstances so painful and distressing to the sufferer, and to those who daily must be a witness of them.

Affairs are at present in such a state of uncertainty here, that one knows not what to do, but I purpose in a few days seeing Lord Wellington, and I shall then communicate my wish to return to England whenever his Lordship may be of opinion that I can do so without sacrificing the duty which I owe to the service. A great deal must depend upon what is going on in Germany, but at all events the Campaign here can scarcely last above two months more. Professionally speaking, I should not wish to desert my post till the struggle for the year 1813 was closed and then indeed I care not if my sword be sheathed for life, for I am heartily sick of the sight of it. A few days more may enable me to speak more positively upon this point.

[1] Mrs C. B. Long had died on June 9, 1813.

Battles in the Pyrenees
TO C. B. LONG

Lecoros, nr. Elizondo,
Valley of Bastan
6 August, 1813

The recent movements of the Army have interrupted so much the regularity of communication, that whilst others have received letters and papers to a very late date it has been my misfortune to get no papers at all, and it was yesterday only that I was favored with your letter of the 29th Inst., and also with one from Kate of the 23rd June.

The last fortnight has been pregnant with interesting occurrences, and much blood has been spilled.

Soult having joined the Army at Bayonne immediately determined to attempt the relief of Pamplona. His Army was concentrated, for this purpose, near St. Jean Pied de Port, and moved in two columns, the right under Count d'Erlon by the Pass of Maya into the Valley of Bastan, the other commanded by himself upon Roncesvalles along the direct road to Pamplona.

Both passes were forced after a considerable but ineffectual resistance, and with much loss on both sides. Lord Wellington appears to have expected a greater degree of resistance on the right, and was rather alarmed at the rapid advance of the Enemy in that direction. On the 26th I retreated with the 13th Dragoons to Lanz, transporting wounded men on the dragoon horses, the only use we could be of.[1] On the 27th Lord Wellington arrived at Lanz, and having given his orders repaired by the Lanz road to Villaba. But on his arrival at Ostiz he found the Enemy in possession of the communication, which obliged him to bear away to his right. He did so, and succeeded in reaching Villaba that evening: he immediately placed what troops he could there collect in position.

The very next day, the 28th July, Soult attacked our position in considerable force, but was everywhere repulsed. His loss on this day is supposed to amount to nearly 6,000 men.

That night and the following day, Lord W. employed in strengthening his position and bringing up his artillery to places almost inaccessible. Count d'Erlon's Corps having also joined Soult, we all expected a renewal of the action on the 30th. A feint indeed was made

[1] It is characteristic that Long omits to mention that by copying and sending on a dispatch from General Cole, who commanded a detached corps and had been driven from his position on July 26, 1813, Long made certain that Wellington was fully informed about an unpleasant situation. Wellington's subsequent orders made the Allied repulse of Soult a certainty.

before daybreak, but it appears to have been a manoeuvre to mask their retreat. The moment Lord W. was aware of this circumstance he made a general and offensive movement upon both flanks of the Enemy, and pressed him so hard, that they were obliged to go off at a full trot, and a considerable number of Prisoners were taken. Soult's retreat was covered by d'Erlon's Corps, who advanced against Sir Rowland Hill, and dislodged him from the first position he occupied, but was unable to drive him from the second.

On the 31st the pursuit was continued in the direction of Roncesvalles, Lanz and Santesteban. Partial but severe actions occurred in the passes and mountains, and the Enemy's loss was considerable. I counted nearly 200 killed at Puerto d'Arraiz on the road to Sanesteban. Of course with wounded and prisoners they must have lost on this spot 1,000 men. The Column that pursued along the road (the Valley of Bastan) overtook a considerable convoy, and made 200 prisoners of the escort. In short this expedition for the relief of Pamplona has cost Soult according to every estimate near 15,000 men killed wounded and prisoners, and our loss I conjecture, can scarcely be less than 8,000. Sir Rowland Hill's Corps has suffered severely, the beautiful brigade[1] (formerly Kenneth Howard's) consisting of the 92nd Highlanders, 50th and 71st Regiments is nearly annihilated, and the havoc among the officers has been most afflicting. Such are the delights of war!

Lord Wellington has, I think, shown himself greater on the recent occasion than ever, and to his personal talent, exertions and presence I ascribe our delivery from a very serious scrape, which, at one moment, threatened the loss of all we had acquired, and made even the Headquarters look very blue. At present affairs are assuming a different complexion, and indicate an intention to carry the war into France. I should hardly have expected or wished for this, until Pamplona was secured. That is the point on which the fate of the Campaign hangs, and it will not astonish me to see Soult repeat his endeavours to keep Lord W. out of France by carrying the war again into Navarre or Arragon.

The French Army advanced with the most perfect confidence of relieving and entering Pamplona, after which we were to have been driven behind the Ebro, according to Napoleon's directions. The poor garrison issued full rations upon the occasion and illuminated the town in the most splendid manner. Judge of the bitterness of their disappointment on seeing the redcoats dislodging their friends from

---

[1] This brigade of the 2nd Division comprised the 50th Foot (Royal West Kent Regiment), the 71st Foot (Highland Light Infantry), and the 92nd Foot (Gordon Highlanders). In the battles of the Pyrenees they suffered over a thousand casualties, and their divisional commander, Colonel John Cameron, of the 92nd, was wounded.

the strong ground they occupied, and their whole force en pleine retraite!

The Cavalry during these operations have had little to do in the fighting way, but plenty in fatigue, and my Brigade, particularly, has come in for an abundant share. The 13th Dragoons are nearly knocked up again. That portion of them that was at Roncesvalles were 70 hours without feeding, and they have now 75 men and horses out of 300 on detached duties or fatigue. The Infantry have run away with the honor and glory, and dearly have they paid for it. A great part of them are in a dreadfully shattered state from fatigue, famine and nakedness. The wounded can be little short of 5,000 men. The Army appears to me to stand in need of repose and refitment, particularly the British part of it, which, as usual, is the first to fire and the last out. Lord W. however, shows too much judgment to admit a doubt about the propriety of his decisions, whatever they may be. I fear the work of blood must continue, for humanity seems to have fled from the earth.

Such are the scenes of desolation going on here, in addition to which I have more particularly to lament the sacrifices imposed upon my friends at home. *You* have been a sufferer, my dear C., in an irreparable manner, and others, I fear, are doomed by fate, to keep your sorrows in countenance. You must bear up against it as well as you can, and make the most of a life that is scarcely worth possessing. I have lately seen so much of death in all its various hues, that I am half in love with it. There is no real peace but in the grave!

The Prince of Orange takes home the dispatches relative to the recent affairs.

I was yesterday on the summit of the Pyrenees near the Puerto de Maya, and nothing could be more magnificent than the prospect, comprehending all the country from St. Jean de Luz by Bayonne towards Bordeaux, and an immense extent of sea coast. The whole, excepting a tract of barren sand called Les Landes, to the north of Bayonne, appeared highly cultivated, and with houses and villages without end. It was most gratifying to see the Vandals encamped at last upon their own soil, and I counted about ten different British encampments along the summit of the Pyrenees overlooking them.

I have just received an order to march back to Lanz, for which I am very sorry, this valley being particularly suited to my tastes. I have not yet communicated with the Lord, but shall do so in a day or two. Tell Kate she shall hear from me next week.

God bless you. Rather hurried and not in the best spirits.

Last Letter Home from the Peninsula
TO C. B. LONG

Santesteban
12th August 1813

 I have this moment received your letter of the 6th ult., and it is a great comfort to me to think and hope that by the end of this month I shall have the opportunity to embrace you all again.

 I apprised you of my intention to see Lord Wellington and arrange if possible a leave of absence with him. I went over to Lesaca for the purpose yesterday, and was rather unexpectedly greeted with the following notification received from the Horse Guards.

Horse Guards, 22 July, 1813

MY LORD,
 I have the Commander-in-Chief's commands to acquaint your Lordship that the Prince Regent has been pleased to remove M. General Long from the Staff of the Peninsula to that of Great Britain, and your Lordship will therefore be pleased to cause that officer to return to this country with his earliest convenience.

     I have the honor, etc., etc.,
        (signed) H. TORRENS

Field Marshal Marquis of Wellington, K.G.

 Having told my mind upon the subject of this unceremonious kind of notification to Lord W. I have felt it a duty to do the same to H. Torrens, for Prince Regent's information, and have accordingly transmitted the following answer.

Santesteban, 12 *August,* 1813

SIR,
 I yesterday received from the Adjutant General of the Forces in this country a copy of your letter of the 22nd July to F.M. the Marquis of Wellington, notifying by command of H.R.H. the Prince Regent my removal from the Staff of the Army in this Peninsula to that of Great Britain.

 I was perfectly aware, Sir, that no services of mine could deserve or obtain a greater reward than what they have received, the thanks and approbation of those who witnessed them, but nothing could be so far from my mind as that they had prepared for me a stigma so distressing and unexpected as I feel to be conveyed by the notification above alluded to, and which construction I apprehend every officer in this Army will put upon it.

 I can only say, Sir, that perfectly conscious myself of having, upon all occasions, discharged my duty to my Sovereign and country to the best of my limited ability and judgment, I should most anxiously court any enquiry that might tend to rectify this supposition if erroneous, and reconcile me to the justice of the step to which I am about to yield obedience by returning immediately to England, or else, which might do away the unfavourable impression that appears to have influenced so prejudicially for my feelings and reputation H.R.H. the Prince Regent's commands respecting me.

At all events I entreat H.R.H. the Commander-in-Chief will allow me to convey thro' his Royal Highness to H.R.H. the Prince Regent my humble request to decline accepting the appointment tendered to me on the Staff of Great Britain, as I should deem it inconsistent with every principle of Honor to hold any military situation at Home, the duties of which I appear not to have discharged satisfactorily abroad.

(Signed) R. L.

Col. Torrens, Etc.

Thus, my dearest C., have I thrown down the gauntlet of defiance to them, and shown my determination not to be "Sladed" in silent passiveness. I care not one farthing what they may think, how they feel, or what they may do in revenge for my presumption; my sword is now sheathed for ever. It has earned me little else but trouble hitherto, and will, I hope, now be laid by without sorrow or regret of any kind. My feelings are those of a person entering a land-locked Harbour after encountering the tempestuous ravings of the Atlantic Ocean. No man ever yet died to the world with greater pleasure than I shall do.

The conviction of this step having been taken to give Col. Grant a Brigade, at my expense, and thus induced him to return to his bread and butter, of course quiets my mind and my feelings upon the subject. But as I cannot be supposed to know this, I must *act* upon other presumptions, and no military man can be removed from active to home service, unless at his own request, without feeling it a slur upon him. I wish the practice to be discontinued, and that they should find out a way to provide for their favorites without offending those whom they determine to supersede. They dare not be honest, and they have not sense enough to be civil. Because they think that every man has his price, and a bribe will set all difficulties at rest. They possess not the delicate sense of Honor which should be the soldier's breastplate. Everything must be carried with the Cat o' nine tails, or rather by the Union of force, fraud and falsehood. They are a precious Junta, and I thank God I have done with them.

Now, my dearest C., pray stop all further correspondence, packets and parcels, and suspend the execution of any commissions I may have

T

given, for I hope this will not be very long in your hand before I have the happiness to squeeze it.

I have an order upon Sir G. Collier[1] for a passage and as soon as my cattle are disposed of, and other arrangements made I shall proceed to the coast for embarkation.

In the meantime every affectionate wish attend you.

R. L.

Apprise Mrs. Nesbitt that I have received her letter of the 3 July, and with God's leave will answer it in person.

Farewell to the Peninsula

Lesaca
17 *Aug*, 1813

Sir Robert Kennedy[2] presents his compliments to Major General Long and begs to enclose two sets of Bills, viz 1st 2nd and 3rd on the Treasury for the sums as per margin requested in his letter of the 15th inst.

[in margin] Major General Long £240 14 9
Captain Dean, A.D.C. £120 7 4

TO C. B. LONG

Renteria
20 *Aug.*, 1813

For security's sake I enclose two bills, and the copy of a third in England. The original of the latter and duplicates of the former, I shall take home with me, and I beg you will keep them till my arrival.

I am only waiting the appointment of a ship of war to embark at Passages. My Horses are all on board a Transport named the "Reward" and will I believe proceed this day to Bilbao to join Convoy. There are three of them, and I have given James orders to proceed with them to Langley, there to wait my further instructions.

In the ardent hope of shaking hands with you my Dearest C. before the lapse of many weeks, I shall add no more at present than my earnest wish to find you as tranquil in your mind as I am in mine.

[1] Sir George Collier had commanded the British naval forces engaged in the first siege of San Sebastian during July 1813.
[2] Sir Robert Kennedy, Commissary General, was in the Peninsula from Wellington's first landing, in August 1808, until Coruña; from June 1810 to November 1811, and from September 1812 until April 1814.

Peninsular Prize Money
1st Class

2nd Payment	£132	14 10½
3rd "	£134	9 10
4th "	£142	5 7½
5th "	£164	17 0
	£574	7 4
Deduct 4 receipt stamps @ 2/6 each		10 0
Nett Amount credited	£573	17 4

Back again in England
TO C. B. LONG

Plymouth
1st Sept., 1813

I arrived here this day from Falmouth where I landed on Monday. As I am suffering a good deal from a rheumatic attack, and travelling annoys me, I purpose remaining here two or three days to try to get rid of my Aitches as well as to satisfy my curiosity, and if I can meet with an opportunity of going round to Portsmouth by sea I shall avail myself of it; if not I must proceed via Exeter, Salisbury, etc. to Langley where I want to get hold of some clothes if possible.

I have just fired off a letter well charged with indignation to the Horse Guards, and I only wish I had the value of my commission in my pocket to speak my mind more freely than my own interest will, at present, permit. However, more upon this, and all other subjects when we meet.

Send me a note to Langley to apprise me where you are to be found, that I may make my ultimate arrangements accordingly, and beg your people there to get me a bed dried, as I may be detained a day or two. I suspect I shall be obliged to attack the warm sea baths, for at this moment I feel half crippled. I dread an English winter after the severe roasting I have experienced for the last two years.

Reflections to a Brother-in-Law
TO HENRY HOWARD

Berkeley Square
Sept. 16th, 1813

Many thanks for your congratulations, altho' under all the circumstances of the case they ought to have been condolements. I am doomed to be at eternal war with Princes, and when we meet you shall see the correspondence that has recently passed between the Horse Guards and myself, and which has terminated in my indignant rejection of their appointment to serve on the Home Staff, which was tendered as a Bribe or sop to stop my mouth and induce me to submit quietly to their own unprincipled arrangements. "They may starve me if they please, but they shall never insult me with impunity." I may therefore now consider myself on the shelf for life, and must lose no time in giving to my Rheumatic bones the best repose a shelf can afford.

The hearts of those I have served with are with me, and I care not a rush for the feelings or opinion of unrestrained or unrestricted power. They have ordered me home in order to accommodate and fulfil their promises to Colonel Grant, who deserved a rod infinitely more than princely submission to his demands. I have no objection to this if carried into effect as becomes a Military Prince in making a military arrangement which should never lose sight of the delicacy and attention due to a soldier's best feelings. But abandoning all principle they fancy they can cut and carve as they please, provided they have a *pecuniary* plaster at hand to apply to the wounds they inflict. They are a dirty-minded despotic set, and I almost thank God that I have done with them.

I have not yet made up my mind in which direction to steer when I quit Town, but it will probably be towards Arundel or Bracknell. Had I arrived sufficiently early to have accompanied you to Wallow I should gladly have done so, for I am a wanderer by habit and predilection. But I believe I must give my bones some rest this winter, and start upon a new life in the Spring.

Carolus met me at Langley and I was happy to find him in better looks and spirits than I expected. He is still at East Cowes but returns I believe to Langley next week. London is quite a Desert.

I must now bid you adieu in order to pay off an epistolary debt which I owe to your Henrietta, who wrote me a long letter to say that Harry was a great Grecian and likely to become a celebrated Carpenter.

The Inside Story

The following undated narrative was found in Long's manuscript. It states quite clearly his own view of the proceedings attending his removal from Spain. The letters mentioned include the official correspondence printed earlier, along with some personal and private notes exchanged by Long and Colonel Torrens, Secretary at the Horse Guards.

Narrative of the circumstances which preceded and attended Major-General Long's removal from the Staff of the Army in the Peninsula to that of Great Britain; to which is subjoined the correspondence which that act of infamy originated.

An honest tale speeds best, being plainly told.[1]

The Campaign of 1813 may be considered as having opened about the 16th of May of that year. At that time (from the absence in England of Lt. General Sir S. Cotton) no Cavalry arrangements were made, Lord Wellington having publickly expressed his determination not to interfere, but to leave the whole concern to the Officer Commanding that Arm. Every General Officer of Cavalry, therefore took the field, as it were, in statu quo; and Colonel Grant commander as Senior Officer, the Brigade of British Hussars that had arrived during the Winter, and which was the finest in the Army, and nearly double the strength of any other.

In consequence of the return of the 9th Light Dragoons to England, M. General Long's Brigade consisted only of the 13th Light Dragoons; to which the 6th Regiment of Portuguese Cavalry (very weak) was afterwards attached. From this miserable force he was directed to detach one Squadron with the 6th Division of Infantry, and one more to make a reconnaissance upon Pancorbo; so that in the Action of Vittoria he could scarcely muster more than three squadrons, a force incompetent for any undertaking of consequence; and this circumstance was rendered more distressing by seeing a very junior officer at the head of 1500 of the best troops in the field, which were equal to any enterprise. Viewing the subject, however, as a temporary evil, General Long said nothing, but did all that lay in his power to forward the public interests.

About two or three days after the Battle of Vittoria Sir Stapleton Cotton arrived, joined the Army in the neighbourhood of Pamplona, and resumed the Command of the Cavalry. The arrangements soon followed. M. General Long received the 13th and 14th Dragoons

[1] *Richard III*, Act IV, Scene 4.

as his Brigade, M. General Victor Alten the 1st German and the 18th British Hussars, and the 10th and 15th British Hussars formed a Brigade, and were placed under the command of Lord Edward Somerset, who had recently, by Brevet, been promoted to the rank of M. General.

It is here to be observed that Lord Edward Somerset, Sir Granby Calcraft,[1] and Colonel Head, had *all* been serving during the war in the peninsula *as full Colonels* at *the head of their respective Regiments*, and all of them were, considerably, *Senior* in rank to Colonel Grant, who, by the arrangement above mentioned naturally reverted to his proper post, the command of the 15th Hussars. If this common practice of the Service was considered by *that* officer as a hardship or degradation, what must be *his* opinion of the treatment experienced by M. General Long, who was displaced from the command of his Brigade, which he had held for three years, in order to make way for *him*?

Nevertheless, on the notification of the above arrangements, Colonel Grant thought himself highly aggrieved in being deprived of the command of the Brigade which he had temporarily held, as Senior Officer; and applied, immediately, for leave to return to England. This was granted; and he quitted his post and repaired to Passages. At that place, or at Renteria, he met Sir S. Cotton and had a long conversation with him on the subject of his alleged grievance. Col. Grant represented that he had received the Prince Regent's promise that he should command the Brigade of Hussars; that in consequence, he had invariably intimated such his expectations to the Army; and that he felt himself degraded by the arrangements which had disappointed those expectations. Sir S. Cotton pointed out to him the irregularity of any such pretensions on his part, shewed the nature of the commands that had been held for years past by officers much his senior, and how inferior those commands were to the one he held then, that of the 15th Hussars, observed upon the indiscretion of going home at such a period, and advised him to consider well the consequence of the step he was about to take.

Colonel Grant, influenced apparently by these suggestions, altered his plan; and is reported to have written to Lord Wellington requesting leave to continue at Passages till he should receive an answer to a communication which he had transmitted to England on the subject of his situation. His request was granted, and it is to be presumed that the very next mail brought him the expected answer, since it conveyed also to Lord Wellington a notification of M. General Long's removal

---

[1] Sir Granby Thomas Calcraft, Lieutenant-Colonel of the 3rd Dragoon Guards, Colonel by brevet July 1810, was in the Peninsula from 1809 to June 1813, when he was promoted major-general.

from the Staff of the Army in the Peninsula to that of Great Britain; which was succeeded by Colonel Grant's appointment to the Brigade late under M. General Long's Command, and originated the correspondence which will be subjoined.[1]

The above details of what passed between Lt. General Sir S. Cotton and Colonel Grant were communicated to M. General Long by the *former*. Of course he could not desire his information from a more authentic source.

On receiving Colonel Torrens' letter of the 22nd July, M. General Long's feelings, as much as the sympathy and opinion of his military friends, sufficiently proved to him that the time had arrived, when, banishing all sense of delicacy and honor, and in violation of every principle of equity, the supreme authority had resolved to make him the victim of its promises or predilections in favor of a *Royal Aide-de-Camp*; and this officer, be it observed was his *junior* Lt. Colonel in the *same* Regiment, and therefore (leaving out of consideration the proceedings that had taken place in the 15th Dragoons) was the very *last person* whom delicacy or honor would have selected to become the instrument of his degradation.

On receiving the notification of his recall M. General Long of course waited upon the Marquis of Wellington, and expressed a hope that no disapprobation of his conduct on the part of his Lordship had caused a measure so unexpected and distressing. Lord W. disavowed all personal implication in the proceedings, declared that the arrangement had originated at *Home*, and that M. General Long must fight his own battle in England as well as he could; that such circumstances were of course distressing to himself, but he washed his hands of all participation in the arrangement.

M. General Long lost not a moment in conveying his sentiments upon the subject to Colonel Torrens, and had the satisfaction, before he embarked, to receive from the officers of the 13th Dragoons (which he had commanded since his arrival in the Peninsula) the most gratifying assurances of their affection, esteem and regret. Nor will it be an unpleasant reflexion to him thro' life, to know that, on the very day selected by the Adjutant General for the transfer of his services from Spain to England, he was actively employed on the Pyrenees in rescuing near 400 wounded British Soldiers, who would otherwise have fallen into the Enemy's power, and in conveying them to the rear, for which duty he received Lt. General Sir Rowland Hill's particular thanks.

It is further to be observed that the Cavalry arrangements which excited Colonel Grant's displeasure took place about the 8th or 10th

[1] Two of the letters have already been printed, in Long's letter of August 12, 1813; the others express Long's attitude of resentment with great clarity and little discretion.

July. Colonel Torrens' first letter is dated on the 22nd of the same month. Nothing can prove more unequivocally that the Carlton House arrangements were made to meet that officer's necessities, at the expense of justice and decorum towards M. General Long; and Colonel Torrens expressly states that he is commanded by His Royal Highness the Commander in Chief to notify the Prince Regent's Honorable decision for Lord Wellington's information.

Long's last paragraph, dated November 24, 1813, reads:

I shall never regret the sacrifices I have made in my profession, and only lament that the poor services I could render my country have necessarily been limited to the extent of very limited abilities; but it shall be my consolation to bequeath to my friends the proud recollection that no earthly consideration or power that ever existed under Heaven could induce me to become an accomplice in the degradation of my own character, or truckle to dishonour!

I have done; and you may depend upon hearing no more from me upon this most disgraceful subject.

Thoughts long afterwards
TO C. B. LONG

Mount Street

10 *Jan.*, 1817

Thanks for your provender. It is enough to last me for a week, and therefore I hope Dean, who is in Town, will assist me in digesting it.

I have recently read thro' the whole of my Peninsula correspondence, and I am justified in saying that my reasoning throughout appears to have been correct, and the greater part of the prediction fulfilled; and there is more than one passage prophetic of the *reward* of my services. I shall put all this some time or another in a more perfect and complete state, and leave it to you as a legacy of incontrovertible truths.

Epilogue

So, with indignation in his heart, Long returned to England. He never served on the active list again, though in due course his name appeared amongst the 1821 promotions as lieutenant-general. Much of his time he spent with Charles. He had various other personal addresses, however, before finally settling at Barnes Terrace, Surrey.

With all the members of his family he maintained the closest possible touch throughout his life. Apart from brothers, sisters-in-law, nephews, and nieces, Long's most intimate friend was Addenbrooke, with whom his first acquaintance had been made while both were young A.D.C.'s of Sir William Pitt at Portsmouth.

Colonel John Peter Addenbrooke, after being Gentleman Usher to George III's Queen Charlotte, joined the staff of the Prince Regent's daughter, Princess Charlotte, when she attained the dignity of a separate establishment, and he was in attendance on her after her marriage to Leopold of Saxe-Coburg.

As a little girl at Weymouth Princess Charlotte had played with and been kept amused by Robert Long, then Lieutenant-Colonel of the York Hussars; and resplendent in the regiment's dashing uniform. She always remembered him as a friend in her lonely life of twenty-one years spent under the shadow of the intrigues of her beastly father and his even beastlier acquaintances. Since at the time of the Princess's residence at Claremont, Robert Long was living at Park Corner House, on the north-east corner of Strathfieldsaye Park,[1] their homes were not far distant. Addenbrooke and Long exchanged long and gossiping letters, but, although constant invitations and kind messages were handed to the General, Long refused to visit the Princess. Leopold naturally formed the topic of many exchanges. When at one time, after the Prince Regent had refused to let him sit in the House of Lords, Leopold seriously proposed standing for the Commons Long was in a state of high excitement. So far as he held any political allegiance he was a Whig. Though he had much contempt for the petty, unhelpful, and purely destructive attitude of the great Whig leaders, he agreed with them in their dislike and hatred of "Prinny," who by 1813 had long ago forgotten his drinking friendship with Charles James Fox,[2]

---

[1] Strathfieldsaye, in Berkshire, near the Hampshire-Surrrey boundaries, was the estate presented to Wellington by the Nation after the wars were over.

[2] Fox, who died in 1806, had a truly liberal outlook, though it was probably the least-pleasant side of his character which attracted the future Regent and George IV.

and was to develop into almost as complete a reactionary as Cumberland himself. Thus the prospect of helping Leopold, who had a very proper and well-founded dislike for his father-in-law, to a seat in the Commons was delightful to Long.

Leopold, anxious to meet this ally and friend of Addenbrooke's, supported his wife's invitations. But Long had had enough of princes, and was too anxious to preserve his own independence. Though Leopold's physician, the celebrated Baron Stockmar, was also among Long's friends, Claremont was never visited by Long, who avoided like the plague any appearance of courting the great and powerful. It was a pity that Leopold and Long never met, for they shared a great deal in common over political matters, both being especially convinced that Catholic Emancipation, an honest Parliament, and a constitutional monarchy were essential for England's honour and safety.

In November 1817 Princess Charlotte died in child-bed. It was this death, and the non-survival of the child, which threw the succession to the throne ultimately to Victoria; and since Leopold's subsequent voluminous correspondence with the young queen had much influence upon her opinions and actions Long's political philosophy was in a manner of speaking vindicated by history.

Addenbrooke did not long survive the break-up of the Claremont establishment. He died in France in November 1821, leaving the bulk of his fortune to his old comrade, "Mons Roblong," as the nickname ran. Long had a sarcophagus built over the vault in the cemetery of Notre Dame at Versailles, where his friend was buried, and also erected a monument in the church at Esher.

Long himself had not much longer to run his course. On March 2, 1825, he died in Berkeley Square, in his fifty-fourth year. At his death he left a tidy little fortune, finally proved at over £6000. His manservant received £500, clothes, and household linen; his literary nephew, Charles Edward, inherited Long's books, maps, gold watch, and plate; two old friends (one, Mrs Nesbitt, the widow of a major-general with whom Robert corresponded a great deal) received £100 each; brother Charles came in for £1000 cash, and also a share, with his three sisters, of all remaining possessions. Typically, Robert Long wrote the whole of his will himself, without witnesses. He directed that he should not be buried in his vault but in the earth, "without any personal pomp and at the least possible expense." His body was placed in the family vault in the church at Seale, Surrey. Here Charles was also buried later, and a monument erected to them both by Charles's children. A memoir appeared in the *Gentleman's Magazine*, and another soldier had slipped almost unnoticed from the scene.

Not until the outburst of pamphlets and recriminations between Napier and Beresford was there a sudden brief revival of interest in Long's military performances, when Campo Mayor, Albuera, and Usagre were fought over again. Charles Edward Long published two slim volumes of extracts from his uncle's papers to vindicate the action taken, and was able to supplement the considerable evidence marshalled by Napier not so much in support of Long as against Beresford. Long, for reasons due to his personal feud with his leader, had never received the gold medal for Albuera, and a posthumous attempt to get this obvious injustice remedied failed before the invincible stone-walling of the Horse Guards.

Robert Long had never agitated himself over this matter, nor is there anything to show that his own often-professed indifference to the end of his military life was not perfectly sincere. To a proud and independent man the satisfaction of his own sense of honour and the considered approval of his family and personal friends were all that in the final account really mattered.

Index

ADDENBROOKE, COLONEL J. P., 24, 98, 121, 125, 151, 183, 192, 297, 298
Alba de Tormes, 210, 230, 234, 235, 236, 239, 271
Albuera, 13, 48, 70, 71, 73, 115, 142, 159, 182, 196, 197, 198, 200, 270, 299; skirmishes before battle of, 83, 87, 90; battle of, 99, 104–112, 117, 118, 121, 123, 124, 151, 172, 174
Alemtejo, 62, 64, 68, 127, 133, 140, 143, 157, 160
Almaraz, 113, 193, 219; bridge destroyed at, 182–189, 190, 192, 194, 195
Almendralejo, 90, 92, 98, 105, 110, 190, 194, 197, 200
Arroyo dos Molinos, battle of, 137–145, 151, 152, 156, 158, 193
Arundel, 15, 49, 50, 97, 153, 269, 292
Azeuchal, 105, 110, 114, 194, 197, 200

BADAJOZ, 48, 56, 59, 61, 62, 64, 67, 69, 70–78 *passim*, 80, 82, 83, 87, 90, 125, 131, 142, 148, 167, 189, 197, 238, 246; first siege of, 87, 95–119 *passim*, 121, 123; second siege of, 158–164 *passim*, 169, 171, 173, 174, 175, 177, 178, 187
Ballesteros, General F., 69, 89, 91, 92, 95, 110, 197, 233
Beresford, Marshal W. C., 47, 48, 59, 62, 67–72 *passim*, 74, 77, 78, 80, 83, 95, 103, 107, 108, 109, 111, 142, 177, 211; character of, 70; General Long's quarrels with, 12, 14, 45, 73, 79, 82, 92, 93, 98, 104, 105, 106, 117, 146–157, 241, 261, 299
Bienvenida, 108, 199, 201, 202, 206
Blake, General J., 95, 104, 110, 119, 156, 158, 162, 167
Bonaparte, Joseph (King of Naples and Spain), 38, 127, 133, 197, 212, 216, 224, 226, 232, 245, 268, 279, 281, 282
Bonaparte, Napoleon—*see* Napoleon I
Bron, General, 138, 141, 142, 145, 156
Brownrigg, General R., 17, 26, 30, 55, 80, 97, 120
Brunn, General—*see* Bron
Burgos, 210, 214, 221, 237, 271, 272, 275; siege of, 224, 227–236

CABECA DE VIDE, 141, 144, 146, 147, 150, 152, 155, 160, 163, 164, 166, 168, 169, 237, 242, 243, 244, 246, 247, 249, 251, 252, 253, 254, 256, 257, 261, 262, 264, 280
Cadiz, 27, 47, 71, 91, 95, 121, 130, 133, 135, 165, 179, 191, 205, 210, 213, 215, 216, 217, 218, 230, 231, 241, 242, 244
Calvert, Sir H., 17, 37, 43, 136, 146, 157
Campo Mayor, 140, 147, 171; battle of, 68–82, 89, 91, 92, 93, 117, 151, 152, 154
Canopus, H.M.S., 167
Ciudad Rodrigo, 99, 121, 123, 135, 143, 150, 165, 174, 187, 232, 234, 235, 238, 271; siege of, 158–164 *passim*
Cobbett, William, 100, 114, 149, 157, 177
Coruña, 59, 70, 271; retreat to, 37–39, 40, 45
Cotton, General Sir Stapleton, 11, 90, 111, 113, 115, 119, 171, 177, 211, 216, 248, 255, 264, 270, 272, 280, 293, 295
Cumberland, Ernest, Duke of, 14, 19, 32, 33, 34, 36, 37, 70, 97, 98, 116, 166, 273, 298
Cummings, Colonel H. J., 126, 136, 164, 263

DEAN, CAPTAIN, 51, 63, 64, 69, 86, 100, 107, 130, 134, 150, 160, 242, 248, 290, 296
Divisions (British Army), nicknames of, 177
Douro, river, 177, 183, 197, 208, 212, 221, 223, 233, 271, 272, 275, 278
Drouet, J. B. (Comte d'Erlon), 55, 113, 133, 186, 188, 191, 195, 196, 197, 198, 201, 202, 204, 229, 285, 286

EBRO, RIVER, 115, 135, 164, 179, 190, 205, 206, 221, 268, 271, 274, 275, 278, 279, 280, 286
Edinburgh Review, 149
Elizabeth, H.M.S., 52, 54
Elvas, 56, 68, 69, 73, 86, 87, 88, 97, 109, 111, 114, 173, 236, 246
Erskine, General Sir W., 11, 66, 108, 110, 111, 115, 119, 134, 152, 155, 177, 180, 200, 216, 248, 252, 261, 266, 270

Estremadura, province of, 47, 87, 95, 102, 122, 133, 143, 154, 155, 165, 203, 212, 215, 221, 227, 276, 279, 282

FANE, GENERAL H., 49, 59, 68, 90, 261, 262, 265, 266, 268, 272, 280
Fuentes de Oñoro, 48, 107, 121, 124
Fuente del Maestro, 87, 180, 191, 194, 200, 201, 206

Ganges, H.M.S., 57
George IV (Prince Regent), 30, 121, 127, 128, 135, 153, 155, 163, 168, 187, 258, 282, 288, 294, 296, 297
Girard, General, 137, 139, 140, 142, 145, 151
Graham, General Sir T., 121, 205, 271, 279, 282
Grant, Colonel Sir C., 37, 38, 268, 277, 289, 292, 293, 294, 295
Greenwood, Mr, 51, 58, 80, 97, 101, 120, 122, 145, 170, 209, 227, 250, 263
Guadiana, river, 70, 82, 84, 88, 96, 101, 102, 111, 115, 128, 130, 144, 159, 160, 188, 193, 205, 207

HILL, GENERAL SIR R., 13, 47, 108, 117, 132, 133, 137, 138, 139, 145, 146, 148, 152, 153, 157, 158, 159, 162, 168, 169, 171, 173, 182, 183, 184, 185, 186, 190, 192, 193, 197, 198, 200, 201, 205, 210, 220, 223, 233, 266, 268, 281, 284, 286, 295
Horse Guards, 34, 124, 151, 216, 268, 277, 288, 291, 293, 299. See also Regiments
Howard, Colonel Sir G., 19
Howard, Colonel H., 81, 97, 116, 146, 155, 163, 167, 194, 203, 262, 266, 269, 273, 291
Howard, General K., 127, 138, 139, 140, 148, 156, 162, 184, 185, 186, 190, 191, 239

Isis, H.M.S., 40

JOSEPH, KING—*see* Bonaparte

LALLEMAND, GENERAL F., 182, 195, 196, 200, 201, 206, 207, 208, 210, 217, 220
Langley Hall, 18, 44, 57, 131, 154, 170, 261, 274, 290, 291, 292

Le Marchant, General J.G., 11, 25, 31, 57, 124, 128, 136, 155, 171, 177, 211, 245
Lisbon, 11, 38, 40, 45, 47, 51, 58, 59, 60, 61, 63, 64, 69, 80, 81, 86, 88, 103, 108, 120, 125, 130, 134, 145, 151, 157, 163, 165, 170, 179, 184, 190, 203, 222, 236, 242, 246, 248, 249, 251, 252, 259, 262, 264, 266, 269
Lisbon Gazette, 209
Llera, 182, 190, 195, 201, 207, 208
Llerena, 92, 108, 109, 113, 202, 205
Long, Catherine Maria (aunt), 203
Long, Mrs Charles (sister-in-law), 243, 249, 251, 254
Long, C. B. (twin-brother), 12, 15, 16, 18, 44, 45, 50, 95, 121, 241, 297, 298
Long, C. E. (nephew), 73, 135, 177, 230, 274, 292, 298, 299
Long, Charlotte Mary (sister), 15
Long, E. (father), 15, 16, 25, 26, 49, 50, 51, 56, 58, 60, 63, 81, 117, 121, 122, 146, 153, 165, 167, 169, 178, 179, 203, 222, 241, 245, 249, 257, 262
Long, E. B. (brother), 15, 17, 55, 63, 174, 175, 203, 256, 261, 267
Long, E. N. (nephew), 17, 40
Long, Elizabeth (sister), 15, 26, 45, 93, 146, 165, 180, 249, 251, 273
Long, H. (nephew), 135, 175, 177, 274
Long, Jane Catherine (sister), 15
Long, Mary (niece), 136, 157
Long, Lieutenant-General Robert Ballard: early education, 14–19; *campaigns and engagements*: Low Countries, 21–23; Coruña, 36–39; Walcheren, 40–43; Campo Mayor, 70–81, 93–94; Albuera, 95–107; Usagre, 108–110; Arroyo dos Molinos, 137–145; Almaraz, 182–189; Ribera, 206–208; Vittoria, 268–276; Pyrenees, 277–287; promotions, 19, 21, 24, 25, 37, 45, 111, 297; *regimental commands*: Hompesch Mounted Riflemen, 25–27; 2nd Dragoon Guards, 31; 16th Light Dragoons, 32; 15th Light Dragoons, 32–36
Long, R. (nephew), 103, 150, 157, 166, 168, 263
Long, S. (great-grandfather), 19
Los Santos, 83, 90, 93, 95, 102, 110, 194, 195, 198, 200, 201, 203, 216

Lumley, General, W., 85, 104, 106, 108, 109, 110, 118, 123, 125, 127
Lynch, J. (groom), 30, 99, 112, 134, 165, 169, 170, 208, 216, 222, 232, 236, 242, 265, 267, 290

MADRID, 99, 123, 133, 167, 190, 205, 210, 212, 213, 215, 216, 228, 229, 230, 233, 237
Madrid Gazette, 247
Madrid Gazetteer, 227
Marmont, Maréchal de France and Duc de Raguse, 119, 121, 133, 135, 143, 156, 161, 162, 171, 173, 174, 193, 194, 197, 198, 199, 205, 206, 207, 208, 210, 211, 214, 215, 219
Masséna, Maréchal de France, Duc de Rivoli, and Prince d'Essling, 46, 48, 52, 56, 61, 65, 99, 100, 102, 107, 121, 142, 143
Merida, 87, 89, 138, 139, 140, 143, 158, 159, 160, 171, 173, 189, 190, 223, 246
Moore, General Sir J., 25, 37, 38, 39, 45, 232

NAPOLEON I, 11, 12, 27, 38, 40, 48, 70, 134, 135, 137, 142, 143, 159, 175, 179, 180, 181, 183, 192, 209, 219, 232, 241, 242, 243, 244, 246, 256, 258, 265, 286

Orion, H.M.S., 57

PAMPLONA, 271, 280, 286, 293; blockade of, 277-285 *passim*
Perceval, Spencer, K.C., 42, 122, 184, 191
Pitt, George (first Baron Rivers), 51, 92, 125, 151, 154, 259
Pitt, Sir William, 24, 25, 26, 27, 297
Portalegre, 64, 67, 70, 73, 128, 130, 131, 132, 134, 141, 144, 148, 152, 171, 186, 241, 242
Prince George (transport), 40

REGIMENTS: Royal Horse Guards (The Blues), 22
    1st Dragoon Guards (King's), 19, 20, 21, 27, 29; 2nd Dragoon Guards (Queen's Bays), 31; 3rd Dragoon Guards, 22, 68, 70, 75, 86, 92, 104, 106, 108, 109, 123, 200, 206; 4th Dragoon Guards, 199, 261; 5th Dragoon Guards, 22, 130

    1st Dragoons (Royals), 22, 180; 4th Dragoons, 68, 70, 75, 86, 92, 95, 104, 108, 123, 143; 5th Dragoons (Royal Irish), 26; 6th Dragoons, 130; 7th Dragoons, 130; 10th Dragoons, 252; 14th Dragoons, 126, 223, 263, 277, 281, 284, 293; 18th Dragoons, 77, 251, 252, 263; 26th Dragoons, 73, 75, 158; 27th Dragoons, 206
    9th Light Dragoons, 141, 165, 182, 232, 237, 252, 257, 261, 263, 265, 293; 11th Light Dragoons, 111, 113, 117, 119, 126, 130, 136, 255, 261; 12th Light Dragoons, 29; 13th Light Dragoons, 12, 70, 71, 72, 73, 75, 77, 82, 83, 84, 85, 86, 90, 91, 104, 106, 109, 110, 113, 137, 158, 159, 182, 190, 211, 232, 237, 252, 262, 266, 268, 283, 285, 287, 293, 295; 15th Light Dragoons (Hussars), 21, 32, 33, 34, 35, 36, 37, 38, 128, 251, 252, 268, 293, 294, 295; 16th Light Dragoons, 22, 32; 17th Light Dragoons, 29, 206; 20th Light Dragoons, 27
    1st Hussars, King's German Legion, 223, 293; 2nd Hussars, King's German Legion, 24, 60, 111, 113, 127, 137, 141, 147, 148, 158, 159, 162, 207; 10th Hussars, 75, 294; 15th Hussars, 294; 18th Hussars, 293; York Hussars, 28, 29, 30, 31, 44, 177, 297
    Coldstream Guards, 17; 3rd Foot (East Kent Regiment—The Buffs), 164; 30th Foot, 29; 33rd Foot (Duke of Wellington's Regiment), 23; 36 Regiment (The Worcestershires), 50, 52, 54; 50th Foot (Royal West Kent Regiment), 182; 59th Regiment (East Lancashire Regiment), 280; 60th Foot (King's Royal Rifles), 27; 71st Regiment (Highland Light Infantry), 133; 79th Regiment (Cameron Highlanders), 54; 85th Regiment of Foot (King's Shropshire Light Infantry), 65; 90th Foot (Cameronians), 137
    Hompesch Mounted Riflemen 25-27, 159; 6th Regiment Portuguese Cavalry, 293; West India Rangers, 54; 4th West India Regiment, 128; York Rangers, 25
Reward (transport), 290

Ribera, 110, 174, 176, 178, 182, 206, 207, 208, 210
Rivers, Baron—*see* Pitt, George
Russia, 179, 180, 205, 209, 210, 213, 222, 242, 247, 255

SAINT VINCENTE, 73, 83, 116, 117, 122, 123, 198, 266
Salamanca, 11, 38, 182, 193, 197, 198, 199, 205, 231, 233, 239, 245, 271, 272; capture of, 210-212
Santarem, 59, 60, 61, 62, 64, 65, 132
Seville, 69, 71, 83, 90, 91, 95, 98, 119, 192, 193, 195, 197, 198, 203, 217, 218
Slade, General J., 11, 60, 66, 73, 177, 180, 182, 195, 196, 200, 206, 214, 216, 221, 223, 232, 242, 252, 254, 255, 257, 261, 262, 264, 266, 267, 268, 269, 272, 273
Snap, brig, 277
Soult, Maréchal de France and Duc de Dalmatie, 38, 39, 48, 71, 95, 98, 100, 104, 105, 107, 113, 119, 121, 123, 131, 133, 145, 163, 174, 188, 190, 193, 194, 196, 197, 201, 204, 205, 213, 215, 216, 219, 221, 223, 225, 229, 230, 233, 234, 242, 244, 246, 254, 269, 277, 285, 286
Stewart, General W., 84, 85, 110, 127, 143, 164, 216, 252, 255, 261, 262, 264, 265
Suchet, Maréchal de France and Duc d'Albufera, 142, 143, 158, 193, 194, 197, 224, 225, 258, 275

TAGUS, RIVER, 48, 59, 60, 61, 67, 88, 96, 113, 127, 128, 133, 162, 165, 182, 184 185, 188, 191, 193, 198, 205, 207, 212, 220, 221, 223, 229, 232, 235, 236, 239, 246, 254
Talavera, 87, 101, 173, 210, 222; battle of, 43, 46, 47, 61, 220, 223
Times, The, 149, 179

Torbay, 53, 55, 56, 57, 58, 59, 62, 81
Tormes, river, 193, 231, 232, 233, 234, 235, 239, 246, 271, 275
Torrens, Colonel H., 44, 47, 288, 289, 293, 295, 296

USAGRE, 108, 112, 113, 123, 142, 182, 188, 190, 195, 199, 201, 202, 206, 299

Venerable, H.M.S., 42
Vengeur, H.M.S., 51, 53
Victory, H.M.S., 49, 52, 53, 54, 58, 162
Villafranca, 61, 63, 64, 92, 95, 98, 101, 108, 110, 111, 112, 115, 117, 160, 189, 191, 193, 194, 200, 206, 211, 214, 217, 223
Villemur, Count P., 103, 110, 115, 140, 192, 194, 200, 201, 223
Vittoria, 279, 281, 282; battle of, 268-276, 278, 293

WALCHEREN, 44, 144; expedition to, 40-43
Wellington, Arthur Wellesley, Duke of, 11, 13, 20, 24, 33, 37, 45-48, 52, 56, 59-73, 79, 82, 89, 95, 96, 99-104, 107, 109, 111, 113, 116, 121, 126, 134, 135, 136, 143, 146, 148, 150, 151, 152, 156-164, 167, 170-174, 177, 183, 186, 189-194, 197, 198, 199, 203-206, 210-219, 222-227, 229, 231, 232, 233, 236-246, 249, 254, 256, 258, 261-265, 268-281, 284-288, 294, 296
Weymouth, 28, 30, 31, 164, 282, 297
Windeler (tailors and hosiers), 100, 129, 145, 147, 167, 170, 227, 228, 259, 264

YORK, FREDERICK, DUKE OF, 21, 22, 27, 28, 31, 37, 111, 114, 225, 241

ZAFRA, 89, 90, 92, 95, 110, 112, 189, 192, 194, 195, 198, 203